THE ROOSEVELT NEW DEAL

A PROGRAM ASSESSMENT
FIFTY YEARS AFTER

EDITED BY WILBUR J. COHEN

CONTRIBUTORS

Henry J. Abraham
James E. Anderson
Gladys L. Baker
David H. Bennett
Clarke A. Chambers
Wilbur J. Cohen
Leonard Dinnerstein
Melvyn Dubofsky
Frank B. Freidel
Ellis W. Hawley
Richard Lowitt
Donald R. McCoy

Ruth M. Milkman
Bruce A. Murphy
Paul L. Murphy
James T. Patterson
Wayne D. Rasmussen
Edward L. Schapsmeier
Frederick H. Schapsmeier
Jordan A. Schwarz
Michael B. Stoff
William M. Stott
Winifred D. Wandersee

Lyndon B. Johnson School of Public Affairs
Lyndon Baines Johnson Library
Virginia Commonwealth University
1986

Library of Congress Card No.: 85-80498
ISBN: 0-89940-416-2
© 1986 by the Board of Regents
The University of Texas
Printed in the U.S.A.

Funding provided by the Lyndon Baines Johnson Foundation and the
  Sid Richardson Chair in Public Affairs
Cover design by Barbara Jezek

CONTENTS

PREFACE

This volume is the second product of a three-day convocation held in March 1983 under the auspices of the Lyndon Baines Johnson Library and Museum, the Franklin Delano Roosevelt Library, Virginia Commonwealth University, and the University of Texas at Austin.

The event, which coincided with the fiftieth anniversary of Franklin D. Roosevelt's first inauguration on March 4, 1933, had two parts: a public gathering primarily of New Deal participants, observers, and critics, and a working symposium primarily of academic scholars who presented and discussed papers on selected New Deal subjects. The proceedings of the public symposium were summarized in *The New Deal, Fifty Years After: A Historical Assessment*, published in December 1984 by the Lyndon B. Johnson School of Public Affairs.

Special thanks are due to Professor Melvin Urofsky of Virginia Commonwealth University, who arranged the symposium and invited the participants. The support of Elspeth Rostow, then Dean of the Lyndon B. Johnson School of Public Affairs, and Harry Middleton, Director of the Lyndon B. Johnson Library and Museum, made the symposium a reality. Dean Max Sherman of the LBJ School lent support in making the publication of the proceedings a reality.

The editing process involved some minor revisions in the papers presented at the symposium, but the objective was always to retain the substance of the presentations. In carrying out my editorial responsibility, I had the able assistance of Marilyn Duncan and Mary Beissner of the Lyndon B. Johnson School Office of Publications. That office also handled the production aspects of the project.

The result of these efforts is, we hope, a book which will be of value to students of history and public affairs, as well as others interested in this significant period in our country's social and political history.

Wilbur J. Cohen

CONTRIBUTORS

HENRY J. ABRAHAM is a world-renowned expert in constitutional law, civil rights, the comparative judicial process, and American and comparative government. Among his recent books are *The Judicial Process: An Introductory Analysis of the Courts of the United States, England, and France* (5th ed., 1985); *Justices and Presidents: A Political History of Appointments to the Supreme Court* (2d ed., 1985); and *Freedom and the Court: Civil Rights and Liberties in the United States* (4th ed., 1982).

Mr. Abraham, James Hart Professor of Government and Foreign Affairs at the University of Virginia since 1978, is listed in *Who's Who in the World, Who's Who in America,* and the *International Who's Who in Education.*

JAMES E. ANDERSON, Professor of Political Science at the University of Houston, has published extensively on public policymaking and economic regulation. His most recent book, *The Management of Macroeconomic Policy during the Johnson Administration* (with Jared Hazleton, 1985), was written in connection with the Administrative History of the Johnson Presidency project at The University of Texas at Austin. Other titles include *Public Policymaking* (1984) and *Politics and Public Policy in America* (1984).

Mr. Anderson served as president of the Southern Political Science Association during 1984-85.

GLADYS L. BAKER, now retired, was Historian in the U.S. Department of Agriculture from 1939 to 1982. She has served as president of the Agricultural History Society and is author of *The County Agent* (1939), *Century of Service* (with others, 1963), and *The Department of Agriculture* (with Wayne D. Rasmussen, 1972).

DAVID H. BENNETT, Professor of History at Syracuse University, specializes in the study of American radical movements.

His publications include *Demagogues in the Depression: American Radicals in the Union Party, 1932-36* (1969); *From Teapot Dome to Watergate* (1974); and, most recently, *From the Know Nothings to the New Right: Anti-Alien Movements in American History* (1986). He has contributed entries to the *Dictionary of American Biography* on Francis Townsend and William Langer (1979).

CLARKE A. CHAMBERS is Professor of History and American Studies at the University of Minnesota. His major publications include *Paul U. Kellogg and the Survey: Voices for Social Welfare and Social Justice* (1971); *Seedtime of Reform* (1963); and *The New Deal at Home and Abroad, 1929-1945* (editor, 1965).

Mr. Chambers served as chairman of the Minnesota Humanities Commission from 1978 to 1980, and since 1964 has been director of the Social Welfare History Archives at the University of Minnesota.

LEONARD DINNERSTEIN, Professor of History since 1970 at the University of Arizona, has written and edited numerous books and articles on American Jewish history. His most recent books are *America and the Survivors of the Holocaust: The Evolution of a United States Displaced Persons Policy, 1945-1950* (1982), and *Ethnic Americans: A History of Immigration and Assimilation* (1982).

Among his many honors and awards have been three fellowships from the National Endowment for the Humanities and research grants from the American Philosophical Society, the Herbert Hoover Library, and the Eleanor Roosevelt Institute. In 1969 he received *Saturday Review*'s Anisfield-Wolf Award for his book *The Leo Frank Case* (1968).

MELVYN DUBOFSKY has authored over twenty-five articles and five books on American history, many on the American labor movement. His books include *The United States in the Twentieth Century* (with Daniel Smith and Athan Theoharis, 1978), and *We Shall Be All: A History of the Industrial Workers of the World* (1969, paperback 1974).

Mr. Dubofsky, Professor of History at the State University of New York at Binghamton, has received research grants and fellowships from the American Philosophical Society, the American Council for Learned Societies, and the National Endowment for the Humanities. In 1977-78 he taught at the University of Tel Aviv in Israel through a Fulbright Senior Lectureship.

FRANK B. FREIDEL, an internationally known Roosevelt historian, has been the Bullitt Professor of American History at the University of Washington since 1981. He taught for over twenty-five years at Harvard University, where he was the Charles Warren Professor of American History.

Mr. Freidel has written extensively on the Roosevelt Presidency, including such books as *FDR: The Ordeal* (1954); *Roosevelt: The Triumph* (1956); *FDR and the South* (1966); and *Roosevelt: Launching the New Deal* (1973). He also edited a series entitled *Franklin D. Roosevelt and the Era of the New Deal.*

ELLIS W. HAWLEY, Professor of History at the University of Iowa, specializes in the study of U.S. economic policy, business-government relations, and economic organization in the 1920s and 1930s. His publications on these subjects include numerous articles, thirty-five book reviews, and his books *The Great War and the Search for a Modern Order* (1979) and *The New Deal and the Problem of Monopoly* (1966).

Since 1976 Mr. Hawley has served on the steering committee for the Center for the Study of the Recent History of the United States (a consortium of the Hoover Library, University of Iowa, and Iowa State Historical Society). He was consultant, annotator, and editorial team member for the *Public Papers of the Presidents: Herbert Hoover* (1974-1978).

RICHARD LOWITT, Professor and Chair, Department of History, Iowa State University, has written or edited seven books on twentieth-century American history, and has contributed to several others. Most notable are his three volumes on George W. Norris (1963, 1971, and 1978), *One Third of a Nation: Lorena Hickok Reports on the Great Depression* (coeditor, 1981), and *The New Deal and the West* (1984).

Mr. Lowitt has been a recipient of numerous awards and grants, including fellowships from the Guggenheim Foundation and the National Endowment for the Humanities.

DONALD R. MCCOY has written or edited eleven books and authored forty articles on U.S. history, many on the era of the 1920s and 1930s. Among his books are *Landon of Kansas* (1966, Landmark ed. 1979); *Angry Voices: Left-of-Center Politics in the New Deal Era* (1958, rpt. 1971); and *Coming of Age: The United States during the 1920s and 1930s* (1973).

A fellow of the Society of American Archivists since 1980, Mr. McCoy received the society's Waldo Gifford Leland Prize in 1979 and the Byron Caldwell Smith Award for Distinguished Writing in 1970. He is University Distinguished Professor of History at the University of Kansas.

RUTH M. MILKMAN, Associate Professor of Sociology at Queens College—CUNY, has written extensively on women's work and labor history. She is editor of *Women, Work, and Protest: A Century of U.S. Women's Labor History* and is currently completing a book on the sexual division of labor in industry during World War II. She also serves on the editorial boards of *Feminist Studies* and *Politics and Society*.

BRUCE ALLEN MURPHY, Associate Professor of Political Science at Pennsylvania State University, specializes in the study of American constitutional law and judicial behavior as well as American government and the American presidency.

In addition to his recent book, *The Brandeis-Frankfurter Connection: Secret Political Activities of Two Supreme Court Justices* (1982), Mr. Murphy has published several articles on Supreme Court justices in such journals as the *Hastings Constitutional Law Quarterly*, the *Georgetown Law Journal*, and the *Michigan Law Journal*.

PAUL L. MURPHY, Professor of History and American Studies at the University of Minnesota, has authored or contributed to over fourteen books and sixty articles and reviews in professional journals. Representative publications include *World War I and the Origin of Civil Liberties in the United States* (1979) and *The Meaning of Freedom of Speech: First Amendment Freedoms from Wilson to FDR* (1972; winner of the American Bar Association Gavel Award in 1973 for an "outstanding contribution to public understanding of the American system of law and justice").

Mr. Murphy, a former Guggenheim Fellow and Senior Fulbright Lecturer at the University of Lagos in Nigeria (1971-72), has been a member of the Joint Committee of Project '87, planning the Bicentennial of the Constitution, and is Chair of its Media Task Force.

JAMES T. PATTERSON is Professor of History at Brown University. Among his recent books are *America's Struggle Against Poverty, 1900-1980* (1981) and *America in the 20th Century: A History* (rev. ed. 1982).

Mr. Patterson has received numerous awards, grants, and fellowships, the latter including Woodrow Wilson, Guggenheim, and National Endowment for the Humanities.

WAYNE D. RASMUSSEN, Chief of the Agricultural History Branch of the U.S. Department of Agriculture, has worked for the USDA since 1937, serving as Historian from the 1940s to the present. In 1976 he was U.S. Information Agency Bicentennial Lecturer on the History of American Agriculture in Iran, India, and Afghanistan. He has served as president of the Agricultural History Society and of the Society for History in the Federal Government. He is a fellow of the American Agricultural Economics Association.

Among Mr. Rasmussen's many publications on American agriculture are *Agriculture in the U.S.: A Documentary History*, which he edited (1975, 4 volumes), and *The Department of Agriculture* (coauthored with Gladys L. Baker, 1972).

EDWARD L. SCHAPSMEIER and FREDERICK H. SCHAPS-MEIER have coauthored seven books, many on the history and politics of American agriculture. Their titles include *The Encyclopedia of American Agricultural History* (1982) and *Abundant Harvests: The Story of American Agriculture* (1973). Their two-volume study of Henry A. Wallace in 1969 and 1970 is *Henry A. Wallace of Iowa: The Agrarian Years, 1910-1940* and *Prophet in Politics: Henry A. Wallace and the War Years, 1940-1965*.

Edward Schapsmeier is currently Distinguished Professor of History at Illinois State University. Frederick Schapsmeier is John McN Rosebush Professor at the University of Wisconsin—Oshkosh.

JORDAN A. SCHWARZ, Professor of History at Northern Illinois University, has written, coauthored, or edited five books and numerous articles on twentieth-century U.S. history, especially the Depression era. Representative titles are *The Speculator: Bernard M. Baruch in Washington, 1917-1965* (1981) and *The Interregnum of Despair: Hoover, Congress and the Depression* (1970).

Mr. Schwarz is completing a book about Adolf A. Berl and will next write a political history of inflation in twentieth-century America.

MICHAEL B. STOFF is author of *Oil, War, and American Security: The Search for a National Policy on Foreign Oil, 1941-1947* (1980; paperback, 1982). His published articles and papers have often focused on FDR, Herbert Hoover, and Harold Ickes.

Mr. Stoff, Assistant Professor of History at the University of Texas at Austin, is currently writing a biography of Ickes.

WILLIAM M. STOTT, Professor of American Studies and English at the University of Texas at Austin, is author of *Documentary Expression and Thirties America* and editor of *Remembering America: A Sampler of the WPA American Guide Series*. He served as historical consultant for "America Lost and Found," a documentary motion picture of the Depression years as portrayed in films, newsreels, photographs, and other media (first broadcast on PBS in April 1980). He is also the author of *On Broadway*, a picture book on the Broadway theater in the 1940s and 1950s, and *Write to the Point: And Feel Better about Your Writing*.

Mr. Stott has received several prestigious honors and grants, including a Fulbright lectureship in London in 1980-81 and a Guggenheim Memorial Fellowship in 1978.

WINIFRED D. WANDERSEE has presented conference papers and published numerous articles on the experiences of American working women in the Depression era. Her book *Women, Work, and Family Values, 1920-1940* was published by Harvard University Press in 1981.

Ms. Wandersee is working on the subject of the youth movement of the 1930s and contributed an essay, "Eleanor Roosevelt and American Youth: Politics and Personality in a Bureacratic Age," to *Without Precedent: The Life and Career of Eleanor*

Roosevelt (1984), edited by Joan Hoff-Wilson and Marjorie Lightman.

Ms. Wandersee is Associate Professor of History at Hartwick College. She has also taught at Syracuse University and St. Cloud State University.

ABOUT THE EDITOR

WILBUR J. COHEN, editor of the volume, has been a Professor at the LBJ School of Public Affairs since 1980. He began his long career in human services in 1934 when he went to Washington as research assistant to the Executive Director of President Roosevelt's Cabinet Committee on Economic Security, which drafted the original Social Security Act. In 1935 he joined the staff of the Social Security Board and subsequently was Assistant Director and then Director of its Division of Research and Statistics. Between 1961 and 1968 he served as Assistant Secretary, Under Secretary, and Secretary of Health, Education, and Welfare, the only person ever to hold all three positions. During that period he also served as chairman of President Kennedy's Task Force on Health and Social Security and President Johnson's Committees on Population and Family Planning and Mental Retardation.

In 1969, Mr. Cohen became Dean of the School of Education at the University of Michigan, a post he held until 1978. He has continued to be active in government and human services through appointments to federal committees and task forces. He was a member of President Jimmy Carter's Task Force on Education (1976), Chairman of Carter's National Commission on Unemployment Compensation (1978-80), and a member of the National Commission on Social Security (1979-81) by appointment of Speaker O'Neill.

STATE OF NEW YORK

EXECUTIVE CHAMBER

ALBANY

FRANKLIN D ROOSEVELT
GOVERNOR

April 16, 1929.

My dear Bishop McConnell:-

Will you please tell the Second
National Conference of Old Age Security of my very
great personal regret that I cannot come, but, as you
know, I shall be in the South on that date?

I am very certain that better
Old Age Security against want is the most immediate
pressing need of our present day civilization. I am,
of course, glad that the Legislature of the State of
New York has gone along with me in authorizing a
Commission to study the whole subject this summer.
I hope that next year we will see many States taking
definite action.

Very sincerely yours,

Franklin D Roosevelt

Bishop Francis J. McConnell,
American Association for Old Age Security,
Room 1603 - 104 Fifth Avenue,
New York City, N. Y.

This historic letter indicates that Franklin D. Roosevelt favored
social security as early as 1929.

Source: Files of the American Association for Social Security (formerly the
American Association for Old Age Security). Copy courtesy of Mrs. Abraham
Epstein, widow of the association's former Executive Secretary.

INTRODUCTION

There is one uncontrovertible fact in the nearly two hundred years of Presidential tenures in the United States: Franklin D. Roosevelt was President longer than any other person in that position. Unless the U.S. Constitution is changed, no future President will be able to challenge that record.

Many newspaper commentators have made the claim that the Roosevelt New Deal political coalition was finally terminated by the Reagan election victories of 1980 and 1984. Whatever may turn out to be the long-run results of these elections, it is still evident that a very large part of the New Deal domestic programs remain basically intact, even if slowed down or modified in recent years.

The sixteen-year administrations of Roosevelt and Truman and the succeeding Democratic and Republican administrations (1953-1980)—Eisenhower, Kennedy, Johnson, Nixon, Ford, and Carter—which in effect built on the New Deal, represent a cycle of far-reaching domestic policy development not comparable to any other period of American history.

In planning a conference to celebrate the fiftieth anniversary of the inauguration of President Roosevelt, it at first seemed appropriate to try to assess the longer-range impact of some of the major programs established by the New Deal. The political revolution of 1933-1938 might be appraised in light of the political revolution of 1981-1983. Yet, it may be too early to make a final evaluation of New Deal programs until the longer-range impact of the Reagan Administration is discernible.

To fully discuss and analyze all the New Deal domestic programs in a one-day symposium would not have been feasible. Consequently, it was decided to organize the discussion around nine important facets of the New Deal: minority groups, radical politics, labor, economic legislation, the welfare state, women, farm policy, advisers, and the courts.

The papers and commentaries on these topics produced a highly successful conference. Collected as a volume, they should enable historians and political scientists to examine the New Deal in terms of more recent political events.

As someone who began his professional career in the New Deal in 1934, I initiated the 1983 commemorative symposium not to heap praises on the Roosevelt Administration, but rather to bring to public attention the need and possibility of further domestic reform uncompleted by the New Deal. If political change goes in cycles, as I tend to believe it does, another opportunity will come in our national life to build upon what the New Deal and the Great Society developed. Consequently, periodic reexamination of the experience with New Deal programs and policies could in itself be a mechanism for considering future changes.

Arthur M. Schlesinger, Jr., has summarized American life as operating "on a thirty-year rhythm, from public purpose to private interest. The 1980s, like the 1950s and 1920s, is a time of respite from seasons of public action, idealism, and reform. But periods dominated by private interest do not go on forever. For rest replenishes the national energies, and problems neglected grow worse, threaten to become unmanageable, and demand remedy. Sometime around the year 1990, if the rhythm holds, we can expect a breakthrough into a new and generous epoch in American life." (CBS Television, "Robert Kennedy: A Representative Man," in viewers' guide to "Robert Kennedy and His Times," broadcast January 27, 29, 30, 1985.)

This volume is offered in the hope it may be of some assistance in preparing for such a breakthrough.

Wilbur J. Cohen

I

KEYNOTE PAPER

The New Deal: Laying the Foundation for Modern America

Frank B. Freidel

In 1983, the fiftieth anniversary of the beginnings of the New Deal, what was once acutely controversial has come to appear with the passage of time as a foundation of modern America. The first great responses to the rapid industrialization and urbanization of the nation were the Populist and Progressive movements. Building upon them, and upon the domestic experience of the First World War, was the New Deal, which together with the administrative innovations of the Second World War, did much to usher in the America in which we live.

The acceptance of the New Deal changes did not come overnight. Eighteen years after they had begun, the bitterness and anger of some Republican leaders was undiminished. In March 1951, the distinguished Robert Taft, "Mr. Republican," came off the floor of the Senate to defend vehemently Senator Joseph McCarthy from the criticism of Doris Fleeson, one of the most notable Washington correspondents. His onslaught curiously swung to the New Deal. Red-faced, he exclaimed to her, "The trouble with you left-wingers is that you will stop at nothing to protect Franklin D. Roosevelt." He went on to charge that "the whole administration of Roosevelt was penetrated by Communists from top to bottom."

Thirty years were to elapse before Ronald Reagan, heir to Taft's Republican conservatism, startled the Republican convention of 1980 that had just nominated him for President by citing Roosevelt twice in his acceptance address. Some of the delegates at first did not seem to know whether to cheer or boo, but soon realized Reagan was paying tribute to Roosevelt. The *New York Times* editorially hailed the nominee the next day as

"Franklin Delano Reagan." As President, Reagan has by no means proclaimed himself an advocate of the New Deal ideology despite his unflagging admiration of Roosevelt. What is more significant is that in the third year of his avowedly conservative administration, the basic programs put in place under the New Deal are still intact in their fundamentals. He has been emphatic, for example, in his assurances that he will not undercut Social Security aid to the aged. Rather, he seems to be whittling away at some of the additions to the programs, especially the accretions in benefits, that have evolved since the Roosevelt years.

The contrast between the angry invective of Robert Taft and the warm tributes of Ronald Reagan indicates on the one hand the way in which time has brought the New Deal into the mainstream consensus of the American political tradition. On the other hand, it points to the obstacles that the New Deal innovators faced at the time, and the serious possibility for nearly a decade after Roosevelt's death that if conservatives had come into power they might well have dismantled the basic New Deal institutions. Taking a long-range view, as the economist Herbert Klein did recently at an American Historical Association session, one can see that without Roosevelt and the New Deal the government of the United States today would probably, like those of other Western nations, bear a large responsibility for the economic and social well-being of the nation. Yet when one remembers the firmly entrenched opposition in the 1930s, one wonders how much change would have transpired and when.

Beyond all doubt almost all the precedents, the building blocks, for a New Deal program for recovery and reform were in place well before March 4, 1933. They were to be found in the Populist tradition, in the progressive proposals of both Theodore Roosevelt's New Nationalism and Woodrow Wilson's New Freedom. They existed too in the World War I agencies which channeled, helped finance, and rationalized both agricultural and industrial production, set working conditions, and settled labor disputes. They were to be found too in modernization of state governments in the 1920s and in state efforts to cope with the Great Depression. Overseas there were European models for electric power development, securities regulation, and social security. There was even, in the spring of 1933, in the Nazi racist atrocities, a mirror in which Americans could examine their own shortcomings, for Hitler, reacting to criticisms of his treatment of Jews, pointed to the second-class citizenship the United States imposed, de facto, upon blacks. American administrators and jurists could in response return to the original intent of the framers of the Fourteenth Amendment—but only faint beginnings of desegregation were to appear during the New Deal.

Above all, there was the acute, terrifying crisis of the Great Depression. The nation had since the War of 1812 undergone cycles of boom and bust, bringing ruin and privation. For a nation basically agricultural, these depressions had been barely tolerable, but there had been food and shelter on farms. Already in the urban America of the 1890s the unemployed had suffered acutely. Modern Presidents, beginning with Theodore Roosevelt, as Ellis Hawley and others have demonstrated, felt that federal intervention in some degree was essential to mitigate economic catastrophe. President Herbert Hoover, seeking to restore prosperity in the Depression of the 1930s, was shocked at the attitude of his Secretary of the Treasury, Andrew Mellon, who regarded depressions as a salutary working of the natural law of supply and demand, weeding out the weak and creating opportunities for the strong. Soon Hoover dispatched Mellon to the Court of St. James, where he could do no harm. Yet Hoover himself, while innovating far beyond any previous chief executive, feared the destruction of state and local responsibilities and of individual initiative if the federal government channeled aid directly to the dispossessed, or sought to aid business or agriculture except through voluntary schemes. The failure of Hoover's limited programs to bring recovery made the electorate receptive to more drastic action.

With the building blocks in place and the catalyst of the acute depression at work, modernization was logical, but not necessarily inevitable. The political and economic leadership of the nation, while not as fundamentalist in its laissez-faire, Social Darwinist views as was Secretary Mellon, nonetheless favored only the slightest changes. Moreover, they dominated the leadership of Congress in both parties. One has only to refer to the hearings of the so-called Depression clinic that Senator Pat Harrison of Mississippi conducted in February 1933 in order to provide guidance to the incoming President. Dignitary after dignitary appeared, including such famous figures as Democrats Al Smith and Bernard Baruch, to affirm that the solution was strict government economy and higher taxes to achieve a balanced budget. Only a few obscure figures, like Mormon banker Marriner Eccles, suggested massive federal spending. The irony is, that as of this time, February 1933, President-elect Roosevelt seemed foursquare behind a program of economy and a balanced budget. Indeed he was permanently in favor of them. It is essential to an understanding of Roosevelt as New Deal President to keep in mind that he always aspired to a balanced budget. Heavy expenditures, whether for relief and recovery or for national defense, were a last resort. Woodrow Wilson was sometimes called a "progressive with brakes on"; Roosevelt never had the appellation tacked onto him, but he was in fact always a "New Dealer with brakes on."

Yet it can be argued that with any likely alternate person in the White House in 1933 and thereafter, there would have been far more brakes than New Deal. If anyone doubts that Roosevelt made a difference, note how different the scenarios would have been if chance had taken a different turn at two critical points. The first was at the Democratic convention of 1932, when although Roosevelt had a majority of the delegates, the Democratic two-thirds rule dating back to the age of Jackson prevailed. The stop-Roosevelt movement was potent and came exceedingly close to forcing the nomination of a compromise candidate. That candidate would probably have been Newton D. Baker, once reform mayor of Cleveland and later Wilson's Secretary of War, who had become a utilities lawyer. What made him so attractive to intellectuals (and prevented in the end his obtaining the nomination) was his support of the League of Nations. But on domestic matters, to judge by his later fulminations against the New Deal from the perspective of Riviera, he would have supported little more than an economy program plus, no doubt, some public works. The best that can be said is that his views on FDR and the New Deal were more temperately phrased than Taft's.

The second point when history could have changed was that February evening in Miami, when the angry Joseph Zangara, firing point-blank with his Saturday night special, quite possibly would have assassinated the President-elect, had not a forgotten heroine, Lillian Gross, tugged at Zangara's arm, spoiling his aim. (It was Mayor Anton Cermak of Chicago who fell victim to the assassin.) If Roosevelt had been killed, Speaker John Nance Garner, a West Texas banker, would have become President.

Garner had a touch of the populist about him, and would have favored heavy taxes on the wealthy, but was far more devoted than Roosevelt to the balanced budget. By 1934, he was reporting to Roosevelt from Texas that the Depression was over, and in his second four years as Vice-President was kept only by party loyalty from going openly into vehement opposition to the President. Who can believe that under either Baker or Garner there would have been much more of a New Deal than, say, a Stanley Baldwin brought to Britain? Add to that the fact that public opinion polls of the late 1930s and congressional elections of the World War II years indicate that a majority of the electorate was willing to accept reform only as an adjunct of recovery. When recovery came during the war, as John M. Blum emphasizes, they lost interest in reform.

Just why Roosevelt could make a considerable difference— indeed be the right President at the right time—takes quite a bit of explaining. Basically, I believe that, together with his other obvious qualifications, it was because he was rooted in the earlier American traditions, yet was receptive to change. Like his generation of Americans he had been born in the nineteenth century with its glorification of laissez-faire and Social Darwinism, but had matured in the early twentieth century when a moral and technical approach seemed to bring a golden age within grasp.

As a college student he was still sufficiently in his father's Cleveland Democratic tradition to criticize President Theodore Roosevelt's energetic intervention in the anthracite coal strike of 1902; fifteen years later he was one of President Wilson's most dynamic young war administrators, proud of his feats in labor relations, construction, and naval innovations. Both as a young progressive and as a middle-aged Governor of New York, he became personally familiar with the people and institutions which could serve as the basis for the New Deal.

His knowledge, while seldom as profound as that of some scholars or technical experts, was nevertheless remarkably broad, and he had a knack for grasping essentials quickly. He was adept at skimming books and at picking brains. It was a logical progression for him to assemble a "brain trust" to research issues when he decided to run for President. After he was elected, he continued to be unusually responsive to new ideas, and was particularly gifted in selling them to the electorate as part and parcel of the American tradition.

He was aware of the cultural lag in America—the fact that technology had brought changes so fast that people's thinking could not keep pace. Realistically he felt that thorough education was essential before proceeding very far. He dreamed large dreams, then acted prudently. "To accomplish anything worthwhile," he had written before becoming President, "it is necessary to compromise between the ideal and the practical." He came into office already firm in his view of presidential leadership—it was one to which the American people responded. He had told Anne O'Hare McCormick:

> The Presidency is not merely an administrative office. That's the least of it. It is more than an engineering job, efficient or inefficient. It is preeminently a place of moral leadership. . . . T.R. and Wilson were both moral leaders, each in his own way and for his own time, who used the Presidency as a pulpit.
>
> Isn't that what the office is—a superb opportunity for reapplying, applying in new conditions, the simple rules of human conduct we always go back to? I stress the modern application, because we are always moving on; the technical and economic environment changes, and never so quickly as now. Without leadership alert and sensitive to change, we are bogged up or lose our way.[1]

Roosevelt was indeed sensitive to the need for change, and managed to make it palatable both to an electorate and a congressional leadership with its ideological roots still half in the nineteenth century.

Roosevelt's leadership modernized the office of President even beyond the changes that his two mentors, Theodore Roosevelt and Wilson, had wrought. He institutionalized the press conferences and systematically used the radio as a means of building public support. After the fiasco of the Supreme Court fight in 1937, he regularized his meetings with congressional leaders, and finally in 1939 he obtained legislation creating the Executive Office of the President, placing the Bureau of the Budget within it under his (rather than Treasury) control, and providing it with a staff of assistants who were supposed to have "a passion for anonymity."

The special sessions and heavy legislative loads of the New Deal years transformed Congress, bringing lengthier sessions and a faster tempo. Staffs remained small, but congressmen could no longer spend the larger part of their time at home among their constituents. The greatest change for Congress was that even more than under earlier progressive presidents, leadership in the legislative process fell upon the chief executive. One indication of the shift was the fact that the focus of news in Washington moved from Capitol Hill to the White House.

The shock of the Great Depression undoubtedly stimulated the innovative side both of Roosevelt and the young experts he enlisted. Until the deepening of the Depression in 1930, Roosevelt's views were certainly no more advanced than Hoover's. That deepening shock led to Roosevelt's easy victory in 1932.

Then, the truly crucial shock—the catalytic agent—was the banking crisis of February-March 1933. By the morning of inauguration day, practically every bank in the nation was closed. Roosevelt as President-elect had remained surprisingly calm and quiet during the growing crisis, and had refused to take responsibility and act before he wielded full presidential power. He had seemed to be confirming [journalist Walter] Lippmann's earlier opinion that he was "a highly impressionable person, without a firm grasp of public affairs, and without very strong convictions."

The more the surprise when in his inaugural address on March 4, 1933, Roosevelt spoke firmly and reassuringly to the frightened, bewildered American people, hungering for action. He urged them to put their fears behind them, and promised them that he would take prompt steps to combat the Depression, and would seek reforms to prevent future depressions. Suddenly the entire nation seemed ready to follow Roosevelt's leadership in new directions. The *Nation* expressed the prevalent mood when it wrote, "Never in our national history has there been so dramatic a coincidence as this simultaneous transfer of power and the complete collapse of a system and of a philosophy."[2] It asserted that America was suddenly being redirected "toward a goal such as Jefferson envisaged—a democracy based on full economic, as well as political, equality."

Roosevelt's first cautious steps, putting into action the sort of program political and business leaders had urged before Congress a few weeks earlier, brought him almost total public support. Some, like the publisher of the *Chicago Tribune*, who later became among his grimmest enemies, for the moment hailed him enthusiastically.

Both Roosevelt's confident air and his immediate success in

ending the banking crisis caused him suddenly to appear in almost superhuman dimensions. The nation for the moment was unified behind Roosevelt. It was one of those rare times when a President has received such strong national backing that he has been able to overturn the dominant restraints of Congress and obtain a comprehensive new program, breaking previously sacrosanct precedents. In the process, even during the first one hundred days when the New Deal was new and full of promise, Roosevelt had to demonstrate his consummate political talents in order to maneuver his program through Congress. Overall, few members of Congress dared thwart the President, and many, as Senator Hiram Johnson noted, went along with Roosevelt even though they did not understand nor trust what he was trying to do. They simply hoped the new measures would work. Yet it was no "rubber stamp" Congress, as a few diehard members charged; it made significant, often constructive, modifications in the President's proposals. Basically it was the public image of Roosevelt as the miracle worker who could bring quick recovery for everyone and a better life for the dispossessed that brought enactment of the New Deal. This image became the lasting view of Roosevelt that millions of people, including some farmers, most laborers, and almost all of the dispossessed, continued to hold.

For many others dazzled with Roosevelt in the spring of 1933, disenchantment ensued, and the hero turned into villain. Quick recovery did not follow. For several months, as there was some rise in economic indices, financiers and businessmen who did not believe in the New Deal did not want to disturb the precarious recovery process by criticizing the President. But in the fall of 1933 when conditions were deteriorating, they reverted to their earlier orthodox views and began to express their alarm. As Roosevelt, to counter the acute deflation of the time, gingerly moved toward inflation, one British economic observer reported the feeling of Wall Street transmitted to the City of London: "Roosevelt is mad and is led by madder professors."[3] That became the view of defenders of the old order both within the United States and out. It was the editorial opinion of some of the nation's most respected journals. It was the view of most of the Republican opposition and, in private, of some of the leaders of Roosevelt's own party in Congress. What seems evolutionary today seemed revolutionary then. Roosevelt obtained additional recovery and reform legislation in 1935, and some legislation as late as 1939, but he did so only by dint of extraordinary effort and at the price of some humiliating setbacks.

New Deal America moved toward both recovery and reform only by fits and starts. Nothing was very certain at the time. There is no need before this assemblage to depict the process. Rather I would like to examine with you, as I have already examined the changes in the Presidency, the way in which New Deal measures came to serve as foundations for future decades.

At the outset, Roosevelt was operating within an overall scheme in sending proposal after proposal to Congress during the first hundred days. The proposals appeared haphazard or ad hoc, but behind them was Roosevelt's intent first to bring quick recovery— he hoped in a matter of months—and then reform to bring a more equitable living standard to Americans and to mitigate the causes of depressions. In practice, there was some reform injected from the outset in the recovery proposals, and the immediate desperate needs of millions of the dispossessed forced heavy relief expenditures. These in turn had an effect upon recovery.

The heavy expenditures were not part of Roosevelt's initial planning. Rather, he had hoped to bring recovery in a way that differed little if at all from the blueprint the conservatives had set forth at Senator Harrison's "depression clinic." It was to be a "bootstrap" program involving in both the industrial and agricultural recovery programs part regulation and part planning. There had to be a good deal of both (a combination, of course, of the essence of both the New Freedom and the New Nationalism) because neither would involve large appropriations or defeat Roosevelt's pledge of a balanced budget. Roosevelt was not so doctrinaire as to think spending was unnecessary; young economists had emphasized the need for "pump priming," to put dollars into consumers' pockets so they could buy the products of factories and farms, but he hoped to keep it to a minimum. The traditional mode of expenditure would be through public works; Roosevelt was determined that they should be both substantial and self-liquidating in expense. He would set up both a regular budget, which through drastic cuts in regular departments he could balance, and an emergency budget to cover relief and public works expenditures. Pressure from Congress forced him to take $3.3 billion; partly because of that prudence but also because of the months it took for engineers to draft construction plans and for lawyers to prepare contracts, little of that money got into the economy during the summer and fall of 1933.

For a while, there was little "pump priming," and serious shortcomings became manifest in the bootstrap National Recovery Administration (NRA) and the Agricultural Adjustment Administration. The NRA was a plan for government backing of business self-regulation along the trade association lines, something that businessmen themselves had wanted. Basically it failed through lack of enforcement, and because the codes of fair practice often favored large enterprise at the expense of small. The demise, after the "Sick Chicken" decision in 1935, was permanent, yet in 1938 when the shift in Supreme Court views on economic powers of the federal government eliminated the question of constitutionality, FDR was once again ready to resort to an NRA-type scheme simply because it would not take a large federal appropriation. What stopped him after several tentative discussions with corporate and labor leaders was the inability of the corporate leaders to agree among themselves. More important still, an NRA-type program could work only if business cooperated with the government. Roosevelt did not want a device in which business sat at the head of the table; and businessmen would not accept one in which government would be in prime control. There were many subtleties and ramifications in the NRA and subsequent New Deal economic programs; in his paper Ellis Hawley has charted and analyzed these definitively.

Despite the shortcomings, out of the corpse of the NRA Blue Eagle came several of the lasting shifts in the functioning of the federal government in the economy. There was the federal setting of a minimum wage and maximum workweek, and the prohibition of child labor through the Fair Labor Standards Act of 1938. The first minimum wage was only forty cents an hour. Also, in the National Industrial Recovery Act, a rather weak Section 7-a wrote into federal law a long-standing goal of labor unions. It legalized the right to join a union of one's own choice and to engage in collective bargaining. In 1935 Congress enacted the far stronger Labor Relations Act, weighted on the side of labor at a time when it was weak, and authorizing a strong National Labor Relations Board. The Wagner Act led to a spectacular growth of unions and more firmly allied labor with the New Deal and the Democratic party. Finally, in the statistical services related to the NRA, embodied in the National Emergency Council, there began to evolve the type of economic planning that was to result after World War II in the creation of the President's Council of Economic Advisers.

Planning, which since the progressive era had been a prime aim of the political scientists and economists, had received government financing in the First World War. As late as the 1930s, President Hoover, who encouraged planning, felt sternly that it should be privately financed and should serve only to provide advice for the government and private enterprise. Thus he had obtained foundation financing for the highly important President's Research Committee on Social Trends, which conducted a broad social survey and drew up a national social plan for the future. One of its recommendations was the creation of a national planning board. The authors of the proposals, especially Professor Charles E. Merriam of the University of Chicago, soon became engaged in planning for the New Deal. The first planning board began operating in the Department of the Interior, and gradually evolved into the National Resources Planning Board. It was government financed, and made plans for action which usually required federal appropriations. To conservatives it seemed dangerous, and Congress during World War II killed it, primarily because it had recommended enlargement of Social Security after the war.

The major advance in planning came through the Agricultural Adjustment Administration, where again, the New Deal moved from the voluntary emphasis of Hoover's Farm Board to a program in which farmers received economic incentives to cut production of basic crops. In one form or another, crop reduction and price support programs have continued ever since.

Similarly, planning entered into the New Deal conservation programs. Roosevelt was particularly knowledgeable about conservation and continued vigorously what had originated in the progressive era. In addition there were the innovations of soil conservation, resettlement of families on poor land, and other programs to alleviate rural poverty. There were protection of grazing lands and forests on a larger scale, the return of wind-eroded plowed fields in the dustbowl to grasslands, the beginnings of shelter belts of trees on the Great Plains, and the building of check-dams in dry areas and of flood control dams in those of heavy rainfall. The Tennessee Valley Authority combined conservation and agricultural rehabilitation with cheap development of public power to stimulate both industry and agriculture. Roosevelt wanted seven valley authorities, but aside from TVA gained only authorization to develop power on the Columbia River in the Northwest. Cheap power brought to farms through the Rural Electrification Administration lightened both farm and household chores. It is pointless to continue this sort of cataloguing, delineating both improvements of earlier programs or innovations. Some, like the Civilian Conservation Corps, disappeared at the federal level during World War II, to be resumed in new guises (like the Job Corps of the 1960s); others have continued, as has TVA, becoming transformed over the decades into quite different sorts of institutions. TVA today is more notable for its steam-run generators than its hydroelectric power.

Much from the outset of the New Deal was in the New Freedom tradition of regulation. Securities regulation came in 1933 and 1934 as a logical response to the Great Crash; the Securities and Exchange Commission, despite Wall Street protests, became permanent. The most important changes were in money and where safety nets came into place. In 1933 Congress enacted, despite Roosevelt's misgivings, legislation establishing Federal Deposit Insurance, a notable success, and in 1935 modernized the Federal Reserve system. There were other regulatory measures, but there is no need to catalog them.

The most significant innovation, coming out of the abandonment of the gold standard in the spring of 1933 and Roosevelt's efforts to bring a mild rise in prices through manipulating the price of gold, was a shift to a managed currency. Gradually economists began to move the government toward monetarism as a means of restoring prosperity and restraining economic declines. It was one of the prime foundations of the new relationship between the federal government and the economy.

Another was, of course, countercyclical spending—what came in far more complicated form to be called Keynesian economics. The move toward spending as a means of obtaining recovery came, as I have already suggested, contrary to Roosevelt's firmest convictions. The downturn in the fall of 1933 promised such acute misery among millions of unemployed that he accepted Harry Hopkins's program to tap the $3.3 billion fund appropriated in the National Industrial Recovery Act to establish a Civil Works Administration (CWA). The CWA would give a few hours of work per week at standard pay to large numbers of the unemployed. By February 1934, Roosevelt and Hopkins were bringing the CWA to an end, hoping that the private sector would provide employment through the summer. The CWA spending was indeed an economic stimulus but was not sufficient to bring much reemployment. Consequently, in the summer of 1934, before the congressional elections, Hopkins planned a two-point security program at Roosevelt's direction. It would involve a larger, longer-lasting work relief program (what became the Works Progress Administration or WPA) intended to give a job to every head of family in need of one, and in addition a Social Security program to provide a safety net for old age and for future times of economic downturn.

Countercyclical spending, together with the stimulus from other spending (especially the payment over Roosevelt's veto of the bonus due to World War I veterans), resulted in a strong economic upturn in 1936 and early 1937. This occurred despite serious underfunding of the WPA. Roosevelt, incorrectly fearing that the upturn could lead to a runaway boom, inflation, and a crash, cut both spending and credit drastically, seeking to balance the budget. The cuts precipitated a sharp recession. For months during the winter of 1937-38, Roosevelt sought through ways other than spending to stimulate recovery. (I should add that through much of this time, Congress, even more anxious than he to cut spending, would have been very reluctant to appropriate new funds.) By April 1938, with the 1938 elections not far off, Roosevelt asked for a heavy appropriation to enlarge the WPA and revive the PWA (Public Works Administration), and Congress quickly responded. The machinery was in place, and both programs spent the money rapidly, bringing some recovery within a few months. Roosevelt himself did not really become a Keynesian. He continued to favor spending only as a last resort. But many of the young economists by the end of 1938 were accepting the Keynesian formula—or to be more precise, an American form of countercyclical spending to stimulate the economy. It was one of the most notable of the New Deal innovations.

It came about in the context of relief spending and Social Security—two areas about which James Patterson and other historians have written comprehensively. Clarke Chambers, in his well-titled *Seedtime of Reform*, has described the way in which social workers perpetuated the social justice objectives during the 1920s. With the coming of federal relief in 1933, the federal government provided funds which private charity and state and local governments could not raise. Along with the funds, which it gave according to dollar-matching formulas, it set minimum national standards for social work. It brought nationally the professionalization of relief. Federally, the WPA and allied programs such as the National Youth Administration (NYA) created other precedents. First under the Federal Emergency Relief Administration and then the NYA came both youth training programs and the payment of monthly stipends to needy youth so that they might continue their education. University students might receive, say, sixteen dollars per month, in return for which they did work for the university at the rate of forty cents per hour. It was a beginning of federal aid for higher education, and in various forms has continued. Other precedents came through the federal art, music, and writers' programs of the WPA. Hopkins's premise was the simple one that these people needed to eat too; work relief was the primary aim. Nonetheless, these programs nurtured writers like Ralph Ellison and artists like Jackson Pollock, together with large numbers of lesser talents. Congress wiped out these programs, along with the rest of the WPA and other programs during World War II, but since then state arts councils have filled some of the same functions, and in more recent years the National Endowment for the Arts and the National Endowment for the Humanities have made grants.

Joseph W. Alsop, Jr., in his luminous appreciation of Roosevelt, has listed as the most singular achievement domestically, transcending even the installation of the welfare state, the fight to attain full rights for all those previously excluded in a WASP America. I would add that the description also could apply to what had been a patriarchal America. Fortunately, several papers in this conference focus on these efforts.

The enumeration could go on and on in specifics. A few more generalizations will suffice.

After his landslide election in 1936, President Roosevelt wished—on behalf of the third of a nation he saw living in a substandard fashion, and also on behalf of those living wretchedly or under tyranny in other nations—to refashion in a grand way both American domestic and foreign policy. In the area of foreign policy, his goal was collective security, and he made a modest beginning with a cruise to Rio and Buenos Aires, where he preached good neighborliness and democracy. The Good Neighbor policy as he tried to develop it was in many ways a prototype of the sort of world order he envisaged—and which in part did unfold after World War II.

At home he wished to modernize the Supreme Court, which he felt was construing the Constitution in a narrow, outmoded fashion, invalidating both federal and state economic regulation. His effort to add justices to the Court failed, in considerable part because in the spring of 1937 the Court began to take a broader view of the Constitution. It is fortunate that Roosevelt failed to enlarge the Court, and one should not forget that thenceforth both states and the federal government have been able to intervene in the economy with little Court interference.

The loss of the Court fight emboldened Congress to defeat by a narrow margin Roosevelt's bill to reorganize the federal administration. Nonetheless, in 1939 he obtained a measure which did bring some changes, especially the major and significant one of creating the Executive Office of the President. The establishment of this office was a major factor in the modernizing of the administration.

Roosevelt lost too in his effort to remodel the Democratic party along New Deal lines. At the state level, old organizations, basically conservative, were dominant, and they helped send traditional-minded politicians to Congress. Roosevelt tried in the 1938 primaries to "purge" some of the Democrats who had thwarted him, with little success. Nevertheless, the New Deal did greatly alter the Democratic party, building the coalition of urban workers together with some farmers that even in 1983 does not seem entirely dead. Blacks shifted from the party of Lincoln to that of Roosevelt, and have remained there. From the age of McKinley to that of Hoover, the electorate was predominantly Republican. Only a third of the registered voters were Democrats in 1932. In contrast, a decided majority of the electorate has been Democratic in registration for nearly fifty years, although they have not always voted Democratic.

Overall, the New Deal program was flawed and limited. It did not bring quick or total recovery, and the reforms did not always work as had been anticipated. But it did bring enormous changes. It did provide the foundations for the role of the federal government for the next half-century. It did prove, as President Roosevelt declared, that the nation could recover without resort to totalitarian dictatorship or to war. The American nation could provide greater security for the American people, and in time it nurtured greater security throughout much of the world.

1. Anne O'Hare McCormick, *The World at Home* (New York: Alfred A. Knopf, 1956), p. 132.

2. *Nation* 136 (March 15, 1933): 278.

3. Nigel Law to M. Craigie, December 8, 1933, FO 371/16609 9082, p. 291, Public Record Office.

II

The New Deal and the Jewish Population

FRANKLIN D. ROOSEVELT, AMERICAN JEWRY, AND THE NEW DEAL

Leonard Dinnerstein

When Franklin D. Roosevelt died in April 1945, no group praised him more lavishly than did the American Jews. "The Jewish people lost its best friend," a California rabbi eulogized. "He gave, for the first time in American history, America's common man a sense of real security; he inspired the common man of the world with tremendous hope in the future. The big man was friend; the little man, his sole concern. His every word and deed vibrated with concern." As if this tribute were not quite sufficient, the rabbi went on, "His garments were justice and humanity; his weapons were words that came from the heart; orphaned America has lost a second Lincoln." Another Jew observed that the active support Roosevelt gave "the cause of liberalism, the preservation of the rights of minorities, and the dignity of the human personality rebounded to the welfare and security of the Jew in this and other lands." And a third proclaimed, "He gave meaning to the words—Liberty and Justice."[1]

Those encomiums were expressed in 1945. Now, with the passage of time and the publication of several major books questioning the depth of Roosevelt's commitment to the Jews and their concerns,[2] I am glad to be able to address the subject of Jews and the New Deal and to put the relationship of Roosevelt and the Jews in a somewhat—but not a radically—different perspective.

Roosevelt and the domestic New Deal undoubtedly did a great deal for American Jewry. The legislation and newly established agencies that the President recommended and/or approved not only laid the groundwork for a more secure and socially just capitalistic system, but provided thousands of new jobs. Sticking to the three Rs—relief, recovery, and reform—the New Deal helped reverse a downward spiraling economy that appeared to be destroying the nation. The New Deal did not end the Depression, but it did deal directly with the dire consequences that befell people during its most severe downturn.

More specifically, the programs enunciated and developed during the New Deal years—such as protection for bank deposits, social insurance, regulation of banks and the stock market, control of the excesses of big business, bills to provide jobs and housing, and aid to students trying to finish school—coincided with Jewish teaching and values. "For just as the New Deal advocated concern for the poor and jobless," one scholar wrote, "so did Judaism." The tradition of *Tsedekah*, emphasizing aid to the less fortunate, goes back to biblical times and has been transmitted from generation to generation, from country to country, wherever Jews have lived. As Lawrence Fuchs of Brandeis has written, "Within the framework of the Jewish cultural tradition, wealth, learning, and other tangible possessions are channeled from the strong to the weak and from the rich to the poor, as a matter of right."[3]

There were other reasons for Jews backing the President. During his twelve years in office, Roosevelt, a master of ethnic politics, appointed more Jews to office—and in especially prominent places—than had any of his predecessors. The same may also be said about Roosevelt and Irish Catholics, Roosevelt and blacks, and Roosevelt and women. Groups that had formerly been ignored were starting to receive recognition.

Although many of these appointments were symbolic, and of slight numerical or political consequence, this was not true about those given to Jews. Because Roosevelt needed, wanted, and felt stimulated by competent, imaginative, and intellectual individuals, he took them wherever he found them. A person's religious or philosophical background seemed irrelevant to the President. "I don't think a man's Jewishness entered his stream of consciousness much more than whether a man had red hair or black hair," his longtime aide, Samuel I. Rosenman, reminisced in the 1970s. And although his own social circle included no Jews aside from Henry and Elinor Morgenthau, Hyde Park neighbors, Roosevelt valued the advice and opinions of Jewish labor leaders like Sidney Hillman and Rose Schneiderman; his "favorite economist," Isador Lubin;[4] and Supreme Court Justices Louis D. Brandeis and Felix Frankfurter.[5] For political and other reasons, at various times he kept Sam Rosenman, Ben Cohen, and David Niles near him in the White House.

But more important than these very visible symbols of Roosevelt's respect for Jews, the establishment of a wide variety of New Deal agencies and the expansion of government employment created opportunities for hundreds, if not thousands, of Jews who would never have been hired by the federal government. To be sure, outside of the White House Roosevelt did not bother with appointments beneath those at the highest levels of policymaking. But by bringing Jews into the White House, and by letting it be known that Professor Felix Frankfurter of the Harvard Law School could supply untold numbers of bright young law school graduates, he signaled his approval to subordinates that they should hire people on the basis of talent and not religious, social, or class background.

Two of his Cabinet members, Frances Perkins at Labor and Harold Ickes in the Interior Department, not only shared the President's openness in this area but also had a high regard for the views of Frankfurter and therefore solicited his advice about policies and personnel. Perkins had worked with Jewish immigrants and labor leaders in New York during most of her adult life and respected them. She told one subordinate, in fact, that she preferred working "with young, alert people of a kind of urban Jewish background." Much of what the Secretary of Labor believed necessary for federal policies to improve labor's lot had already been called for by New York's lower east side Yiddish newspaper, the *Forwards*. She favored legislation which would provide "these natural, effective protections, like reasonable hours, subsistence wages, protection against damage to life and limb, protection against bad sanitation and all that kind of thing," and she hired bright young men and women to help her obtain these goals.[6]

In the Interior Department, Ickes, upon the advice of Frankfurter, took on Nathan Margold as Department Solicitor. Margold, in turn, looked to Frankfurter and Brandeis for suggestions on staff appointments and "procedures for exercising authority."[7] Perhaps no other Cabinet department, aside from Labor, included so many Jews in high-level positions during Roosevelt's lifetime. In addition to Margold, Abe Fortas served as Director of the

Division of Manpower and later Undersecretary, Saul K. Padover worked as Ickes's assistant, Michael W. Straus became Director of the War Resources Council, and Ernest Gruening was appointed Governor of Alaska. [8]

Jews in the Department of the Interior, in fact, absolutely dominated American Indian policy. Although John Collier, the Commissioner of Indian Affairs, framed the philosophical issues, that is, cultural pluralism and tribal sovereignty, the real architect of the Indian New Deal was Felix Cohen, a militant New York attorney, and son of Morris Raphael Cohen, the great guru of City College students. Felix Cohen wrote the Indian legislation with Nathan Margold; later Fortas figured prominently as a defender of Indian rights. It is interesting to observe that although Jews in the New Deal did little to promote civil rights for Jews, they were instrumental in contributing to reforms in Indian affairs.[9]

By the end of the 1930s, Jewish attorneys appeared disproportionately concentrated in the Department of Labor, parts of the Justice Department, the Securities and Exchange Commission, the National Labor Relations Board (NLRB), and the Social Security Administration. During the early period of the New Deal they had also appeared prominently in the Agricultural Adjustment Administration (AAA), and their presence made them a target for bigoted attacks. Adlai Stevenson of the AAA complained, "There is a little feeling that the Jews are getting too prominent." Southern and Western farmers also made it clear that they did not like dealing with large numbers of Jewish lawyers at the AAA. Moreover, in December 1938, the chairman of the Institute of Human Relations Conference meeting in Houston, Texas, charged that there were too many Jews in the NLRB and the Department of Labor, and a year or two later one person told a journalist, "You can't find an official in the whole [government] who hasn't got a damned Jew lawyer sitting by him at his desk."[10]

Many of the people who did not like Jews did not like the President either. The businessmen and upper classes of society who denounced the Administration and its policies—the so-called Jew Deal—also frowned upon the numbers of Jews they saw about Roosevelt. Rumors passed about Roosevelt's alleged Jewish heritage and the influence of the left-leaning Jewish "radicals" who were responsible for the New Deal policies.

"The anti-Semitic and racial overtones which marked so many of the anti-Roosevelt stories and which soon became an obsession among the members of the country-club establishment were not accidental," E. Digby Baltzell later wrote.[11]

Jews represented the new breed in Washington and the new directions marked out by the government. Although many members of the WASP elite feared the erosion of their positions, New Deal policies should have reinforced their feelings of security rather than threatened them. The reverse seems to have been true. Moreover, with Roosevelt so popular, it was much easier to attack the Jews than the President and make them the culprits for the unwelcome changes. "Thus," one scholar tells us, "the onslaught began, the slurs, the snide comments, the whispering campaign that Jews were running the New Deal, that Roosevelt was a tool of the Jews, that Jews were responsible for the administration's allegedly leftist policies."[12]

Roosevelt weathered the attacks on both his Administration's policies and the numbers of Jews that he brought into government. At the very time that most of society was excluding Jews, he drew them closer to his side. In 1936, for example, he wanted Judge Samuel Rosenman, who had been his chief aide when he was Governor of New York, to be with him during the election campaign. Rosenman questioned whether it would be politically wise for a Jew to accompany the President on a tour through the Bible Belt in the Midwest, but Roosevelt dismissed the objection. "That's no way to handle anti-Semitism," the President supposedly replied in anger. "The way to handle it is to meet it head-on."[13] The prime opposition again came from other Jews who feared an increase in American anti-Semitism when Roosevelt indicated he would go ahead with his desire to appoint Felix Frankfurter to the Supreme Court. But again the President knew what he wanted to do and he did it.[14] For support of this kind, therefore, most American Jews warmly embraced Roosevelt as their champion.

However, in areas where the President had to rely on the initiative and approval of both Houses of the Congress, Roosevelt acted more cautiously and responded more politically. And it is in these areas—immigration policy and aid to Jews victimized by Hitler in Europe—that more recent historical analyses have questioned whether American Jews should have so revered Franklin Roosevelt.

When Roosevelt took office in 1933, immigration policy had not only been settled but created no divisions in the country. No recent immigration group, and that included the Jews, indicated any desire to change the established quota policy.[15] As the 1930s went on, however, and as Hitler's treatment of the Jews in Germany became more restrictive and brutal, individual Jews made some informal attempts to have the President liberalize the State Department's interpretation of immigration policy. This Roosevelt refused to do. Keenly attuned to the isolationist and restrictive sentiments that pervaded the United States (in 1939, 85 percent of the Protestants and 84 percent of the Catholics opposed less restrictive immigration laws to aid refugees),[16] Roosevelt did almost nothing to prevent the extermination of six million European Jews between 1939 and 1945.[17]

Not until 1944, in fact, did the President establish the War Refugee Board to help rescue those Jews who still might be saved. But he did that (1) after the Senate Foreign Relations Committee passed a resolution recommending that the President establish a commission "to assist rescue of Jewish victims of Nazi persecution"; (2) after Supreme Court Justice Frank Murphy, Vice-President Henry Wallace, and former Republican presidential nominee Wendell Willkie headed up a group called the National Committee Against Nazi Persecution, calling for a "sustained and vigorous action by our government and United Nations to rescue those who may yet be saved"; and (3) after Secretary of the Treasury Henry Morgenthau presented the President with a report entitled "Acquiescence of This Government in the Murder of the Jews" in January 1944. In other words, not until sufficient political pressure had been put upon him did Roosevelt attempt anything of consequence to rescue European Jews from Hitler's ovens.[18]

But American Jews, for a variety of reasons, never put the kind of pressure on Roosevelt to do something to save their European brethren that many American Jews in subsequent generations think they should have. There were several reasons for this. The increase and pervasiveness of anti-Semitism, along with a cultural pressure in the United States calling for the assimilation of Jews into the dominant society,[19] made American Jews reluctant to speak out as members of a minority group. Furthermore, American Jews did not look kindly upon an influx of European Jews because they assumed that the presence of the newcomers would exacerbate American anti-Semitism. Third, the fragmented nature of the American Jewish community and its lack of adequate leadership precluded any concerted political efforts. And finally, not until 1942 or 1943 did a large number of American Jews understand the enormity of the Holocaust then underway.[20]

The ambiguity of American Jewish attitudes during the New Deal years must also be explored to understand American Jewish reservations about boldly calling for assistance for their European coreligionists. The middle- and upper-class Jews, whether succumbing to pressures against parochialism, or out of a real desire to assimilate the values of the dominant society, were not quite sure how to behave. To speak up for increased Jewish immigration smacked of parochialism; to acquiesce in allowing existing immigration policies to stand meant a rejection of their heritage and ignoring the plight of their European brethren.[21]

The most famous American Jewish spokesman of the era, Rabbi Stephen S. Wise (who represented only a small segment of American Jewry at that time) perhaps captured the American Jewish dilemma when he testified at a 1938 congressional hearing in support of a proposed bill to bring twenty thousand German children to the United States. While favoring the measure, he also stated quite clearly: "I want to make it plain that, so far as I am concerned, there is no intention whatsoever to depart from the immigration laws which at present obtain. I have heard no sane person propose any departure or deviation from the existing law now in force." He then added that if there were any conflict between the needs of the children and those of the United States, "I should say, of course, that our country comes first."[22]

Although Wise did not hesitate to speak out as a Jew, many Jews were so eager to be accepted as full-fledged Americans, indistinguishable from others except for nominal religious affiliation, that they prostituted themselves in the most embarrassing fashion. Perhaps the worst example of this occurred when the *Saturday Evening Post* published Judge Jerome Frank's essay "Red, White and Blue Herring" the day before the Japanese attack on Pearl Harbor in 1941. Frank tried to assure readers of that archetypical American magazine that most American Jews had rejected "all or most of the old Jewish customs," that they thought "as Americans . . . not as Jews," and that they voiced the same opinions, saw the same movies, and rooted for the same ball teams as their Christian neighbors. He went even further by asserting that the religion practiced by most American Jews "is clearly closer to liberal Protestantism than to Jewish orthodoxy." Frank elaborated: "For those American Jews who broke the hold of the old Jewish code, what remains of the historic Jewish religion consists principally of some noble ethical principles and special values. . . . To call them 'Jewish' is to be a pedantic antiquarian." Frank dismissed the fervent Zionists as "a small group of fanatic Jewish nationalists," and told readers that all shades of American Zionist opinion at that time constituted "only a small percentage of the American Jewish population." The judge even acknowledged that in the past he had been upset that "because I was a Jew, I was barred from fraternities in college, [and] when I found I was not wanted in a hotel or club, I didn't like it, of course. But . . . I accepted such social disabilities with a sense of humor." Nonetheless, he identified himself completely as an American and said that "however much I might be anguished at the plight of the oppressed peoples in other countries, Jews or Gentiles, I [do] not believe that America should sacrifice its welfare to rescue them." He assumed that most American Jews shared his sentiments.[23]

With such self-effacement, which probably represented the thoughts and actions of many Jews who aspired to be accepted as Americans and not Jewish Americans, Roosevelt did not have to concern himself too much about changing American immigration policies or spending any of his political capital trying to rescue Jews desperate to escape from Germany. In fact, it would probably be most accurate to state that the intensified anti-Semitism in the United States during the New Deal era, and the fearful responses of the Jews to it, contributed more toward Roosevelt's attitudes on increased immigration than any callousness or calculation on his part.

Roosevelt was a realistic politician who rarely bucked the tide of public and congressional opinion. He helped Jews indirectly with his New Deal programs and directly with his appointments. But he never tried to do more than he knew he could accomplish for them, and he was unwilling to expend his political capital on an issue that he probably saw as politically destructive for other policies that he wished to pursue. An all-out attempt to rescue Jews would have resulted in a direct confrontation with the Congress and an aroused and hostile American public, and a threat to the harmonious pursuit of wartime and planned postwar policies.

How, therefore, should we evaluate Franklin Roosevelt and his relationship to American Jews? Was he saint or sinner? Should he be revered or excoriated? Well, if Roosevelt is praised for what he did, he should also be censured for what he did not do, namely for not moving vigorously and imaginatively to give refuge to the threatened Jews of Europe.

1. *Emanu-El* (San Francisco), April 20, 1945, pp. 2, 3; William B. Furie, "Jewish Education," *Jewish Advocate* (Boston), April 19, 1945, p. 12; *Buffalo Jewish Review*, April 20, 1945, p. 73.

2. See, for example, Henry L. Feingold, *The Politics of Rescue* (New Brunswick: Rutgers University Press, 1970); Saul S. Friedman, *No Haven for the Oppressed* (Detroit: Wayne State University Press, 1973); Bernard Wasserstein, *Britain and the Jews of Europe* (New York: Oxford University Press, 1979); and David S. Wyman, *Paper Walls* (Amherst: University of Massachusetts Press, 1968).

3. Myron I. Scholnick, "The New Deal and Anti-Semitism in America" (Ph.D. dissertation, University of Maryland, 1971), p. 22; Lawrence H. Fuchs, "American Jews and the Presidential Vote," *American Political Science Review* 49 (June 1955): 400.

4. Rosenman quotation is from Samuel I. Rosenman Oral History Memoir, William E. Wiener Oral History Library, American Jewish Committee, New York City, Tape 2, p. 18. Forrest Davis, "Minister to Moscow," *Saturday Evening Post* 217 (June 16, 1945): 17.

5. On the influence of Brandeis and Frankfurter, see Bruce Allen Murphy, *The Brandeis/Frankfurter Connection* (New York: Oxford University Press, 1982).

6. Frances Perkins Oral History Memoirs, Columbia University Oral History Collection, vol. 1, pp. 57, 61; vol. 3, pp. 522, 590; vol. 7, p. 16. See also *Brandeis/Frankfurter Connection*, p. 114; Michael E. Parrish, *Felix Frankfurter and His Times* (New York: Free Press, 1982), p. 225; Benjamin Stolberg, "Madam Secretary," *Saturday Evening Post*, July 27, 1940, p. 9. Quotations are from Charles E. Wyzanski, Jr., Oral History Memoir, Columbia University Oral History Collection, p. 185; and Perkins Memoirs, vol. 1, p. 57.

7. Murphy, *Brandeis/Frankfurter Connection*, p. 114.

8. Milton Persitz, "Jews in Government Service," *Jewish Chronicle* (Indianapolis), March 27, 1942, in folder, "U.S.—Politics and Government—Jews," in Blaustein Library, American Jewish Committee, New York City.

9. Interview with Allison Bernstein, who is compiling a dissertation on New Deal Indian policy at Columbia University.

10. W. M. Kiplinger, "The Facts About Jews in Washington," *Reader's Digest* 41 (September 1942): 3; *The New Dealers*, by an unofficial observer (New York: Literary Guild, 1934), p. 322; Albert Jay Nock, "The Jewish Problem in America, II," *Atlantic Monthly* 168 (July 1941): 74. Quotations are from Jerold S. Auerbach, *Unequal Justice* (New York: Oxford University

Press), p. 188; and "Too Many Jews in Government?," *Christian Century* 55 (December 28, 1938): 1614.

11. "Anti-Semitism Is Here," *Nation* 147 (August 20, 1938): 167; George Wolfskill and John A. Hudson, *All But the People* (New York: Macmillan Co., 1969), p. 86; *The New Dealers*, p. 322; Marquis W. Childs, "They Still Hate Roosevelt," *New Republic* 96 (September 14, 1938): 148; E. Digby Baltzell, *The Protestant Establishment* (New York: Random House, 1964), p. 248.

12. Scholnick, "The New Deal and Anti-Semitism," pp. 76-77.

13. Samuel I. Rosenman Oral History Memoir, William E. Wiener Oral History Library, American Jewish Committee, Tape 2-19, 20.

14. Stephen S. Wise to Milton Krensky, September 23, 1938, in Carl Hermann Voss, *Stephen S. Wise: Servant of the People* (Philadelphia: Jewish Publication Society of America, 1970), pp. 229-30; Rabbi Ferdinand M. Isserman, "FDR and Felix Frankfurter," *National Jewish Monthly* 80 (November 1965): 16; Joseph P. Lash, *From the Diaries of Felix Frankfurter* (New York: W.W. Norton & Co., 1975), p. 64; Parrish, *Felix Frankfurter and His Times*, p. 276.

15. David Brody, "American Jewry: The Refugees and Immigration Restriction (1932-1942)," in Abraham J. Karp, ed., *The Jewish Experience in America*, 5 vols. (Waltham, Mass.: American Jewish Historical Society, 1969), 5:340.

16. "The Fortune Survey: XX," *Fortune* 19 (April 1939): 102.

17. Henry L. Feingold, *Zion in America* (New York: Twayne Publishers, Inc., 1974), p. 276; Melvin I. Urofsky, *A Voice That Spoke for Justice* (Albany, N.Y.: State University of New York Press, 1982), p. 136; Robert Dallek, *Franklin D. Roosevelt and American Foreign Policy* (New York: Oxford University Press, 1979), p. 446.

18. Isaiah Berlin, *Washington Despatches, 1941-1945*, ed. H. G. Nicholas (Chicago: University of Chicago Press, 1981), p. 295; Leonard Dinnerstein, *America and the Survivors of the Holocaust* (New York: Columbia University Press, 1982), pp. 4, 5; Urofsky, *A Voice That Spoke for Justice*, p. 330. See also, Naomi W. Cohen, *Not Free To Desist* (Philadelphia: Jewish Publication Society of America, 1972), p. 170.

19. For articles typical of the type that put pressure on the Jews to assimilate, see the following in *Christian Century*: Alfred William Anthony, "Explaining the Jew," 50 (August 16, 1933): 1034-36; Joseph Ernest McAfee, "Jewish Solidarity in America," 51 (January 10, 1934): 52-53; "The Jewish Problem," 51 (February 28, 1934): 279-81; Albert Levitan, "Leave the Jewish Problem Alone!," 51 (April 25, 1934): 555-57; "Jewry and Democracy," 54 (June 9, 1937): 734-36. In the last, the author wrote, "The situation in which the Jewish problem arises is in large measure Jewry's own creation" (p. 736).

20. Cohen, *Not Free to Desist*, pp. 194, 204.

21. Brody, "American Jewry," pp. 324, 326, 332, 334, 338.

22. Wise's comments are quoted in ibid., p. 331.

23. Jerome Frank, "Red, White and Blue Herring," *Saturday Evening Post* 214 (December 6, 1941): 9, 10, 83, 84, 85.

III

RADICAL POLITICS IN THE THIRTIES

Could the New Deal Have Taken America to the Left?

David H. Bennett

It has been fifty years since that grim winter of 1932-33 in America. But the somber spectacle of millions in despair is easier to recall now because of the reminders everywhere in contemporary life. Today there are two million homeless across this nation, and the tent villages on the outskirts of Houston and other communities evoke memories of the Hoovervilles of yesterday. The "new poor" is a term used widely by those unaware that its first appearance in America was in the Great Depression. The pictures of soup kitchens and long lines of discouraged job seekers, the desperate testimony of the unemployed at congressional hearings, seem lifted from the crisis of a half-century ago.

Of course, yesterday's crisis was much more severe and its impact more cruelly felt. Unemployment approached 25 percent then, twice the toll of today's recession, and because there had been no New Deal, the victims of 1933 were much more vulnerable. At least twenty-nine persons starved to death in New York City alone that year and admissions to state hospitals for the mentally ill tripled. Anger born of desperation led to violence or to the fear of violence and to repression. The crushing of the Bonus Army the year before and the Farm Holiday Association's food blockades would be followed by the forty-eight-mile-long "coal caravan" of ten thousand striking miners in southern Illinois, the seizure of the county-city building in Seattle, the raids on grocery stores by gangs of the unemployed in Detroit, the mass refusal to pay streetcar fares in Des Moines, and assorted acts of defiance of the law and theft of public and private property coast to coast. From many quarters came a call to overturn an economic and social system which had failed, which some insisted had been the root cause of the abyss into which so many hopes and dreams had disappeared.[1]

It was not only the melodramatic magazine writers calling for the appointment of a dictator or labor leaders warning darkly that "revolutions grow out of the depths of hunger." Numerous political activists believed that a crucial choice was at hand: capitalism under the centralized authoritarian control of Fascism, Communism, or some Socialist middle ground. The European revolutions were on many minds and the alternatives seemed clear—the road to Berlin, the road to Moscow, or an American radical alternative which preserved democracy while abandoning capitalism.[2]

The New Deal was born in what many viewed as the perfect setting for making radical change in the United States. But it did not produce radical change. Some of Franklin D. Roosevelt's bitterest critics thought they could discern a revolution under way; Herbert Hoover filled the pages of *The Challenge to Liberty*, published the year after the Hundred Days, with dire warnings that "Regimentation" (always with a capital R) was replacing the "true domain of Liberty." But few would agree across the years. In the fifties and after there were collections published with titles like *The New Deal: Evolution or Revolution*, but it was not "revolution" in the way it was seen in 1933 that these editors had in mind. Most of them would agree with Frances Perkins in her most frequently quoted passage: "Roosevelt took the status quo in our economic system as much for granted as his family. They were part of his life and so was our system; he was content with it." FDR would be what his predecessor was not—flexible, experimental, and in its broadest meaning, pragmatic. He was sensitive to suffering and he was humane. His Administration would address the enormous problem of alleviating hunger and of replacing fear and anxiety with hope for the future. When his New Deal was over, the government had assumed wide responsibility for achieving and maintaining prosperity; some federal bureaus had been vastly expanded and many new ones created; institutional arrangements in America had changed in ways many saw as permanent. Franklin Roosevelt had become the political master of his age, the dominant political figure of the century. But he had not taken America to the left as many had hoped and a few had predicted. Instead, he had produced a reform Administration which Perkins rightly characterized in her famous memoir as "a little left of center."[3]

But the central questions from the winter of 1932-33 endure. Should the New Deal have moved the United States to the left? Could it have done so? The argument that the New Deal should have taken the nation to the left is informed by the critics' negative assessment of the achievements of the Roosevelt Administration. Contemporary analysts of a more radical persuasion had assailed FDR as a shrewd political manipulator without vision or principle, a clever confidence man who gained the esteem of the poor and the middle class while helping the rich to maintain power and privilege. In 1935, Benjamin Stolberg and Warren Jay Vinton compared the New Deal to a hurricane: "a lot of activity and no lasting change, an attempt to evade the fundamental contradictions of our economy" which became a "synthesis of errors." In the sixties, the emergence of what was then called by some a "new left" historical analysis produced a more sophisticated critique. Howard Zinn dismissed the New Deal in 1966 as merely "refurbishing middle class America," which had taken a dizzying fall in the Depression, and giving "just enough to the lower classes to create an aura of good will." Paul Conkin saw it as Edmund Wilson had: "a promise betrayed, essentially misdirected from the beginning." In an influential essay, Barton J. Bernstein noted the conservative "achievements" of this liberal reform: while creating no significant redistribution of power in American society, "the New Deal failed to solve the problem of the depression, it failed to raise the impoverished, it failed to redistribute income, it failed to extend equality . . . it failed . . . to make business more responsible to the general welfare or to threaten business's pre-eminent political power." Quoting Raymond Moley that "if ever there was a moment when things hung in the balance, it was on March 5, 1933— when unorthodoxy would have drained the last remaining strength of the capitalist system," Bernstein concludes that FDR ignored the golden opportunity. He operated only within safe and narrow channels and "not only avoided Marxism and the socialization of property, but also . . . other possibilities—communal direction of production or the organized distribution of surplus," with the result that "the marginal men trapped in hopelessness were seduced by rhetoric, by style and movement, by the symbolism of efforts seldom reaching beyond words."[4]

The New Deal not only missed its chance to bring radical and lasting change, we are told, but it is attacked for destroying this opportunity for others. In its successful relief programs, the cutting edge of the crisis was blunted; the Federal Emergency Relief Administration (FERA) and the Civil Works Administration (CWA), the Works Progress Administration (WPA) and the Public Works Administration (PWA) put so many people on government payrolls that the mounting anger and despair dissipated and the setting for radical action disappeared. In this sense, worse than a do-nothing or an incompetent in the White House, Roosevelt was the savior of a destructive and inequitable system. If he had not been so adroit, so persuasive, so responsive to the need for minimal action, the United States might have had its chance; there might have been built a better new world in the ashes of the old.

In 1983, these memories of lost opportunities and failed alternatives have a peculiar poignancy. Fifty years after the first inauguration, America has a President who derides many of the programs of the Roosevelt Administration, who refers to fifty years of failed federal initiatives, who seeks to make these years a referendum not only on the nation's future but also on a past dominated by the heritage of Franklin D. Roosevelt. The contemporary assault on the New Deal casts different shadows on the decades-long debate over the choices available in 1933. In the end, the question of should the New Deal have taken America to the left cannot be resolved. It may be more passionately debated at certain junctures—as in the sixties—or more deeply felt at other times, such as our own. But the discussion will continue as long as people with different values and different visions read and write history.

That other question, however—could the New Deal have taken America left—may be more usefully addressed today. The answer I propose here: probably not.

For the purposes of the inquiry, let us first avoid the obvious objection that FDR never intended to achieve radical change. What if he had been different, what if an Administration with different goals and objectives had begun its work that morning a half-century ago? Could America have been led down the road to a new order, to a radically transformed social and economic system?

In pursuing that question, we might begin by considering the fate of those radical leaders and movements proposing such alternatives in the thirties. If America could have been taken to the left, what of these options? What was the nature and the fate of the radical movements which were on the scene?

The Communist Party seemed to have the right program for America at the right time when the Great Depression began. When the Sixth World Congress of the Communist International dictated a change in the Communist line in 1928, leaders of the party in the United States were forced to go along despite grave reservations. Those who refused were expelled as rightist deviationists, their claims to an "American exceptionalism" dismissed by Stalin, who was shaping world Communist policy in response to internal Soviet needs. Thus, at the high tide of prosperity in the roaring twenties, American Communists were asked to declare the bankruptcy of capitalism, to become resolutely militant, to prepare for revolution. It seemed suicidal.

But then came the Great Depression. Now, with the mounting numbers of unemployed and the growing feeling that the free enterprise system was a dismal failure, the new Communist line called for radical change, a clean break with the capitalist past. In the worst economic crisis in the history of any industrial society, American Communists—through no work of their own— had what seemed to them the perfect program in place. By 1932, with upwards of fifteen million unemployed, the Communists reviled "both main bourgeois parties" for "fully supporting the policies of finance capital." When FDR was elected, he was seen as "just the same as Hoover before him . . . the New Deal is not developed fascism, but in political essence and direction it is the same as Hitler's program." But the party which was preparing for revolution in 1931, which had its youth affiliate, the Young Storm Leaders (studying street fighting, barricade building, and rifle shooting), did not succeed with its militant program before or after the coming of the New Deal. Its presidential candidate polled a disappointing 103,000 votes in 1932 despite the most extensive campaign it ever conducted. Party membership rose only from a miniscule 7,500 in 1929 to less than 24,000 in 1934— in a nation of 130 million. And the party was not even keeping the members it recruited. From 1930 to 1934 approximately 50,000 new members were enrolled, and the leaders wondered why "two out of every three recruited members have not been retained in the Party."[5]

Was there a setting for truly radical change in 1933? Were

Americans ready to abandon capitalism and the social and political institutions supporting it? Certainly not in favor of a Communist alternative. Of course, Communism did prosper in the Depression decade, reaching its point of greatest strength and influence in America during this time. But this happened only after the hard-line policy had been completely transformed and American Communists made peace with the presiding system and with the New Deal. The success of American Communism in the thirties appears paradoxical; in fact, it tells us much about the enduring appeals of the system which FDR "took as much for granted as his family."

In August 1935, the Seventh World Congress of Comintern heard General Secretary Georgi Dimitrov announce a new direction for world Communism. The Soviet Union needed allies to contain the expansionist plans of Adolph Hitler. Stalin could not reach out to the Western powers for such an alliance if he was actively fomenting revolution in the West. Now the U.S. party, among others, was instructed to build the Popular Front, an anti-Fascist coalition of labor, liberal, and leftist forces in domestic as well as international affairs. In practice, this meant that the American Communist Party (CPUSA) would embrace FDR and the New Deal.[6]

"Communism is twentieth century Americanism" became the widely advertised new anthem. It was not only the pictures of Jefferson and Jackson displacing those of Lenin and Stalin at headquarters but the rejection of radical tactics and even radical objectives. The Communists' treatment of Franklin D. Roosevelt was turned upside down: in the *Daily Worker*, the *New Masses*, and the *Communist*, the running dog of finance capital and Fascism became "a man who sincerely believes in democracy," a man with "the stature of a major statesman" offering a "program of material well-being for the people." While it ran a candidate once again in 1936, the party made it clear that the choice was really between Roosevelt and Landon and that it was the President who should receive members' support. Leaders pledged their full support to him by 1937: "We Communists welcome his speeches, agree with their central thoughts and quietly and calmly tell President he has nothing to fear from us, on the contrary, he will receive our help." By 1938, Communist leaflets were circulating bearing the title *We Do Not Propose to Let the President Down.*[7]

CPUSA membership rose to over one hundred thousand during this period, and membership in fellow-traveler organizations like the League for Peace and Democracy swelled to many times this number. It had been only when the party became nonrevolutionary, when it rejected radical alternatives, that its appeal as an anti-Fascist movement found a substantial audience. Before the Popular Front, when the Depression was at its worst, the deviant nature of the Communist program doomed it to failure. These radical ideas had little appeal even in capitalism's darkest hour.

The Socialist Party experienced a different fate in these years, but its failure is as significant as the curious if limited success of Popular Front Communism. Under the leadership of Norman Thomas, Socialists never embraced FDR. With no Comintern dictating their policy, they became increasingly hostile to the New Deal across the decade and paid the same price for their radicalism as had the Communists before 1932 and 1935: their membership shriveled, and their angry speeches fell on deaf ears.

In 1929, Socialist Party membership hovered at only 9,500, but the crisis of American capitalism promised to bring vast new support. It did not. Membership in the organization which for three decades had called for an end to capitalism rose to less than 17,000 in the grimmest year of the Depression. Thomas, the Socialist candidate, polled almost 900,000 votes that year, but his call to "bring about the social ownership of land, natural resources and the principal means of production" elicited little interest outside those precincts which had voted for the party in earlier and less critical elections. Now, the movement which had failed to win a following with Herbert Hoover in the White House would have to contend with Franklin D. Roosevelt. [8]

Norman Thomas was unimpressed by the New Deal. Noting those hysterical attacks in which Al Smith and the Liberty League accused FDR of carrying out most of the demands of the Socialist Party platform, Thomas angrily responded: "What Roosevelt has given us . . . is not socialism . . . it is state capitalism which the Fascist demagogues of Europe have used when they came to power." Thomas moved his party to the left in these early years of the New Deal. Siding with the faction of younger militants in the savage fratricidal struggle which rocked Socialism in 1934, he so alienated that old guard of venerable New York regulars—veterans of decades of Socialist organizing but counselors of moderation in the months after the Hundred Days—that these old-timers were forced out of the party. The militants in control were not necessarily revolutionaries, but an influential faction—the Revolutionary Policy Committee—did talk of resisting Fascism by any means necessary. Such a theme would attract few followers in the United States, and Socialist Party membership declined by almost a third by September 1935. The party never recovered. Thomas polled a disastrous 187,000 votes in 1936—a small fraction of his earlier total—and acrimonious ideological quarrels, incursions by Trotskyists, and other factional disruptions marked a movement in decline and disarray through the end of the decade.[9]

Why did Socialism founder in the period of capitalism's greatest failure? Some writers have pointed to the internecine struggles, sympathizing with Thomas's plight or blaming him for siding with the left wing of his party. Others have argued that the party in the thirties—as throughout its history—was led by unrealistic men and women, people unable to shape policies to reconcile Socialism with the overwhelming reality of New Deal success. In the end, Norman Thomas seemed to sadly accept the view that the New Deal destroyed his chances; he noted in his memoirs that "what cut the ground out pretty completely from under us was . . . Roosevelt in a word. You don't need anything more." But, of course, it was not only Roosevelt, or else the party would have been making headway before its virtual disintegration. The failure of the Socialist dream in the thirties—as those who left because of their "conservative" obstinacy in 1934 recognized—was that America was not ready to go left even in those months of greatest despair. The fate of Socialism at this time, like Communism, is a monument to the dilemma of radical activism in the United States.[10]

So, too, was the fate of those individuals seeking a non-Socialist, non-Communist cooperative commonwealth. Whether it be Alfred Bingham and Selden Rodman, those non-Marxist radicals who inaugurated their journal *Common Sense* in late 1932 in the belief that the time was ripe for the making of a new industrial democracy based on government planning and "production for use," or their sometime colleagues, Stuart Chase, Paul Douglas, and John Dewey—radical insurgents who also envisioned an emerging collective state—there were many intellectuals dreaming of what George Soule called the "coming American Revolution" in his 1934 volume by that name. But their plans never even began to materialize; their dreams died in gestation. Within a year, *Common Sense*, whose editors expected fifty thousand readers, was barely functioning with two thousand sales. The League for Independent Political Action (LIPA), which Bingham, Dewey, and others hoped would encourage an independent Socialist Party, was foundering. When Howard Y. Williams and Thomas R. Amlie, those gifted progressives from the upper Midwest, joined Bingham and his fellows in organizing the Farmer Labor Political Federation, which they hoped might give their ideas a chance to be heard at last in the larger nation, they met further disappointment. The cooperative commonwealth was not to be; neither LIPA or its allies—the Wisconsin Progessive Party of 1934 or Floyd Olson's Minnesota Farmer Labor Association—survived as radical alternatives through 1936. They were all undone not only by the appeal of the New Deal but by popular indifference to their ideas. FDR's agenda was born of the crisis; their agenda seemed irrelevant because it appeared abstract. FDR's program offered jobs and food, clothing and shelter—not a sophisticated scheme for overturning institutions. But they also ran afoul of the resistance to the specter of radicalism. As Alfred Bingham observed, Americans could never easily be recruited to a party offering to build an equitable, classless society because Americans believed they already were living in a classless society. Even the poor, the laborers, and the lower middle classes—propertyless and exploited and desperate in 1933—could not be reached on this point. Americans identified not with the class they belonged to, Bingham would say, but with the class in which they thought they belonged. That Americanist ethos, that middle-class mindset, could not be reshaped even by sensitive radical thinkers who rejected a rigid Marxist dialectic.[11]

Indeed, the only truly successful "radical" activists of the thirties endorsed and embraced the American Dream, proclaimed their devotion to individualism, and called for neither a planned economy nor the end to private property. The achievements of Father Charles Coughlin, Huey Long, and Dr. Francis Townsend suggest not that radicalism was a viable alternative in 1932, but instead how difficult it would be to take America to the left.

Coughlin's rise to national prominence was meteoric in the

early thirties. The radio priest of Royal Oak with the mesmerizing speaking style tailored perfectly to the new medium—"without doubt one of the great voices of the twentieth century," an observer had written, "a voice made for promises"—became the greatest radio star of the age, a clergyman with a weekly audience of tens of millions for his Sunday sermons on economics and politics. Charles E. Coughlin built a political movement to mobilize that audience in service of his plans for America. The National Union for Social Justice (NUSJ) had recruited "at least" 5,267,000 members, he announced in January 1936 (although on another occasion he referred to "1.6 million active and 6 million passive members"); it had units in 302 of 435 congressional districts. What Coughlin proposed was to defeat the Depression through a program of cheap money. His inflationary schemes changed across the years, but the point remained the same: prosperity was denied only because certain men of influence and great wealth made money and credit hard to obtain. All that was necessary was to establish a government-owned central bank and to manipulate the money supply; to give the less affluent, the workers, small businessmen, and other debtors access to credit; and to "lift the crushing taxation from the slender resources of the laboring class."[12]

Coughlin had made his mark before 1933, when he built his following by attacking Herbert Hoover, Andrew Mellon, and what he called their "bankster" allies. While he initially supported FDR as a fellow inflationist and dreamed of becoming the Richelieu of the Roosevelt era, his feud with the President would soon become famous; he would assail that "Great Betrayer and Liar . . . Franklin Double-Crossing Roosevelt." But the radio priest was not calling for a truly radical alternative: "I am no Socialist, no Communist, no fascist and against . . . any un-Americanism," he exclaimed. "Capitalism is . . . the best system of economics provided it does not run counter to the laws of morality." The famed Sixteen Principles of the NUSJ called on his followers to pledge: "I believe in upholding the right to private property." Father Coughlin's ideas owed much to the Populist tradition; he believed with these predecessors that America was so rich that no revolution was needed here, the wrong people were in control of the government and its currency, and their replacement would bring a better tomorrow.[13]

There is a historical debate over whether Coughlin's appeal

should be characterized as demagogic. I believe that many of his followers did think of him as a millennial savior and that there was an ugly hidden agenda to his sermons that helped create the frenetic response to his leadership. At the national convention of his movement in 1936, there was a unanimous endorsement by ten thousand delegates of a resolution proclaiming him "The Greatest American of all time." Delegates compared him to Christ; resolved that "we give thanks to the mother of the Reverend Charles E. Coughlin for bearing him"; and shouted across the hall, "Father Coughlin, test us, try us, lead us." But whether critical of the radio priest's charismatic style and political management or sympathetic to this "voice of protest" in the dark days of the early thirties, many of us would agree, in the words of a recent book, that his followers were imperiled members "in a world of modest middle-class accomplishments"; that they were "no more eager to see the state encroach on their lives than they were to accept the influence of great private interest"; and that they "sought a system of decentralized power, limited ownership and small scale capitalism." Whatever the sources of his success, Coughlin was not going to take the country to the left.[14]

Nor was Huey Long. The Kingfish of Louisiana insisted he was no Socialist and no Communist: "Just say I'm sui generis and leave it at that." But Long's idea's were not merely unique, they were uniquely American. Like Coughlin, his Share-Our-Wealth scheme owed much to the Populist tradition. He embraced private property and proposed to end poverty by providing every family a patrimony of "at least $5000 debt free" (plus an adequate pension, home, automobile, radio, and college education for the kids) by simply taxing the rich. All savings would be seized above a certain figure, set at first at $10 million, lowered later to $1.7 million. His scheme, of course, was only a wild dream. In computing the national wealth to be divided, he included latent resources; only by some miracle could forests and mines, highways and schools, oil wells and factories be converted to a house and a bank account for each family.

Economists dismissed Share-Our-Wealth as a hoax, and one called it "a monstrous and tragic joke . . . based upon either demagogic hypocrisy or else ignorance so abysmal as to inspire awe." But the validity of Huey Long's panacea was no more important than Coughlin's inflationary schemes in gauging his appeal. Long spoke for the scared and angry people whose families were hungry, whose hopes were blasted in the Depression. He believed he could gain the White House because "I can outpromise Roosevelt." It was not necessary, it was not wise, and it was never intended to offer a truly radical alternative to the capitalist system. Whether or not there really were 7.6 million Share-Our-Wealth members by 1935 (or three million as alleged at another time that year); whether or not the "27,431 Share-Our-Wealth clubs in 8000 communities" really functioned and the organization "voiced the demands of 12 million people," as his paper alleged; Long's popularity and his Share-Our-Wealth movement's appeal were real enough. But the movement would not have survived if this remarkable man had promoted a radical agenda. He promised the world, but it was his style and his colorful assault on enemies that elicited support; the program was preposterous but it was also safe because—like Coughlin's—it was not truly radical.[15]

The same was true of Dr. Townsend's Old Age Pension plan. The aging physician from Long Beach, California, had hit on the idea of ending the Depression through saving the old people of America—who faced unparalleled privation in the thirties—by providing a $200-a-month pension to every citizen sixty years old and over, provided the recipient agreed to spend the money within thirty days. If these "civil veterans of the republic," as he called his pensioners, poured their over $20 billion into the economy each year, people everywhere would prosper as factories reopened, unemployment shrank, and prosperity returned to the land. It was a hyperinflationary concept, linked in many ways to Coughlin's and Long's but even more bizarre. Critics ridiculed the Townsendites' argument and their turnover taxing program. One said that the doctor was trying to "teach people to believe in Santa Claus again"; another said that "what the Townsendites are really demanding is a revision of the science of arithmetic by law." The plan would not have saved the nation; in practice it would have meant only that a new privileged class—the elderly—had been established with fiat money. It would make our present Social Security dilemma pale in comparison; the plan called for spending more than half the gross national product in 1932 on pensions.[16]

But Townsend's program, despite its wild extravagance and obvious shortcomings (one cynic suggested everyone be given $200 every week—if the government could afford $24 billion, it could afford $2,400 billion), was not really radical. The old doctor embraced capitalism and celebrated the American Way of Life. His movement was not left wing in any way. One could be a Townsendite without being called a "red," and as one member put it, "The Plan stands for everything a nice person ought to favor." Dr. Townsend was the repository and embodiment of the Protestant ethic, and individualism was central to his movement. These old folks had "earned their vital role as circulators of money," and Townsend even declared that "the Plan will save America from Radicalism." With such an appeal, the organization recruited 2.2 million members by late 1935; over 3.5 million were claimed by 1936, with over 7 thousand local Townsend clubs operating across America. As with the other mass movements, Townsendism prospered not by offering a turn to the left, but by promising prosperity in a quintessentially American context.[17]

Could FDR have taken America to the left? The radical alternatives offered by so many others in the early thirties suggest that there was no audience for the challengers of the traditional socioeconomic system, only followers for messiahs who endorsed the American Way. But could FDR have done it? He had the charismatic authority, the political skills, the bully pulpit of the Presidency. If only he had been different. Ultimately, the left opportunity argument must swing on FDR's personal power, magnetism, and motives: not any radical, not any President, but only an FDR might have taken America to the left.

But could even *he* have done it? Recognizing the fate of his radical adversaries, if he had tried would it have worked? There are several problems here, even in dealing with such a hypothetical question.

First, there are the structural obstacles he would have encountered. Conservative forces were present throughout America even in 1933. Would the Supreme Court have remained silent if a truly radical agenda was proposed by the President and somehow successfully piloted through Congress? The Court's declaration of the National Industrial Recovery Act (NIRA) and the Agricultural Adjustment Act (AAA) as unconstitutional suggests otherwise; the massive resistance to Roosevelt's effort to circumvent a negative Court is a matter of record, one of the relatively few examples of political insensitivity and ineptitude by the Chief Executive in the New Deal years. But would such an agenda ever have survived a congressional debate? Conservative opinion surely would have been mobilized from every corner: in the press, in the private sector, in the House and Senate. Would the huge Rooseveltian majorities have held on issues much more divisive than the relief, recovery, and reform programs of 1933-35? The Liberty Leaguers at the time assailed the "dole" as un-American, and the National Recovery Administration (NRA) was attacked as a statist perversion of the American system. But the nation had voted overwhelmingly to do something about the plight of the hungry and unemployed, and the business community—as critics point out so well—was given a dominant voice in the NRA. Would a Congress in which defenders of traditional political and economic arrangements were still present (and with growing cohesiveness after 1934) have accepted a very different approach, a program of wide-ranging nationalization of basic industries and realignment of institutional arrangements? Such plans would have received little encouragement in many influential sectors. Economic conventional wisdom still advised great caution lest the crisis deepen. State and local governments were often controlled by those who would resist radical change, who were devoted, as one analyst put it, to "traditional attitudes regarding self-help, private initiative and local responsibility." The forces militating against a successful effort to move to the left were formidable indeed.[18]

But what of that perfect setting for radical opportunity in March 1933? Was there not the fear of revolution which would have allowed an FDR to successfully act against all these constraints? The question here is whether there truly was such a setting in 1932-33. Several students of the period have insisted, in William E. Leuchtenburg's words, that "the mood of the country during the winter of 1932-33 was not revolutionary . . . the country was less rebellious than drifting." It was not until 1934 that the setting changed, for "the revolutionary spirit burgeons not when conditions are at their worst but as they begin to improve." As Jerold S. Auerbach observed, radicalism flourished in the wake of the New Deal reforms, not in anticipation of them; the "sense of possibilities" galvanized activists. Irving Bernstein, citing the 1856 work stoppages involving 1,470,000 workers, argued that it was "in 1934 (that) labor erupted . . . labor's mood was despair compounded with hope." That there was a popular setting for radical activity as FDR took office seems more wishful thinking than hard reality.[19]

Finally, more important than the fierce and broad-based opposition which a radical Roosevelt would have faced or the lack
of a setting in which he could act, was the omnipresent fact of
the American resistance to radical ideas. It was in 1906 that
Werner Sombart had posed the question in the title of his book
Why Is There No Socialism in the United States? His oft-cited
conclusion that it was "on the reefs of roast beef and the shoals
of apple pie" that "socialistic utopias of every sort are sent to
their doom" came after he pointed to America's open frontiers,
the opportunities for social ascent through individual effort,
and the perception that things would improve for those who
were hard working. This creed of egalitarianism in a nonfeudal
society, this American Lockian faith, as Louis Hartz described
it, did not disappear even in the crisis hour of 1933. It was not a
question of whether social and economic mobility was fact or
myth, whether access and opportunity existed in the way the
celebrators of this American ethos always insisted. It was the
enduring belief in this American Dream which mattered in the
depth of the Depression, as throughout the nation's history.
Tocqueville reappears in years of conservative ascendancy because in these periods we can see most clearly the force of his
central insight: this was land in which most people believed
they were masterless and separate, believed in the possibilities
for individual achievement, believed that almost anyone might
grasp that success which beckoned so seductively that it created
frustration and "inquietude," so that "life would hold no relish
for Americans if they were liberated from the anxieties which
harrass them." Dimissed by some as an apologia for inaction,
this Tocquevillian analysis is instead essential for all who would
ask how and why changes in institutional arrangements occurred
in the past and how they might be made in the future. Tocqueville
lives. When Ronald Reagan was floating his proposal to tax
unemployment benefits—a scheme to force those he believes are
malingerers off the rolls and into the jobs which must be there
because of all those "help wanted" advertisements he reads in
the *Washington Post*—the response by some of those very objects
of his concern who were interviewed at the Syracuse, New York,
unemployment office was, "I understand what he is trying to
do." The victims have not abandoned the faith even when they
are reviled for their alleged "failure" in an age of economic

distress. America does have an ideology—as powerful as the Socialist dream—and it was present in 1933 as it is in 1983.[20]

Of course, Franklin Roosevelt was a product of this ideology. He rejected the argument that America was a "class-conscious society," as he put it in his first Fireside Chat of 1936, for the United States was different than "those other countries." He embraced the individualist ethos, as he told the Young Democratic Club in 1935: "I do not believe in abandoning the system of individual enterprise. . . . the freedom and opportunity that have characterized American development in the past can be maintained" if only "we recognize the fact" that individualism "in our day" needs reform, "the collaboration of all of us to provide security for all of us." FDR would never have attempted to take the nation to the left because he was no radical. He feared radicalism and was contemptuous of radicals. He was the brilliant reform politician who embraced traditional values, a leader a "little left of center."[21]

But could he have achieved even a small part of the radical agenda if he had been a different kind of thinker? Some scholars of different persuasions have suggested that he might have won at least congressional ascent to the socialization of the banking industry in 1933. (James M. Burns speculates that he might have done the same with railroads.) There seems little possibility of anything more. Of course, he did not attempt even this move to the left. Yet is it reasonable to conclude that his New Deal consequently was a fraud or a failure—in one critic's words, a program which "solved a few problems, ameliorated a few more, obscured many, and created new ones"? I think not. For while the New Deal did not take America to the left, it did change America and the role of the national government in America. What seems remarkable now is not its failure to do something else in 1933, but to achieve what it did given the constraints in this society.[22]

The New Deal was more than just a relief expedition for a desperate middle class in the depth of the Depression. Its significance is more enduring than implied even in those terms of admiration and support used by its scholarly champions: "guarantor state," "welfare state," "interventionist state." It did establish the federal government's responsibility to intervene in order to guarantee the "collaboration of all of us to provide security for all of us." But beyond these reformed institutional arrangements and the heritage of its relief and recovery programs lay its larger achievement, the recognition that social and economic problems in this great nation required national political solutions and national political responsibility, that the old order would not and could not work any more. More important than its inconsistencies or its faltering conception of economic planning was this signal accomplishment. Franklin Roosevelt's New Deal did not bring the egalitarian utopia of the cooperative commonwealth, and it did not dramatically redistribute wealth or attend to racial wrongs and shames of the past. It brought no radical change, but it did create significant change. Yet even this required not only the skillful leadership of the President but the unparalleled collapse of the economic order in the Great Depression. Its very success is a measure of not what might have been, but a testament to how hard it is to make any significant new departures in political and socioeconomic relationships in America.[23]

Since the end of the New Deal there has been little evidence of continued movement in this direction. Save for Lyndon B. Johnson's remarkable attempt to build the Great Society in 1964-65—an effort to address an agenda left over from the Depression decade, more an extension of the New Deal than another new departure—there has been no sign of success. The failure of Harry S. Truman's Fair Deal and John F. Kennedy's New Frontier before LBJ's Presidency would be followed by the growing resistance to any effort even to formulate a reform agenda for the seventies and eighties. Now the heirs of the New Deal and Great Society have been silenced; it is the heritage of the New Deal which has become the object of attack. The "faceless bureaucracies" of the inefficient and bloated federal government, the financial albatross of the "swollen social programs"—these are the favorite subjects of those who speak of "fifty years of failure." Even in the heart of the severest recession since Roosevelt's day, even in the face of a program which redistributes income by widening the gap between the rich and the rest during economic crisis, little has been heard in defense of yesterday's reforms. For admirers of the New Deal, it is a sorry spectacle.

It took a huge economic shake-up to produce the setting for the New Deal, and to make the changes achieved in those years. That FDR did not take the United States to the left is obvious, but the success of Roosevelt's present-day critics and the confused silence of his later-day disciples make the reason why clear once again. The power of that older vision of atomistic individualism and private sector freedom resonate in the speeches of today's Chief Executive. It is still a fighting faith in the eighties. It was the massive resistance to challenges to the American Dream which sealed the fate or shaped the success of radical movements in the thirties, which built the insuperable political obstacles a radical in the White House could not have overcome in those years. Given this opposition to any meaningful change, it was only the economic collapse of 1933 which allowed the achievements of Franklin D. Roosevelt, modest only by comparison to some radical ideal. But what upheaval will be needed by leaders of the future who hope to build on that foundation?

1. Dixon Wecter, *The Age of the Great Depression* (New York: MacMillan, 1948), pp. 39-40; William E. Leuchtenburg, *Franklin D. Roosevelt and the New Deal* (New York: Harper and Row, 1963), pp. 24-25.

2. Walter Johnson, *1600 Pennsylvania Avenue* (Boston: Little, Brown, 1960), pp. 20-21; Norman Thomas, *America's Way Out* (New York: Macmillan, 1931), pp. 306-7.

3. Herbert Hoover, *The Challenge to Liberty* (New York: Charles Scribner's, 1934); Edwin C. Rozwenc, ed., *The New Deal: Revolution or Evolution?* (Boston: D.C. Heath, 1959); Otis Graham, Jr., ed., *The New Deal: The Critical Issues* (Boston: Little, Brown, 1971), a collection juxtaposing selections on "The Revolutionary New Deal" and "The Conservative New Deal"; Frances Perkins, *The Roosevelt I Knew* (New York: Viking Press, 1946), p. 328. FDR's "radicalism" is also denied by many sympathetic scholars. Among them: Daniel R. Fusfeld, *The Economic Thought of Franklin D. Roosevelt and the Origins of the New Deal* (New York: Columbia University Press, 1954), pp. 226-27; James MacGregor Burns, *Roosevelt: The Lion and the Fox* (New York: Harcourt, Brace, 1956), p. 331; Robert Lekachman, *The Age of Keynes* (New York: Random House, 1966), pp. 140-43; Thomas H. Greer, *What Roosevelt Thought* (East Lansing: Michigan State University Press, 1958), pp. 38-39.

4. Benjamin Stolberg and Warren Jay Vinton, *The Economic Consequences of the New Deal* (New York: Harcourt, Brace and World, 1935); Howard Zinn, ed., *New Deal Thought* (New York: Bobbs Merrill, 1966), pp. xvi-xxiii; Paul K. Conkin, *FDR and the Origins of the Welfare State* (New York: Thomas Y. Crowell, 1967), pp. 104-6; Barton J. Bernstein, ed., *Towards a New Past: Dissenting Essays in American History* (New York: Pantheon, 1968), pp. 246, 268, 281. See also Rexford G. Tugwell, *In Search of Roosevelt* (Cambridge: Harvard University Press, 1972), p. 330. Tugwell on the demise of the NRA: "A great collectivism might have ... come out of it, so that all the enormous American energies might have been ... channeled in one national effort to establish well-being"; instead, ineffective administration led to the big businessmen's vision of "a great supertrust, manipulating supplies, controlling prices."

5. Central Committee, Communist Party, USA, *Toward Revolutionary Mass Work* (New York: Workers Library Publishers, May 1932), pp. 3-4; Earl

Browder, *Communism in the United States* (New York: International Publishers, 1935), pp. 14, 31, 66-71; Irving Howe and Lewis Coser, *The American Communist Party* (New York: Frederick A. Praeger, 1957), pp. 234-35.

6. Georgi Dimitroff, *The United Front* (New York: International Publishers, 1938), p. 15.

7. Earl Browder, *The People's Front* (New York: International Publishers, 1938), p. 198; A. B. Magil, "The New Deal: 1933-1938," *New Masses* (July 5, 1938): 6; Browder, *The Democratic Front for Jobs, Security, Democracy and Peace* (New York: Workers Library Publishers, 1938), p. 10; Browder, "The People's Front Moves Forward," *The Communist* (December 1937): 1095; District Communist Party, *We Do Not Propose to Let the President Down*, Washington, D.C., 1938. (Pamphlet.)

8. Edward Levison, ed., *A Plan for America: Official 1932 Campaign Handbook of the Socialist Party* (Chicago: Socialist Party of America, 1932), pp. 10-11; Norman Thomas, *Why I am a Socialist* (Chicago: Socialist Party of America, 1932), pp. 9-10.

9. Norman Thomas, *Is the New Deal Socialism? An Answer to Al Smith and the American Liberty League* (Chicago: Socialist Party of America, 1936), p. 7; Daniel Bell, "The Background and Development of Marxian Socialism in the United States," in *Socialism and American Life*, ed. Daniel Drew Egbert and Stow Person, vol. I (Princeton: Princeton University Press, 1952), pp. 378-84; Thomas, *A Socialist Looks at the New Deal* (Chicago: League for Industrial Democracy, 1934), p. 15; Thomas, *The Choice Before Us: Mankind at the Crossroad*, (New York: Macmillan, 1934), pp. 158-59.

10. Bernard K. Johnpoll, *Pacifists' Progress: Norman Thomas and the Decline of American Socialism* (Chicago: Quadrangle Books, 1970), p. 177, attacks Thomas for siding with the militants. Thomas is defended by Frank Warren III in *An Alternative Vision: The Socialist Party in the 1930s* (Bloomington: Indiana University Press, 1978), pp. 5-19. See also Daniel Bell, "The Problem of Ideological Rigidity," in *Failure of a Dream: Essays in the History of American Socialism*, ed. John M. Laslett and Seymour Martin Lipset (Garden City, N.Y.: Anchor Books, 1974), p. 89. Thomas is quoted on Roosevelt in David A. Shannon, *The Socialist Party of America* (New York: Macmillan, 1955), p. 235.

11. See Donald L. Miller, *The New American Radicalism: Alfred M. Bingham and Non-Marxian Insurgency in the New Deal Era* (Port Washington, N.Y.: Kennikat Press, 1979), pp. 34-136; Stuart Chase, "The Age of Distribution," in Zinn, *New Deal Thought*, pp. 24-27; and Frank Warren III, *Liberals and Communism* (Bloomington: Indiana University Press, 1966), pp. 23-25.

12. See David H. Bennett, *Demagogues in the Depression: American Radicals and the Union Party, 1932-1936* (New Brunswick: Rutgers University Press, 1969), pp. 29-72; Charles E. Coughlin, *The New Deal in Money* (Royal Oak, Mich.: Radio League of the Little Flower, 1933); Charles E. Coughlin, *Eight Lectures on Labor, Capital and Justice* (Royal Oak: Radio League of the Little Flower, 1934); and Charles E. Coughlin, *Driving Out the Money Changers* (Detroit: Radio League of the Little Flower, 1933).

13. See Bennett, *Demagogues*, pp. 13, 51, 69-70; Charles E. Coughlin, "How Long Can Democracy and Capitalism Last?", *Today* 3 (December 29, 1934): 6-

7; Coughlin, *Money! Questions and Answers* (Royal Oak: Social Justice Publishing Company, 1936); and Coughlin, *A Series of Lectures on Social Justice, 1935-1936* (Royal Oak: Radio League of the Little Flower, 1936), pp. 11-12.

14. Bennett, *Demagogues*, pp. 16-17, 54-67; and Alan Brinkley, *Voices of Protest: Huey Long, Father Coughlin and the Depression* (New York: Alfred A. Knopf, 1982), pp. xi, 144, 154, 198, 202-3.

15. Bennett, *Demagogues*, pp. 118-30; Huey Long, *Every Man a King* (New Orleans: National Book Co., 1933); *American Progress*, January 4, 1935; Long, *My First Days in the White House* (Harrisburg: Telegraph Press, 1935); Long, *Share Our Wealth* (Washington, D.C., 1934), pp. 1, 7-16.

16. David H. Bennett, "The Year of the Old Folk's Revolt," *American Heritage* 16 (December 1964): 48-51, 99-107; Francis E. Townsend, *The Townsend National Recovery Plan* (Chicago: Townsend National Recovery Inc., 1941); *The Townsend National Weekly*, November 2, December 21, 1936.

17. Francis E. Townsend, *New Horizons* (Chicago: J. L. Stewart, 1943); Bennett, *Demagogues*, pp. 156-69, 173.

18. Otis L. Graham, Jr., "New Deal Historiography: Retrospect and Prospect," in Graham, *The New Deal*, pp. 174-77; Ellis W. Hawley, *The New Deal and the Problem of Monopoly* (Princeton: Princeton University Press, 1966), pp. 55-57; James T. Patterson, *Congressional Conservatism and the New Deal* (Lexington: University of Kentucky Press, 1967), pp. 70-71, 74-75; John Braeman, Robert H. Bremner, and David Brody, eds., *The New Deal: The State and Local Levels*, vol. II (Columbus: Ohio State University Press, 1975), pp. x-xi. See particularly David J. Mauser, "Relief Problems and Politics in Ohio," pp. 75-102; and James T. Patterson, *The New Deal and the States* (Princeton: Princeton University Press, 1969).

19. Leuchtenburg, *Roosevelt and the New Deal*, pp. 26, 95; Jerold S. Auerbach, "New Deal, Old Deal or Raw Deal: Some Thoughts on New Left Historiography," *Journal of Southern History* 35 (February 1969): 24; Irving Bernstein, *Turbulent Years* (Boston: Houghton Mifflin, 1971), p. 217.

20. Werner Sombart, "American Capitalism's Economic Rewards," in Laslett and Lipset, *Failure of a Dream*, pp. 593-608; Louis Hartz, *The Liberal Tradition in America* (New York: Harcourt, Brace and World, 1955), pp. 259-83.

21. Samuel I. Rosenman, ed., *The Public Papers and Addresses of Franklin D. Roosevelt* (New York: Macmillan, 1938-1950), vol. IV, pp. 338-39, 341. On FDR's attitude toward radicals and radicalism, see Greer, *What Roosevelt Thought*, pp. 38-40, 208-10.

22. See Bernstein, *Towards a New Past*, pp. 267-68; Tugwell, *In Search of Roosevelt*, p. 272; and Burns, *The Lion and the Fox*, p. 243. The critic cited is Conkin, *FDR and the Origins*, p. 106.

23. See, among others, Carl Degler on the achievement of "the guarantor state," in *Out of Our Past* (New York: Harper and Row, 1959), pp. 379, 416. In John Braeman, Robert H. Bremner, and David Brody, eds., *The New Deal: The National Level*, vol. I (Columbus: Ohio State University Press, 1975), the centralizing impact of the New Deal is considered in a number of essays. See particularly Richard S. Kirkendall, "The New Deal and Agriculture," pp. 83-109; Milton Derber, "The New Deal and Labor," pp. 110-32; and Jerold S. Auerbach, "Lawyers and Social Change in the Depression Decade," pp. 133-69.

NATIVE RADICALS IN THE THIRTIES

Donald R. McCoy

Franklin D. Roosevelt was indisputably the commanding figure of the 1930s in the United States. So too the New Deal coalition was the dominant political movement. It is neither surprising nor wrong that scholars have devoted most of their attention to Roosevelt and the New Deal in considering the history of the decade. Yet American politics during the 1930s involved diverse ideas, interests, and personalities, which resulted in an exceptionally wide range of thought and of contests for power. Scholars have also been rightly concerned with other elements, whether to the right or the left of the President and his administration. After all, these forces had influence in their time, too, and they must be considered if we are to understand the period.

The Great Depression of 1929 to 1939 was the most traumatic experience suffered by the American people since the Civil War. The capitalistic system then seemed to be collapsing both in the United States and elsewhere in the world. Moreover, democracy was in jeopardy, as were traditional social structures. The old certainties were vanishing, dreams were being shattered, and misery stalked the globe. Confusion and even chaos were common by 1933. In the United States many voters shifted their party allegiances, and probably more people became politically active for the first time as a result of the turmoil of the times.

Americans struck out in many different directions in searching for solutions and the power to implement them. This is not surprising, given the diversity of the people and their interests, the nation's size, and its federalism and localism. Moreover, this pluralism was bolstered by the strength of individualism, pragmatism, and personal freedom in the United States. One of the most interesting manifestations of all this was the development of native radical thought and action during the 1930s. It is little wonder that radicalism in America would more often than not reject the forms then popular elsewhere; it is less wonder that native radicalism would be highly variegated. Marxism had not significantly appealed to Americans earlier, and it would become only relatively more attractive during the Great Depression. There were many reasons for this, among them that appeals for class action fell upon so many deaf ears among a people attuned to individualism and local action; the identification of Marxism with foreigners in a yet considerably xenophobic land; the distorted interpretations of Marxism by its often ill-tutored prophets in America; the frequent and bitter schisms among American Marxists; and the dogmatic nature of most Marxists in a pragmatic country. No, Marxists during the 1930s would go their own interesting ways, whether as Communists, Socialists, Socialist Laborites, various kinds of Trotskyists, or what have you. They would, however, carry few Americans with them, and many of these not for long.[1] Poorly grounded in any philosophy and bred to resist political discipline, those Americans who were tempted to undertake radical action were most likely to devise their own radicalism, one that was not constrictive and was not necessarily very radical.

Having said this by way of introduction, I want to say that my purpose in this paper is to comment on the nature of native radicalism in America during the 1930s and on the problems of scholars in dealing with it. Let us begin with the troubles scholars have experienced in considering native radicals. I can speak with some authority on this, for I was among the first historians to deal with the subject.[2] One problem is that so much of the investigation of the native radicals of the 1930s has been localized. Take, for example, the large amount of scholarly literature on the Wisconsin Progressive party, which had radical flashes.[3] This outpouring is understandable because the party was prominent, partly because of its success and partly because of its well-known leadership, especially Governor Philip F. La Follette and Senator Robert M. La Follette, Jr. The Wisconsin Progressive party has thus been prized by many scholars as a well-defined, dramatic, and highly documented topic for articles, theses, and even books. Surprisingly, its match in interest and success, the Minnesota Farmer-Labor party, has not been explored as often. There is, nevertheless, considerable literature on this subject, most recently Millard L. Gieske's *Minnesota Farmer-Laborism: The Third Party Alternative.*[4] Usually ignored have been Raymond Haight and his California Progressive movement, Commonwealth movements in Oregon and, until recently, Washington, and even New York's American Labor party.[5] One appreciates those state studies which have been done and hopes that similar investigations will be conducted elsewhere. The problem is, however, that they are by their nature restricted in scope.

Related to this problem of localization, for similar reasons, is that much of the remaining pertinent scholarly literature, however excellent, is on individual regional or national movements. One can think here of David H. Bennett's *Demagogues in the Depression: American Radicals and the Union Party*[6] and John L. Shover's *Cornbelt Rebellion: The Farmers' Holiday Association.*[7] Also related are appropriate biographies, which have many of the advantages and disadvantages of studies of individual state, regional, and national movements. Coming to mind as examples are Sheldon Marcus's *Father Coughlin: The Tumultuous Life of the Priest of the Little Flower*[8] and T. Harry Williams's *Huey Long.*[9] Of course, the studies of movements and of individuals vary in quality, but they all make contributions to knowledge about native radicalism. Again one would appreciate having more of them. It is clear, however, that they only incidentally or partially deal with the national dynamics of native radicalism during the 1930s. What we need is more attention paid to the relationships of native radical movements and leaders with each other and with other groups and leaders as well as the measure of their radicality.

A second category of problems is seen in theme studies. Basically, only two themes have thus far been studied, politics and ideas. Most of the scholarly literature, as we have seen, has dealt with politics. Less has dealt with ideas. One can think here of R. Alan Lawson's *The Failure of Independent Liberalism, 1930-1941*[10] and Richard H. Pells's *Radical Visions and American Dreams: Culture and Social Thought in the Depression Years.*[11] Despite their other problems, Lawson's work offers the advantage of trying to deal with American independent liberal and native radical thought as a whole and Pells's work of trying to consider American radical thought overall. Their chief problem is that they do not seem to understand that ideas came from sources other than the intelligentsia and that intellectuals were seldom influential leaders. For example, Governor Floyd Olson of

Minnesota reached many Americans because as a successful politician he commanded an audience that such as thinker Alfred M. Bingham could only envy.

There are other problems with theme writers. One is obvious, which is that a theme is only part of the whole. Not only is there no work that treats native radicalism in terms of both ideas and politics, but there are several largely ignored themes. One of these themes concerns economics, for example, the production-for-use and cooperative movements.[12] Another is the activity of those native radicals who were elected to Congress and even state and local legislatures.[13] What about lobbying activities and appeals to trades unions, agricultural organizations, religious groups, women, and other special interests? Perhaps there is not enough documentation for major works on these more specialized themes. Overall, there is enough on them, however, to allow for better studies of native radicalism within states, by movements, biographically, and intellectually. Another hope is that future works dealing generally with the economics, politics, and society of America during the 1930s will reflect research on native radicalism better than those larger canvases do now. It is frustrating to comment on research opportunities for students of native radicalism when the work they have already done is only occasionally used decently by other scholars.

Another problem faced by writers on native radicalism is that of definition. This comes in two major categories, the first of which is what to include. Scholars have readily admitted to the fold John Dewey's League for Independent Political Action (LIPA) and its offspring, the Farmer-Labor Political Federation and the American Commonwealth Political Federation, as well as the Minnesota Farmer-Labor party, the Wisconsin Progressive party, and Upton Sinclair's End Poverty in California movement. Philip La Follette's National Progressives of America of 1938 is usually included, despite serious reservations, because of its close relationship to the Wisconsin Progressive party. There is trouble after these. Perhaps because of their paucity of knowledge, scholars handle gingerly if at all Raymond Haight's California Progressive party, Peter Zimmerman's Oregon Commonwealth Federation, and Homer Bone and Lewis Schwellenbach's Washington Commonwealth Federation.

There are other troublesome questions. To what extent were any of the aforementioned radical? To what extent was native radicalism reflected in the Farmer's Union and the Farm Holiday Association? What was the nature of the third-party sentiment among labor unions, for example, the American Federation of Hosiery Workers and the United Textile Workers? To what extent were political eruptions in North Dakota and South Dakota and even the activities of the American Labor party and the Southern Tenant Farmers' Union native radical manifestations?[14] Another big problem is what to do about the Union party of 1936, its presidential nominee, William Lemke, and its related groups, Father Charles Coughlin's National Union for Social Justice, Gerald L. K. Smith and the late Huey Long's Share Our Wealth organization, and Francis Townsend's Old Age Pension Plan.[15] Part of the problem of definition stems from insufficient knowledge, but part of it results from our propensity for hair-splitting and our difficulty in conceptualizing.[16]

Clearly, the problem of definition also applies to individuals. There seems to be agreement on the native radical status of Congressman Thomas Amlie, Governor Floyd B. Olson, Alfred Bingham, philosopher John Dewey, and economist Paul H. Douglas. Yet there are problems, many problems, with others. Was novelist Upton Sinclair too influenced by his earlier Socialism to be anything but a goat mixing with the sheep? Was Philip La Follette an opportunist or a reformer, or something else? Was Huey Long only a Southern demagogue or Charles Coughlin only an anti-Semite? What exactly were A. J. Muste and Stuart Chase, not to mention the Technocrats Harold Loeb and Howard Scott?

All this is interesting in the cases of individual persons and organizations, but it does not answer the question of what was native radicalism. Its difference from Marxist or even Fascist radicalism is fairly clear. Native radicals were pragmatic, eclectic, and individualistic. There was no sworn oath to a pat ideology for them. Thus they could appear as reformers as well as radicals and yet run politics as usual. Many of them could switch from one movement to another, if necessary. This organizational and intellectual mobility as well as their radicality, whatever its degree, also distinguished them from Democrats and Republicans. Yet the native radicals avoided a foreign coloration, going to great lengths to demonstrate that they were as American as apple pie. They may have been searching for an ideology, but it was a flexible, American one. Indeed it is more likely that they were looking for American solutions to American problems.

This fits well with their backgrounds. They were, after all, the children of a land relatively isolated from other nations, a pluralistic country of pragmatists, a unique nation that had largely rejected foreign politics and economics. Thus they sought to take chunks of American concepts and add bits of foreign ideas in order to devise programs that might be both workable and politically appealing. John Dewey's LIPA could talk of public ownership of key industries in the context of relief for workers and farmers. Floyd Olson and the Minnesota Farmer-Laborites could press for the development of cooperative enterprises and yet encourage small agriculture and business. Philip La Follette and the Wisconsin Progressives could speak of planning and state controls and yet do business as usual with the private economic sector. If they and other native radicals could not agree upon what to emphasize, they all believed in mixing radical and reform proposals—making sure there was something for everyone—and couching everything in American terms. They could thus raise the questions of collectivism and even class without repudiating pluralism, freedom, and democracy. To the extent that they were radicals, they were intentionally very cautious ones.

The native radicals were sensitive to the nature of the citizenry to which they had to appeal. They knew of America's remarkable diversity, socially, occupationally, economically, intellectually, and thus politically. This, as well as their own very American individuality, accounts for the pluralism of their appeals. The native radicals were not unsympathetic to formulating a national program. Their political experience dictated, however, that it had to be fine-tuned to state and local constituencies. That same experience led them to disagree on what should be emphasized in a national program. Thus they resisted attaching themselves to a national anchor that might jeopardize what they had gained in their home constituencies. As local considerations led some political figures to radicalism, so such concerns diluted the radicalism of others and led native radical leaders to be part of a loose American (usually non-Marxist) left-of-center coalition.

Additionally, there is the almost pathological American interest in personalities to be taken into account. There were few well-known leaders among the native radicals, and it was difficult to develop new ones quickly. It was all the more difficult given the occasional jealousies among these leaders and especially their differences on what appeals to emphasize. It is not surprising that familiar names came to the fore in the leadership of the native radicals, such as those of John Dewey, Philip La Follette, Floyd Olson, Upton Sinclair, and even Huey Long. It is also no surprise that occasionally the assistance of well-established reformers such as Fiorello LaGuardia and George Norris should be solicited. The accepted answer of the native radicals to the American hunger for brand names was to develop leaders based on their local and state accomplishments. In the long run, this was self-defeating, for it required time that was not available, as most of the newer leaders became known too slowly.

This is not to say that the strategy was not credible. The objective was clear. Bring along leaders slowly, but solidly. Keep them in touch with one another so that they could seek opportunities for joint action and ultimately federation into a successful national movement. This is precisely what the native radicals dreamed of doing; it just did not work. In 1929, the League for Independent Political Action was established to be the grand clearinghouse for native radical ideas and action. LIPA tried to promote cooperation among established elements, such as the Minnesota Farmer-Labor party, sympathetic trade unions and farmers' groups, Democratic and Republican reformers, and even Socialists; to organize new affiliates; and to publicize common aims. By 1932, thanks to the drastic worsening of the economy, there seemed to be a chance to federate in order to contest the national elections. This did not come about because potential constitutent groups and leaders were not ready for joint action. The signs seemed more favorable for them either individually or in cooperation with the Democrats. Moreover, the odds seemed against voters switching in massive numbers from the major parties to any untried national movement. The idea of giving it a go in 1932 in order to prepare for a great effort in 1936 appeared unappealing in view of the fates of Robert M. La Follette's 1924 and Theodore Roosevelt's 1912 progressive presidential candidacies.

If Franklin D. Roosevelt's smashing success at the polls in 1932 confirmed the wisdom of postponing coordinated native radical action, the cards dealt by his New Deal in 1933 indicated that scattered radical action could not work. The future, it seemed to many, belonged to those who were ready to unite to

bring thoroughgoing change to America. If many analysts see
the New Deal as a triumphant movement in 1933, 1934, 1935,
and 1936, there is another way to view affairs. Despite all the
New Deal's efforts, recovery and large-scale reform had been far
from achieved by 1936. Native radical leaders and ideas had
increasingly become a known though varied quantity. The
Farmer-Labor party had become entrenched in power in Minnesota. In Wisconsin, progressive Republicans had returned to
power in 1934 as the state's Progressive party. The Farm Holiday
Association had become a force to reckon with, and many labor
union leaders were talking of third-party action. Upton Sinclair's
End Poverty in California had burst upon the scene. Indeed, he
captured the Democratic nomination for governor there in 1934,
and he and Raymond Haight, the California Progressive nominee, had won a majority of the votes in the gubernatorial election.
Promising mass movements had emerged in Oregon and Washington, and some senators and representatives were associated or
flirting with the native radicals. Alfred Bingham's *Common
Sense* had become the chief periodical forum of the movement.
Republican fortunes had taken another downward turn in the
1934 elections. And in January 1936 the Gallup poll recorded
half of its respondents against the New Deal and only 51 percent
favorable toward electing Democrats to the Senate. By then it
seemed to many radicals that their best chance for electoral success
was developing. Even the Communists had proclaimed the need
for a United Front, Coughlin was straining at the bit, and many
native radicals were planning for a consolidated national campaign in 1936.

President Roosevelt and his aides were alarmed during the
winter of 1935-36 by the diminishing popularity of the New
Deal and the aggressive stirrings among Republicans and on the
left. Yet the attack from the right was no more successful at the
polls in 1936 than Herbert Hoover's defense had been in 1932,
and the threat from the left largely evaporated. What happened
was that the New Deal leadership summoned great resources
and employed them masterfully in attracting votes for Roosevelt
and his supporters, whether they were Democrats or others. While
Roosevelt's forces mounted a massive frontal assault against the
Republicans, they used a flanking movement against the radicals
with even more effective consequences. This flanking movement
was based on the idea that a new coalition party of independent

progressives and radicals could not win in 1936, that the only practical result of such an effort would be to elect the Republicans. That, many declared, would be a disaster for liberals, progressives, and radicals.

By the end of May 1936 when native radicals met in Chicago to discuss forming a new national party, this supposed disaster was something most of their leaders were eager to avoid. By then Roosevelt had rebounded politically, talking aggressively against big business and reminding Americans of how far the nation had progressed economically since early 1933. Moreover, adverse Supreme Court actions, congressional tantrums, and the increasingly aggressive talk of Republican leaders and dissident conservative Democrats made it seem that the New Deal was in trouble. This added force to the argument that disaster could result if liberal and native radical forces failed to support the President's reelection campaign in 1936. That this argument was effective and that most native radical leaders thought little of a new party's chances for success were clear by the time of the Chicago convention in May. As Floyd Olson declared, a third-party presidential campaign might well lead to the election of a "fascist Republican."[17] The Chicago meeting was, therefore, only a rump convention of radical leadership, which postponed the question of forming a new broad-based radical party.

This left the door open for the entry of a farm club team of native radicals and what not, the Union party, into the 1936 presidential campaign. Initially, this seemed an alarming development to many what with its leadership of the popular radio priest Father Charles Coughlin; Huey Long's chief organizer, the Rev. Gerald L. K. Smith; and, though erratically, Dr. Francis Townsend. There was also Congressman William Lemke of North Dakota, who became the new party's presidential nominee. The fear was that the Union party might significantly attract Catholics, fundamentalist Protestants, the elderly, farmers, and the poor since its program and leadership were wide-ranging enough to appeal to right- and left-wing elements. There need not have been much worry. What Norman Thomas labeled "a union of two and a half Messiahs plus some neo-Populists" contained the seeds of abysmal failure. The bigoted, demagogic, and often contradictory declarations of the Union party's leaders, as well as their incompatible backgrounds, were too much for even their own admirers to stomach. Moreover, the threat they seemed to pose spurred Roosevelt's supporters to greater effort on his behalf.[18]

The politics of 1936 decided the fate of native radicalism in America. Although the Wisconsin Progressives and the Minnesota Farmer-Laborites fared well at the polls, and the American Labor party gave promise in New York State, they and related groups had lost their best chance, however small, to seek national power. In effect, they had traded whatever long-term national potential they had for short-term local support from the New Deal. They had assumed that they would have another opportunity to gain national power. In this they were wrong, and for many reasons.

First, their individuality and pluralism would continue to obstruct them from uniting on national action. The ideas their leaders had used to develop their movements had been translated with different emphases in their various constituencies. There was a great deal of difference in their style and concepts, not to mention organization, among California, Minnesota, New York, North Dakota, Oregon, Washington, Wisconsin, and elsewhere. This guaranteed that the much better nationally organized Roosevelt forces would be at an advantage in keeping independent progressive and native radical elements off balance and indeed in recruiting them for the New Deal.

Second, no dominant leader emerged—no elder La Follette, Teddy Roosevelt, or even Eugene V. Debs—who could by force of personality, thought, or ability mold the disparate native radical and progressive elements into a united force. Neither Philip La Follette, Floyd Olson, nor Upton Sinclair was able to transcend his state constituency in order to accomplish this, nor could an Alfred Bingham or a John Dewey develop a national constituency to match his transcendent thoughts. Only Huey Long before his assassination gave promise of appealing nationally to voters, but he was an anathema to other established leaders.

Third, too few native radicals, either leaders or followers, were committed enough to a new national movement to follow Paul Douglas's advice to stick to the job even if it meant "going down under a worthy flag."[19] Not even Douglas could do it, as he became a Democrat before the decade was out.

Fourth, if native radical leaders could not unite, how could they expect their followers to do so? The rank and file, actual or potential, were also products of a pluralistic, pragmatic, and individualistic society. They wanted action more than ideas, and they were likely to follow whoever gave results. It is not surprising that most of them and indeed the native radical leaders could unite only on Roosevelt, for he gave the most in results.

Fifth, native radicals were seldom philosophically sophisticated. People who often had at best been schooled in Henry George and Edward Bellamy were at a disadvantage not only in the quality of their thought but also in their command of logic. Adequate and even trenchant critics they may have been, but one can suggest that they were often deficient in the development of positive, broad thought. This may not, of course, have been a political disadvantage in America.

Sixth, it is questionable whether native radicals, even if united with independent progressives, had the necessary critical mass of adherents to become politically powerful in the United States. They had good bases only in Minnesota and Wisconsin, perhaps in New York, the Dakotas, and the three Pacific coast states. Was this plus scattered outposts over the country enough to launch an effective national party? No one will ever know. One thing is sure, and this is that the native radicals failed to act when by 1936 they had the closest thing available to a critical mass of followers. When Philip La Follette made the attempt in 1938 with his National Progressives of America, it was too late. The process of the scattering of native radicals and independent progressives, begun in 1936 as a result of Roosevelt's reelection campaign, had proceeded too far by 1938 for union to be accomplished. Not only had the New Deal become too attractive a lure for many of them and the Republicans shown recuperative powers, but the terrifying issues of Communism, Fascism, and war were rapidly replacing the traditional native radical questions and polarizing radicals as well as progressives. The low level of commitment and discipline of native radicals, as well as their marked individualism, were telling. It is little wonder that the National Progressives were virtually ignored and that the Minnesota Farmer-Laborites and the Wisconsin Progressives, among others, went down to defeat in the 1938 elections.

The native radicals of the 1930s had substantially proved to be rhetorical radicals. By 1940 they largely either had been absorbed by Roosevelt's New Deal or were fighting the President on foreign policy issues. Gone was the vision of an indigenous radical transformation of American society. Like the progressives, the native radicals had ultimately accepted less than half the loaf. And why not, considering that their constituents were satisfied with the traditional American promise of opportunity now that the New Deal had added a modicum of security to it. The really radical development of the post-World War I period had been the emergence of the mass production-mass consumption sytem. Once it gave promise of functioning adequately again, it is no surprise that most Americans lost interest in an alternative. Whatever chance for success there was for radicals (including Marxists) had occurred between 1930 and 1936. Although it was not much of a chance, they had failed to seize it. Scholars who overlook this are deluding themselves. It just will not do to mistake articulateness for power, imaginativeness for persuasiveness, and promises for what might have happened.

Native radicals along with progressives did, of course, have influence on the course of events during the 1930s. After all, the New Deal made concessions in order to neutralize them, and native radical ideas, even outside of Minnesota and Wisconsin, influenced people and governments. How much, we have yet to discover. How radical, we have yet to assess. It is time that historians got on with these chores, started searching for the actual impact and operation of native radicals nationally. Long ago, scholars stopped assuming that the New Deal governed by presidential fiat, and they concluded that it was a manifestation of interaction among various elements. This work rightly continues. It has a long way to go, however, before it takes into account the influence of all involved, including the native radicals.

1. There is an abundance of literature on Marxist parties. Among the most pertinent volumes for the 1930s are Constance Ashton Meyers, *The Prophet's Army: Trotskyists in America, 1928-1941* (1977); Roger Keeran, *The Communist Party and the Auto Workers Unions* (1980); Frank A. Warren, *Liberals and Communism: The 'Red Decade' Revisited* (1966), and *An Alternative Vision: The Socialist Party in the 1930s* (1974); Lowell K. Dyson, *Red Harvest: The Communist Party and American Farmers* (1982). See also David A. Shannon, *The Socialist Party of America: A History* (1955); and Donald D. Egbert and Stow Persons, *Socialism and American Life*, 2 vols. (1952).

2. See Donald R. McCoy, "The Development of the Wisconsin Progressive Party of 1934 to 1946" (M.A. thesis, University of Chicago, 1949); "The Formation of the Wisconsin Progressive Party in 1934," *Historian* 14 (Autumn 1951); *Angry Voices: Left-of-Center Politics in the New Deal Era* (1958); and, later, *Radicalism in America During the 1930s* (Forum Series, 1974, 1978).

3. See John E. Miller, *Governor Philip F. La Follette, the Wisconsin Progressives, and the New Deal* (1982) for an excellent bibliography, pp. 217-23.

4. (1979).

5. See, though, Bob Barger, "Raymond L. Haight and the Commonwealth Progressive Campaign," *California Historical Quarterly* 43 (September 1964); Hugh T. Lovin, "Toward a Farmer-Labor Party in Oregon, 1933-38," *Oregon Historical Quarterly* 76 (June 1975); and Albert Acena, *Washington Commonwealth Federation, 1935-1945* (1982).

6. (1969).

7. (1965).

8. (1973).

9. (1969).

10. (1971).

11. (1973). It is also instructive to read Donald L. Miller, *The New American Radicalism: Alfred M. Bingham and Non-Marxian Insurgency in the New Deal Era* (1979), who, unlike Lawson and Pells, makes an attempt to incorporate political history into his intellectual study.

12. See, though, Theodore Rosenof, *Dogma, Depression, and the New Deal: The Debate of Political Leaders Over Economic Recovery* (1975).

13. See Theodore Rosenof, "The Political Education of an American Radical: Thomas R. Amlie in the 1930s," *Wisconsin Magazine of History* 58 (Autumn 1974).

14. Pertinent works include Karel D. Bicha, "Liberalism Frustrated: The League for Independent Political Action, 1928-1933," *Mid-America* 48 (January 1966); Bruce B. Mason, "The EPIC Movement," *Arizona Quarterly* 11 (Winter 1955); Charles Larsen, "The EPIC Campaign of 1934," *Pacific Historical Review* 27 (May 1958); Donald L. Singer, "Upton Sinclair and the California Gubernatorial Campaign of 1934," *Southern California Quarterly* 56 (Winter 1974); Hugh T. Lovin, "The Persistence of Third Party Dreams in the American Labor Movement, 1930-1938," *Mid-America* 58 (October 1976); Donald H. Grubbs, *Cry from the Cotton: The Southern Tenant Farmers' Union and the New Deal* (1971); H. L. Mitchell, *Mean Things Happening in This Land: The Life and Times of H. L. Mitchell, Co-founder of the Southern Tenant Farmers Union* (1979); and Lowell K. Dyson, "The Southern Tenant Farmers Union and Depression Politics," *Political Science Quarterly* 88 (June 1973).

15. On the problem of the Union party, see Bennett, *Demagogues in the Depression: American Radicals and the Union Party* (1969); Edward C. Blackorby, *Prairie Rebel: The Public Life of William Lemke* (1963); and Alan Brinkley, *Voices of Protest: Huey Long, Father Coughlin, and the Great Depression* (1982). A similar problem of categorization concerns 1930 and 1932 independent gubernatorial candidate John R. Brinkley of Kansas. See Gerald Carson, *The Roguish World of Doctor Brinkley* (1960).

16. Obtaining more data is no great problem. With respect to hair-splitting, one problem is that some scholars have been relatively uncritical toward those whom they have studied or overly critical of those who have studied some other

aspect of the subject. As for conceptualization, more attention needs to be paid to defining radicality, both Marxist and native. (Indeed, the relative isolation between historians of native radicals and those of Marxists should be broken down.) Moreover, scholars should ask why the word "radical" is normally only applied to those on the far left of the political spectrum.

17. George H. Mayer, *The Political Career of Floyd B. Olson* (1951), p. 297. There was also a return by May 1936 on the part of some to going it alone.

18. Norman Thomas, *After the New Deal, What?* (1936), pp. 5-6. Regarding the efforts of Roosevelt's supporters to rally progressive, native radical, and other nontraditional voters to his cause, see Donald R. McCoy, "The Progressive National Committee of 1936," *Western Political Quarterly* 9 (June 1956), and "The Good Neighbor League and the Presidential Campaign of 1936," *Western Political Quarterly* 13 (December 1960); and Thomas T. Spencer, "The Good Neighbor League Colored Committee and the 1936 Democratic Presidential Campaign," *Journal of Negro History* 63 (Fall 1978).

19. Paul H. Douglas, *The Coming of a New Party* (1932), p. 224.

COMMENT BY WILLIAM M. STOTT

Professors Bennett and McCoy leave me exasperatingly little to disagree with. Had I been in their shoes, I think I might have pointed out the obvious: one good reason to remember the radicals of the 1930s—including, of course, the Marxists—is that in general they were right. Most of the radicals said that more centralized planning and control was the way to improve the economy. Indeed it was; we know this conclusively. Our mobilization for World War II proved it. True, Franklin Roosevelt also advocated centralized planning and control, but intermittently and at times half-heartedly. This was in part because he wasn't sure which plans to follow and in part because he didn't think he could get Congress, the Supreme Court, and the American people to put up with the necessary regimentation. No doubt *he* was right, too. I will talk about Americans' uneasiness about regimentation in a few minutes.

Professor McCoy says the native radicals of the thirties were "pragmatic, eclectic, and individualistic"; small wonder Roosevelt, who was all these things also, found it pretty easy to head them off at the pass. Professor Bennett says the New Deal probably couldn't have taken the United States any further left because the American people didn't want to; I agree. Looking at thirties media—ads, films, radio—I have been struck by the residue of twenties style and ideology in them.

Why didn't America go farther left in the 1930s? Why is our system notably less socialistic than that of most other industrialized countries? Professors Bennett and McCoy have given good answers to this question, and Professor Bennett has cited Alfred Bingham's good answer (lower-class Americans consider themselves middle class) and those of Werner Sombart.

All these answers are, I think, versions of the pursuit-of-happiness theme. We Americans, even if we are poor, are reluctant to change our system because we think we may get rich, and we don't want anything to stand in our way. George McGovern said that he was persuaded to withdraw his idea of imposing a 100 percent tax on estates worth more than $100,000 by factory workers who said they thought they might strike it rich and wanted to be able to hand on most of their wealth to their kids. If the pollsters are right, a sizable percentage of unemployed black ghetto youngsters think there's a good chance they will be rich. We Americans feel free to better ourselves, and we like that feeling. Call us greedy—we probably won't mind; to us greedy means trying to get ahead, looking out for Number One. Call us aggressive—we'll take it as a compliment. (In most civilized societies the word *aggressive* is a pejorative. I know a French woman who has the occasion to read many letters of recommendation written by Americans on behalf of American students and teachers. Before she came to the States the first time, she was afraid to come, she tells me, because we had all those aggressive people. She had a vision of walking down the street and being punched in the nose.)

One reason socialism has failed in America, then, is that most Americans aspire to rise in the world to a position of power and want to feel free to do it. Another reason socialism has failed is, I think, just the opposite. I think many Americans fear falling under the power of some authority and not being free to rise. I think Americans are generally opposed to centralized planning and control—wage controls—because we fear that we, individually, will be shortchanged. Many British people speak with pride of having a "caring" society. Such talk sounds intimidating to us—as well as maudlin. Caring, all right, but how can we be sure somebody else wouldn't get all the care, and none left over for us? Besides, who's in charge of the caring? Who takes care of the caretakers? With a New Class running the new regime, we could be kept from getting a piece of the action by some bureaucratic foul-up or rule. We would be the helpless objects of our leaders' interest, enlightened or not—which is to say, objects of coercion. We prefer to care for ourselves, thanks all the same.

"Anything like revolution means to the American mind just one thing," wrote Sherwood Anderson in 1935. "There is the picture of men standing, with their backs to the wall, in the act of being shot. Your average American doesn't think of himself as being one of those who are doing the shooting. 'It would be just my luck to be one of those standing there, with my back to the wall,' the average American says" (*Puzzled America*, Scribners, p. 241). Most Americans agree with the dictator in George Orwell's *1984*: "Power is not a means; it is an end. . . . The object of power is power." I don't know why we feel this way when most of our European friends don't seem to. Maybe the Protestant belief in human depravity and Original Sin haunts us harder. Maybe, like my French friend, we are frightened by the aggressiveness we feel in ourselves.

"Nobody is good enough to be a socialist," an ex-radical of the 1930s once told me. John Steinbeck said the same thing in his *In Dubious Battle*, the decade's best "socially conscious" novel. John Dos Passos said the same thing in two astonishing sentences in *U.S.A.* In "Camera Eye (46)" Dos Passos walks the streets of New York near Union Square and comes home to

> read (with some difficulty in the Loeb Library trot) the
> epigrams of Martial and ponder the course of history
> and what leverage might pry the owners loose from
> power and bring back (I too Walt Whitman) our
> storybook democracy
>   and all the time in my pocket that letter from
> that collegeboy asking me to explain why being right
> which he admits the radicals are in their
> private lives such shits. (Modern Library, 1939, p. 150.)

Men can't be trusted to be their brother's keeper. It isn't an ennobling idea, but I think it says a good deal about why America didn't go left in the 1930s and isn't likely to any time soon.

IV

THE NEW DEAL
AND LABOR

THE NEW DEAL
AND THE AMERICAN
LABOR MOVEMENT

Melvyn Dubofsky

Few today would disagree with the assertion that the 1930s were indeed the "turbulent years" of the American labor movement. Workers, as never before, acted with an unparalleled militancy and solidarity. In early 1933, fewer than three million workers belonged to trade unions, and they were mostly an elite of skilled craftspeople outside the basic industries and affiliated to the cautious organizations associated with the American Federation of Labor (AFL). By 1941, however, total union membership had surged to nearly 10.5 million; a new, more militant center for trade unionism had been established in the Congress of Industrial Organizations (CIO); and for the first time in American history, masses of unskilled and semiskilled mass-production workers embraced unionism.

The rise of mass-production unionism won workers a new place in national politics, economics, and society. No longer could giant corporations treat their employees with impunity or assume worker passivity and trade union docility. No longer could politicians dismiss organized labor as a marginal voting bloc; nor could they rely on partisan divisions among labor barons to vitiate working-class suffrage. During that fateful decade, many contemporary analysts immodestly predicted that the rise of mass-production unionism would inaugurate a new era in which class solidarity would overcome ethnic and religious divisions, radicalism would run riot, and workers' power would fundamentally restructure the American nation.

For the most part, historians agree on the main contours of what happened to the American labor movement in the 1930s. In their narratives they give a central place to the mass militancy of 1934—especially the Toledo Autolite conflict, the Minneapolis teamsters' struggle, and the San Francisco general strike. So, too, do they emphasize the AFL's inability and unwillingness to organize the great mass of industrial workers and the consequent emergence of the CIO. Finally, historians focus on three developments which solidified the triumph of the CIO and the victory of mass-production unionism: (1) the Roosevelt reelection landslide of 1936; (2) the 1937 Flint sit-down strike and the United Auto Workers' victory over General Motors; and (3) the Steel Workers Organizing Committee-United States Steel agreement of March 1937.[1]

In bare outline that is what we know about labor in the 1930s. Concerning the eruption of mass militancy in 1934 and 1937, the CIO's contribution to worker organization, the importance of the Flint strike, and labor's new-found political muscle, there can be little dispute. But precisely how all this related to the policies of Franklin D. Roosevelt and the New Deal remains a murkier and more complicated question. On the surface, the question how, if at all, the New Deal changed the history and dynamics of the American labor movement seems deceptively simple. Yet in reality, it requires exceedingly complex answers.

The historian David Brody has frequently pointed out the central irony or paradox involved in the history of the New Deal and labor. As Brody perceives the situation, the impetus for basic reform in the 1930s originated neither with Franklin D. Roosevelt nor the labor movement, as it existed and behaved in the first years of the New Deal. Still and all, however, there was something undefinable about the interaction between the New Deal as a political movement and the upsurge of trade union militancy which produced a real shift in domestic political and economic power.[2]

In this essay, I want to examine perhaps the most decisive aspect of that transformation, the labor upheaval of 1936-37, and why its impact and effects were not deeper and even more transformative. Let me spell out what I mean by the upheaval of 1936-37: (1) the surge of militancy and strikes in such mass-production industries as rubber, steel, and automobiles; (2) the association of CIO and a so-called new unionism with this militancy; and most important (3) the apparent triumph of unionism in the mass-production, basic industries.[3]

We must, however, bear in mind certain essential characteristics about this labor upheaval. From its start to the collapse of the New Deal as a domestic reform movement was a short time indeed—at most from the summer of 1936 to the fall of 1938. The core of the labor upheaval itself was of even shorter duration, at best from summer 1936 to summer 1937, but more accurately from January 1937 to May-June 1937. Thus by the fall of 1938 both the New Deal and the new labor movement had lost their momentum. What, then, was there historically in the relationship between organized labor and the New Deal which led to such an outcome?

Precisely what, if anything, did Roosevelt and his New Deal do for workers which sparked the upheaval of 1936-37? Clearly, the initial New Deal labor policies associated most closely with Section 7a of the National Industrial Recovery Act (NIRA) had failed trade unionism in the mass-production industries. Time and again in 1933 and 1934 Roosevelt and his lieutenants made decisions about the rise of worker militancy in the mass-production industries which crippled unionism, especially in automobiles and steel. The Roosevelt Administration also did nothing during the great textile workers strike of 1934 (the most massive single-industry strike in American history up to that time) to dissuade Southern state officials from using state power to break the strike. By the end of 1934, labor militancy seemed to have dissipated and the major corporations appeared in firm control of their labor forces. In no small measure, Franklin Roosevelt had assisted corporate executives in containing worker resistance.[4]

Yet corporate leaders perceived Roosevelt and his New Deal through a set of distorted lenses. Where Roosevelt struggled to implement reforms which aimed to ameliorate the immediate social and economic crises caused by the Great Depression without altering the basic structure of American capitalism, corporate executives saw creeping socialism. Indeed it would not be an exaggeration to suggest that between 1934 and 1937 most capitalists let their imaginations run riot, their neuroses about Roosevelt's policies distorting for them the reality of what was happening. Hence, for corporate America, as Roosevelt shifted to the left in 1935, his new reform agenda—Social Security, the Public Utility Holding Company Act, the Revenue Act of 1935 (the so-called wealth tax), and the Wagner, or National Labor Relations Act (which the President came to endorse only reluctantly)—signified only the first stage in an insidious plot to collectivize and socialize capital in the interests of labor. The inability of most corporate executives to comprehend Roosevelt's essential conservatism and his commitment to "free enterprise" capitalism, as well as their tendency to perceive New Deal America through lenses better suited for seeing events in a European context, made the President seem in fact the advocate of a workers' republic.[5]

All capital's fears about Roosevelt and the American workers' tendency to identify the President as their advocate were intensified by the politics of 1936. During the campaign Roosevelt did not hide his commitment to labor, especially to the newly formed CIO, which poured more than half a million dollars and thousands of precinct workers into the President's reelection effort. That summer Roosevelt and John L. Lewis, the CIO leader, had several private White House meetings at which the President promised the labor leader support for CIO's aims and a firm offer of Administration cooperation in Lewis's effort to unionize the steel industry. And when Lewis initiated the steel-industry organizing campaign in a July 1936 national radio address, he linked it directly to the approaching presidential election. The steel-industry organizing campaign and the 1936 national election, Lewis stressed, were over the question of "whether the working population of this country shall have a voice in determining their destiny or whether they shall serve as indentured servants for a financial and economic dictatorship which would shamelessly exploit our natural resouces and debase the soul and pride of a free people. On such an issue there can be no compromise."[6]

The 1936 election results magnified the worst fears of corporate America and stimulated the aspirations of labor leaders. As Lewis told a meeting of the CIO executive board convened immediately after the election: "We must capitalize on the election. The CIO was out fighting for Roosevelt and every steel town showed a smashing victory for him. We wanted a President who would hold the light for us while we went out and organized." Less than two months later, on the first night of the Flint sit-down strike, Lewis told a national radio audience:

> The people of our nation have just participated in a national referendum. By an overwhelming majority they voted for industrial democracy, and reelected its champion, Franklin Delano Roosevelt. Labor will expect the protection of the Federal Government in the pursuit of its lawful objectives.[7]

In the event, Roosevelt delivered on his promises to labor.

While the New Deal Democratic governor of Michigan, Frank P. Murphy, refused to use state power to enforce legal injunctions against the sit-down strikers and instead urged General Motors' executives to negotiate with labor, Franklin D. Roosevelt pursued a similar policy behind the scenes. The result was a victory for the strikers in Flint, the United Automobile Workers' (UAW) union, and the CIO. [8] Moreover, only three weeks after General Motors formally recognized trade unionism in its industrial empire (February 11, 1937), U.S. Steel did the same without even risking an open confrontation with its workers or the Steel Workers Organizing Committee (SWOC). The chief executive officer of U.S. Steel, Myron Taylor, recognized the new political situation. Rather than hazard a bitter conflict with labor in which he could no longer rely on the aid of friendly governors or a supportive White House, Taylor beat a strategic retreat. [9]

The CIO's triumph over General Motors and over U.S. Steel within three weeks of each other (something that the AFL had been unable to accomplish in more than half a century) represented the pinnacle of the New Deal labor revolution, one in which labor had simultaneously reshaped national politics to its own advantage and conquered the commanding heights of the economy. John L. Lewis told his fellow CIO executive board members on March 9, 1937: "As years go by, this period will be marked as epoch in [the] life of labor organizations— and [in the] economic, social, [and] political history of America. Gigantic implications." Or as the jounalist Benjamin Stolberg observed in the *Nation* in February 1937, "The CIO has changed significantly the relation of social forces in American industry. It is profoundly affecting our two major political parties. It is transforming the relationship of government to industry." [10]

But the honeymoon between the new labor movement (CIO) and the New Deal proved briefer than expected. By the spring and summer of 1937, friction between Lewis and Roosevelt, and between the CIO and the New Deal, became more evident than cooperation. Roosevelt's political calculus had changed greatly between November 1936 and April-May 1937. In the aftermath of the CIO triumphs over General Motors and U.S. Steel and the surge of sit-downs and worker militancy that followed in their wake, a substantial part of the electorate had second thoughts about where the labor upheaval was taking the American nation. The daily press and corporate opinion-shapers laid down a heavy barrage of anti-CIO propaganda. Even several AFL leaders joined in the chorus which condemned the CIO as a subversive influence in national affairs. By the spring of 1937, Roosevelt's advisers were warning him that the labor situation was full of political dynamite, that he must be more cautious and less partisan in his relationship with Lewis and the CIO. The President took such advice to heart. When CIO-SWOC and the so-called Little Steel companies locked in deadly industrial conflict in May-June 1937, Roosevelt turned a deaf ear to appeals from Lewis for support. As the Little Steel companies used all their time-tested antilabor tactics to break the strike, SWOC found itself unable to devise an effective counterattack. After the infamous Chicago Memorial Day massacre in which city police attacked a peaceful assembly of steel strikers and their families, Lewis turned to the President for assistance. Roosevelt responded by declaring "a plague on both your houses" (labor and capital), behaving precisely as his political advisers had counseled.[11]

The CIO's defeat in the "Little Steel" strike proved only the first in a series of setbacks which further strained the relationship between the new unionism and the New Deal. The brisk economic recovery of 1936-early 1937 ended in the summer of 1937. It was followed by the so-called Roosevelt depression of 1937-38, which saw production and employment tumble even more rapidly than they had between 1929 and 1930. To an extent this economic setback to the New Deal's efforts at recovery made the President and the CIO more dependent on each other than previously. Rising unemployment in the mass-production industries reduced dues-paying CIO membership across the board and paralyzed almost all the organization's ambitious schemes for promoting unionization. It became ever more dependent on federal pump-priming programs to maintain employment levels and National Labor Relations Board's (NLRB) support for its organizing efforts. Roosevelt, in turn, needed CIO backing to protect him on his left flank politically and also to provide the mass support he needed in order to ward off attacks from the right, which were rising in intensity. Yet the "Roosevelt depression" weakened the CIO unions precisely at the moment the President most needed their support to complete his program of domestic reform. And as Roosevelt's domestic reforms lost momentum, many on the CIO left began to turn against the President.[12]

Simultaneously with the decline of the CIO, the AFL discovered new life. In the spring of 1937, after its victories over General Motors and U.S. Steel, the CIO claimed one to two million more members than the AFL. Only a year later, at the time of the CIO's founding constitutional convention in October 1938, the AFL had at least 1.5 million more members than the CIO, and the disparity in size between the two competing national labor centers was to continue to grow in favor of the AFL. Moreover, AFL membership growth, as contrasted with that of the CIO, threatened vital aspects of the New Deal-labor political coalition. Several AFL leaders were still allied to the Republican Party. Others accused the CIO and its New Deal friends of Communist sympathies. And still others retained the AFL's traditional distrust of all state welfare programs. Moreover, the AFL leaders, as a group, joined with corporate officials in condemning the NLRB and New Deal labor policy as too sympathetic to the CIO and too open to Communist influence.[13]

The Roosevelt depression, the AFL's revival, and the emergence of a conservative coalition of Northern Republicans and Southern Democrats in Congress spelled the end of the New Deal as a successful domestic reform movement and meant paralysis for the CIO. As opposition to Roosevelt rose on his right in 1937 and 1938, he turned to his labor and CIO friends for political support as never before. He implored labor to back him in his effort to reform the Supreme Court (the so-called court-packing scheme of 1937) and to lobby Congress for passage of the final New Deal domestic reforms: the Fair Labor Standards Act, the Wagner-Steagall public housing bill, and a more expansive program of public works. The CIO did what the President asked, and it indeed helped Roosevelt gain his goals, except reform of the Supreme Court. As the 1938 off-year elections approached, Roosevelt again turned to his friends in the CIO to help him cleanse the Democratic Party, that is, to defeat a group of conservative, antilabor Democratic candidates in the party primaries. Both the 1938 primaries and the general election spelled disaster for Roosevelt and his allies in the CIO. In the primaries, with one exception, those Democratic candidates selected for defeat by the President triumphed. In the general election, the Republican Party experienced a resounding revival. Nowhere was the defeat for the New Deal and the CIO more evident than in the state of Michigan. There the CIO used all its financial and human resources to promote the reelection of

Frank Murphy, the governor so responsible for the UAW's victory at Flint in 1937. In the event, Murphy and his Democrat ticket went down to defeat, a result celebrated by Republicans, corporate leaders, and even several AFL chieftains.[14]

The end of the year 1938 found the CIO at an organizational and political impasse. Organizationally, it had lost all its momentum and ability to grow. Politically, it had no alternative to Roosevelt and his New Deal, nor could the CIO effectively pressure the President from the left. Much as some CIO leaders, notably John L. Lewis, threatened to form an independent farmer-labor party of one sort or another, they knew, in reality, that they had few troops to enlist in such a cause. Roosevelt had thoroughly captured the working-class vote and there was little the CIO leaders could do to change that fact.[15] Even among workers who belonged to unions with a long independent and even socialist political tradition, such as the Jewish-American garment trades unions, Roosevelt's political appeal was unsurpassed. As a veteran Tammany Hall politician quipped, "The Jews have *drei veltn—di welt, iener welt, un Roosevelt*"[16] (three worlds—this world, the other world, and Roosevelt). The same sentiments were reflected in song verse by Alabama and West Virginia coal miners. A black Alabaman sang

> In nineteen hundred an' thirty three
> when Mr. Roosevelt took his seat,
> He said to President John L. Lewis
> "In union we must be."

> Hooray, Hooray!
> Fer de union we must stan.
> It's de only organization
> Protects de laborin man.

> Boys, it makes de women happy
> Our chillen clap deir hands
> to see de beefsteaks an' de good po'k chops
> Steaming in dose frying pans.

And in West Virginia, the coal miners sang,

> Some people don't know who to thank,
> for this "State of McDowell" that's so free;
> Give part of the praise to John Lewis
> and the rest of it to Franklin D.[17]

At the same time, the rapprochement between the AFL and corporate America became warmer and firmer than ever. AFL attorneys and officials joined with their counterparts in the National Association of Manufacturers, the Chamber of Commerce, and the Conference Board to propose amendments to the National Labor Relations Act which would serve to dilute some of its most prolabor aspects. Many of these amendments were subsequently incorporated into the Taft-Hartley Act of 1947. AFL leaders also continued to testify against the CIO before the House Committee on Un-American Activities and to unleash a relentless barrage of anti-CIO propaganda. And the AFL continued to back politically antilabor Republicans opposed by CIO-endorsed Democrats. Faced by a corporate-AFL coalition on one side and conservative Southern Democrats on the other, Roosevelt by 1939 prepared to replace "Dr. New Deal" with "Dr. Win-the-War." The President restaffed the NLRB with members more sympathetic to the AFL and business, and he generally withdrew his Administration from its more advanced prolabor positions.[18] Had war not come, the CIO and its new unions might have faced a parlous situation. For militant and widespread as was the labor upheaval of 1936-37, its depth was shallow and its staying power limited.

To understand better what actually happened during the 1930s and why the relationship between the New Deal and the labor movement took its particular and peculiar shape, we must grasp more clearly why, in the end, corporate America proved more adept than Franklin D. Roosevelt in influencing the AFL's hierarchs. We also must probe more fully into the question of whether the structure of federalism and the constitutional separation of powers diluted the popular basis for a more radical domestic New Deal, or whether, in fact, popular support for Roosevelt's unachieved yet ambitious and radical proposals was more apparent than real, more shallow than deep. There can be no doubt that the "Roosevelt revolution" transformed the place and role of organized labor in American life. Still, questions abound concerning why that transformation was neither fundamental nor enduring in a radical sense.

1. For these events, see Irving Bernstein, *Turbulent Years: A History of the American Worker, 1933-1940* (Boston, 1969); and Walter Galenson, *The CIO Challenge to the AFL: A History of the American Labor Movement, 1935-1941* (Cambridge, Mass., 1960).

2. David Brody, *Workers in Industrial America* (New York, 1980), ch. 4. For a somewhat different analysis, see David Montgomery, *Workers' Control in America* (New York, 1979), ch. 7.

3. For a fuller version of aspects of this upheaval, see my own "Not So 'Turbulent Years': Another Look at the American 1930s," *Amerikastudien* 24, no. 1 (1979): 5-20.

4. For the general contours of these developments, see Bernstein, *Turbulent Years*, ch. 6. On automobiles, see Sidney Fine, *The Automobile under the Blue Eagle* (Ann Arbor, 1963), chs. 7-10.

5. For these developments, see Arthur M. Schlesinger, Jr., *The Politics of Upheaval* (Boston, 1960), chs. 16-23; and William E. Leuchtenberg, *Franklin D. Roosevelt and the New Deal* (New York, 1963), chs. 7-8.

6. Melvyn Dubofsky and Warren R. Van Tine, *John L. Lewis: A Biography* (New York, 1977), pp. 248-52.

7. Notes on CIO Meeting, November 7-8, 1936, Katherine P. Ellickson Papers, Franklin D. Roosevelt Library; typescript of speech, "Industrial Democracy," John L. Lewis Papers, State Historical Society of Wisconsin.

8. Sidney Fine, *Sit-Down: The General Motors Strike of 1936-1937* (Ann Arbor, 1969), chs. 9-10; and *Frank Murphy: The New Deal Years* (Chicago, 1979), ch. 8.

9. Dubofsky and Van Tine, *Lewis*, pp. 273-77.

10. Notes on CIO Executive Board Meeting, K. P. Ellickson Papers; *Nation*, February 20, 1937, pp. 203-05.

11. Harry Hopkins to Franklin D. Roosevelt, July 2, 1937, FDR Papers, OF407B, Box 27; Dubofsky and Van Tine, *Lewis*, pp. 312-15.

12. Leuchtenberg, *FDR*, pp. 243-44; Dubofsky and Van Tine, *Lewis*, pp. 316-17, 325-29.

13. Christopher L. Tomlins, "AFL Unions in the 1930s: Their Performance in Historical Perspective," *Journal of American History* 65 (March 1979): 1021-42.

14. Leuchtenberg, *FDR*, pp. 271-73; Samuel T. McSeveney, "The Michigan Gubernatorial Campaign of 1938," *Michigan History* 45 (June 1961): 115.

15. For a recent analysis of these political developments, see Seymour Martin Lipset, "Roosevelt and the Protest of the 1930s," *University of Minnesota Law Review* 68 (December 1983): 273-98.

16. Irving Howe, *The World of Our Fathers* (New York, 1976), p. 393.

17. George Korson, *Coal Dust on the Fiddle* (Hatboro, Pa., 1965), pp. 301-05.

18. James A. Gross, *The Reshaping of the National Labor Relations Board: National Labor Policy in Transition, 1937-1947* (Albany, 1981), chs. 4-5, 8, 11.

V

THE ROOSEVELT ADMINISTRATION AND ECONOMIC LEGISLATION

THE CORPORATE IDEAL AS LIBERAL PHILOSOPHY IN THE NEW DEAL

Ellis W. Hawley

In the older frameworks that long dominated the writing of American history, periods of reform were of necessity periods of business-government conflict, and it was as such a period that the era of Franklin D. Roosevelt's New Deal was usually depicted. Like Jackson's war on the bank or Theodore Roosevelt's prosecution of the Northern Securities Company, the struggle for a New Deal was seen as pitting popular democracy against a business system naturally inclined toward undemocratic features. And from it, so it was held, had emerged a modern democratic state so designed as to force the economic order to serve the "people."

With this reading of New Deal history, I still find myself in partial agreement. It captures well, I think, that part of the New Deal most apparent in the years from 1935 through 1938. What it leaves out, however, are those facets of the new state that owed their creation to business interests or modernizing elites rather than popular forces. And what it leaves out as well, I would argue, is an influential stream in the period's reform thought, a stream that viewed the business sector not as an entity to be mastered and constrained but as one to be equipped with a higher rationality, assisted in developing responsible self-government, and then brought into a social concert or partnership with new capabilities for solving national or societal problems. Despite considerable recent revisionism,[1] the extent to which the architects of the New Deal saw themselves as attempting to build an organizational commonwealth rather than a regulatory state has remained unrecognized or misunderstood;[2] and it is as a modest contribution toward correcting this situation that I offer what is to follow. In it I propose to reconstruct the major outlines of this story, focusing in turn on the kind of thinking involved, on its relationship to what was done in 1933, on its persistence during the so-called Second New Deal that followed, and on its resurgence in the late 1930s.

The most prominent manifestation of this kind of New Dealism was, of course, the system of industrial codes, public-private continuums, and economic councils established under the National Industrial Recovery Act and its counterparts in the fields of agriculture, transportation, and conservation.[3] Usually, this has been depicted as a product of crisis improvisation and interest group maneuvering,[4] and clearly both were involved. But it was also, I would argue, the creation of individuals holding certain organizational ideals and finding themselves now in positions where they could apply these to legislative and organizational activity. In essence, the idea was to use the state, not as a regulator or enterpriser, but as a tool for coaxing from modern organizational society a new network of quasi-public associations, one that in theory could be so constituted as to preserve liberty while utilizing new forms of social power to resolve both national and segmental problems. Instead of a modern state, as this had developed in Europe and been foreshadowed in the regulatory commissions of the progressive era, there was to be a modern organizational commonwealth that would allow America to do without such a state.

This was an idea, moreover, that was neither new to American thinking nor confined solely to crisis situations. In somewhat variant forms it had appeared earlier, notably in the "new associationalism" of the pre-World War I period, in subsequent efforts to adapt the war experience to peacetime needs, in the Hoover-promoted associationalism of the 1920s, and in a variety of proposals during Hoover's Presidency.[5] It could be and had been offered as an American idea, not because America had the kind of feudal survivals or corporative traditions often associated with such designs in Europe, but because its "most modern of societies" had begun and continued in a rejection of European-style statism, had sought traditionally to meet its coordinative needs through machinery operating outside the state, and had developed most of its administrative resources under private auspices.[6] In such a society the envisioned commonwealth could appear as a further extension and application of Americanism.

It should be emphasized, too, that the appeal of the idea did extend to people that historians have usually classified as political liberals. One of the major revelations of recent scholarship has been the fascination within liberal reform circles, especially among those viewing themselves as defenders and appliers of the Wilsonian heritage, with such corporative ideas as functional representation, concerts of interest, public-private continuums, and elitist engineering of harmonious abundance.[7] In liberal programs the conception of antidemocratic interests forced through "good government" to serve the needs of the "people" remained an important conception. But competing with it were visions of a "new commonwealth" in which "responsible interests," so constituted as to make gains for the masses their primary goal, would take their place as honorable and trustworthy social partners, govern themselves in a socially reponsible fashion, and work together to develop the coordinative machinery and social intelligence needed for continuing progress.

In part these visions were projected by interest group leaders who felt both a need to preserve group autonomy and a need for new forms of social action. But to see them only as a kind of interest group ideology, be it business or labor, is to miss much that helps to explain why the early New Deal took the form that it did. Also involved, just as they were in developing the parallel visions of a new regulatory state, were individuals who saw themselves not as segmental leaders but as representatives of a special group uniquely equipped to further the processes of societal development. More specifically, one can discern in early New Deal circles three differing types of such individuals.

One such type we might designate as a kind of "modern gentry." Deriving partly from the aristocratic survivals of the South and the Hudson Valley, partly from the "commercial gentry" that had emerged in a number of midwestern cities, such individuals aspired to play key roles in a modernized Jeffersonianism. And unlike similar figures deriving from New England or older mercantile traditions, they had long been associated with the Democratic Party and had been especially prominent among Woodrow Wilson's war managers and councillors.[8] They were in a position to shape what emerged in 1933; and with their memories of the war experience lustered by time and myth making, they seemed confident that their special perspectives and capabilities could turn organized interest groups into social partners working together as a national team.[9]

A second type was the "new professional" turned systems builder and organizational engineer. Trained for professional careers (mostly in law, engineering, or applied science), such individuals had made their marks as builders of the private bureaucracies, ententes, and technical systems that had come to dominate much of American economic life. Within limited spheres they had functioned as institutional engineers; and the lessons learned there, so it was argued, could be applied to the larger problem of a disordered, dysfunctional, and uncoordinated society. Given the opportunity, they could use their special talents and skills to coax the needed cohesion and managerial capabilities from the organizational resources that had developed in the private sector—a feat, so they tended to believe, that had been accomplished during World War I.[10]

The third type was the "new social scientist" turned provider of a new social intelligence. In part such individuals were products of the growing informational sector supported by business firms and interest group organizations. But more generally, they had ties to academia, the media, or the new foundation-supported research institutes, thus allowing them to claim the status of an independent and socially concerned intelligentsia. They saw themselves as the fillers of an informational and analytical gap that was largely responsible for institutional backwardness. And in the 1910s and 1920s some of them had come to see the filling of this gap as the way to secure the kind of institutional development that would allow Americans to remain free of European-style statism. Given the opportunity, they believed, their activities as fact finders, social tutors, and advisory planners could coax from America's new organizational society the needed institutional framework; and in Roosevelt's New Deal some hoped to be given that opportunity.[11]

There were also people, of course, who can be seen as combinations of these types. Among the old Wilsonians and former war managers—for example, groups that contemporaries often referred to as the Baruch, McAdoo, or Baker men—there were people who combined gentry credentials or pretensions with reputations for modern organizational genius. Among the new cadre of professionals were people who could be seen both as organization builders and as developers of social intelligence. And in some cases, best exemplified perhaps by a man like Frederic Delano,[12] membership might logically be claimed in all three groups. But the point is not that the individuals involved fit neatly into the ideal types. It is rather that the Roosevelt Administration, as put together in 1933, included several sorts of people whose visions of the organizational future looked to corporative as opposed to statist development. It was so constituted as to make the chartering of "social partnerships," to be informed and guided by special social expertise, one of the likely responses to crisis conditions and interest group clamor. And in practice this kind of thinking quickly meshed with that of interest group leaders seeking to balance their desires for continuing autonomy with their desire to curb and control "destructive forces" in the society at large— the result being the National Industrial Recovery Act and its counterparts in the agricultural, transportation, and conservation sectors.[13]

The early New Deal, it now seems clear, was shaped by a stream of liberal thought that the older historical readings of the period have usually ignored or misrepresented. Much of it came from people who saw themselves not as the builders of a modern state or agents of a resurgent populism but as the creators of new societal machinery that would allow the emergence of a new organizational commonwealth. Even the so-called left wing of the Brains Trust, as represented by Rexford G. Tugwell, saw its calls for redistributions of power as leading to this ultimate goal.[14] And for the so-called center and right, as represented by the old Wilsonians, former war managers, and admirers of the modern corporation and modern associational development, the existing structure of power did not appear as any major obstacle. Their emphasis was upon making such power "responsible" and "public spirited," thus allowing an organizational capitalism to function without a European-style state; and they believed themselves capable, as the Hooverites had not been, of providing the leadership, expertise, and social spirit necessary to accomplish this task.

"Many good men," said the new President as he launched his industrial program, "voted this new charter with misgivings." But he did not share "these doubts." He had, he said, taken part in the "great cooperation of 1917 and 1918," and it was his faith that "we can count on our industry once more to join in our general purpose to lift this new threat and to do it without taking any advantage of the public trust which has this day been reposed without stint in the good faith and high purpose of American business." Nor was the occasion without similar words from those about to assume the roles of "social partners." For Henry Harriman, President of the United States Chamber of Commerce, the new charter marked the beginning of a "new dispensation" under which "destructive competition" would give way to "constructive cooperation." "In Franklin D. Roosevelt," he declared, "business greets a leader of courage, resourcefulness, and trustworthiness. It glows in the audacious pioneering spirit in which he is tackling our common problems."[15]

That the resulting structure of codes, councils, and committees could ever have realized its officially proclaimed goals now seems dubious. As various students of the subject have pointed out, it could not recreate the "great cooperation of 1917 and 1918," at least not without resort to forms of repression or public spending that were unattainable in the political climate of 1933. And having failed to bring forth the envisioned social concert, the "new dispensation" ended up providing legal permits for restrictionist cartels and predatory combines rather than concerted programs of market expansion and reemployment.[16]

This economic failure, moreover, acerbated the political problems with which the system was now confronted. It was unable to develop effective ways for bringing in or neutralizing small business and consumer groups, for giving industrial labor and its associations a satisfactory role, for grounding itself in a settled body of constitutional law, or for maintaining the concordance and reputation of the social elites and "wise men" who in theory were supposed to keep autonomous groups working together. All of these problems became increasingly acute, producing divisive rifts and policy deadlocks, and generating demands for the very kind of regulatory statism that the system was supposed to prevent.[17] Whether it had to be is debatable. But the tendency, clearly apparent by early 1934, was toward an increasing reliance on governmental rather than social power, and upon administrative resources developed under public rather than private auspices. While the conventional wisdom is otherwise, the opening through which an American version of the modern state finally emerged seems to have been created less by the failure of Hooversim than by the failure of what followed.

In part the emergence of the new state came through the transformation of the failed mechanisms of an envisioned corporatism into operating parts in an expanding federal bureaucracy. Such was the pattern, for example, in agriculture and in a number of extractive, processing, and transportation industries—all areas, generally speaking, where the administrators involved not only had bureaucratic "pork" to dispense but also saw themselves as part of a previously formed segmental establishment. Agriculture, to be sure, was for a brief period a partial exception. But this was no longer the case after the so-called purge of Jerome Frank and his lieutenants in 1935.[18]

Outside the areas noted, however, the turn toward public administration was accompanied by far more heat and friction. For most industries operating under the National Recovery Administration (NRA), there was no previously developed group of public administrators capable of translating demands for statist action into establishment usage of governmental power and resources. Instead, they were confronted with a group that tended to attach themselves to antiestablishment forces, especially new forms of labor, consumer, and small business militancy, and to see their roles not as industrial problem solvers but as public managers or new instruments for maintaining proper bargaining strengths and power balances. Such administrators were emerging now in the NRA's planning, research, consumers, and industrial relations sections. And the result, in much of the business world, was strong resistance to their expanding role and a return to traditional forms of antistatist rhetoric.[19]

It was this conflict, of course, emerging during the later stages of the NRA and forming the backdrop for continued business protests about an "un-American statism," that does fit well the conceptual framework associated with the older history. Nor can one deny either its reality or its importance. Those portions of the new American state charged with regulating industrial relations, protecting consumer welfare, correcting undesirable inequalities, and managing aggregate demand did emerge in the face of fierce business opposition. They were outgrowths of the new adversarial bureaucracy linked to antiestablishment militancy, and they were staffed, at least initially, by people who tended to see businessmen more as "economic royalists" or "social malefactors" than as potential partners in a social concert.[20] On these matters revisionist efforts to substitute a "corporate liberal" scenario for the older history have not been persuasive.[21] But one should recognize as well that these portions of the new American state were far from being its entirety, and that even as they were being created the kind of thinking from which the measures of 1933 had sprung retained a remarkable hold over a number of their original sponsors. For a continuing nucleus of those attached to the Roosevelt Administration, the answer, despite the failure of the NRA, was a state helping to develop "responsible social partners," not one engaged in adversarial regulation.

Prior to the Schechter decision in 1935, the NRA's code authorities and other administrative units served as the primary base for continued articulation and defense of this associative vision.[22] But similar arguments also continued to come from agencies in or attached to the Commerce Department. There the taint of Hooverism had contributed to purges and transfers of previously developed agencies. But Secretary Daniel C. Roper, an old Wilsonian attracted by corporative ideals, had succeeded in 1933 in establishing the Business Advisory and Planning Council (BAPC), which he saw as the germ from which a national economic parliament might develop. And working now with the council's leaders, Roper kept trying to establish a new nexus of trust and understanding within which "progressive" businessmen could join with other social groupings in putting "their shoulders to the wheel of recovery." To Roosevelt he talked of a confused "business mind," needing only responsible assurances and calls to action to bring it back to a "constructive and helpful" position; and in talks to business groups he stressed the "interdependence" linking "every important element in our national structure," giving each a stake in the success of the others, and requiring "constant and consistent partnership."[23]

In addition, such notions continued to rear their heads in various other quarters. In the Tennessee Valley Authority, Arthur E. Morgan deplored the growth of antibusiness militancy and urged a "developmental planning" in which experts, public administrators, and responsible private interests would work together to secure new social benefits.[24] In the new Social Security Advisory Council, the idea that social insurance programs should be grounded in modern business and labor organizations rather than in a European-style state was strongly argued, both by the council's business members and by the "Wisconsin group" that dominated its academic components.[25] In Frederic Delano's National Resources Board, a "plan for planning" had taken shape, one in which scientifically informed experts would evolve and implement national plans through a network of functional representatives and associations.[26] And in a newly formed Committee for Economic Recovery, put together in late 1934 by presidential advisers Raymond Moley and Donald Richberg, the vision being articulated was one of "intelligent cooperation" saving America from both disintegration and regimentation.[27]

Even in the post-NRA period, moreover, as conflict between the Administration and organized business intensified, there continued to be groups and individuals hopeful of developing a societal alternative to the "statification" upon which the New Deal had now embarked. Somehow, they seemed to believe, the process of building modern social partnerships and national teams could be restarted; could, once under way, reestablish its credibility; and could, as a consequence, eventually refill the policy vacuum into which the "statists," "radicals," and "reactionaries" had now moved. Amid mounting conflict and invective, such groups clung to remnants of the 1933 machinery, urged actions that could "crystallize" cooperative impulses, and, periodically, lent their support to organizational promoters claiming a capacity to engineer structures within which new agencies of social cooperation could be incubated and brought to life.

In the Commerce Department, for example, Roper was successful, despite a number of resignations and threats of others, in maintaining the BAPC mechanism. As the Business Advisory Council (BAC), it continued to bring government officials together with "sympathetic" business leaders and to generate a variety of designs and initiatives for transforming conflict into cooperation.[28] And while the Committee for Economic Recovery had now faded from the scene, Donald Richberg had not. In a series of speeches and memoranda, he was calling for another comprehensive effort to forge a concert of interests, offering suggestions as to how the "problems that wrecked the N.R.A." could be resolved, and trying to mobilize support from such groups as the American Bar Association and the American Trade Association Executives. In a memorandum to Roosevelt submitted in late 1936, he insisted that his ideas were again gaining the support of "representative industrialists, economists, lawyers, publicists, and officials."[29]

Running parallel, moreover, to the Roper and Richberg operations were efforts to turn the skeletonized remains of the NRA into the envisioned incubator of a new harmony. In June 1935 Congress had agreed that these remnants might continue for another nine months; and under this measure there developed not only an unsuccessful effort to promote voluntary codes but also a series of plans for finding the extended agency a permanent home, either in the Commerce Department, a new Industrial Council, or a reorganized Federal Trade Commission. Entering the picture, too, in late 1935, was a newly created Coordinator for Industrial Cooperation, a position to which Roosevelt had appointed former labor leader and NRA administrator George Berry. In December, Berry convened what was billed as a national gathering of all economic interests; out of the conference came the Council for Industrial Progress, organized along corporative lines and aspiring to be the structure from which new mechanisms of social cooperation would emerge.[30]

In addition, the period witnessed a variety of lesser initiatives seeking generally similar ends. There was, for example, an effort to create a "constructive business league," which as envisioned would accomplish what the BAC and the Berry Council had been unable to. This was the project of Peter Van Horn, another former NRA official. There was also the effort of Fred I. Kent, a New York banker with whom Roosevelt continued to correspond, to win support for a National Industrial Board, designed both to organize recovery and to develop a "strong intelligent force" operating outside of government and capable of containing the "political forces" demanding harmful legislation. And there were the continued activities of the "planners" operating under the auspices of the National Resources Committee. Their solution, by 1937, was a "national productivity conference," out of which could come a "truly cooperative attack" on the nation's problems.[31]

How Roosevelt himself regarded such initiatives is difficult to say. At times he seemed to view private power as something to be broken and subjected to controls exercised through new governmental institutions, at times as something to be interacted with in a game of power politics, and at times as something to be "socialized" and rendered "responsible" through the kinds of organization, information, and leadership advocated by his corporative-minded advisers. His rhetoric kept vacillating, from calls for "all-America recovery teams" to indictments of "economic despotism" to conceptions of a new and fairer balance of power—all of which may have been no more than political weapons in the arsenal of what one historian has called a "total politician."[32] But a number of those involved believed that the President's heart really lay in the vision of a "new commonwealth," that his encouragement of those keeping the vision alive represented more than efforts to divide his business enemies, and that under the right circumstances he would again assume leadership in efforts to turn the vision into reality.[33]

For some, moreover, the right circumstances were those arriving with the recession of late 1937. The new downturn, they believed, had shown again where destructive conflict, persisting institutional vacuums, and consequent misuses of both public and private power could lead, thus opening the way for a new period of "constructive cooperation." It had, in the words of New York merchant Benjamin Namm, made conditions "very ripe" for new organizational initiatives like those that Berry had attempted earlier. And while others were skeptical about Berry's efforts as a model, they were ready with their own suggestions. Appearing now were updated versions of the Roper, Richberg, and Kent proposals, a variety of schemes for "national organizations" or "central boards," and attempts by such former Brains Trusters as Adolf Berle and Rexford Tugwell to create a "national policy committee" as a vehicle for business-government-labor collaboration. As envisioned, this would refocus energies on producing new wealth rather than waging internal warfare.[34]

For a brief period, too, particularly in January and February of 1938, these new initiatives seemed on the verge of bringing the New Deal back to its 1933 orientation. The President, so Berle thought, "really wanted the N.R.A. back," and seeming to bear this out were his new willingness to consult with Roper's Business Advisory Council, his discussions with the press on "cooperative planning," and his decision to confer with groups put together by Richberg and Berle. In operation by late January were efforts to expand the BAC into a larger "national council," something Roper had long urged, plus an ad hoc "unification committee" composed of Berle and Charles Taussig, labor leaders John L. Lewis and Philip Murray, and business leaders Owen D. Young and Thomas Lamont. Also in operation shortly thereafter was another initiative from the "planners" of the National Resources Committee. Under their scheme they would provide guidance to the President in implementing the "idea of industry-government cooperation."[35]

As it turned out, the hopes raised by such developments were again to be dashed. The recession, it quickly became apparent, could also be used to argue for new attacks on private power or new efforts to liberate businessmen from the New Deal state. And when Roosevelt lent encouragement to the antitrust senti-ment, perhaps in an effort to make uncooperative business leaders more thoughtful about their alternatives,[36] key figures in the new organizational initiatives took umbrage at what they viewed as "third-rate politics" and proceeded to withdraw their support.[37] The outcome in 1938 would be a national "monopoly inquiry," a reactivated Antitrust Division, and further additions to the new regulatory state, not new institutions for nurturing and harnessing a societal corporatism. Yet as the year ended, several developments were under way that would subsequently allow this envisioned alternative to modern statism to reestablish some of its credibility and influence.

One such development was the emerging legislative stalemate in Congress, thwarting both "regulationists" and "business liberationists," yet also acting to reduce their fears of what the other might do and thus to create new opportunities for those claiming to have a "middle way" capable of providing both regulation and liberty. A second was the emergence of a new preparedness movement, shifting concerns now to a type of endeavor for which corporative formulas had retained more of their credibility.[38] And a third was the appearance, mostly from the same quarters that had kept the associative ideals of 1933 alive, of new theoretical formulations in which "progressive government" would function both as a "constructive" regulator and as promoter and developer of responsible "self-government" and "social planning" in the private sector. In these formulations the key conception was still national progress through societal as opposed to statist development. But added to this now was the idea that securing the first would require some of the second and that the two could be harmonized through formulas stressing responsibility, reasonableness, and mutuality. More specifically, the threatening forms of statism that had emerged between 1934 and 1938 were to be rendered "progressive" and "American" through the development of a commercially oriented Keynesianism, a "reasonable" antitrust, a "cooperative" welfarism, and a "responsible" industrial relations policy.[39]

From 1939 on, moreover, the general trend in public policy was away from antibusiness liberalism and back toward the view that organized interest groups had unrealized potentials for social partnership. This was a trend, to be sure, that proceeded haltingly, blocked or obscured at times by businessmen and bureaucrats who persisted in viewing each other as obstructionists or aggrandizers. But the overall drift was unmistakable. The administrative vacuums opened by the exigencies of rearmament and war were being filled by a system assuming partnership rather than adversarial roles.[40] And while some viewed this as a temporary product of war conditions, a growing number saw it as a development upon which the nation's "forward-looking elements" could build for a better future. Such was the message of a newly formed and increasingly influential Committee for Economic Development; and such were the implications of the "New Charter for Labor and Management" endorsed by public and private leaders in early 1945. Under it, if rhetoric meant anything, business, labor, and government were to become postwar partners operating within a framework recognizing their joint interests in full employment, high wages, collective bargaining, capitalist enterprise, and functional specialization.[41]

The result was not another NRA. But the postwar period did bring the Maximum Employment Act of 1946, new trade and aid programs, and new quasi-official boards and councils that were essentially of the sort advocated by the intellectual heirs of the NRA vision. It also brought a tendency to attribute postwar economic growth to the increasing responsibility and consensuality within America's organizational society; and as fears of a postwar depression faded, it brought a further retreat of antibusiness liberalism accompanied by a transformation of federal regulatory activity along the lines envisioned by the 1938 proponents of a "constructive" statism.[42] Liberalism, so it was said, had triumphed and become the new consensus.[43] But the liberalism that had done so seemed to be that of the NRA vision, the National Resources Committee's "cooperative planning," the Berle "unification committee," and the Committee for Economic Development, not that rooted in popular democracy or in a public administration committed to institutionalized warfare with would-be oppressors of the people.

How, then, should the older history's reading of the New Deal period be altered? In answer to this, I would make essentially three points, one having to do with what we should retain of it, the other two with what needs to be added or reconceptualized.

The first point is the continuing validity of the older history as a reading of what happened between 1935 and 1938. The revisionist notion that the state building of that period was being managed by a sophisticated corporate elite intent upon preserving its power and privileges simply does not square with the known facts about how the reform measures were passed and implemented.

The second point is the need to recognize another stream of liberal thought during the period, one that would cope with modern social problems through an organizational common-wealth rather than a regulatory state, and one that helped to shape the early New Deal, that persisted after the failure of the NRA system, and that in somewhat altered form regained much of its influence and credibility after 1938. In the older history most of this was either not recognized or badly distorted, partly because the progressive-conservative dichotomy that this older history employed had little place for it.

Finally, there is the need to recognize that this stream of thought and activity was more than the ideology of certain interest group leaders. It came, like the parallel visions of a new managerial state, from a combination of segmental leaders and people who saw themselves as being uniquely equipped or positioned to further the processes of modern institutional devel-opment. And in a society where history, organizational develop-ment, and political structure had all worked to produce strong resistance to managerial statism, it would continue to have a larger appeal. Its persistence and revival, despite the failure of the NRA system, bear witness to persisting hopes that Americans can find an answer for market failures without turning to statist regimentation and direction.

1. The literature doing so has come chiefly from neoleftists, organizational historians, and antistatist economists. For discussions of it, see Otis L. Graham, Jr., "The Age of the Great Depression," in William H. Cartwright and Richard L. Watson, *The Reinterpretation of American History and Culture* (Washing-ton, D.C., 1973), 498-503; and Thomas K. McCraw, "Regulation in America," *Business History Review* 49 (Summer 1975): 164-79.

2. Hostile interpreters have tried to link it to the corporatism of Fascist theory, while friendly ones have tended to dismiss too easily some of its antidemocratic implications. See, for example, William E. Leuchtenburg, "Franklin D. Reagan's Reach for a Legacy," *Washington Star*, October 5, 1980, F-1, 4, which was written in response to assertions about New Dealism by Ronald Reagan and Professor Melvyn B. Krauss.

3. I have in mind particularly the Agricultural Adjustment Act, the Emergency Railroad Transportation Act, and the Taylor Grazing Act, all of which shared with the National Industrial Recovery Act a common core of assumptions, ideas, promoters, and implementing strategies.

4. See, for example, the explanations in Bernard Bellush, *The Failure of the NRA* (New York, 1975); and Robert F. Himmelberg, *The Origins of the National Recovery Administration* (New York, 1976).

5. See Jerry Israel, ed., *Building the Organizational Society* (New York, 1972); Kim McQuaid, "Coporate Liberalism in the American Business Community," *Business History Review* 52 (Autumn 1978): 342-68; Ellis W. Hawley, "Herbert Hoover, the Commerce Secretariat, and the Vision of an 'Associative State,'" *Journal of American History* 61 (June 1974): 116-40; Ellis W. Hawley, "Antitrust and the Association Movement," in *National Competition Policy* (Washington, D.C., Federal Trade Commission, 1981), 97-119; and Patrick D. Reagan, "The Architects of Modern American National Planning," Ph.D. dissertation, Ohio State University, 1982.

6. These are points well made in Stephen Skowronek, *Building a New American State* (Cambridge, 1982), pp. 19-46; Barry Karl, *An Uneasy State* (Chicago, 1983), 9-33; and Robert D. Cuff, *The War Industries Board* (Baltimore, 1973), 1-12.

7. See, for example, Jordan A. Schwarz, *The Speculator* (Chapel Hill, 1981), 207-70; David A. Horowitz, "Visions of Harmonious Abundance," Ph.D. dissertation, University of Minnesota, 1971; Gerald Nash, "Experiments in Industrial Mobilization, WIB and NRA," *Mid-America* 45 (July 1963): 157-74; Thomas E. Vadney, *The Wayward Liberal* (Lexington, 1970); James Weinstein, *The Corporate Ideal in the Liberal State* (Boston, 1968); and Edward Berkowitz and Kim McQuaid, *Creating the Welfare State* (New York, 1980), 44-95.

8. See Robert D. Cuff, "We Band of Brothers—Woodrow Wilson's War Managers," *Canadian Review of American Studies* 5 (Fall 1974): 135-48.

9. In recent years several scholars have noted the myths and selective memories about the war experience. See Schwarz, *The Speculator*, 50-51, 88, 106; Cuff, *War Industries Board*, 265-69; and Paul A.C. Koistenen, Review of Jordan A. Schwarz, *The Speculator*, in *Journal of American History* 68 (March 1982): 968-69.

10. The clearest examples of the type are such "corporate liberals" as Owen D. Young and Gerard Swope. But it included professionals-turned-modern-organization-builders in such areas as philanthropy, education, scholarship, and community development as well as business. One of the best discussions of the making of such types is in Reagan, "Architects of Modern National Planning," 270-87. See also David F. Noble, *America by Design* (New York, 1977).

11. Two major links through which social scientists of this sort moved from the projects of the New Era to those of the New Deal were the Committee on Recent Economic Changes and the Research Committee on Social Trends. See Reagan, "Architects of Modern National Planning," 122-30, 292-96; and Guy Alchon, "Technocratic Social Science and the Rise of Managed Capitalism, 1910-1933," Ph.D. dissertation, University of Iowa, 1982.

12. Delano was not only the "President's uncle" but also an important figure in bringing "partnership" concepts and their promoters into the early New Deal. The best account of his career, intellectual development, and influence is in Reagan, "Architects of Modern National Planning," 24-67. See also Daniel Delano, Jr., *Franklin D. Roosevelt and the Delano Influence* (Pittsburgh, 1946).

13. A recent study making this clearer than most of the older accounts is Peter H. Irons, *The New Deal Lawyers* (Princeton, 1982). See especially pp. 17-26 and 111-18. But see also Himmelberg, *Origins of NRA*, 181-212; Raymond Moley, *The First New Deal* (New York, 1966); Bellush, *Failure of NRA*, 1-29; Van L. Perkins, *Crisis in Agriculture* (Berkeley, 1969); and Frank Freidel, *Franklin D. Roosevelt: Launching the New Deal* (Boston, 1974).

14. Bernard Sternsher, *Rexford Tugwell and the New Deal* (New Brunswick, 1964), 92-106.

15. Franklin D. Roosevelt, *Public Papers and Addresses*, vol. 2 (New York, 1938), 252-53; *Washington Star*, May 7, 1933; *New York Times*, June 25, 1933, sec. 8, p. 1.

16. Bellush, *Failure of NRA*, 55-83, 176-77; Ellis W. Hawley, *The New Deal and the Problem of Monopoly* (Princeton, 1966), 53-110; Michael M. Weinstein, *Recovery and Redistribution under the NIRA* (New York, 1980).

17. Hawley, *New Deal and Monopoly*, 72-110; Arthur M. Schlesinger, Jr., *The Coming of the New Deal* (Boston, 1959), 119-76; Kim McQuaid, "The Frustration of Corporate Revival during the Early New Deal," *Historian* 41 (August 1979): 682-700.

18. The process is detailed in Kenneth Finegold and Theda Skocpol, "Capitalists, Farmers, and Workers in the New Deal," Paper presented at the American Political Science Association Convention, Washington, D.C., August 31, 1980; Hawley, *New Deal and Monopoly*, 205-46; and Irons, *New Deal Lawyers*, 156-81.

19. For fuller accounts of this, see Theda Skocpol, "Political Response to Capitalist Crisis," *Politics and Society* 10 (1980): 167-201; McQuaid, "Frustration of Corporate Revival," 695-702; Irons, *New Deal Lawyers*, 215-34; Howell John Harris, "Responsible Unionism and the Road to Taft-Hartley," paper presented at the Colloquium on Job Control and the State, Cambridge, England, September 1982; and Ellis W. Hawley, "The New Deal and Business," in John Braeman et al., eds., *The New Deal: The National Level* (Columbus, 1975), 62-71.

20. Skocpol, "Political Response," 179-81, 191-94; McQuaid, "Corporate Liberalism," 362-64; Hawley, *New Deal and Monopoly*, 153-58, 283-303; Arthur M. Schlesinger, Jr., *The Politics of Upheaval* (Boston, 1960), 270-74, 319-20.

21. This is true of Ronald Radosh, "The Myth of the New Deal," in Adoush and Murray Rothbard, eds., *A New History of Leviathan* (New York, 1972), 146-87; G. William Domhoff, "How the Power Elite Shape Social Legislation," in *The Higher Circles* (New York, 1971), 156-250; and Barton J. Bernstein, "The New Deal: The Conservative Achievements of Liberal Reform," in Bernstein, ed., *Towards a New Past* (New York, 1967), 263-88. For the abandonment of such views by some neo-Marxists, see Fred Block, "Beyond Corporate Liberalism," *Social Problems* 24 (1976-77): 352-61.

22. McQuaid, "Frustration of Corporate Revival," 700-1; Hawley, *New Deal and Monopoly*, 111-24; William H. Wilson, "How the Chamber of Commerce Viewed the NRA," *Mid-America* 44 (April 1962): 104-6; Henry Harriman to Franklin D. Roosevelt, September 24, 1934, OF 105, Roosevelt Papers, Roosevelt Presidential Library.

23. Kim McQuaid, "The Business Advisory Council of the Department of Commerce," *Research in Economic History* 1 (1976): 172-78. See also Daniel Roper to Franklin D. Roosevelt, September 28, 1934; and Roper, "Mutual Responsibilities of Government and Business," December 8, 1934, both in OF 3, Roosevelt Papers.

24. Thomas K. McCraw, *TVA and the Power Fight, 1933-39* (New York, 1971), 87-89.

25. Berkowitz and McQuaid, *Creating the Welfare State*, 100-2.

26. Reagan, "Architects of Modern American National Planning," 305-12.

27. Memorandum re Committee for Economic Recovery, November 9, 1934, and Allie Freed to Franklin D. Roosevelt, November 24, December 24, 1934, both in OF1354, Roosevelt Papers; Hawley, *New Deal and Monopoly*, 153.

28. McQuaid, "Business Advisory Council," 179-80; Ernest Draper to BAC, July 5, 1935, and Draper to Roper, October 28, 1935, both in OF 3-Q, Roosevelt Papers; Roper to Roosevelt, November 5, 1935, OF 3, Roosevelt Papers.

29. Vadney, *Wayward Liberal*, 172-78; Donald Richberg, "Civilizing Competition," November 16, 1936, PPF 2418, Roosevelt Papers; Richberg, "Fair Competition and Wages and Hours," February 1937, OF 1961, Roosevelt Papers; Hawley, *New Deal and Monopoly*, 164-65.

30. James O'Neill to Roosevelt, June 28, 1935, OF 100, Roosevelt Papers; Prentiss Coonley to Roosevelt, December 5, 1935, PPF 3174, Roosevelt Papers; Ernest Draper to Roosevelt, November 5, 1935, and George Berry to Roosevelt, December 11, 1935, both in OF 2452, Roosevelt Papers; Berry to Roosevelt, January 3, 1936, OF 466, Roosevelt Papers; Coordinator for Industrial Cooperation, *Council for Industrial Progress* (Washington, D.C., 1936); Hawley, *New Deal and Monopoly*, 159-63.

31. Peter Van Horn to Marvin McIntyre, May 12 and November 9, 1936, and Van Horn to Roosevelt, August 10, 1936, all in OF 1974, Roosevelt Papers; Fred I. Kent to Roosevelt, June 10, 1935, and May 2, 1938, and Roosevelt to Kent, June 13, 1935, all in PPF 744, Roosevelt Papers; Harold Ickes to Roosevelt, March 29, 1937, OF 1092, Roosevelt Papers; Charles Merriam to Ickes, March 12, 1937, with accompanying memorandum, Industrial Committee—Production File, National Resource Planning Board Records, National Archives.

32. Albert U. Romasco, *The Politics of Recovery* (New York, 1983).

33. See, for example, the Adolf Berle Diary, December 14, 1937, Box 210, Berle Papers, Roosevelt Presidential Library.

34. Memorandum of call from Benjamin Namm, December 10, 1937, Matthew Reilly to Roosevelt, December 23, 1937, Leonard Dreyfuss to Roosevelt, October 22, 1937, and C.H. Heppenstall, "Central Board Plan," December 3, 1937, all in OF 172, Roosevelt Papers; Daniel Roper, "Counselling for Progress," December 1, 1937, OF 3, Roosevelt Papers; Roper to Roosevelt, January 5, 1938, OF 3-Q, Roosevelt Papers; Berle Diary, December 14, 16, 23, 1937, Box 210, Berle Papers; Fred I. Kent to Roosevelt, May 2, 1938, PPF 744, Roosevelt Papers; Vadney, *Wayward Liberal*, 177-78.

35. Berle Diary, December 14, 1937, January 17, 1938, Box 210, Berle Papers; McQuaid "Business Advisory Council," 180-81; Vadney, *Wayward Liberal*, 178-79; Hawley, *New Deal and Monopoly*, 396-97; Frederic Delano to Harold Ickes, April 9, 1938, with memorandum on "Industry Regulation," OF 1092, Roosevelt Papers; Josephine Y. and Everett N. Case, *Owen D. Young and American Enterprise* (Boston, 1982), 695-98.

36. This was the perception of people as diverse as Ickes, Tugwell, and Berle. See Hawley, *New Deal and Monopoly*, 398, and Berle Diary, December 30, 1937, Box 210, Berle Papers. It also fits the findings about Roosevelt's antitrust views and commitments in Wilson D. Miscamble, "Thurman Arnold Goes to Washington: A Look at Antitrust Policy in the Later New Deal," *Business History Review* 56 (Spring 1982): 1-15.

37. Berle Diary, January 31, 1938, Box 210, Berle Papers; Case, *Owen D. Young*, 699-700.

38. Richard Polenberg, "Decline of the New Deal," in Braeman et al., eds., *The New Deal*, 246-64; Schwarz, *The Speculator*, 356-58.

39. One expression of these ideas was in *Toward Full Employment* (New York, 1938), written by Henry S. Dennison, Ralph Flanders, Morris Leeds, and Lincoln Filene, with assistance from John K. Galbraith. Also involved in developing and promoting them were presidential adviser Beardsley Ruml, a "Chicago group" put together by William Benton and Paul Hoffman, and the Commerce Department's Business Advisory Council. See Robert M. Collins, "Positive Business Responses to the New Deal: The Roots of the Committee for Economic Development, 1933-1942," *Business History Review* 52 (Autumn 1978): 369-91, and Reagan, "The Architects of Modern American National Planning," 338-50.

40. David Brody, "The New Deal and World War II," in Braeman et al., eds., *The New Deal*, 267-305.

41. Collins, "Positive Business Responses," 384-90; Karl Schriftgiesser, *Business Comes of Age* (New York, 1960), 9-59; Paul Hoffman, "Business Plans for Postwar Expansion," *American Economic Review Papers and Proceedings* 35 (May 1945): 85-89; Jesse Jones to Roosevelt, August 29, 1944, OF 5384, Roosevelt Papers; "A Proposal for Industrial Peace," March 5, 1945, "New Charter for Labor and Management," March 28, 1945, and Roosevelt to Philip Murray, William Green, and Eric Johnston, March 28, 1945, all in OF 407, Roosevelt Papers.

42. Reagan, "Architects of Modern American National Planning," 397-409; Robert M. Collins, "The Persistence of Neo-Corporatism in Postwar Business-Government Relations," Paper presented at Organization of American Historians Convention, Detroit, Michigan, April 2, 1981; Robert Griffith, "Dwight D. Eisenhower and the Corporate Commonwealth," *American Historical Review* 87 (February 1982): 87-122; Bernard Sternsher, "Liberalism in the 1950s," *Antioch Review* 22 (1962): 315-31; David Lilienthal, *Big Business: A New Era* (New York, 1953); Adolf A. Berle, *Twentieth Century Capitalist Revolution* (New York, 1954).

43. Eric Goldman, *The Crucial Decade: America, 1945-1955* (New York, 1956).

THE NEW DEAL, CAPITALISM, AND THE REGULATORY STATE

James E. Anderson

The election of 1932 was what political scientists have come to designate as a critical or realigning election. (Others in this category include the elections of 1860 and 1896.) A realigning election involves major readjustments in the relations of power in society and is productive of significant changes in the nature and direction of public policy. As Walter Dean Burnham has commented,

> Realignments are themselves constituent acts: they arise from tensions in society which, not adequately controlled by the organization or outputs of party politics as usual, escalate to a flash point; they are issue-oriented phenomena, centrally associated with these tensions and more or less leading to resolution adjustments; they result in significant transformation in the general shape of policy; and they have relatively profound aftereffects on the roles played by institutional elites.[1]

The election of 1932, which focused on the broad issue of how the national government should deal with the effects of the Great Depression, brought to power Franklin D. Roosevelt and the New Deal. Large majorities of Democrats were elected to the House and Senate and, in the electorate, the Democratic Party replaced the Republican Party as the majority party. Roosevelt and the Democrats believed they had a mandate to act, and act they did. In the next half-dozen years (the 1936 election confirmed the 1932 realignment), more important economic regulatory and social welfare legislation was adopted than in the previous 140 years of the nation's history.[2]

This paper will focus on the nature and general consequences of the New Deal legislation for the regulation of private economic activity. Economic regulatory legislation is distinguished from other categories of economic legislation by its use of control or restraint *to limit the discretion*, the freedom of action, of persons involved in economic activity by prescribing some actions and proscribing other actions. It substitutes public purpose for private (although the two are not necessarily and always antithetical). The control or restraint involved may take a variety of forms— rules, orders, licensing requirements, price or rate controls, standard-setting, inspections, informal processes (e.g., bargaining, threats to prosecute), taxation, and so on. The substance of regulation may be shaped either directly by the legislature or by administrative agencies exercising legislatively delegated authority.

In the following sections of the paper, I will comment on some general theories of New Deal regulatory activity, survey New Deal regulatory legislation, and make an appraisal of the New Deal regulatory experience.

Some Theories of Regulation Briefly Treated

This paper sets forth no overarching or grand theory to explain New Deal economic regulatory activity. Others have left us with a variety of alternatives. Aruthur Schlesinger, Jr., organized his volumes *The Age of Roosevelt* around the theme of conflict between business and reformers. Regulation is seen essentially as an effort to promote the public interest and control abuses by business. Gabriel Kolko, in contrast, has contended that national economic regulation, both during the Progressive and New Deal periods, was generally designed and secured by the regulated to serve their own ends. Business interests rather than the public interest were the prime beneficiaries of regulatory programs. The regulators were the "captives" of those ostensibly regulated.[3] Others have contended that business "capture" of regulatory programs occurs not at their inception but over time.[4]

Another writer contends that "the New Deal may be best understood as a series of attempts to save capitalism by further regulating and rationalizing the economy, by bringing important elements of the labor movement into established political life, and by staving off social revolution through expansion of the welfare role of the state."[5] It is his view that the New Deal reforms, regulatory and otherwise, were unable to solve "the basic structural problems" of a capitalist society. These include unemployment, inequality, production for profit rather than for use, and inadequate social control of productive processes. Obviously his view of the New Deal differs markedly from that held by the National Association of Manufacturers and the Liberty League.

A recent entry into the theoretical sweepstakes holds that, after 1933, New Deal regulatory activity can be explained in terms of middle-class bureaucratic interests. To wit:

> The creation and expansion of numerous regulatory agencies pro- vided new jobs and expanded jurisdiction for the Brain Trusters and commissioners who wrote the new statutes. Furthermore, the expansion of the administrative apparatus in Washington and the requirement that many thousands of new program administrators pass civil service exams were applauded by the middle class of the 1930's. The federal government nurtured the middle-class intelligentsia by providing its members with economic security and the status and excitement of a new mission. The expanding state thus created a new public servant class that functioned, in turn, as a major support group for the administrative state.[6]

Members of Congress, especially Democrats, were willing to support the enactment of regulatory legislation delegating broad power to administrative agencies for two reasons. One was partisanship. The second was that "ambiguously worded statutes" increased the opportunities for members of Congress to influence the agencies' conduct of public policy.

None of these theories adequately explains the New Deal's economic regulatory activity. Some of the New Deal legislation enjoyed broad public support, and some did not. None was enacted in the face of general public opposition. Business groups supported some acts (e.g., the Communications Act and Civil Aeronautics Act) while they strongly opposed others (e.g., the Wagner Act and the Public Utility Holding Company Act). Farm groups generally supported the Agricultural Adjustment Act (1933) but were largely indifferent to the Agricultural Market- ing Agreement Act. Some New Deal legislation did originate with the administrative agencies, did delegate substantial dis- cretion to agencies, and did provide employment for middle- class persons. That, however, does not adequately explain the enactment of it. The New Deal was broadly conservative in that it sought to reform and retain rather than replace capitalism. It also brought about changes of much benefit to nonbusiness groups, such as organized labor.

Professor Thomas McCraw has remarked that in the United

States, regulation "has been a multi-functional pursuit, a circumstance that has offered scholars a choice, when they generalize
about the regulatory process as a whole, between extreme caution
on the one hand, and exteme likelihood of error on the other.
Regulation is best understood as an institution capable of serving
diverse, even contradictory ends, some economic, some political,
some cultural."[7] Although McCraw's remarks were directed at
regulatory experience over the past century, they seem apropos
when focused on the New Deal experience alone. That, of course,
is not a narrow focus, as we shall see.

New Deal Regulatory Activity

In this section my focus is mostly upon the domestic economic
regulatory legislation enacted between 1933 and 1938. (International trade and tariff legislation is not treated.) The intent is to
capture the magnitude, extent, and diversity of legislation in
this area, and to lay the basis for a general appraisal of economic
regulation during the New Deal era. The discussion is organized
around several conventional substantive categories. (A chronological tabular listing of "major" regulatory legislation is included in a table.) No claim is laid to comprehensiveness.

Antitrust. Antitrust policy, which has been a cardinal feature
of American public policy, is concerned with the maintenance
of competition and the prevention of monopoly. In this policy
area the New Deal followed a rather erratic course; a consistent
position on antitrust was never developed. The initial effort in
this area was the National Industrial Recovery Act (NIRA),
which authorized industrial groupings to set up "codes of fair
competition" to govern themselves, with the codes being subject
to presidential approval.[8] Initially the business community was
highly supportive of the NIRA, but by 1935, when the act was
declared unconstitutional by the Supreme Court, they had lost
faith in it. So had many others. The codes of fair competition, it
should be noted, were exempt from the antitrust laws. In effect,
the NIRA constituted a suspension of antitrust.

The Robinson-Patman Act (1936) and the Miller-Tydings Act
(1937) are later statutes which fall within the antitrust area.
They, however, were really contradictory to the broad goals of
antitrust. Both were parts of the effort in the 1930s to protect
small businesses against the pressures of their larger, more effi-
cient competitors—department stores, chain stores, and discount

houses.[9] (State legislation in this regard included chain store taxes, minimum markup laws, and resale price maintenance or "fair trade" laws.) The Robinson-Patman Act was intended to strengthen the Clayton Act's prohibition on price discrimination, while the Miller-Tydings Act exempted agreements under state "fair trade" laws from antitrust prosecution. These laws could be construed as setting a level of competition, thus being consistent with antitrust. However, they were widely viewed as supporting "soft" or nonprice competition. (The Miller-Tydings Act was repealed by Congress in 1975.)

In 1938, when Thurman Arnold became head of the Antitrust Division, the New Deal moved to intensify enforcement of the antitrust laws to combat the exercise of monopoly power. During the 1939-41 period, nearly two hundred antitrust cases were filed. Mention here should also be made of the establishment of the Temporary National Economic Committee by Congress, at the President's recommendation, to investigate the concentration of economic power.

Industry Regulation. Much of the New Deal regulatory legislation was focused upon particular industries and variously involved governmental control of such matters as entry into the industry, rates or prices, standards of service, finances, and competitive relationships. (At the present time, such regulation is often referred to as "economic regulation." It is distinguished from "social regulation," which is concerned with the social consequences of economic activity—for example, health and safety hazards and environmental pollution. The distinction, in practice, is not especially sharp or highly useful.)

Industries which came under initial or increased regulation during these years included banking, securities exchanges, communications, electric power, soft coal mining, motor carriers, shipping, and commercial air transportation. Regulation of these industries was based on two assumptions. First, private ownership was desirable. Public ownership was never really seriously considered as an alternative, except in the area of electric power production. Second, competition could not be relied upon adequately to protect the public interest. Many members of the affected industries were not wildly enthusiastic about unrestricted competition and favored government action to lessen or restrain competitive pressures. For example, in 1933, as Hawley states, "Many truckers welcomed the establishment of a NRA code."[10] When the NIRA was declared unconstitutional, many truckers, including the American Trucking Association, supported enactment of the Motor Carrier Act.

The patterns of industry regulation varied from one industry to another, which makes generalizations difficult. The Motor Carrier Act, for instance, authorized the Interstate Commerce Commission (ICC) to control entry, set minimum and maximum rates, supervise the issuance of securities, and regulate labor and safety practices of common carriers. A somewhat similar pattern was established for commercial airlines by the Civil Aeronautics Act, which also gave the Civil Aeronautics Authority (now the Civil Aeronautics Board, or CAB) authority to control mergers and provide subsidies for airlines. Thus, something closely akin to traditional public utility regulation was applied to these industries.

In comparison, regulation of the securities and soft coal industries was more limited in scope. In the case of securities, the Securities Act of 1933 sought to ensure that the prospective buyers of securities were provided with accurate information. The use of false, misleading, or fraudulent statements in the sale of securities was prohibited; the filing of detailed registration statements was required; and various corporation officials were made liable for the accuracy of statements. The Securities Exchange Act of 1934 extended regulation to the stock exchanges, prohibited various forms of stock manipulation, and gave the newly created Securities Exchange Commission much discretion in regulating various dealers and trade practices. Control over margin requirements for the purchase of stocks was assigned to the Federal Reserve Board. The concern of the two securities statutes was to prevent unfair practices and abuses and to establish open, fair competition in the sale and purchase of securities.[11]

The regulation of the soft coal mining industry under the Bituminous Coal Conservation (Guffey-Snyder) Act of 1935 and the Guffey-Vinson Act of 1937 was sought by segments of the industry following the demise of the NRA's coal code. The soft coal industry was a good illustration of a "sick" industry, being characterized by excess production, low or nonexistent profits, erratic prices, and low wages. The 1935 legislation established a coal commission with authority to regulate prices and trade practices. Some provisions of benefit to labor were also included.

When the Supreme Court declared the act unconstitutional in

1936, the supporters of regulation sought a second statute to meet constitutional objections. The result was the Guffey-Vinson Act, which, omitting any labor provisions, provided for a complicated price-setting scheme for coal. Much controversy attended the passage of both statutes. Support came from the United Mine Workers and unionized northern producers. In opposition were southern producers and large users of coal, such as the railroads.

The 1937 legislation was never effectively administered and expired during World War II. Johnson concludes that this episode "was not a story of regulation in the 'public interest,' although some saw it as such. Nor was it a tale of businessmen controlling or coopting government agencies. The politics of soft coal was rather a story of a splintered industry unable to find a means to save itself through industrial self-government."[12] Here regulation was sought to ease the pain of competition. The effort ultimately failed. Soft coal thus stands in contrast to the motor carrier and commercial airline industries, where the regulatory schemes were generally successful.

Agriculture. American farmers had long benefited from a variety of promotional programs—research and education, marketing services, and credit facilities. The New Deal expanded activity in these areas and added a significant new element—the regulation of agricultural production as part of the effort to increase farm prices and incomes. It is this aspect of New Deal agricultural policy that is pertinent here.

The Agricultural Adjustment Act (AAA) of 1933, agreed to by farm leaders and the Roosevelt Administration, provided for production controls ("domestic allotments" to reduce the supply of farm products to bring supply and demand into better balance and thereby raise farm prices). The goal here was parity: "the establishment of prices to farmers at a level that will give agricultural commodities a purchasing power with respect to articles farmers buy equivalent to the purchasing power of agricultural commodities in the base period . . . August, 1909-July, 1914." (Only in recent years did the parity concept disappear from price support legislation.) Farmers who agreed to restrict production were eligible for cash benefits financed by a tax levied on the processors of farm commodities. Commodity loans were available to cooperating farmers, and direct purchases of surplus commodities were also authorized. Legislation enacted in 1934 made production quotas mandatory for cotton and tobacco when approved by two-thirds of the producers voting in a referendum.

The AAA came to an end in 1936 when it was declared unconstitutional by the Supreme Court. It was quickly replaced by the Soil Conservation and Domestic Allotment Act, which provided for payments to farmers who took soil-depleting crops out of production. The "soil-depleting" crops happened to be those in excess supply.

In 1938 Congress adopted a second Agricultural Adjustment Act. Price supports were authorized in a range from 52 to 75 percent of parity. Farmers who stayed within their voluntary acreage allotments were eligible for commodity (nonrecourse) loans, parity payments, and/or soil conservation payments. When necessary to reduce excess production of wheat, corn, cotton, tobacco, and rice (and later, peanuts), the Secretary of Agriculture could impose mandatory marketing quotas with the approval of two-thirds of the growers voting in a referendum. A variety of surplus disposal programs (e.g., a food-stamp program and subsidization of the export of cotton and wheat) was also provided. The second AAA remains in the statute books as "permanent" farm legislation.

Regulation of production was the price farmers agreed to pay in turn for higher prices and incomes.

Labor. New Deal labor policy can be described as involving protection and positive support for unionization, collective bargaining, and workers. This involved regulation of some of the activities of employers. Leaving aside the labor provisions of the National Industrial Recovery Act (Section 7a), two statutes are noteworthy.

The National Labor Relations Act (or Wagner Act) guaranteed the right of workers to organize and bargain collectively through unions of their own choosing, free from employer interference.[13] The law then prohibited a number of unfair employer practices, such as discriminating against workers because of union membership and refusing to bargain collectively in good faith. The National Labor Relations Board was created to enforce the law and to assist in the choice of union representation. The agency was given no authority to involve itself with the substance of labor disputes. The act's guarantees and restrictions on employers created a favorable legal context for unionization and contributed to the development of unions as an important economic and political force in society.

The Fair Labor Standards Act (1938) set minimum labor standards for a large portion of the labor force. Southern spokesmen stoutly opposed the law because they did not want their region to lose the attractiveness of low wages and a general absence of protective labor legislation. The Fair Labor Standards Act provided initial minimum standards of twenty-five cents an hour and a forty-four-hour workweek, with forty cents an hour and a forty-hour workweek as goals to be reached within eight and three years respectively. The act also excluded from interstate commerce goods made by "oppressive child labor," that is, children under sixteen years of age. For hazardous occupations the minimum age was eighteen years. Agricultural labor, professional workers, fishermen, domestic workers, and others were exempted from the act's wage and hour provisions.

Consumer protection. Protection of consumers was essentially a peripheral part of the New Deal for a number of reasons. Consumers were poorly organized. Most persons were more concerned with improving their lot (i.e., their incomes) as producers. Also, the United States had not yet become a high mass-consumption society. The 1930s consumer was not confronted with the vast array of complex products, hazardous substances, drugs and medical devices, and credit arrangements which served as the subject matter for the outpouring of consumer legislation in the 1960s and early 1970s. Other public problems attracted the attention of most people.

Nonetheless, two important pieces of consumer legislation were enacted in 1938.[14] The Wheeler-Lea Act plugged a judicially created loophole in the Federal Trade Commission (FTC) Act's prohibition of unfair competition. The Supreme Court had held that the act protected only competitors and not consumers. The Wheeler-Lea Act amended the FTC Act so as to prohibit "unfair or deceptive acts or practices" as well as unfair methods of competition. This gave the commission clear authority to act to protect consumers. The act also expanded the jurisdiction of the FTC to include the false and misleading advertising of drugs, cosmetics, and therapeutic devices.

The Food, Drug, and Cosmetic Act broadened the definitions of adulteration and misbranding in earlier legislation and expanded the coverage of law to include cosmetics and therapeutic devices. Inspection of factories making foods, drugs, and cosmetics was authorized. New drugs could not be marketed until they had been tested and proven safe to use. (In 1962 the requirement of effectiveness was added.) For food products, the Secretary of Agriculture was empowered to set standards for identity, quality, and fill. Penalties for violations were increased. The enactment of this statute was facilitated by two factors: some of its key provisions were moderated and conflicts of interest among some of the affected industries reduced their political power.[15]

Appraisal and Commentary

Regulation has frequently been depicted as a moderate approach for dealing with the economic problems of an industrial society. As Professor Lloyd Musolf has contended:

> In ideological terms, regulation has drawn strength from the general belief that it is a halfway house between laissez faire and socialism. If the former became increasingly inappropriate as the Industrial Revolution continued, the latter appeared equally inappropriate in an economy largely based on vigorous private enterprise. Certainly regulation lacks the ideological appeal of the other two, but America has not been fertile ground for elaborate ideologies. Regulation permits, and even invites, the piecemeal, pragmatic approach to specific public problems that seems to fit the American temperament.[16]

Musolf's comments are quite applicable to the New Deal. The Great Depression and the attendant economic problems clearly made laissez faire an outdated concept for all but the most conservative.[17] On the other hand, socialism had little popular appeal. Norman Thomas and the Socialist Party received less than two hundred thousand votes in the 1936 presidential election. The radical movements of the 1930s focused more on schemes to redistribute income than to socialize property. The Townsend Movement and Huey Long's "Share the Wealth" movement are illustrative.

During the Progressive Era, regulation had become established as the dominant method used by government in dealing with economic problems when, one should add, they were dealt with by government. Until 1933, the national government's economic regulatory activity was, with some exceptions, as George Steiner states, "within the scope of a liberal interpretation of the limited-government doctrine.[18] National economic regulation was largely confined to antitrust (necessary to maintain competition), the railroads (a "natural monopoly"), banking (a precondition for a modern economy), and some consumer protection legislation.

This situation changed drastically with the flood of regulatory legislation enacted during the New Deal years. The regulatory state, which had flowered during the Progressive Era, reached maturity. Laissez faire, as an operative concept, was put to rest by the legislation sketched in the previous section and listed in the appendix. (In addition to that, a lot of "minor" legislation was enacted which collectively added to the weight of regulation.)

As noted earlier, regulation in the United States has been a "multifunctional pursuit." This phrase well describes the New Deal regulatory experience. A variety of functions or purposes, often overlapping and sometimes contradictory, can be identified.[19] These include at least the following:

1. Control of monopoly power
    Public Utility Holding Company Act
    the revival of antitrust enforcement
2. Cartelization of some industries
    National Industrial Recovery Act
    Civil Aeronautics Act
3. Promotion of group interests
    National Labor Relations Act
    Robinson-Patman Act
4. Consumer protection
    Wheeler-Lea Act
    Food, Drug and Cosmetic Act
5. Resolution of group conflicts
    Glass-Steagall Act (banks and depositors)
    Guffey-Vinson Act (northern and southern operators)
6. Provision of information and disclosure
    Securities Act
    Food, Drug and Cosmetics Act
7. Legitimizing capitalism
    prevention of abuses in banking, securities, and utility holding companies
8. Support of state regulatory activity
    Connally Hot Oil Act
    Miller-Tydings Act

New Deal regulation, as should be apparent, was characterized by experimentation and pragmatism rather than planning and philosophic consistency.

One thread that does run through much of the New Deal legislation is a lack of affection for competition as a regulating force in the economy. The Great Depression and revealed economic abuses gave competition something of a bad name. Unrestrained competition was seen as productive of abuses of power, economic dislocation, and misuse of resources, and hence of limited utility as a regulator of economic behavior. For many industries and for parts of agriculture, "regulated competition" was substituted for "free competition." If this was often agreeable to the regulated, who saw it as in their self-interest, so was it also to other segments of society, who saw it as in the public interest. Rarely, if ever, was there complete conflict between group and societal goals.

Much of the attention of the deregulation movement of recent years has been focused on industry regulatory programs—for airlines, motor carriers, natural gas, banking—that were originated or significantly expanded during the New Deal. (Railroad regulation is the major exception.) Where once the market was regarded as an inadequate source of control, it is now seen as preferable to government regulation. This change in view toward the market is not fully explainable in terms of economic and technological changes. Rather, it also seems to rest upon two separate strands of thought. One is the notion that regulatory agencies have been "captured" by the regulated industries and converted into tools of the industries' self-interest. That the CAB was the captive of the commercial airlines, for instance, is a widely expressed viewpoint in regulatory literature. Thus, deregulation is required to break up the alliance between captor industry and captive agency. Second, there is a revival of belief (or faith) in the market as an effective and beneficent allocator of economic resources. The affection for the market of the "Chicago school" of economists, which has been quite influential, borders on idolatry. Neither of these strands of thought was of much influence in the 1930s.

New Deal regulatory activity involved heavy reliance upon administrative agencies as an enforcement mechanism. Administrative regulation supplanted judicial regulation as the dominant mode. Regulatory statutes typically delegated broad discretion of action to regulatory agencies, which more often than not took the structural form of independent regulatory commissions. The Securities and Exchange Commission, National Labor Relations Board, Federal Communications Commission, Civil Aeronautics Board, and Federal Maritime Commission were created in the 1930s. Also, the Federal Power Commission was converted from a conservation agency into a regulatory commission, while the Federal Reserve Board was restructured and given substantially greater authority.

New Deal regulatory administration was based upon several premises.[20] First, effective regulation required a reliance on expertness. Understanding of the relevant social, economic, and technological factors was required to shape regulatory programs effectively to ameliorate the problems at which they were directed. This expertness could best be secured by reliance on administrative organizations and personnel.

Second, administrative agencies should be insulated from direct political control, hence the reliance upon independent regulatory commissions. Effective regulation required dispassionate action, continuity, and adaption of policy to changing conditions, which could best be secured if there was not continued political intrusion in agency action. As New Deal regulator James M. Landis remarked:

> Those with experience in legislative matters or with an insight into the difficulties attendant upon bridging the chasm between the phrase "Be it enacted" and law in the sense of controlling human affairs recognize that it is easier to plot a way through a labyrinth of detail when it is done in the comparative quiet of a conference room than when it is attempted amid the turmoil of a legislative chamber or committee room.[21]

Third, effective regulation required considerable flexibility by administrative agencies. The legislature should avoid binding agencies tightly with detailed legislative provisions or instructions. Rather, general policy guidance should be the legislature's concern. This would be conducive to the taking of initiative and the assumption of responsibility for action by agencies.[22]

Fourth, it was believed that the courts should exercise only limited control over administrative agencies, especially on substantive matters. The Logan-Walter bill, which sought to place severe procedural constraints on agencies to provide for extensive judicial review of agency actions was vetoed in 1941 by President Roosevelt. The bill reflected the disenchantment of lawyers and conservatives (the two categories are not mutually exclusive) with the expansion of administrative regulation.

In conclusion, the New Deal can be appropriately viewed as broadly conservative in that it sought not to replace the nation's capitalist economic system but to reform it. Regulation was one facet of the reform effort; the development of a variety of social welfare programs was another. On the other hand, the changes the New Deal made in regulatory policy and practice were sufficiently sweeping that they can fairly be described as revolutionary in their impact on government-business relationships. Henceforth, government would play a major role in the operation of the economy and the shaping of business decisions. Although some would have preferred otherwise, the government-business relationship continued to be primarily adversarial in nature. Moreover, the maturation of the regulatory state made it a more potent adversary.

1. Walter Dean Burnham, *Critical Elections and the Mainsprings of American Politics* (New York: Norton, 1970), p. 10.

2. For a discussion of how such changes are brought about by realigning elections, see David W. Brady, "Critical Elections, Congressional Parties and Clusters of Policy Change," *British Journal of Political Studies* 8 (1980): 79-99.

3. Gabriel Kolko, *The Triumph of Conservatism* (Glencoe: Free Press, 1963); and *Main Currents in Modern American History* (New York: Harper and Row, 1976).

4. See, for examples, Marver Bernstein, *Regulating Business by Independent Commission* (Princeton: Princeton University Press, 1955); and Theodore J. Lowi, *The End of Liberalism*, 2d ed. (New York: Norton, 1979).

5. Edward S. Greenberg, *Understanding Modern Government: The Rise and Decline of the American Political Economy* (New York: Wiley, 1979), p. 70.

6. Elizabeth Sanders, "Business Bureaucracy and the Bourgeoisie: The New Deal Legacy," in Alan Stone and Edward J. Harpham, eds., *The Political Economy of Public Policy* (Beverly Hills: Sage Publications, 1982), pp. 135-36.

7. Thomas K. McCraw, "Regulation in America: A Review Article," *Business History Review* 49 (Summer 1975): 159-83.

8. The NIRA and its administrative agency, the National Recovery Administration, are ably discussed in Ellis W. Hawley, *The New Deal and the Problem of Monopoly* (Princeton: Princeton University Press, 1966), chs. 1-7.

9. Joseph C. Palamountain, Jr., *The Politics of Distribution* (Cambridge: Harvard University Press, 1955).

10. Hawley, *The New Deal and the Problem of Monopoly*, p. 232.

11. Cf. Michael E. Parrish, *Securities Regulation and the New Deal* (New Haven: Yale University Press, 1970).

12. James P. Johnson, *The Politics of Soft Coal* (Urbana: University of Illinois Press, 1979), p. 245.

13. Good accounts of the enactment of the Wagner Act can be found in Arthur M. Schlesinger, Jr., *The Politics of Upheaval* (Boston: Houghton Mifflin, 1960); and J. Joseph Huthmacher, *Senator Robert F. Wagner and the Rise of Urban Liberalism* (New York: Atheneum, 1968).

14. Charles Jackson, *Food and Drug Legislation in the New Deal* (Princeton University Press, 1970).

15. Ibid.

16. Lloyd D. Musolf, *Government and the Economy* (Chicago: Scott Foresman, 1965), pp. 35-36.

17. One who clung to his beliefs in a severely limited government was James M. Beck. See Morton Keller's biography of Beck, *In Defense of Yesterday* (New York: Coward-McConn, 1958), ch. 10.

18. George A. Steiner, *Government's Role in Economic Life* (New York: McGraw Hill, 1953), p. 87.

19. McCraw, "Regulation in America," pp. 180-81.

20. This discussion draws upon Bruce A. Ackerman and William T. Hassler, *Clean Coal, Dirty Air* (New Haven: Yale University Press, 1981), ch. 1.

21. James M. Landis, *The Administrative Process* (New Haven: Yale University Press, 1938), p. 70.

22. Ibid., pp. 75-77.

TABLE
New Deal Regulatory Legislation, 1933-38

YEAR	STATUTE	PURPOSE
1933	Agricultural Adjustment Act	Provided for control of farm productions. Payments to cooperating farmers were financed by a tax on food processing. Also authorized marketing agreements.
	National Industrial Recovery Act	Authorized industries to develop "codes of fair competition" subject to presidential approval. Codes were to contain wage, hour, and collective bargaining guarantees for labor.
	Securities Act	Required corporations to provide prospective buyers with extensive, accurate information on stock issues. Registration statements must be filed with the Federal Trade Commission (FTC).
	Glass-Steagall Act	Compelled divorce of commercial and investment banks. Gave Federal Reserve Board (FRB) more supervisory authority over national banks. Created Federal Deposit Insurance Corporation to insure bank deposits in most banks.
1934	Securities Exchange Act	Created Securities and Exchange Commission (SEC) to enforce Securities Act and regulate Stock Exchanges and margin requirements. Legislation passed in 1936 and 1938 extended authority of SEC to dealers in unlisted securities.
	Communications Act	Created Federal Communications Commission (FCC) with authority to regulate all radio services and interstate telephone and telegraph companies.
1935	Banking Act	Reorganized FRB; created the Federal Open Market Committee. Gave FRB power over reserve requirements and discount rates. Strengthened central control of banking.

YEAR	STATUTE	PURPOSE
	Federal Power Act	Gave the Federal Power Commission (FPC) authority to regulate the security issuances, rates, and other aspects of interstate electric companies. Converted FPC into a regulatory body.
	Connally Hot Oil Act	Prohibited shipment in interstate commerce of oil produced in violation of state production control laws.
	Bituminous Coal Conservation Act	Set up Bituminous Coal Conservation Commission to set minimum prices for coal, and in some instances maximum prices. A penalty tax was imposed on violators of the law. Provided some benefits for labor.
	Motor Carrier Act	Brought interstate motor common carriers under control of Interstate Commerce Commission (ICC), which could set minimum rates for all regulated carriers.
	National Labor Relations Act	Established National Labor Relations Board (NLRB). Guaranteed right of labor to organize and bargain collectively. Banned a series of unfair employer practices.
	Public Utility Holding Company Act	SEC was given broad authority to regulate utility holding companies. "Death Sentence" clause directed SEC to simplify holding company structures. Systems containing more than three tiers were to be abolished.
1936	Merchant Marine Act	Replaced Shipping Board with Federal Maritime Commission (FMC). Authorized FMC to regulate rates, routes, trade practices, and other aspects of shipping companies. Also authorized to subsidize the construction and operation of American merchant ships.
	Soil Conservation and Domestic Allotment Act	Took place of first Agricultural Adjustment Act (AAA). Provided payments to farmers who reduced production of soil-depleting (i.e., basic) crops.
	Robinson-Patman Act	Strengthening prohibition of Clayton Act against price discrimination to protect small businesses.

TABLE (cont.)
New Deal Regulatory Legislation, 1933-38

YEAR	STATUTE	PURPOSE
1937	Guffey-Vinson Act	Replaced unconstitutional 1935 act. Contained modified price fixing, marketing, taxing, and fair practices provisions. Omitted labor provisions. Enlarged the Coal Commission.
	Agricultural Marketing Agreement Act	Authorized marketing agreements for milk, fruits, vegetables, and nuts to ensure orderly marketing and help achieve parity prices.
	Miller-Tydings Act	Exempted state resale price maintenance laws from the antitrust laws.
1938	Agricultural Adjustment Act	Provided for average allotments and production quotas to control farm production. Crop loans and parity payments to farmers authorized. In effect, provided a minimum price for some products.
	Civil Aeronautics Act	Set up Civil Aeronautics Authority (later Board) to regulate entry routes, rates, mergers, and so on of commercial airlines.
	Fair Labor Standards Act	Provided for twenty-five-cents-an-hour minimum wage and forty-four-hour workweek for workers in interstate commerce. Wage to increase to forty cents in eight years, hours to decrease to forty in three. Various workers exempted.
	Food, Drug, and Cosmetic Act	Food and Drug Administration (FDA) improved to license new drugs, which must be proved safe. Therapeutic devices and cosmetics brought under control. Department of Agriculture could establish identity and quality standards for food products.
	Natural Gas Act	FPC authorized to regulate interstate pipeline companies and sale of natural gas.
	Wheeler-Lea Act	Empowered FTC to prohibit "unfair deceptive acts or practices," thus giving the agency clear power to protect consumers.

VI

THE NEW DEAL
AND THE WELFARE
STATE

Comparative Welfare History: Britain and the United States, 1930-1945

James T. Patterson

Studies of developments in welfare policy in Britain and the United States between 1930 and 1945 stress two points. First, these years were fundamentally important in forming welfare states.[1] Second, unprecedented crises—war in Britain, depression in America—prompted these important changes.[2]

Of course, revisionists have challenged these conclusions. On the left, writers have maintained that the changes did nothing to promote greater equality, and that the new policies arose either to promote economic efficiency or to protect elites fearful of social unrest.[3] Economic historians, meanwhile, have minimized the effect of these public policies, and some economists have employed models purporting to prove that welfare programs retarded recovery in the short run and economic growth in the long run. It would have been better, some of these writers conclude, if the welfare state had never developed at all.[4]

Whatever the merits of these arguments, they rarely compare the experiences of the two nations. Such a comparison will suggest some of the strengths and weaknesses of general theories of comparative welfare. It highlights the peculiar values, economic ideas, and institutions of Britain and the United States. In particular, it reveals the power of historical constraints stemming from ideological and institutional forces.[5]

A glance at the overall chronological trend of national government policies in both countries is likely at first to reveal differences between the two nations. Britain, it seemed, went slowly from right to left. According to this common interpretation, the British

people shed an inept Labour government in 1931, endured
standpat administrations under Ramsay MacDonald and Stanley
Baldwin throughout the 1930s, and turned to the left only between
1942 and 1948, when the ideas of the Beveridge Report catalyzed
a great and lasting liberalization of the country's welfare state.[6]
United States policy, by contrast, was left of center in 1933-36.
This liberal phase was apparently short-lived, however, with
conservatives surging back into control after 1938 and dominating
during and after the war. As Roosevelt observed ruefully, "Dr.
Win the War" replaced "Dr. New Deal."[7]

This picture needs a revision that highlights some similarities
between the two countries. Most important, the standard view
exaggerates the ineptitude of the Labour government in 1929-31
and the "conservatism" of Hoover prior to 1931. Both governments, in fact, moved to combat the Depression—the Labour
Administration by sextupling the amount spent on "transitional
benefits" for the long-term unemployed, the Hoover Administration by lowering taxes and increasing spending for public
works. Compared to earlier years, the period between 1929 and
1931 is best seen as a time of growing centralization and expansion of the anti-Depression role of government in both nations. [8]

Social policies during the next few years in both countries—
until 1933 in the United States, and 1934 in Britain—were similar
also in that fiscally conservative political leaders tried to control
this tide of centralization. The new National government of
1931 cut transitional benefits by 10 percent, thereby forcing the
needy to exert greater pressure on local poor relief authorities
until 1934. The cuts were then restored, and a new, national
Unemployment Assistance Board (UAB) began to take over
some of the functions of the local Public Assistance Committees.
Hoover, meanwhile, refused to involve the federal government
in relief—except grudgingly and indirectly with loans administered through the Reconstruction Finance Corporation in 1932.
Thus it is that central government policies of 1931-32 seem
"conservative," especially in the United States, where the shock
and duration of the Depression were so much greater, and the
need so much more pressing, than in the 1920s.

In fact, however, it is perhaps more revealing to look at
overall public policies, local as well as national. From that
perspective, it is accurate to see these years (1931-32) as a time of
temporarily arrested centralization. In both countries, the over-

all amount spent for unemployment relief—through local as
well as national authorities—grew slightly, especially when
deflation is taken into account. In both countries, local (or state)
governments took up the slack while the national authorities
struggled for time.

Welfare policy then took a more national turn in both nations.
Compared to what had come before, the break was indeed greater
in the United States than in Britain, where the Conservative
Party grew in strength after 1934. It is very misleading, however,
to assume that policy in Britain was "conservative" after 1934,
or that the shock of World War II, important though that was,
alone transformed welfare there. The fact was that British unemployment benefits improved considerably after 1934. So did
the terms of eligibility, the coverage, and the spirit of welfare
administration. Moreover—and this deserves special emphasis—
British social policy throughout the decade was advanced in any
comparative sense. "Cash relief," one scholar writes, was in
Britain "given to a larger percentage of jobless workers, on
generally less rigorous conditions, than in other countries with
a comparative problem." Another scholar adds that British social
services—which well before the Beveridge Report included not
only incomparably costly unemployment benefits, but also old
age pensions, sickness benefits, and public housing—were "the
most advanced in the world."[9] Modest economic recovery, meanwhile, returned by 1936 in Britain, at least in the South, which
began to prosper as never before.[10]

For these reasons, the contrast between a supposedly conservative Britain and a dynamically liberal New Deal in the mid-
1930s is overdrawn. Social policymakers in Britain did not have
nearly as far to go as is usually depicted, and therefore did not go
much farther than where they had started in 1934. In both
countries, the basic trend between 1934 and 1938 was toward
greater centralization of social policy, and more comprehensive
social welfare. In both countries, the percentage of the GNP
spent on social welfare increased slightly. Most of the unemployed
in Britain as well as in the United States were better off than they
had been before 1934.[11]

Most significant, both countries emerged from the mid-1930s
with a stronger consensus in favor of centralized social policy.
In so doing, they slammed the door on the minority who clung
to dogmas about self-help. "During the ten years between 1929

and 1939," one informed social worker wrote of American policy in 1940, "more progress was made in public welfare and relief than in the 300 years after this country was first settled."[12] To be sure, this "progress" stalled in America after 1937—"Dr. New Deal" took second place. Moreover, hostile popular attitudes toward the "undeserving" poor remained potent in the United States, perhaps strengthening in the 1980s. But the policies of the New Deal, once initiated, were liberalized in 1939, and proved capable of virtually fantastic expansion in the 1950s and 1960s. They also proved resistant to conservative political pressures.[13]

What of the 1940s? In Britain, of course, the changes of the 1940s were dramatic. When Beveridge made public his report in December 1942, he basked in a favorable response that was "well-nigh universal." He commented of his public appearances at the time, "It's like riding on an elephant through a cheering mob." While the consensus behind the report was not so solid as it seemed, it helped to promote legislative action between 1944 and 1948, by which time Britain led the world in the overall quality of its social services.[14]

But these changes were not solely the result of the war, dramatic though that impact was in Britain. Rather (as the "well-nigh universal" response suggested), the stage had already been set by Britain's experience with poverty well before the 1930s, and by the social welfare institutions that dated to the Liberal reforms of 1908-11. In this sense, the Beveridge Report may be seen not as a dramatic break but as a logical extension of the major trend of social welfare policy in Britain in the 1920s and 1930s: incremental centralization. In Britain, as to a lesser extent in the United States, the 1940s represented what one writer has aptly called the stage of "consolidation" of public welfare. Policy became more national and more uniform in both countries. Bureaucracies developed with stakes in the existing social welfare system. Popular expectations of governmental activism increased. And benefits, however inadequate, were established that politicians of the future dared not take away. It was this consolidation of social policy—enacted as part of a developing political consensus, or ideology of social welfare—that is the most distinguishing and lasting legacy of public policy in both countries. In this way, as in others, the British and American experiences with depression and war reveal fundamental similarities, not differences.[15]

The policies themselves also reveal similarities, especially in their limitations. One such limitation concerned family policy. Programs in both countries tended to emphasize the individual needs of male workers and therefore to slight the problems of the family unit. In America, work relief under the Works Progress Administration (WPA) ordinarily went to only one member of a household—no matter the size of the family or the extent of need. Until liberalized in 1939, social security did not provide for insurance to surviving widows or to dependents. Britain did provide supplementary payments for dependents of the unemployed, but in a striking anomaly it did not do the same for families whose heads received sickness benefits. Until 1941, British policy included a "household means test" by which earnings of all people in a household were calculated before unemployment benefits were granted. This test revealed that family considerations did exist in Britain. But, like the WPA's policy of helping only one member of the family, the household means test may have induced some income-earning members of households to leave the family unit so as to increase the benefits available to the rest.[16]

These aspects of policy reveal interesting, and mostly parallel, attitudes toward women and children. In both nations, policymakers—while celebrating the need to preserve the nuclear family—tended to focus less on the family unit than on ways of assisting able-bodied male workers. And though Beveridge strongly advocated children's allowances as a way of reaching a "national minimum," he did not succeed in making these an imporant part of the British welfare state. In the United States, meanwhile, few experts (Daniel Moynihan excepted) raised the issue before the 1970s.

This is another way of saying that neither country developed social policies aimed single-mindedly at alleviating all types of need. Rather, policies in both nations—even in Britain post-Beveridge—concentrated on helping the two most politically influential and "deserving" groups of poor people at the time: the aged and the unemployed. By contrast, other politically less powerful but equally needy groups—notably members of female-headed families, and the low-wage working poor—received short shrift.[17] In Britain, many of these people had to turn to the hated poor relief authorities until 1948; in the United States, they had to depend either on general assistance administered ungenerously at the state and local level, or on ill-financed and mean-spirited categorical assistance (to the blind, disabled, indigent old, and dependent children).

This term "category" indeed underlined a popular assumption of welfare policy that was especially strong in the United States: poverty was vaguely immoral. Rather, poverty afflicted certain vulnerable groups, some of which were in need because of their own making. In Britain, by contrast, lengthy experience with poverty had led experts to seek a "national minimum" income, below which no person should fall. Categorically oriented British policies, such as old age assistance, were supported as means to this inclusive end, not as ways of making sharp distinctions between people. Policy in the United States did more to underline such distinctions between various groups of "deserving" and "undeserving" poor, and to increase the stigma attached to the undeserving.

These differences notwithstanding, British and American policies were similar in two fundamental respects. First, politicians focused less on poverty per se than on unemployment. That is not to say that they were unaware of studies of poverty.[18] But in the 1930s they were understandably mesmerized by unemployment, and they therefore devoted their scarce fiscal resources to alleviating it. Second, they championed social insurance—not welfare—as the underpinning of the social state. For both FDR and for Beveridge, the faith in contributory social insurance—as opposed to means-tested public assistance—was fundamental and axiomatic. Both men, like their contemporaries, hoped that social insurance would in time conquer want—that somehow a broader poverty would "wither away," and that welfare before too long would become virtually unnecessary.[19] It was not until the 1960s that a "rediscovery" of poverty in both countries revealed the illusiveness of this notion.

These limitations reflected the continuing power in both countries of historically durable ideas. These included faith in the work ethic; the assumption (especially strong in the United States) that widespread poverty was unnatural, indeed un-American; and the continuing appeal of orthodox fiscal policies even amid depression. Policy in both nations also reflected an obvious fact about the democratic process, whether in a parliamentary or representative federal system: fiscal resources are directed at those groups that appear to be most numerous and most politically threatening.

Public programs in the two countries, however, revealed significant differences as well as similarities—differences that suggest broader generalizations about the values and institutions of the two nations. Of these differences, four are particularly interesting. First, the United States spent billions of dollars on work relief and public works; Britain, by contrast, relied on the dole, spending virtually nothing on work relief.[20] Second, unemployment compensation and old age pensions under the new Social Security Act in the United States depended on contributions from employers and employees; there was no direct public subsidy. In Britain, by constrast, the government subsidized both programs from the beginning in 1908-11. Third, social security in the United States was mainly earnings based, both at the stage of contributions and in the ultimate benefits. By contrast, flat-rate contributions and flat-rate benefits remained in order in Britain until the 1960s.

The fourth difference was perhaps the most significant. By the mid-1940s Britain had evolved a philosophy of welfare, as reflected in the Beveridge Report, which contrasted with that in the United States. The British ideal was not only the relief of destitution and protection against want, but also fair shares for all, so that society itself would be composed of citizens standing together. In America, however, the goal remained more one of prevention. The welfare state was not supposed to aim at producing equality or social solidarity. It was to *prevent* conditions under which want might develop, thereby (in the long run) eliminating the need for welfare. Prevention was explicitly the goal not only of social insurance, but also of the "public welfare amendments" of 1962, of the "war on poverty," and of other liberal programs of the early 1960s.

Why these differences? Concerning public works, the editors of the *Economist* in 1937 had an ingenious explanation. Public works, they said, was an "unduly expensive form of increasing employment . . . it is only a rich country that can afford to deal with its unemployment in this expensive, unremunerative way."[21] By this statement the editors did not mean, of course, that the United States at that time was rich—merely that work relief, for which materials and supervisors are necessary, was costlier than a dole. (One estimate figured the cost as 37 percent higher.)[22] This explanation is useful to the extent that it highlights the staunch opposition in Britain—especially by Chamberlain—to deficit spending. In Britain the fiscal orthodoxy of the "Treasury view" easily triumphed over Keynesian notions of compensatory public spending.

Longer-range historical forces also help explain the different attitudes toward work relief. One of these was the virtually unanimous view in Britain that public works was "unremunerative" in the sense that it competed with private enterprise, thereby nullifying any potential gains. As the American experience during the Depression years suggests, this negative view of public works was not necessarily accurate in times of economic depression. But experts in Britain thought that was so, and their opposition was decisive.

Second, of course, one must look to history. That is, Britain already had unemployment insurance well before the Depression of the 1930s. This insurance was so well established as an institution, and so expensive, that it could hardly have been abolished or easily supplemented with still more costly work programs. It was simpler to tinker with existing institutions. In America, by contrast, limited experience with public works before 1929 had evoked mixed responses—and economists there were a little more receptive to the idea. More to the point, Americans viewing the British experience with the "dole" in the 1920s considered it a disastrous business. Wilbur Cohen and others who studied foreign welfare systems for the Committee on Economic Security in 1934 adamantly opposed a dole in America.[23]

Perhaps the largest obstacle in the way of work relief in Britain was also historical: the lengthy experience there with the hated mixed workhouses, which were central to the contemporary consciousness in ways that were not the case across the Atlantic. As late as 1929, official British policy had sought to deny insurance to unemployed people who could not demonstrate that they were "genuinely seeking work." Any talk of instituting work relief in Britain therefore evoked bitter debate by conjuring up among working-class voters the specter of the "poor law." Indeed, it was in part to avoid the social divisiveness of means-tested work relief that Beveridge championed the ideal of social insurance. The National Assistance Act of 1948 opened with the ringing declaration, "The existing poor law shall cease to have effect." In the United States, however, virtually all the experts, led by Harry Hopkins, thought that a dole harmed "morale."

Work, it was thought, promoted the work ethic, conserved skills, and resulted in useful construction. In these ways, as in many others, the historical experience of each country placed real constraints on the options of policymakers in the 1930s.

In accounting for the second difference—the lack of public subsidies for American social insurance—the role of corporate models, and of business thinking, was significant. When American planners set about the task of developing a social security system in the early 1930s, they did not have any public models at home to copy. Instead, they studied a few existing corporate plans for old age pensions. These, of course, operated according to "insurance" principles, and were therefore financed via worker and/or company contributions. The "reserve" system of financing that these planners devised for the social security system stemmed from their attention to these private models.

Roosevelt, too, stood firmly against general revenue financing for social security. His role was decisive in this respect. He worried, of course, about the expense that such subsidies would involve, and about the likelihood that the Supreme Court would strike down nationally financed programs of social insurance. As is well known, however, he thought above all in political terms. Recognizing the power of conservative ideas about public welfare in America, he pressed for social policy that future Congresses could not sabotage. With this end in mind, he stood firmly for contributory social insurance, and he resolutely opposed general revenue financing even in 1939, by which time virtually all the experts in the field had abandoned the faith in a reserve fund or in the strict insurance notion of social security. This stand was perhaps his greatest contribution to the social security program. At least in the short run, it amply revealed his political savvy.

Again, however, long-range historical forces also proved important in accounting for the different attittudes toward public subsidies. One was the power in America of faith in decentralization—a faith enshrined in the federalism underlying the Constitution. Americans distrusted the central government. The one federal program that had historically given out large sums of public money to people—to veterans—has long been regarded as expensive and wasteful. Americans, lacking a well-established, generally respected civil service such as existed in England, resisted the idea of turning over scarce public dollars to social welfare bureaucrats. Under the circumstances, it was perhaps remarkable that the categorical assistance programs—which did authorize the outlay of tax dollars to "deserving" categories of people, passed at all. Surely it was the least popular and least well financed aspect of social policy in 1935.[24]

To these historical forces and perceptions operating against public subsidies in America may be added another historical reality. This was the role of very real fiscal constraints that stood in the way of American policymakers, who were attempting not only to start programs from scratch but also to make them relatively comprehensive. It seemed impossible to support these programs, even partly, with public revenue (which was needed, among other things, for work relief and for categorical assistance). In Britain, however, such subsidies for unemployment and old age insurance had begun in 1908-11, with the avowed goal of covering only certain classes of workers. For such carefully limited programs, the government had therefore been willing and able to offer a small subsidy. Having done so at the start, it could hardly renege when the original programs grew—as they did in the 1920s—far beyond the expectations of the framers. The initial design of social programs in both countries—designs produced in very different historical circumstances—proved durable indeed.[25]

The heritage of existing policies, and of values, also helps to explain the third difference—that British social insurance used a "flat-rate" system of contributions and benefits as opposed to an equity-based system in the United States. One basic explanation—again—was that Britain in 1929 was already operating such flat-rate programs; it was bureaucratically logical to continue to do so. Indeed, Britain made no important change in its flat-rate sickness or old age pension programs in the 1930s; it did not superimpose equity-based programs until the 1960s, long after the flat-rate benefits (low because they did not go much beyond what the poorest could afford to pay) were shown to be woefully inadequate. The United States, by contrast, had no such flat-rate public programs. What it did have—again—were the pension plans operated by a few corporations. These private plans were equity based. In adapting this idea to the social insurance program in the 1930s, the New Dealers deliberately rejected the flat-rate system of England and installed the equity model closer to home.[26]

The historical circumstances under which the two nations adopted their social insurance programs deeply affected these decisions of policymakers. Britain's plans were originally intended to cover only workers in a few trades. Workers in stable trades stoutly resisted being drawn into a pooled government scheme of unemployment insurance, which they thought could require them to make contributions to support the jobless in more vulnerable occupations. Those who were included in the original scheme—people with roughly comparable wages—could therefore be expected to pay about the same in contributions and to get the same in benefits. In that sense, the British system promised to be equitable. American planners in the 1930s, however, were faced with a world of massive unemployment. They knew they were devising a scheme that must ultimately cover millions of workers earning vastly different wages. They thought that they could not do other than base the contributions and the payments on income.

The role of the left in Britain, stronger politically than in the United States, was also relevant in this context. Some British spokesmen, notably trade union leaders, resisted governmental competition in the area of social welfare. Others, more numerous, strongly opposed the very idea of employee contributions of any magnitude. The government, they said, should pay for the programs out of progressive taxes. Many others were willing to support the idea—enshrined in policy after 1911—of nominal employee contributions, but they refused to jettison the flat-rate concept. Earnings-based contributions, they thought, were reminiscent of hated means-tested poor relief. Equity-based benefits would prop up a nonegalitarian social system. This working-class opposition to wage-based social insurance persisted into the late 1950s in Britain, where it was strong enough politically to prevent major changes in policy. In the United States, however, no political force on the left was strong enough to block equity-based programs. On the contrary, such programs jibed well with a predominant value: to each according to his income.[27]

Why, finally, did Britain develop, under the Beveridge reforms, a philosophy of welfare that placed considerable emphasis on equality and on social solidarity? Here, traditional answers are useful. World War II had a profound impact on British opinion, bringing the social classes closer together and helping to develop a sense of common purpose that was lacking in America. More-

over, the Beveridge Report—to repeat—was in many ways a
logical extension of social policies already well established. The
centralizing thrust of the Beveridge plan was yet one more step in
an incremental process dating at least to 1908.[28]

This very incrementalism provides another clue to explaining
the diverging philosophies of the two countries. Britain, like
Sweden, Denmark, and other nations that early developed systems
of social insurance, was a comparatively small and ethnically
homogeneous nation. By the 1940s, with social policies in place
for several decades, it could contemplate a comprehensive expansion of programs already in operation. Policymakers in the
United States had no such luxury. It was then inconceivable that
a country so vast and diverse as the United States could jump
immediately to a scheme as venturesome as Beveridge's. In all
countries, social policies have grown incrementally; the United
States was surely no exception.

Finally, contrasting perceptions of the social order helped
explain the different welfare philosophies of the two nations.
Beveridge, like many of his contemporaries, considered class
conflict the bane of twentieth-century Britain. He hoped that a
comprehensive system of social insurance might alleviate class
tensions. Most American policymakers, however, did not perceive class as such a divisive social problem. Those who did
doubted that the working classes—even in the turbulent 1930s—
had much potential political power. For most American planners,
therefore, the practicable ideal was to strengthen economic opportunity and social mobility. Those planners who wished to
move in Beveridge's direction—as did the writers of the National
Resource Planning Board's report of 1942—received a poor hearing not only in Congress, which abolished the agency the next
year, but within the executive branch. Roosevelt in effect sup-
pressed the report for a year.

The differences, therefore, between the social policies of the
two nations stemmed from a wide range of important forces.
These included not only contemporary fiscal, constitutional,
and political considerations, but also longer-range ideological
and institutional matters. These in turn were rooted historically
in the sometimes differing value systems and social orders of the
two countries. Together, these forces reveal the centrality of the
particular historical circumstances that facilitated adoption of
original policies, and of the great constraints that stood in the

way of free choices for policymakers. It is hardly surprising that
the policies, like the nations themselves, therefore differed in
significant ways.

Constraints or no, the United States managed to launch, and
Britain to consolidate, welfare states during the 1930s and 1940s.
So have all other industrial nations. It is pertinent to ask what
forces—other than the obvious "external" ones of depression and
war—facilitated this change.

Scholars in the field of welfare policy offer a variety of interpretations that seek to explain such forces. One interpretation, of
course, is the traditional progressive view. Especially popular
among mainstream New Deal historians, it emphasizes the role
of Roosevelt, Hopkins, Frances Perkins, and others who seized
the moment to introduce progressive social reforms. A variant of
this argument maintains that social welfare states depend on the
coming to power of left-of-center and working-class political
parties. Welfare states, in short, owe much to humanitarianism
and to left-liberal politics.[29]

Other scholars downplay the importance of altruism. This
second view, sometimes expressed as a conspiracy thesis, stresses
the role of social unrest. Welfare, it is argued, functions as a
means of social control. It is ordinarily ungenerous and stigmatizing, in order (among other things) to ensure that employers will
always have ample cheap labor. Moreover, welfare becomes more
generous only when economic elites fear that unrest will undermine social stability. At that point—the 1930s were supposedly
such a time—welfare states grow, at least until the threat from
below subsides.[30]

A third and related argument stresses the role played by calcu-
lating political actors, usually in league with the economic elites.
This view contends that politicians ordinarily ignore the poor,
who after all lack power. But under special circumstances—
when the poor begin to organize, and when the opposition
threatens to win elections—the politicians will move to secure
their flanks.[31] As Hopkins was reputed to have said, the key to
Democratic Party success was "spend and elect, spend and elect."

A fourth view—one that resembles the previous three—con-
centrates on the part played by expert social engineers, who
seek ways of promoting national unity and efficiency. Experts
such as these are not left-of-center altruists or social democrats.
They do not worry much about mass unrest or winning elections.

Rather, like Bismarck, Theodore Roosevelt, Beveridge, and many advocates of family allowances, they seek to accelerate national development.[32]

A fifth hypothesis emphasizes the role of bureaucratization and of political centralization. Decentralized countries (such as the United States or Canada) find it difficult to establish large and respected public bureaucracies, and are therefore slow to enact welfare states. But once nations attain the necessary levels of bureaucratization and centralization, the welfare state can not only begin, but can also expand incrementally. For it is above all the social welfare bureaucrats who possess the expertise, the position, and the self-interest to expand what they have started.[33]

A final view, which owes much to the work of the sociologist T.H. Marshall, talks of "concepts of citizenship." This is less a theory of welfare growth than a taxonomy of it. These concepts, he argued, evolve. People first imagine that they have political and legal rights. Then (as industrialization promotes economic progress and erases Malthusian pessimism), people seek social and economic rights. Equality becomes a widely shared goal. Policymakers share this vision: it affects elites as well as ordinary people, and becomes part of a consensus. At this point the welfare state becomes an irreversible fact.[34]

Which of these interpretations are most helpful in accounting for the changes in Britain and the United States in the 1930s and 1940s? The answer, it will be apparent, is that most of these theories are useful—the conspiracy idea excepted—but that no single view suffices.

The progressive view, for instance, is of some use in explaining British development in 1908-11 and after 1945. It is even more obviously relevant in accounting for the left-of-center innovations in American policy during the early New Deal. In neither country before 1945 did a Socialist or Labour Party legislate great changes in welfare policy. Progressive leaders took the lead in identifying social needs, and used the political arena to advance welfare legislation. As the roles of leaders like Lloyd George and Roosevelt suggest, there is much life yet in the "old" progressive view of social reform.

The conspiracy view is less satisfactory—at least in its most reductionist forms. As applied, for instance, to the American scene in the 1930s, the argument that elites devised welfare as a means of social control ignores the solid progressive credentials of people like Roosevelt and Harry Hopkins, and it exaggerates the perceived threat of social unrest. Still, it is obvious that the growing involvement of working-class groups in politics could not be ignored by political leaders in both countries. As early as 1908-11 in Britain, and after 1933 in the United States, such pressures sensitized policymakers to consider seriously a range of public programs to help the aged and unemployed.

Social engineers were also present and influential in both countries. Beveridge was the example par excellence. Advocates of social security in the United States included experts—and politicans—who stressed that old age pensions would take supposedly inefficient, unproductive people out of the work force and contribute to national growth and efficiency. The inspiration for social welfare in America and Britain came from social engineers in the center as well as from pressure from liberals and the left.

The bureaucratic context was also relevant. Britain, like Sweden and Germany, was able to play the role of pioneer in part because it was a relatively homogeneous and centralized nation with a fairly well-developed and respected civil service. The more decentralized United States, lacking such a public bureaucracy, necessarily moved more slowly. These fundamental differences, indeed, played very large roles in accounting for the social welfare experiences of the two countries in the 1930s and 1940s.

The historian, in short, must remember the obvious: multiple causes lay behind the changes in social welfare policies in the two countries in the 1930s and 1940s. No single, overarching social theory provides the answer. Moreover, the theories can slight the special role played by particular historical experiences and perceptions. These historical experiences were especially significant in explaining the differences in the actual *content* of policies in the two countries, which after all were initially enacted at different times and under different political and economic situations. Without focusing on these historical contexts, the student of comparative welfare runs the risk of letting overarching interpretations take the place of historical research into the particular circumstances and ideas that have decisively affected the development of social welfare in the twentieth century.

1. Major sources include: for Britain, Noreen Branson and Margot Heine-mann, *Britain in the 1930s* (London, 1973); Sean Glynn and John Oxborrow, *Interwar Britain: A Social and Economic History* (London, 1976); John D. Millett, *The Unemployment Assistance Board* (London, 1940); and especially Bentley B. Gilbert, *British Social Policy, 1914-1939* (London, 1970). A relevant article on Britain is Eric Briggs and Alan Deacon, "The Creation of the Unemployment Assistance Board," *Policy and Politics* 2 (December 1974): 43-62. For the United States, see Josephine C. Brown, *Public Relief, 1929-1939* (New York, 1940); Barbara Blumberg, *The New Deal and the Unemployed: The View from New York City* (Lewisburg, Pa., 1979); Arthur J. Altmeyer, *The Formative Years of Social Security* (Madison, Wis., 1966); Edwin E. Witte, *The Development of the Social Security Act* (Madison, Wis., 1963); and Donald Howard, *The WPA and Federal Relief Policy* (New York, 1943). Articles include Clarke Chambers, "Social Service and Social Reform: A Historical Essay," *Social Service Review* 37 (March 1963): 76-90.

2. For the impact of war in Britain, see Paul Addison, *The Road to 1945: British Politics and the Second World War* (London, 1975); and the classic essay, Richard Titmuss, "War and Social Policy," in *Essays on the Welfare State* (London, 1963). For the Depression in America, consult Charles H. Trout, "Welfare in the New Deal Era," *Current History* 65 (July 1973): 11-15ff.

3. For examples relating to America, see Frances Fox Piven and Richard Cloward, *Regulating the Poor: The Functions of Public Welfare* (New York, 1971); and William Graebner, *A History of Retirement: The Meaning and Functions of an American Institution* (New Haven, Conn., 1980). For Britain, consult Norman Ginsburg, *Class, Capitalism, and Social Policy* (London, 1979).

4. Relevant works include Daniel K. Benjamin and Lewis A. Kochin, "Search-ing for an Explanation of Unemployment in Interwar Britain," *Journal of Political Economy* 87 (June 1979): 441-78; and Jens Albers, "Government Responses to the Challenge of Unemployment: The Development of Unem-ployment Insurance in Western Europe," in *The Development of Welfare States in Europe and America*, ed. Peter Flora and Arnold Heidenheimer (New Brunswick, N.J., 1981), pp. 151-83.

5. Important efforts to compare social policy in various nations include Hugh Heclo, *Modern Social Politics in Britain and Sweden: From Relief to Income Maintenance* (New Haven, 1974); Heclo, "Income Maintenance Patterns and Priorities," in *Comparative Public Policy: The Politics of Social Choice in Europe and America*, ed. Arnold J. Heidenheimer, Hugh Heclo, and Carolyn Teich Adams (New York, 1975), pp. 187-226; John A. Garraty, *Unemployment in History: Economic Thought and Public Policy* (New York, 1978); and Gaston V. Rimlinger, *Welfare Policy and Industrialization in Europe, America, and Russia* (New York, 1971). Also relevant are Harold Wilensky, *The Welfare State and Equality: Structural and Ideological Roots of Public Expenditures* (Berkeley, 1975); and W.J. Mommsen, ed., *The Emergence of the Welfare State in Britain and Germany, 1850-1950* (London, 1981).

6. For British policy from 1929 to 1931, see Robert Skidelsky, *Politicians and the Slump: The Labour Government of 1929-31* (London, 1967), pp. 67-77. For the 1930s, see Gilbert, *British Social Policy*, pp. 162-254, and F.M. Miller, "National Assistance or Unemployment Assistance? The British Cab-inet and Relief Policy, 1932-33," *Journal of Contemporary History* 9 (April

1974): 163-84. For the 1940s, see the fine study by Jose Harris, *William Beveridge: A Biography* (London, 1977).

7. See William Leuchtenburg, *Franklin D. Roosevelt and the New Deal, 1932-1940* (New York, 1963), especially chapter 6; Richard Polenberg, *War and Society: The United States, 1941-45* (Philadelphia, 1972); and John M. Blum, *V Was for Victory: Politics and Culture During World War II* (New York, 1976).

8. See especially, Ross McKibbin, "The Economic Policy of the Second Labour Government, 1929-31," *Past and Present* 68 (1975): 95-123; and Albert Romasco, *The Poverty of Abundance: Hoover, the Nation, the Depression* (New York, 1965).

9. Citations are from Miller, "National Assistance," pp. 163-84; and Addison, *Road to 1945*, p. 33.

10. For assessments of the impact of depression on employment, see H.W. Richardson, "The Economic Significance of the Depression in Britain," *Journal of Contemporary History* 4 (October 1969): 3-20. For America, see Bernard Sternsher, "Counting the Unemployed and Recent Economic Developments," in *The New Deal*, ed. Bernard Sternsher (New York, 1979), pp. 101-3.

11. For British statistics, see Alan T. Peacock and Jack Wiseman, *The Growth of Public Expenditures in the United Kingdom* (Princeton, 1961), pp. 42, 85-86, 106-7; Brian R. Mitchell and Phyllis Deane, eds., *Abstract of British Historical Statistics* (Cambridge, 1971), pp. 366-71, 399-400, 418, 426; and Glynn and Oxborrow, *Interwar Britain*, pp. 258-67. For the United States, the basic source is Bureau of the Census, *Historical Statistics of the United States, Colonial Times to 1957* (Washington, D.C., 1960), pp. 140, 722-23. Governments (local, state, and national) in both countries spent about 5-6 percent of GNP on social welfare (health, social insurance, and public assistance) in the middle and late 1930s, or a percentage point or two higher than in the late 1920s. If education is included as a social welfare item, the percentages rise to between 8 and 11 percent by the late 1930s. In both countries, social welfare (including education) amounted to between 30 and 40 percent of total public expenditures. These figures do not include nongovernmental contributions for social insurance. These were considerable in Britain (44 percent of unemployment insurance expenditures in 1935), but virtually nonexistent in America until the late 1930s.

Such comparisons of spending ought also to consider—but rarely do—the extent of need. During the 1930s, this was probably greater in the United States, where the percentage of the labor force that was unemployed was generally twice that in Britain. From this perspective, it is fair to conclude that Britain, in devoting a comparable percentage of its GNP to public welfare, was doing a more thorough job of meeting need than was the United States. Studies of welfare "effort" in Western countries since World War II, when statistics are more complete, tend to support this hypothesis concerning the 1930s. These studies uniformly show that the United States was a laggart in the percentage of its GNP spent on public welfare after 1945. See, for example, Henry J. Aaron, "Social Security: International Comparisons," in *Studies in the Economics of Income Maintenance*, ed. Otto Eckstein (Washington, D.C., 1967).

Other problems plague this complex business of comparative statistics on welfare. Should private charity, and plain neighborliness, be figured in as well? And what of the quality of public welfare? Was American public welfare given in a specially patronizing or stigmatizing manner? There are no easy answers to these questions, but I conclude that private charity for welfare purposes was relatively unimportant in both countries after 1930, and that quantitative measures of public aid are the best way of getting at the question of welfare effort. Concerning the quality and efficiency of public programs, suffice it to say that the workhouse/almshouse spirit appalled humanitarian observers in England as well as in the United States. See, for example, Richard Lowitt and Maurine Beasley, eds., *One-Third of a Nation: Lorena Hickok Reports on the Great Depression* (Champaign, Ill., 1982); George Orwell, *Road to Wigan Pier* (London, 1937); and H. L. Beales and R. S. Lambert, eds., *Memoirs of the Unemployed* (London, 1934.)

12. Brown, *Public Relief*, p. ix. For Britain, see Millett, *The Unemployment Assistance Board*, pp. 19-27, 223-87.

13. James T. Patterson, *America's Struggle Against Poverty, 1900-1980* (Cambridge, 1981), pp. 56-77, 157-84.

14. Addison, *Road to 1945*, pp. 217, 17. For postwar British programs, see V. N. George, *Social Security: Beveridge and After* (London, 1968). A less favorable assessment, reflecting the pessimism of the 1970s, is Philip Abrams, ed., *Work, Urbanism, and Inequality: UK Society Today* (London, 1978).

15. This emphasis on centralization and consolidation is Heclo's, in his *Modern Social Politics*. See also T. H. Marshall, "Citizenship and Social Class," reprinted in *Sociology at the Crossroads and Other Essays* (London, 1963).

16. For the operation of work relief in the United States, see Jonathan R. Kesselman, "Work Relief Programs in the Great Depression," in *Creating Jobs: Public Employment Programs and Wage Subsudies*, ed. John L. Palmer (Washington, D.C., 1978), pp. 153-240. Useful information on British policies, much of it critical, exists in Gilbert, *British Social Policy*, pp. 162-254; and Ginsburg, *Class, Capitalism, and Social Policy*, pp. 60-66.

17. Works emphasizing the role of political pressure groups include Frances Fox Piven and Richard Cloward, *Poor People's Movements: Why They Succeed, How They Fail* (New York, 1977); and Rimlinger, *Welfare Policy*, pp. 112-36, 203-5. For Britain, see Gilbert, *British Social Policy*, 66; Frederic Miller, "The British Unemployment Assistance Crisis of 1935," *Journal of Contemporary History* 14 (1979): 329-51; and Maureen Turnbull, "Attitude of Government and Administration towards the 'Hunger Marches' of the 1920s and 1930s," *Journal of Social Policy* 2 (1973): 131-42.

18. For British awareness, see Asa Briggs, *Social Thought and Social Action: A Study of the Work of Seebohm Rowntree, 1871-1954* (London, 1961), pp. 296-98; and Lady Juliet Rhys Williams, *Some Suggestions for a New Social Contract: An Alternative to the Beveridge Report Proposals* (London, 1942). For the United States, see Harry Hopkins, *Spending to Save* (New York, 1936); and Abraham Epstein, *Insecurity: A Challenge to America* (New York, 1933).

19. For Beveridge, see his report, *Social Insurance and Allied Services* (New York, 1942). For Roosevelt, See Leuchtenburg, *FDR and the New Deal*, pp. 118-42.

20. Gilbert, *British Social Policy*, p. 193, maintains that the largest number of men employed on public works at any time in Britain was 59,000, and that by 1937 the total had dwindled to 303. Others, of course, were employed building houses erected by local public authorities, but this practice preceded the Depression of the 1930s and was not thought to be work relief. In the United States, relief rolls of the WPA often exceeded 3 million.

21. Editors of *Economist, The New Deal: An Analysis and Appraisal* (New York, 1937), pp. 26, 14.

22. Kesselman, "Work Relief Programs," p. 162.

23. Relevant discussions of public works policies in the 1930s include McKibbin, "Economic Policy of the Second Labour Government"; and Rimlinger, *Welfare Policy*, pp. 150-51, 217, 222-32.

24 Indirectly, of course, public dollars supported unemployment insurance in the United States, where states, not employers or employees, ultimately bore most of the burden.

25. See especially, J. D. Brown, "British Precedent and American Old Age Insurance," *American Labor Legislation Review* 27 (March 1937): 18-23.

26. Edward Berkowitz and Kim McQuaid, "Businessman and Bureaucrat: The Evolution of the American Social Welfare System, 1900-1940," *Journal of Economic History* 38 (March 1978): 120-42.

27. See George Hoshimo, "Britain's Debate on Universal or Selective Social Services: Lessons for America," *Social Services Review* 43 (September 1969): 245-58.

28. Titmuss, "New Guardians of the Poor in Britain," in *Social Security in International Perspective*, ed. Jenkins, pp. 151-70; and Heclo, *Modern Social Politics*, pp. 143-47.

29. Examples include Allen Davis, *Spearheads for Reform: The Social Settlements and the Progressive Movement* (New York, 1967); and Robert Bremner, *From the Depths: The Discovery of Poverty in the United States* (New York, 1956).

30. Major works in this vein include Piven and Cloward, *Regulating the Poor*; and William Ryan, *Blaming the Victim*, rev. ed. (New York, 1976). For a critique, see Gerald Grob, "Reflections on the History of Social Policy in America," *Reviews in American History* 7 (September 1979): 293-308.

31. Piven and Cloward, *Regulating the Poor*.

32. See especially Rimlinger, *Welfare Policy*, pp. 75-80.

33. Arnold J. Heidenheimer, "The Politics of Public Education, Health, and Welfare in the United States of America and Western Europe: How Growth and Reform Potentials Have Differed," *British Journal of Political Science* 3 (July 1973): 315-40.

34. Marshall, "Citizenship and Social Class."

Social Security: The Welfare Consensus of the New Deal

Clarke A. Chambers

In addressing the subject of welfare and the New Deal, this paper is primarily an attempt to assess the centrality of the Social Security Act of 1935 in defining a new consensus in economic and social policy that emerged quickly in the Roosevelt years. I will explore a few issues, addressed over the past half-century by many scholars, most notably those relating to the process by which a set of policies and programs so long delayed in the United States came to be embraced with joyful enthusiasm, despite sharp reservations on the left and lingering skepticism on the right.

The social security package of 1935 entered mainstream American politics quickly and thoroughly.. Over four decades, while many other New Deal measures were being dropped, modified, amended, restricted, or transformed, social security gathered momentum. The swirling debate in the winter of 1983 never challenged fundamental principles of policy, but sought rather to salvage social security by tactics both economically sound and politically feasible. Social security is not a matter to be dismissed as "academic," nor is the debate carried on only by stodgy and tenured historians.

Let me first, briefly, explain with what trepidation I nuzzle up to this assignment. All of our most prominent New Deal historians have had their say. We are beneficiaries of a number of solid monographic studies—by Achenbaum, Hirshfield, Holtzman, Leotta, Lubove, Nelson, Schlabach, Tishler, and more recently by Berkowitz and McQuaid, Graebner, and Patterson. Distinguished social scientists have added their not inconsiderable bits—Cates, Gronbjerg, Levitan, Rimlinger, Steiner, Wilensky, and the caustically brilliant Martha Derthick. Scholarly practitioners of public affairs—Winifred Bell, Josephine Brown, and Eveline Burns—have provided significant insights. Finally, and with great authority, our understanding has been enriched by extended scholarly reminiscences of the pioneers themselves, who created and shaped the system—Arthur Altmeyer, J. Douglas Brown, Frances Perkins, Edwin Witte, and today's commentator, Wilbur Cohen. I know of no development in social policy more extensively and critically recorded by so many movers and shakers than is the story of social security. Here is a body of literature weighty enough to give even the most sanguine of scholars pause. I take seriously, moreover, the authoritative caveat of Wilbur Cohen that "it is very difficult to obtain a clear picture of all the forces at work in the legislative process. The process is frequently so complex that it is either oversimplified or neglected. . . . While economic and social forces may be at work, they only operate through human beings who react in terms of their own experience and knowledge." Agreed! As one social historian has observed, "History as it is made is always more untidy than what gets written down."[1]

Of all the New Deal projects, social security must be counted as the one of most lasting significance. Since January 20, 1981, we have witnessed a series of turnabouts: regressive tax strategies have replaced progressive; regulatory powers of federal government have been weakened, allowed to lapse, or perverted. Knights on white chargers, their shields blazoned "Supply-Side Economics," have bested economists mounted on tired Keynesian nags (although in fairness it must be said that for most citizens *both* economic theories have remained more in the realm of Merlin than of Arthur). But until the winter of 1983's funding crisis, social security for nearly a half-century enjoyed expansion and enlargement, especially in years divisible by two and four, under a succession of Presidents, four Democrats and three Republicans.

J. Douglas Brown, the distinguished Princeton economist who helped draw up the old age insurance titles, 1934-35, and subsequently became one of the nation's chief counselors guiding its expansion, summed it up in 1969:

> Thirty-five years ago, this vast enterprise in preventing hardship and dependency was but a tenuous idea in the minds of a few deeply concerned individuals. Seldom in modern times has an

idea, hammered out by a small group of planners, become in a single generation such a pervasive and practical part of the way of life of a people. Social Security is now taken for granted. In September 1934 even the term was unknown.[2]

That social insurance, a strategy of income support for persons in need through no personal fault of their own, had been launched in other modernized industrial nations of the Atlantic community, albeit tentatively and modestly, a generation and more before the United States inaugurated its own system in 1935 raises questions of timing that historians of welfare have had to address. However much such scholars have differed in emphasis and detail, they are agreed in their identification of a number of basic factors that tended to retard the adoption of social security in this country.

They point, for example, to the federal nature of American government that, under the Tenth Amendment to the Constitution, reserved the authority to deal with issues of health and welfare for the several states. Harold Wilensky's comparative analysis of the coming of the welfare state indeed demonstrated that the degree of governmental centralization in a given nation bore far greater weight in defining the extent and strength of its social insurance system than did its *form* of government or the nature of its economy.[3] In the United States, the Supreme Court had for generations acted as a brake on the creation of national initiatives in the realm of human welfare policies, and as recently as 1934, when the social security bill was being written, had found the Railroad Retirement Act to exceed the legitimate authority of Congress under the commerce clause. The decision of the Committee on Economic Security to rest the establishment of a fully federal system of old age insurance on the power of Congress to tax for the general welfare proved to be a shrewd maneuver, but when in 1937 the Court affirmed the constitutionality of that legal tactic, it was by a bare majority of five to four.

Ideological resistance put up other barriers. Americans had traditionally cherished a cluster of value assumptions, rooted in a Victorian bourgeois ethos, that celebrated the primacy of individualism, work, thrift, and personal self-reliance, each tub on its own bottom. No province of the English-speaking world remained more fiercely loyal to the poor law precepts of Elizabeth I than did the American. The assumption that families must bear the first responsibility of caring for their own, with local government having a secondary obligation, continued to be reflected in the severe American opposition to all forms of public outdoor assistance. In a society dedicated to success, to getting ahead, or at the least to keeping up, there was little sympathy for those who could not even get along. That the system appeared to work so effectively for so many for so long—especially throughout an era of prosperity and rising material standards, 1900-29, during which many other Western nations had begun to experiment with social insurance—undoubtedly held back public interest in the United States.[4]

Related to such factors was the lack in America of working-class consciousness and the absence of a labor-based, social democratic political movement. Pork chop issues dominated the agenda of craft unions; the AFL committed itself to winning immediate gains through processes of collective bargaining; Gompers's skepticism of government welfare—what the state offered it could withdraw—was widely shared. Although organized labor came to be the most assertive and powerful lobby working for the expansion of social security in the 1950s and 1960s, by far the most effective political force making possible the enactment of Medicare and Medicaid, its support for social insurance in the early thirties had been hesitant and mild.

Less obvious, perhaps, but carrying substantial influence, was the ethnic and racial pluralism of American society. Welfare programs and policies in Dickensian England, particularly following the new poor of 1834, can hardly be described as humane or benign, but the sharply punitive temper of benevolence in America, for all its rhetoric of reconciliation and amelioration through "friendly visiting," exceeded the severity that prevailed in Victoria's island realm. Ruling elites throughout the Atlantic community suffered deep anxiety regarding the potentially disruptive force of the "dangerous classes," and such uneasiness proved often to be a spur to the inauguration of state welfare programs, as in Germany in the 1880s. In the United States, however, governing majorities perceived the poor and needy to constitute not only a separate class but a radically different culture. Irish and German immigrants, later a swarm of strange folk from southern and eastern Europe, Chicanos and Hispanics in more recent decades, and always blacks—were seen by influential segments of the host society as subversive of republican principles. "They" seemed always so profoundly different from "us." The kind of national and racial divisions that retarded the development of industrial unionism also worked against the elaboration of a sense of reciprocal responsibility expressed for society through the state.[5]

In Europe, where elements of a welfare system developed relatively early, statesmen of differing tendencies and dispositions made little distinction between society and the state. What Daniel Levine has written of Denmark holds true in varying degree for other countries of northern and western Europe: "Rather than see 'government' . . . as one of many institutions in society with important but limited spheres of activity, government was society manifest." That organic sense of a shared nationality was deficient in America; social mobility, a myth that informed so much of public policy in the United States, had little force in Denmark where there was, consequently, no expression of fear that social insurance might dampen human incentive. In Europe there lived a tradition of social authority and responsibility for which there was no strong counterpart in the New World.[6]

Perhaps the bracing of will for empire and war played a part in tipping European states toward welfare systems designed to secure the loyalty of working classes, to strengthen health, to facilitate the mobilization of human resources, and to equalize sacrifice in times of conflict. Such motives undoubtedly underlay Bismarck's initiative and that of the Liberals in England in the years immediately preceding the coming of the First World War. And, in the United States, it is of more than casual significance that Theodore Roosevelt's New Nationalism, not the New Freedom, embraced schemes for comprehensive social insurance in 1912.[7]

All said, how are we to explain the broad acceptance of social security and related welfare measures at such a quick pace in the mid-1930s? Hard times is credited first, of course. After several years of economic slump, with millions of citizens down and out for the first time in their lives, persons with long records of continuous work experience suffering prolonged unemployment for the first time in the Great Depression had moved from self-blame to the commonsense conclusion that hard times derived from forces quite beyond their personal control. Such persons were ready, by 1933, to support welfare measures of all sorts and to vote for politicians who had seized the initiative in providing relief, work, and some promise of security, however partial and modest such measures may seem in retrospect. [8]

Mass unemployment may also have served to provoke an interest, especially among younger workers, in finding ways to encourage the permanent retirement of older workers; justifications for old age insurance, in fact, included labor market arguments. In a recently published study, William Graebner has proposed that private corporate pension plans, and public pension systems covering a variety of civil servants, had accustomed many citizens by 1930 to the function of retirement mechanisms. Once in place, moreover, old age insurance subsequently inspired a substantial expansion of private retirement systems through union contracts that often included provisions for pensions among other fringe benefits, and through the enlargement of established programs in government and education. It was also the case, in Graebner's interpretation, that a small cadre of experts who exercised decisive influence in the drafting of the old age sections of the Social Security Act—Barbara Armstrong, Murray Latimer, J. Douglas Brown, and Otto Richter—came to their task from a background of wrestling with labor and pension legislation.[9]

One must consider also the readiness of a few corporate executives and conservative public officials—Edward Filene, Henry Dennison, Gerard Swope, Owen Young, Marion Folsom, and Walter Teagle, among others—to press for national governmental progams of social insurance. Such business figures had pioneered pension programs in the private sphere, many of which were rendered defunct by hard times following the Panic of 1929. Their social theories of unemployment and old age insurance placed primary emphasis on the bureaucratic/business values of efficiency, coordination, rationalization, cost-effectiveness, stabilization of production, and regularization of employment. A recent study by Edward D. Berkowitz and Kim McQuaid, which extends the "conservative-roots-of-reform" hypothesis elaborated earlier by Gabriel Kolko and James Weinstein, demonstrates the influence of such corporate pioneers of welfare capitalism in promulgating a philosophy of social engineering and corporate responsibility. FDR called upon such persons to enlist support for the bill brought to Congress by his Committee on Economic Security; the personal prestige and authority of Teagle, Swope, and Folsom carried weight with some conservatives in Congress and helped to offset the reservations of Secretary of the Treasury Henry Morgenthau, Jr.[10]

Although we have no monographic studies on the subject, it is probably safe to speculate that the experience of immigrant workers who had created mutual benefit societies to provide a measure of security against the economic consequences of incapacity and death must have inclined many of them, by the 1930s, toward an unquestioning acceptance of social insurance. Such associations had served a variety of functions, of course, some of them not directly related to mutual aid—the lodges created networks through which their members found leads to employment, and they were a chief means through which diverse groups were able to sustain national identity and community solidarity in a hostile environment—but they also undoubtedly developed a reservoir of implicit support on which proponents of social insurance could draw. That the descendants of immigrant groups from southern and eastern Europe provided enthusiastic mass support for Roosevelt and the New Deal and that they added substantially to Democratic electoral victories can be attributed in some part to the success of New Deal welfare programs in fulfilling a tradition of mutual assistance. It was also the case that industrial union leaders, many of them of immigrant stock—Sidney Hillman, David Dubinsky, Philip Murray, and their successors—became the single most powerful political bloc pressing forward the expansion of social insurance.[11]

As for the unemployed and the aged themselves, there existed no effective, popular, organized movement before 1935 to fight for social security. The Townsend movement was barely underway when Roosevelt charged his Committee on Economic Security in June 1934. Politicians of all persuasions, it is true, looking forward to 1936, were made uneasy by the rise of protest movements whose leaders—Father Coughlin, Huey Long, and Dr. Francis Townsend—could not be contained within the two-party system. Given widespread disaffection and the persistence of hard times, everything was up for grabs; and this volatility surely provoked the President to be nimble and quick. Unless constructive measures were enacted, and quickly, the nation might be seduced by unsound panaceas. When the social insurance bill was before Congress in the winter and spring of 1935, the testimony of Townsendites received wide press coverage, but the net effect of their witness was probably to reveal the fiscal absurdity of the Townsend proposal and thereby to draw support to the Administration program. The judgment of the Townsend movement's chief historian, Abraham Holtzman, confirms the published recollections of Perkins, Witte, and Altmeyer: it "compelled an immediate consideration of old-age secuirty legislation"; it "crystalized tremendous popular sentiment in favor of old-age security"; and it "weakened conservative opposition" to the Administration's bill.[12]

By the mid-1930s, then, there existed a broad (if often undefined, unrecognized, and implicit) popular readiness to accept the principles of social security once its mechanisms were clearly set forth. For citizens generally, insurance had appeal as a way to avoid the always-demeaning needs test for persons who suffered through no fault of their own. There was insurmountable opposition to health insurance, namely the American Medical Association, so the Administration moved quickly to postpone its consideration in order to salvage other parts of the package; but no self-interest group had reason to oppose old age insurance, or for that matter unemployment insurance, because employers routinely passed along their share of the cost to the consumer. Although the American Federation of Labor (AFL) originally resisted the imposition of an unemployment insurance tax on workers, arguing that regularity of employment was the responsibility solely of employers, organized labor cheerfully endorsed the fifty-fifty formula for financing old age insurance on the grounds, in the words of William Green, that "everyone gets old."[13]

As for other sections of the 1935 act, they were little noticed or debated, and they built on assorted programs that state and federal government had experimented with in recent years. Federal grants to state assistance programs for the blind and aged made sense given the inadequacy of state finances. There was sound precedent in the Sheppard-Towner program, 1921-29, for federal grants-in-aid for public health, vocational rehabilitation, and for maternal and infant welfare. Local government programs to assist mothers competent to provide "suitable homes" for their dependent children, in place in most of the states for two decades or so, had largely run out of funds in the early thirties. On the urging of social workers and allied reformers, who coordinated their lobbying efforts through the Children's Bureau, Congress accepted as part of the social security bill federal assistance to the states. It seemed the only decent thing to do, especially because it was assumed that such assistance would go to strengthen "worthy" families whose mothers had been left financially stranded by death or divorce, and that in time such welfare payments would fade away with the implementation of expanded social insurance coverage.

After generations of resistance to federal welfare, the American public was implicitly prepared to welcome social security as the keystone of the New Deal. The means for implementing both unemployment and old age insurance, moreover, were deliberately shaped to conform to traditional, prudential American values of self-help and planning ahead for when one might again be out of work owing to a cyclical downswing in business, or for a time to enjoy hard-earned leisure in retirement. That benefits would be linked to contributions and would reflect a given person's history of work and the level of wages he had earned reassured blue-collar and white-collar workers alike that benefits would come not from paternalistic generosity but as earned rights, with maintenance of a delicate balance between the principles of equity and adequacy. The old age titles seemed to represent a carrying forward of a cherished system of family obligation by which the young had cared for the old in the expectation that when they in their turn became old their children would assume responsibility for them. In social security that intergenerational implied contract was rationalized and underwritten by the fiscal resources of national government.[14]

From the mid-1930s until his death in 1960, Edwin E. Witte, whose instinct for the broad center of American life made him a logical spokesman for a program whose chief architect he was, continued to explain social insurance in basically conservative terms. "Failure to insure the essentials of life breeds communism and revolution," he declared in 1958. "Society and state are not synonymous" in America, but in a secular state, government must assume a major responsibility for insurance and for rehabilitative programs that promise to restore the individual to self-support. "Responsibility for his support and that of family rests primarily on the individual," he concluded. "Social security is grounded in the philosophy that everyone must put forth his best efforts and rests on the assumption that in all normal circumstances most individuals, at least during the productive years of life, are able to support themselves and their families."[15]

The Social Security Act, however, did not just happen. Action waited on efforts conceived by a coalition of politicians, independent reformers, and a cadre of experienced experts, themselves committed by professional training and social inclination. Introduced as a state senator to the insecurities that pervaded life and labor in an industrial society, Franklin Roosevelt continued to be influenced by friends and associates like Frances Perkins, Harry Hopkins, Robert Wagner, Molly Dewson, and Lillian Wald. Agitation for social insurance had been sustained by scholars and publicists who, however sharply they disagreed on details, did agree on the basic principle—Abraham Epstein, Isaac Rubinow, Paul Douglas, John B. Andrews, Florence Kelley, Grace Abbott, Paul U. Kellogg, and a host of others from whose work the pioneers of 1935 drew. And we count the builders, of course—Arthur Altmeyer, Barbara Armstrong, Bryce Stewart, J. Douglas Brown, Thomas Eliot, and their chief, Edwin Witte—whose task it finally was to devise a workable and constitutional bill behind which the Administration could muster an effective majority.

This is no occasion to offer a detailed critical analysis of the act itself, but some simple facts stand clear. The President's role was crucial. Publicly committed as early as 1930 to the principle of comprehensive insurance, it was his initiative to create the Committee on Economic Security. After a hesitation, potentially fatal, in November 1934, when he appeared to be backing away from the old age titles, his insistence on a comprehensive, integrated single legislative act held wavering congressmen in line. His was the decision to establish the principle firmly and quickly, in the full knowledge that amendments would come easily in time.[16] It was a jumble of separate measures, eclectic in social theory, regressive in its form of taxation, deflationary in net effect, modest in the benefits it promised for the short run, restrictive in the constituents it covered. It promised security down the line for millions of citizens without the introduction of any fundamental changes in the economic or social order. It was, then, profoundly conservative.

But it did establish a national, compulsory, contributory system of old age insurance which, in the blunt words of FDR at the time, "no damn politicians [could] ever scrap."[17] It created a system of unemployment insurance that offered stability of income to unemployed workers and a way to sustain purchasing power in times of recession. Over the following years, it did more to reduce poverty than any other New Deal program—or any measure of the Great Society or the War on Poverty, for that matter. Its popularity was assured when it became clear to millions of older citizens that with normal (and increasing) life expectancy, they got out in benefits far more than they had put in, and when it became clear in times of recurring recession that unemployment benefits were crucial in seeing families through rough times and in sustaining levels of purchasing, a process so essential to the profit and economic stability of small retail establishments.

Modes of implementation, worked out in early years, brought assurance to organized labor—to qualify for unemployment benefits a worker had to be ready and willing to accept employment, but not if a firm were being struck, not if he would be required to join a company union, and only at accustomed tasks and prevailing wage rates. Professional social workers were bound to be pleased with administrative procedures for old age assistance and old age security that set forth clear and explicit criteria for eligibility, assured confidentiality to clientele (no more publishing of pauper lists), provided for fair hearings and for appeal, and offered assistance in cash (not kind) which recipients were free to spend without surveillance. Federal guidance implied that county welfare boards would, with surprising speed, adopt uniform rules of administration enforced by qualified civil servants hired and promoted by merit standards.

The centrality of social security to the creation of a government welfare system was evidenced in the steady expansion and enlargement of insurance programs by incremental steps, some short and stumbling, others giant strides, with almost every Congress. The 1939 amendments substantially increased coverage and benefit levels and inaugurated the principles of adequacy of benefits and the entitlement of survivors. During the Eisenhower years more than ten million new constituents were added, including farm operators and many categories of the self-employed and professional persons; benefits for all recipients were raised, and benefits for the totally disabled introduced. In the tumultuous and generous sixties, the federal government picked up three-quarters of the costs of providing social services through social security (most notably family and job counseling), and added Medicare for senior citizens. During the presumably fiscally prudent years of the Nixon Administration, benefit payments came to be linked to the cost of living index—a logical enough tactic at that time, but one which placed an ever-larger burden on the OASI system as inflation ravaged the nation's economy.

Prime moving forces in the achievement of these measures were members of a series of advisory councils who provided both a broad consensus supportive of the expansion of social security and expert advice on concrete details. As it was with the original act, however, new designs arose chiefly from social security professionals, leaders such as Arthur Altmeyer, Robert M. Ball, and Wilbur Cohen, who had the determination, the managerial skill, and the political savvy to build from strength. Accepting the unlikelihood of a coherent federal program of public family assistance ever being created, these administrators, with the knowing complicity of presidential and congressional leaders, followed a strategy of relying primarily on social security to extend the principles of a welfare state.

1. The quotation from Cohen is in "Factors Influencing the Content of Federal Public Welfare Legislation," *Social Work Forum* (New York, 1954), 215. Cohen further observed specifically of social security legislation over the years: "I have yet to see a consideration by Congress of legislative proposals in social security that did not result in a reconsideration of what were believed to be basic principles or produce some surprises in the form of amendments which nobody could have predicted would have been enacted or considered" (ibid., 211). The social historian is Paul A. Carter in *Another Part of the Twenties* (New York, 1977), 15. Literature on the history of social security includes the following (which is far from a definitive listing, of course):

William Leuchtenburg, *Franklin D. Roosevelt and the New Deal* (New York, 1963), 130-133, and passim; Arthur M. Schlesinger, Jr., *The Coming of the New Deal* (Boston, 1959), ch. 18, and *The Politics of Upheaval* (Boston, 1960), ch. 3, and 613-14, 635-40; W. Andrew Achenbaum, *Old Age in the New Land: The American Experience Since 1790* (Baltimore, 1978), 127-38; Daniel S. Hirshfield, *The Lost Reform: The Campaign for Compulsory Health Insurance in the United States from 1932-1942* (Cambridge, Mass., 1970); Abraham Holtzman, *The Townsend Movement: A Political Study* (New York, 1963); Louis Leotta, "Abraham Epstein and the Movement for Old Age Security," *Labor History* 16 (Summer 1975): 359-77; Roy Lubove, *The Struggle for Social Security, 1900-1935* (Cambridge, Mass., 1958); Daniel Nelson, *Unemployment Insurance: The American Experience, 1915-1935* (Madison, Wis., 1969); Theron F. Schlabach, *Edwin E. Witte: Cautious Reformer* (Madison, Wis., 1969), chs. 5-7; Hace Tishler, *Self-Reliance and Social Security, 1870-1917* (New York, 1971); Edward D. Berkowitz and Kim McQuaid, *Creating the Welfare State: The Political Economy of Twentieth-Century Reform* (New York, 1980); William Graebner, *A History of Retirement: The Meaning and Function of an American Institution, 1885-1978* (New Haven, 1980); James T. Patterson, *America's Struggle Against Poverty, 1900-1980* (Cambridge, Mass., 1981); Jerry R. Cates, *Insuring Inequality: Administrative Leadership in Social*

Security, 1935-1954 (Ann Arbor, Mich., 1982); Kristen Gronbjerg, David Street, and Gerald D. Suttles, *Poverty and Social Change* (Chicago, 1978); Sar A. Levitan et al., *Towards Freedom from Want* (Madison, Wis., 1968); Gaston V. Rimlinger, *Welfare Policy and Industrialization in Europe, America and Russia* (New York, 1971); Gilbert Y. Steiner, *Social Insecurity: The Politics of Welfare* (Chicago, 1966), and *The State of Welfare* (Washington, D.C., 1971); Harold L. Wilensky, *The Welfare State and Equality: Structural and Ideological Roots of Public Expenditures* (Berkeley, 1975); Martha Derthick, *Policymaking for Social Security* (Washington, D.C., 1979). Winifred Bell, *Aid to Dependent Children* (New York, 1965); Josephine Chapin Brown, *Public Relief, 1929-1939* (New York, 1971); Eveline M. Burns, *The American Social Security System* (Boston, 1949); Arthur J. Altmeyer, *The Formative Years of Social Security: A Chronicle of Social Security Legislation and Administration, 1934-1954* (Madison, Wis., 1968); J. Douglas Brown, *An American Philosophy of Social Security: Evolution and Issues* (Princeton, N.J., 1972), esp. ch. 1; Frances Perkins, *The Roosevelt I Knew* (New York, 1946), 105-8, 278-300; Edwin E. Witte, *The Development of the Social Security Act* (Madison, Wis., 1962); Witte, "Organized Labor and Social Security," in Milton Derber and Edwin Young, eds., *Labor and the New Deal* (Madison, Wis., 1957), 239-74; Robert J. Lampan, ed., *Social Security Perspectives: Essays by Edwin E. Witte* (Madison, Wis., 1962); Charles McKinley and Robert W. Frase, *Launching Social Security, A Capture-and-Record Account, 1935-1937* (Madison, Wis., 1970).

2. J. Douglas Brown, *The Genesis of Social Security in America* (Princeton, N.J., 1969), 1. This was a major argument of mine in *Seedtime of Reform: American Social Service and Social Action, 1918-1933* (Minneapolis, 1963), see especially chs. 7 and 10; and more recently, "Social Reform, Social Work, and Social Security: A Subject Revisited," in John N. Schacht, ed., *The Quest for Security* (Center for the Study of the Recent History of the United States, 1982), 1-17. I have drawn from some parts of the latter essay for this paper.

3. Wilensky, *The Welfare State and Equality*, ch. 2.

4. Ibid., 62-63. Here Wilensky argues with plausibility, if without final and sure proof, that opposition to welfare programs ran especially strong in societies in which many citizens had experienced some self-employment and independent entrepreneurship, and in which artisans, professional persons, and shopkeepers constituted significant proportions of the citizenry. He asserts that by such criteria, the United States ranked relatively high.

5. Gronbjerg et al., *Poverty and Social Change*, 6-9; Eveline Burns, discussion report of paper by Gaston V. Rimlinger, in William G. Bowen et al., eds., *The Princeton Symposium on the American System of Social Insurance* (New York, 1968), 239.

6. Daniel Levine, "Conservatism and Tradition in Danish Social Welfare Legislation, 1890-1933: A Comparative View," *Comparative Studies in Society and History* 20 (January 1978): 54-69. The direct quotation is from p. 57.

7. The great mobilization in America, 1939-1945, substituted "Dr. Win-the-War" for "Dr. New Deal," but welfare policy objectives enunciated in the war years by the National Resources Planning Board (NRPB) provided a blueprint to which social planners referred, successfully, in the 1950s and sixties. The G.I. Bill of Rights and the Full Employment Act of 1946 may be taken as

evidence of the immediate impact of modern war on the state's responsibility in the welfare arena. See, for example, such NRPB Reports as: *After the War—Full Employment* (January 1942); *Post-War Planning: Full Employment, Security, Building America* (September 1942); *Human Conservation: The Story of Our Wasted Resources* (March 1943). See also Wilbur J. Cohen, ed., *War and Post-War Social Security* (Washington, D.C., 1942). One historian's estimate of the "waning of the New Deal" is Richard Polenberg's *War and Society* (New York, 1972), ch. 3.

8. Such an obvious point hardly calls for citation, but one study, among many others deserving of note, provides explicit analysis of the complex relationship between hard times, social analysis, and political action: Bernard Sternsher, "Victims of the Great Depression: Self-Blame and Non-Self-Blame, Radicalism and Pre-1929 Experiences," *Social Science History* 1, no. 2 (Winter 1977): 137-77. Also useful is John Garraty, "Unemployment During the Great Depression," *Labor History* 17, no. 2 (Spring 1976): 133-59.

9. Graebner, *A History of Retirement.* See also his succinct restatement of the hypothesis: "From Pensions to Social Security: Social Insurance and the Rise of Dependency," in Schacht, ed., *The Quest for Security,* 19-33. Graebner's thesis adds a salutary correction to other standard accounts, even though his survey falls short of providing a comprehensive new explanation of the origins and significance of social security. Explicit labor participation concerns can be taken as important but hardly primary given all the other factors operating during the 1930s. The place of retirement in justifying old-age insurance is noted in Wilbur J. Cohen, *Retirement Policies Under Social Security* (Berkeley, 1957), esp. 3, 21.

10. Berkowitz and McQuaid, *Creating the Welfare State.* See also Brown, *An American Philosophy of Social Security,* 21-22. In Theron Schlabach's judgment, Eastman Kodak's treasurer, Marion Folsom, did more than any person other than E. W. Witte to persuade some skeptical legislators that unemployment and old age insurance provided practical solutions to very real and pressing problems (Schlabach, *Edwin E. Witte: Cautious Reformer,* 144). Folsom would continue to play an influential role in the expansion of the social security system and subsequently in welfare programs in general as Secretary of Health, Education, and Welfare. John G. Winant, a main-line patrician Republican, provides a parallel illustration of a public figure whose reputation and talents helped to establish the acceptability of social insurance.

11. Here is a theme that historians are just beginning to explore. For a preliminary comment that does not, however, hint at my suggestion, see: Immigration History Research Center, *Records of Ethnic Fraternal Benefit Associations in the United States: Essays and Inventories* (St. Paul, 1981); the volume contains essays detailing opportunities for doing research on these subjects by Michael G. Karni, John Bodnar, Robert F. Harney, John Modell, June Alexander, and Frank Renkiewicz. The speculation is my own. See also Robert Park and Herbert Miller, *Old World Traits Transplanted* (New York, 1921), 119-44.

12. Holtzman, *The Townsend Movement,* 27, 87. For Frances Perkins' assessment see her foreword to Witte, *The Development of the Social Security Act,* vi; for Witte's comments, see ibid., 95-96; Derthick, *Policymaking for Social Security,* 193-95.

13. Quoted by Brown in *American Philosophy of Social Security*, 84.

14. Edward Cowan, in Michael J. Boskin, ed., *The Crisis in Social Security: Problems and Prospects* (San Francisco: Institute for Contemporary Studies, 1977), 2, makes that point.

15. Edwin E. Witte, "The Objectives of Social Security," an address at the Meeting of the Catholic Economic Association at Chicago, December 28, 1958, in Lampard, ed., *Social Security Perspectives*, 101-11. Here was a retrospective commentary that differed in no substantial way from an address of June 17, 1938, in which Witte elaborated similar themes of self-support, self-respect, encouragement of thrift, and prevention of dependency: "Social Security: A Wild Dream or a Practical Plan?," address to the Wisconsin Alumni Institute, in ibid., 3-14. The thesis pursued by Alan Brinkley in his recent study of the popular movements led by Huey Long and Father Coughlin— *Voices of Protest: Huey Long, Father Coughlin, and the Great Depression* (New York, 1982)— may speak to this point. He proposes that their followers were moved primarily by their uneasiness with distant, centralized political power, that they longed for ways to strengthen the autonomy of individual and community against the corporation and the modern state. To such citizens the appeal of earned rights appears obvious, while the promise of security was bound to alleviate their feelings of helplessness.

16. J. Douglas Brown summed it up in his *An American Philosophy of Social Security*, 24: "A great President, when convinced of the feasibility of the program, was ready to take bold advantage of a uniquely favorable political situation to push through legislation. The need was for a workable plan which matched the predisposition of the American people, if not the constitutional precedents of the country."

17. Roosevelt quoted in McKinley and Frase, *Launching Social Security*, 17.

COMMENT BY WILBUR J. COHEN

When Franklin D. Roosevelt became President in 1933, only two major legislative proposals relating to social welfare had significant congressional support: federal aid for old age assistance to the needy and federal legislation to ensure that all states establish state unemployment insurance laws. There was no widespread support for social security in another form, or for national health insurance. Harry Hopkins, Federal Emergency Relief Administrator, was concerned about the broad problem of unemployables who could not be assisted by a work program. Secretary of Labor Frances Perkins was concerned about long-term programs of social insurance. Together they persuaded FDR to establish a Cabinet Committee on Economic Security to study the entire economic security problem and to make recommendations to him.

The selection of fewer than two dozen key intellectuals, academics, or members of the elite (as you may choose to call them) for the committee's ideas led to the development of a vastly more comprehensive program. In addition to the two programs of old age assistance and unemployment insurance, the following far-reaching proposals were added to the legislation:

1. Social security—old age entitlement;
2. Aid to needy dependent children;
3. Aid to the needy blind;
4. Maternal and child health grants;
5. Crippled children grants;
6. Child welfare grants;
7. Public health grants;
8. Permanent authorization of vocational rehabilitation grants;
9. Grants for administration of unemployment insurance;
10. Creation of a Social Security Board; and
11. Authorization of research in the broad field of social security.

While it is not correct to say FDR initiated the "safety net" or modern welfare legislation (there were three or four other such

161

programs or agencies in existence when FDR took office), it is fair to say he catapulted it into a working mechanism by effective use of a "brain trust."

But here we must be careful. FDR was, despite popular thought, really a fiscal conservative. He strongly advocated social insurance in order to cut down on future federal and state expenditures on what was then called "relief" and what today we call "welfare" in a pejorative sense. When the issue of utilizing federal general revenues to subsidize the old age entitlement program came to him for decision in 1935, he decided against it in order to protect the Federal Treasury. In 1939, when the issue of providing low-income states with a higher proportion of federal matching by use of per-capita income came to him for decision, he decided against it.

In my judgment, FDR balanced radical, liberal, and conservative elements to forge an effective political instrument. He was not afraid to use any or all of the rhetoric of these three elements to experiment. I think his approach was mainly intellectual but was accompanied by a pragmatic conviction that he wanted steps taken "then and now."

One major FDR policy decision has had the long-term impact of basically precluding the widening of the welfare state. In 1934, as a result of pressure from medical sources, he decided not to include any health insurance program within the omnibus social security package. He concluded that such a program might adversely affect the enactment of other elements. But he encouraged further efforts to study the problem, including the development of a postwar program which eventually resulted in the Truman advocacy of health insurance (1945), the inauguration of the Hill-Burton program of hospital construction (1946), and the eventual enactment of Medicare and Medicaid (1965). In this way, FDR left available for private insurance a wide but not complete field. It is doubtful whether that was his intention, but that was the result.

Another comment: FDR, along with many others, including myself, had no idea that the Aid to Families with Dependent Children (AFDC) program would become so large, so important, so controversial, and so recognized as "the" welfare program. Nor did I realize in the late thirties, the forties, or the fifties that I would become a significant actor in the expansion of this program in the sixties. There seemed no other alternative in the thirties; work relief programs were limited. AFDC became the welfare program which nobody had really planned to become so controversial.

FDR's advocacy of social security and unemployment insurance was his permanent contribution to a significant change in the American socioeconomic structure. This point has been made many times and is well accepted. What is not as well appreciated by current thought is how his actions and programs saved the state-federal system as well as the banking system and other key elements in the competitive free-enterprise system.

Could FDR have pursued and achieved a more radical program? Could we have become more of a welfare state than we are today? My answer is a clear yes. Even Ronald Reagan, who voted for FDR in 1932, 1936, 1940, and 1944, probably would have voted for him even if he had been more radical, or more welfare oriented.

One reason why Roosevelt and his 1934 advisers were not more comprehensive or radical in their program advocacy is because they were deeply concerned about administrative implementation. They recognized the limitations of human competence in handling new problems and programs. They thus became advocates of incrementalism, of careful administrative planning, and of a professional public service. This was all before the day of the computer; they were willing to feed in only as much as they thought the system could digest without getting an administrative stomachache. They derived this concern from their labor legislation expertise. The leading advocate of this concern was John R. Commons, whose influence persuaded Altmeyer, Witte, and also myself, as one of his students, of the truth of his repeated advice that if you ever have a choice between a good law that will be badly administered and a less desirable law which will be well administered, always choose the latter.

Over the past fifty years I have kept the advice I received when I was twenty years old—advice, I would add, that is still relevant.

VII

WOMEN AND THE NEW DEAL

THE NEW DEAL, THE CIO, AND WOMEN IN INDUSTRY*

Ruth M. Milkman

Recent reconstructions of what had been an obliterated history of women's relationship to the New Deal have demonstrated that women were deeply involved in the development of the innovative labor and social welfare policies of the period, and also that feminist ideology and activism survived during the Depression decade. The pathbreaking work of Lois Scharf and Susan Ware, in particular, suggests that "social feminists"— for whom women's emancipation was part of a broader program of social reform—enjoyed better opportunities to pursue their longstanding goals under the Roosevelt Administration than ever before. The individual careers as well as many of the collective reform objectives of the elite women who held policy-making positions in New Deal agencies were fulfilled in the 1930s, and their work helped bring substantial material improvements to the nation's working women.[1]

This is an important history, but it offers at best a partial, top-down account of the impact of the New Deal on women workers. To be sure, the "social feminists" who became government officials in this period, faithful to their Progressive legacy of professional concern for the working-class woman, consistently advocated and worked to implement policies beneficial to women workers. But at the same time, and almost completely unconnected to the work of these female New Dealers, there was an upsurge of unionization among women workers themselves, associated with the dramatic growth of the labor movement as a whole in the 1930s. While many of the "social feminists" who

* This article includes material from Ruth Milkman's forthcoming book on the sexual division of labor in industry. Permission to publish this material has been granted by the University of Illinois Press. Copyright © 1985 by Ruth Milkman.

were incorporated into the Roosevelt Administration had worked closely with the labor movement in the years before World War I, by the 1930s their alliance with organized labor was more nominal than real. Even the Women's Trade Union League was remarkably disconnected from the revitalization of the unions. And what few ties remained were with the old American Federation of Labor (AFL) leadership, so that the women New Dealers were particularly distant from developments within the dynamic new industrial unions of the Congress of Industrial Organizations (CIO).[2]

In what follows, I will explore this other dimension of women workers' relationship to the New Deal period. The CIO upsurge was at least as beneficial to women in industry as the New Deal measures with which the "social feminists" were associated, and in some ways more so. This was true despite the fact that what self-conscious feminist impulse there was during this era was certainly not concentrated in the labor movement. On the contrary: feminism was anathema to most unionists, and even in the CIO relatively few labor leaders evinced any serious concern with women workers in particular. This set definite limits on the extent to which women shared in the achievements of the unions in the 1930s. And yet, the CIO's commitment to industrial democracy and to nondiscrimination meant that the burgeoning of industrial unionism offered enormous benefits to women in industry.

The analysis below focuses on two of the major industrial unions which emerged in the 1930s, the United Automobile Workers (UAW) and the United Electrical, Radio, and Machine Workers of America (UE). The two cases offer somewhat different insights, since while the production workforce in auto was almost entirely male in the 1930s, women were better represented in the electrical manufacturing workforce than in the wage labor market as a whole, and made up a higher percentage of the production workforce there than in any other durable goods industry. This meant that for the UE, almost from the beginning, successful organizing demanded serious attention to the specific concerns of female workers. In auto, however, while women production workers were included in the unionization process, their status as a small industrial minority meant that UAW organizers could, and often did, achieve their goals without addressing themselves to women workers in particular.

The Impact of Unionization on Women Workers in the 1930s

The formation of the CIO in 1935 led almost immediately to a dramatic increase in the unionization of women workers. In 1900, only 3.3 percent of the women in the paid workforce had been union members. The proportion dropped still lower by 1910, to 1.5 percent, and then rose to a peak of 6.6 percent in 1920. In contrast, 21 percent of the much larger number of male workers were union members in 1920. As industrial unionism swept the nation in the late 1930s, organization among women workers quickly surged upward. By 1940, 800 thousand women were organized into unions—a 300 percent increase over their numbers ten years earlier, and twice the 1920 figure (which had been the high point of the AFL period).[3] The new CIO unions were committed to organizing workers in mass production industry without regard to skill, race, or sex—a radical departure from the timeworn organizing strategy of the AFL craft unions which had dominated the American labor movement during the preceding half-century. The AFL had focused its efforts on the protection of skilled workers, and viewed women, most of whom were unskilled, as "unorganizable." With some important exceptions, like the garment and textile industries (which together accounted for over half of all female union members in 1920), the AFL unions included very few women in their ranks, and many of them actively excluded women from the occupations which they represented.[4]

Women production workers in industries organized by the new CIO unions, like their male counterparts, benefited enormously from the organizational breakthroughs of the 1930s. In the auto industry, women's average hourly wages rose from 54 cents in 1936 to 65 cents two years later, while men's wages rose from 81 to 98 cents over the same period. Wages in electrical manufacturing had always been lower than those in auto, but they too rose dramatically with unionization. Between July 1936 and July 1937, women production workers in electrical saw their wages rise by 17 percent, to a 55-cent hourly average, while men's pay rose 15 percent, to 81 cents. In both industries, these gains were maintained in spite of the 1937-38 economic downturn, and by 1941 the unions had won substantial additional increases.[5]

In the electrical case, there were some serious efforts to narrow sex differentials in wages. The women's committee of UE Local

601, for example, pursued this issue at the East Pittsburgh Westinghouse plant, although due to management's intransigence on the issue they made little headway.[6] Although it was not achieved, the CIO did have a serious (if abstract) commitment to working for the systematic narrowing, and ultimately the eradication, of inequalities in wages and working conditions imposed on distinct groups of workers.

Both the UE and the UAW advocated "equal pay for equal work" for women, and often won contract clauses to this end. However, this policy was double-edged. Women did benefit, but the primary purpose of the demand was to prevent the use of female labor to undercut men's wages. Since most women in industry did not do the same jobs as men, large differentials between "men's" and "women's" jobs persisted well after unionization in both auto and electrical manufacturing, even where equal pay clauses were written into union contracts. Still, if women did not achieve parity with men, they did share in the wage increase which resulted from unionization.

Other than increasing wages, the major achievement of the CIO unions was the institutionalization of seniority systems for layoff and rehiring. This was particularly important in auto, where this sort of job security was a radical departure from established managerial practice. There were many abuses of the management-initiated seniority systems in electrical manufacturing during the Depression, so that the issue was a serious concern of electrical workers, although the overall seniority principle had long since been established there. At General Electric (GE), indeed, the company's existing seniority policy was simply added to the union contract.[7]

Seniority systems gave women some protection from sexual favoritism and harassment for the first time. "I can think of some of the gals who actually had to sleep with some of these guys," recalled Sadie Rosenberg of UE Local 427, "and you'd expect the hands to creep as the foremen walked up and down the aisles. . . . I don't think it was ever completely eliminated, but certainly the situation improved during the period of the union's strength increasing." Similar reports came from the auto industry, where sexual harassment and favoritism had also been widespread. [8]

But this was an indirect benefit of the overall seniority victory. Its direct effects offered men significantly more protection than women. After the Flint sit-down strike, when General Motors agreed to use seniority as the major criterion for layoffs and rehiring, management insisted that married men be given precedence in the event of long-term reductions in employment. In addition, many companies had separate seniority lists for women (and sometimes separate lists for married women). In the electrical manufacturing case, seniority did not become the predominant consideration in layoffs until the 1940s, with "need" weighted very heavily, as it had been previously.[9]

The CIO unions were primarily concerned with consolidating their organizational inroads in the 1930s, and that was difficult enough without the additional burden of developing a special commitment to challenging sexual inequality. Organizing women qua women was simply not a priority for the CIO, partly because most women workers were employed outside the mass production industries which were the main target of the organizing drives, and partly because of the widespread acceptance within the labor movement of the dominant social ideology which proclaimed that "woman's place is in the home." There were some important efforts to address women workers' needs in the CIO of the 1930s, but these almost always came from individual female union organizers, including leftist (but rarely "feminist") women, rather than from the top union leadership.

In both the UAW and the UE, women activists offered initiatives in "women's issues" in the early organizing drives. The UE women seem to have gotten more encouragement than their counterparts in auto from the union leadership, simply because women workers in the electrical industry were too numerous to be ignored. "If women could be attracted . . . to take a more active interest in our organization," UE national secretary-treasurer Julius Emspak wrote to Bertha Scott and other female organizers in May 1936, "it would be of great organizational value."[10]

Women's leadership was actively cultivated on the local level as well. Many UE locals established special "women's committees" in the late 1930s. Local 601's first constitution went so far as to empower the women's committee, made up of assistant shop stewards from each department in the plant, "to sit in on all standing committees and to offer suggestions so that the proper women's appeal shall be made in all the affairs of this union."[11]

During World War II, the UAW would develop similar organizational forms and take a more extensive interest in women's concerns, as its female membership expanded with the economic mobilization. But in the 1930s, women's concerns were marginal to the auto workers' union, except in locals with large female representation (especially parts plants). Even in the UE, where the importance of involving women was recognized, their role was quite circumscribed in this period. "They knew they had to fight for the rights of women . . . in the UE," recalled Mary Voltz, a UE organizer based in St. Louis. But her personal experience was difficult. "I was not accepted by the other representatives of the UE," she remembers. "They were men. And they tried very hard to make me into an office clerk."[12]

It was not uncommon for the women most active in the UE to be assigned to such positions. Even Margaret Darin, who was active in the East Pittsburgh Westinghouse local from the outset, and who attended the early national EU conventions faithfully, as well as organizing the first women's conference ever held by the union, ended up as a specialist in the UE's office work. Having served as Local 601's Recording Secretary and as an Executive Board member for several years, she visited various locals to teach them to improve their record-keeping systems. She was also a business agent for a year in Lima, Ohio's Local 724, and recalls that there "some of them came up to me and said that . . . I had too much power for a woman."[13]

There was resistance to the idea of employing women organizers with specific responsibility for organizing female workers. When a resolution was introduced at the 1939 UE national convention, calling for the immediate employment of an International Woman Representative with such duties, the union's Committee on Resolutions recommended against the proposal, arguing that all organizers should be hired based on "ability regardless of sex." Those favoring the resolution argued that women would be more effective than men in approaching women workers, having a better understanding of their special needs and problems. "We have to show the girls in our shops that there is not a position in our organization that is not open to them," implored Ruth Young, who would later become the first female member of the UE's International Executive Board. "In my local [Local 475 in Brooklyn]," she went on, "girls don't come to meetings because they feel the men have built the union and probably know how to make a point of order better than they do. If we go out of our way to educate these girls, I am sure these girls can and will show they are capable of leadership."[14] That this debate took place at all in the UE in the 1930s distinguished it from the other new mass production industrial unions. The fact that women were so numerous in the industry alone generated some legitimacy for the dedication of special resources to women workers, but the 1939 convention debate also revealed the limited commitment to such work within the union.

There were also external obstacles to women's full participation in the new industrial unions. Even though the CIO was far more hospitable to women's involvement than the AFL had been, many of the traditional impediments remained. Especially crucial was the fact that family obligations and authority structures constrained women's participation in such activities as unionism, for both daughters and wives. Significantly, Ronald Schatz found that female activists in the early UE were unlike most women workers in the 1930s in that they enjoyed some measure of independence from "traditional" family ties. Ruth Meyerowitz found the same to be true of women UAW activists in the 1940s.[15]

Despite such difficulties, women were active contributors to the building of the new industrial unions in the 1930s, especially at the local level. At the East Pittsburgh Westinghouse plant, they signed up workers, became shop stewards and organizers, and developed local women's conferences to discuss and plan campaigns intended to equalize male and female wage rates and other concerns specific to women. Much of their work remained invisible, however. As Margaret Darin recalled, "Their activity in the union was overshadowed by the activity of the men that took the leadership role in it. Their role, in those early days, was a little bit clouded."[16]

The electrical workers' union did give women more attention than most of the other new CIO unions. But for the UE as for the others, the main emphasis was on organizing the industry's large plants, like GE's headquarters in Schenectady and the East Pittsburgh Westinghouse plant. These factories, "the central fortresses of the industry," produced heavy industrial equipment and employed relatively few women. The overwhelmingly female Cleveland lamp division, in contrast, was the last part of General Electric to be organized. This reflected the logic of CIO unionism, which was directed toward the strategic core of American industry—an emphasis reinforced by the low priority accorded to organizing women.[17] It is significant in this regard that the principle of industrial unionism was rarely extended to the substantial numbers of female clerical workers employed by industrial corporations in the 1930s. In at least a few recorded instances, moreover, the CIO bargained away the contract rights of clerical workers and failed to resist wage cuts, layoffs, and speedups to which office workers were subsequently subjected.[18]

The CIO and the "Family Wage" Ideology

Without apologizing for the sexually discriminatory aspects of industrial unionism in the 1930s, it is important to recognize that in American society as a whole, women workers were seen not as "workers" but as women who happened to be employed. Their primary role was in the home and family, whether or not they worked for pay, in this culturally dominant view, and they certainly did not have the same rights as men in the labor market. The adherence of unions to such attitudes as these did not distinguish them from other social institutions, and indeed, it seems quite difficult to imagine how the labor movement could have held a different view during this era.

The social impact of the Depression strongly reinforced conventional sex role ideology, as men's ability to maintain their status as family "breadwinners" became increasingly precarious. Unemployment hit men harder than women, simply because the fields of work women were concentrated in contracted less, and later, than did predominantly male occupations. The "white collar" jobs which already comprised the bulk of the female labor market had lower rates of unemployment than the manufacturing and mining sector, where men were more heavily represented.[19] Moreover, in manufacturing, which was hit hardest by the economic slump, there were frequent complaints that management was substituting women for men as a means of cutting wages. In early 1935, Nathan Sleames, who had been laid off after working seven years in an auto parts plant, reported to the National Recovery Administration (NRA) that his former employer was "printing great write ups in the daily paper about how they are hireing and adding to their force but it is the wimmen & girls they have hired and there is nothing said about the men that are let go."[20] Similarly, General Electric workers in Lynn, Massachusetts, complained in 1935 of management's eagerness to substitute women for men. "If a woman can do a job, and does it," they lamented, "it then becomes a woman's job."[21]

In working-class communities, the main effect of female substitution was to strengthen the hold of the "family wage" ideology, according to which the male breadwinner should earn enough to support an entire family. This ideal, which had been weakened somewhat with the growth in female labor force participation in the 1910s and 1920s, enjoyed a tremendous resurgence as a result of the severe unemployment the Depression brought. It was frequently suggested that the flocking of women into the workforce in the preceding years had contributed to the scarcity of jobs for men, and incidents of female substitution deeply reinforced this perception.[22]

Working-class women themselves agreed with the male workers' sentiment that women, and especially married women, should not take jobs while male "breadwinners" were desperate for work. Women workers were often quite reluctant to cooperate with changes in the sexual division of labor which involved directly replacing men with women. "I refused to take a man's job which would have taken from him, his wife, and his children his weekly wage," said a single woman who had worked in the auto industry until she was laid off in 1931.[23] The idea that women, like men, were entitled to jobs, simply had no legitimacy in the 1930s, even for women themselves. Instead, the class ideal was the "family wage."

One of the major ways the CIO incorporated women into organizing, the women's auxiliaries, reflected this same view of the relationship of class and family. In the sit-down strikes in auto, the "place of women was in the auxiliaries, many of which included women workers as well as the wives and daughters of male workers. It was considered inappropriate for women to occupy the plants along with the men, even though they had participated actively in the organizing which culminated in the sit-downs. In the 1936-37 Flint strike, for example, the women working in the cut-and-sew department of GM's Fisher Body Plant No. 1 were told to leave the factory when the strike began. "The press and the radio were so eager to say there was sexual mingling," recalled Genora Johnson Dollinger, the leader of the Women's Emergency Brigade, which played a key role in this strike, supporting the workers from outside the occupied plants. "A few of them offered to stay, but they were asked, 'No,

don't do it because we can't give General Motors any propaganda.' " This was the typical pattern in the auto sit-downs, although
at the Detroit Bohn Aluminum plant the women refused to
leave the shop during the January 1937 strike.[24]

The Flint Women's Emergency Brigade was probably the
most developed example of the auxiliary, playing a critical
military role in protecting the occupied plants from the police
assault in the famous Battle of the Running Bulls. Women won
enormous praise throughout the CIO for their activity in the
auxiliaries. "You gals who want to be free, just take a tip from
me," the popular labor song "Union Maid," written in 1940,
tellingly recommended. "Get you a man who's a union man
and join the ladies' auxiliary."[25]

While greatly appreciated during the sit-down wave, the role
of the women's auxiliary and the Emergency Brigade was all
but forgotten in the aftermath of the UAW's triumph. "Following the strike the Emergency Brigades were effectively dispersed,"
recalled Genora Johnson Dollinger. "Everybody in it [the strike]
said, 'Thank you ladies. You have done a wonderful job. But
now the laundry is piled up, the dishes are piled up and the kids
need attention, and what else could a woman do?' " Even though
it involved them in quite unconventional activities, the women
active in the Brigade and other strike support work defined
their contribution, as Ruth Meyerowitz has pointed out, "as an
extension of their family responsibilities to support and help
their men."[26] After the strike, women indeed returned to their
old "place" in the home, and the minority of women with jobs
in the auto industry returned to work perhaps more marginalized
than before, having been excluded from the galvanizing strike
experiences of men inside the plants.

Women's greater representation in the electrical manufacturing workforce, and the relatively peaceful transition to the CIO
era which occurred in that industry (where union recognition
was generally achieved through elections, not sit-down strikes),
gave women a more stable, if still subordinate, role in the UE
than in the UAW. While they were excluded from the upper
ranks of union leadership in both cases, women in the UE did
penetrate the lower levels of the union bureaucracy and carved
out a space in which to pursue issues of particular concern to
female workers. Where there were protracted strikes—as for
example at the Newton, Iowa Maytag plant—women's auxiliaries

did emerge and played a role like that in auto. But in most UE locals, in the absence of this kind of struggle for union recognition, auxiliaries played a marginal role, if they existed at all.[27]

The family wage ideology left its mark on the UE in a different way, particularly in the controversies within the union over married women's employment. The issue caused serious divisions within many UE locals. The layoffs of the 1937-38 downturn, which followed union recognition for many locals, aroused much sentiment among UE members in favor of discrimination against married women. Other members argued that differential treatment for any group of workers was out of keeping with the principles of industrial democracy and nondiscrimination which the CIO represented. The disagreement did not break down neatly along sex lines, but divided women themselves as much as men. Even women who were active in the union and presumably had some appreciation of the general principle of nondiscrimination sometimes favored barring married women from employment. At the District 6 Women's Conference in 1938, Margaret Darin recalled, "There was disagreement amongst the women. Oh, sure. Some felt that married women had a husband to take care of them, therefore why should they be taking jobs. It was a question of jobs."[28]

The issue was resolved differently in different locals. At the General Electric plant in Lynn, Massachusetts, management's policy had always been not to hire married women. But after a protracted internal debate on the issue, UE Local 201 arrived at the position that length of service at the plant should be the sole factor governing the order of layoffs.[29] At the Westinghouse plant in Mansfield, Ohio, in contrast, the union played just the opposite role. In this plant, marriage had been made a criterion for dismissal for women workers early in the Depression decade, but management had not enforced this policy rigorously, making numerous exceptions. The UE local here took it upon itself to insist that the company adhere to its official policy, and a clause to that effect was written into the union contract. A U.S. Women's Bureau investigator found that the union had succeeded in persuading the firm to lay off numerous married women from the plant, and moreover, that the contract agreement to this end was made by the union officers without the consent of women union members themselves.[30]

In another UE plant, the company policy of discrimination

against married women directly impeded the organization of female workers into the local, and the union eventually took up the issue as a means of attracting women to its ranks. The question arose when Emma Hebble, a married woman who had worked in the Decatur, Indiana, GE plant for years while keeping her marriage a secret, sued for divorce in 1940, and was thereupon dismissed. She was a union member, and came to UE Local 924 for help. "The women will not attend open meetings," a local union official reported. "It is known to us that several of the women are married, and because they are still employed we believe that they desire to continue as such." The plant employed ninety-two women, but only five of them had joined the union by late 1940.[31] Although the policies on the employment of married women adopted in the early 1930s had been popular among workers, management could clearly use those policies to advantage in situations like these.

When Local 901 in Fort Wayne, Indiana, was unable to resolve the issue of married women's rights, the local officers wrote to the UE national office for guidance in January 1938. "We realize there is considerable feeling as to what should be done in this matter," replied UE President James Carey. "We also know from past experience, if a local union can be used as a pawn by the company on a question such as this, the company is only too glad." But even as it recognized the dangerously divisive character of the issue, the national office refused to take a firm stand on the question, referring it instead to a conference of GE locals.[32] By the time of the 1939 UE national convention, however, a resolution in favor of "equal rights for married women" was adopted with no debate. The resolution noted that married women were only 6 percent of the nation's labor force, and that discrimination against them "would serve as an opening wedge for discrimination against different groups and sections of our population."[33] However, individual locals continued to do as they pleased on the issue, even after the resolution was passed.

The issue also arose in the UAW, although it was less central simply because female employment was far smaller in the industry. Some UAW locals entered agreements with management which provided for discrimination against married women in layoffs. But most auto union leaders took the position that while the family wage ideal was a desirable one, it was simply unrealistic in view of the need of families for income. The vice-president of UAW Local 2 replied to a letter from the wife of a member who suggested that married women be expelled from the plant in 1939 in these words: "Some day," he wrote, "I hope we will reach that economic ideal where the married woman will find her place in the home caring for children, which is God's greatest gift to women and her natural birthright." However, this was impractical, he suggested, for several reasons: "The union must protect their seniority; many women must work to support large families because their husband's income is inadequate; many pose as single girls."[34] Here, the principle of nondiscrimination together with the practicalities of maintaining unity between male and female union members prevailed over the family wage ideal in shaping the union's policy.

Feminism, Class Solidarity, and the CIO

Two counterideologies were potential sources of opposition to the dominant social ideology of "woman's place" and the working-class "family wage" ideal. One possible vehicle for challenging discrimination against women as dictated by the dominant culture was feminism. But by the 1930s, the first "wave" of feminism survived only in a rather limited form. The "social feminists" in the New Deal Administration were a dying breed—a "generation on the wane," in Susan Ware's phrase.[35] While their work did bring important benefits to women workers, most of these achievements were secured in the name of social reform and democracy—not feminism.[36]

Feminism had in any case been associated primarily with educated, professional women rather than working-class women—although there were moments where class alliances among women were effective. In the 1930s, however, this did not occur, and class divisions among women were exacerbated due to the differential impact of the economic crisis on professional women, who faced blatant discrimination, and working-class women, who found themselves with somewhat better employment levels than their husbands, fathers, and brothers. The intensification of the "family wage" ideology in working-class communities made feminism less relevant than ever before to women in industry.

However, the second source of opposition to the conventional sex role ideology did resonate among working-class women, as well as their male allies in the CIO. This was the ideology of working-class solidarity, which included the principle of non-discrimination among working people. The tension persisted between opposition to sex discrimination and the "family wage" ideal, as we have seen. But the CIO's class unity ideology could and often did serve as a meaningful avenue of change for women workers. In addition to the material improvements women workers enjoyed as a result of the CIO's rise (improvements in wages, working conditions, and job security), the rise of industrial unionism opened up new opportunities for a challenge to the legitimacy of discrimination.

As long as depression conditions persisted, these opportunities were pursued only in a limited way. Economic insecurity among men remained a barrier to the full pursuit of class solidarity, even though the ideological commitment was there. But during the Second World War, when full employment at least temporarily eliminated the fears and insecurities which prevailed in the early years of building the CIO, women workers were able to challenge discriminatory practices far more effectively. The wartime demand for "womanpower" in industry pulled women in huge numbers into the CIO strongholds, and the unions gained greater stability as well in the full employment economy. By the war's end, all AFL and CIO unions were free of restrictions barring women from membership, and female union membership reached an all-time high. Women's representation on union staffs increased dramatically as well, especially in the CIO, and women's issues were taken up in almost all the major industrial unions.[37]

If the potential gains available to women workers through the CIO were more fully realized in the 1940s, nevertheless the late 1930s also brought important improvements. The CIO's impact on women was only indirectly linked to the official New Deal policies emanating from the Roosevelt Administration, but the achievements of industrial unionism nevertheless deserve a central place in the story of the New Deal and women workers.

1. See Lois Scharf, *To Work and To Wed: Female Employment, Feminism, and the Great Depression* (Westport, Conn.: Greenwood Press, 1980), especially Chapter 6; Susan Ware, *Beyond Suffrage: Women in the New Deal* (Cambridge: Harvard University Press, 1981); and, for background on "social feminism" in the previous decade, J. Stanley Lemons, *The Woman Citizen: Social Feminism*

in the 1920s (Urbana: University of Illinois Press, 1973).

2. See, in addition to the sources in note 1, Gladys Boone, *The Women's Trade Union Leagues in Great Britain and the United States of Ameria* (New York: Columbia University Press, 1942), pp. 190-221.

3. John B. Andrews and W.D.P. Bliss, *History of Women in Trade Unions*, Senate Report on the Condition of Women and Child Wage-Earners in the U.S., 61st Cong., 2d sess. S.Doc. 645 (1911), p. 138; Leo Wolman, *The Growth of American Trade Unions, 1880-1923* (New York: Bureau of Economic Research, 1924), pp. 85, 105, 137-45; Gladys Dickason, "Women in Labor Unions," *Annals of the American Academy of Political and Social Science* 251 (May 1947): 71.

4. For a fuller discussion, see Ruth Milkman, "Organizing the Sexual Division of Labor: Historical Perspectives on 'Women's Work' and the American Labor Movement," *Socialist Review* 49 (January-February 1980): 95-150.

5. "Annual Averages of Hourly and Weekly Earnings and Average Hours per Week for Male and Female Wage Earners in the Automobile Industry," June 28, 1944, Research Department, UAW-CIO, in UAW Research Department Collection, Wayne State University Archives of Labor History and Urban Affairs [hereafter WSU Archives], "Employment, Detroit, 1941-1947," Box 10, Folder 10-19; Milton Derber, "Electrical Products: Local Surveys of Four Leading Companies," in *How Collective Bargaining Works*, ed. Harry A. Millis (New York: Twentieth Century Fund, 1942), pp. 760, 769, 804; Leo Jandreau to Dear Sir and Brother, July 24, 1941, Records of United Electrical, Radio, and Machine Workers of America (UE) District 3, UE Archives, University of Pittsburgh Library, File Folder 166 [GE 1941 wages]; keysheets in Margaret Darin Stasik Papers, University of Pittsburgh Archives, File Folders 6 and 14 [Westinghouse 1937 and 1940 wages].

6. See *Wayne-UE Victory News*, August 14, 1942, p. 3. (Copy in Stasik papers, File Folder 27.)

7. W.H. McPherson, "Automobiles," in *How Collective Bargaining Works*, ed. Millis, pp. 617ff; Ronald W. Schatz, *The Electrical Workers: A History of Labor at General Electric and Westinghouse, 1923-60* (Urbana: University of Illinois Press, 1983), pp. 105-11, and "GE Contract Clauses on Seniority in Layoffs," in *Exhibits in Case of EEOC Charges TNP4C-2002 and TNP4C-2000 against General Electric*, January 2, 1976, p. 1411. (Copy in the UE Archives.)

8. Sadie Rosenberg Interview, January 11, 1979, untranscribed tape, Oral History of the American Left Tamiment Library; an incident of this sort is also recorded in a "Note," March 19, 1939, from UE Local 924, in the Records of UE District 9, UE Archives, File Folder 594: Ruth Meyerowitz, "Women in the UAW," unpublished manuscript in author's possession, pp. 33ff.

9. Irving Bernstein, *A History of the American Worker: Turbulent Years, 1933-1941* (Boston: Houghton Mifflin Co., 1969), p. 551; Jonas Silver and Everett Kassalow, "Seniority in the Automobile Industry" (U.S. Bureau of Labor Statistics, Washington, D.C., 1944, mimeograph); Schatz, *Electrical Workers*, pp. 113-14; and "GE Contract Clauses," pp. 1411ff.

10. Julius Emspak to Bertha Owens Scott, May 26, 1936, Records of UE District 9, UE Archives, File Folder 185.

11. "Local 601 Constitution," Stasik Papers, File Folder 1.

12. Meyerowitz, "Women in the UAW"; Mary Voltz Interview, The Life and Times of Rosie the Riveter Film Project, Series IV, Oral History of the American Left Collection, Tamiment Library, pp. 1, 20 of transcript.

13. Stasik Papers, File Folder 7; Linda Nyden, "Women Electrical Workers at Westinghouse Electric Corporation's East Pittsburgh Plant, 1907-1945," M.A. thesis, Department of History, University of Pittsburgh, 1975, pp. 50-60.

14. Proceedings of 1939 UE Convention (New York: UE, 1939), p. 141.

15. Ronald Schatz, "Union Pioneers: The Founders of Local Unions at General Electric and Westinghouse, 1933-1937," Journal of American History 66 (December 1979): 586-602; Ruth Meyerowitz, "Women Unionists and World War II: New Opportunities for·Leadership," paper presented at the Organization of American Historians' Meeting, San Francisco, April 1980. See also Theresa Wolfson, The Woman Worker and the Trade Unions (New York: International Publishers, 1926).

16. Nyden, "Women Electrical Workers," p. 52.

17. James J. Matles and James Higgins, Them and Us: Struggles of a Rank-and-File Union (Boston: Beacon Press, 1974), pp. 53-55; Julius Emspak to Stanley Newton, September 22, 1939, Records of UE District 4, UE Archives, File Folder 336.

18. See Sharon Hartman Strom, "Challenging 'Woman's Place': Feminism, the Left, and Industrial Unionism in the 1930's," Feminist Studies 9 (Summer 1983): 359-86. At the 1946 UAW convention, one delegate alluded to this problem in the course of a debate over a resolution urging the organization of white collar workers: "I recall that in the original Ford contract the payroll department was organized and then it was cancelled out of the contract, due to some finagling. . . . I recall at the time the members of the payroll department picketed the members of the International Union for being sold out." Proceedings of the 1946 UAW Convention (Detroit: UAW, 1946), p. 41.

19. See Ruth Milkman, "Women's Work and the Economic Crisis: Some Lessons from the Great Depression," Review of Radical Political Economics 8, no. 1 (Spring 1976); 73-97.

20. Nathan D. Sleames to Dear Sir, January 5, 1935, Records of the National Recovery Administration, National Archives, Record Group 9, Box 7682, Folder: "Automobile Industry: Letters Received in Washington."

21. Finn Theodore Malm, "Local 201, UE-CIO: A Case Study of a Local Industrial Union," Ph.D. dissertation, Massachusetts Institute of Technology, Department of Economics, 1946, pp. 278-79.

22. See Scharf, To Work and To Wed, and Jane Humphries, "Women: Scapegoats and Safety Valves in the Great Depression," Review of Radical Political Economics 8, no. 1 (Spring 1976): 98-121.

23. U.S. Women's Bureau, Women Workers in the Third Year of the Depression Bulletin No. 103 (Washington, D.C., 1933), p. 10.

24. Dollinger oral history, cited in Meyerowitz, "Women in the UAW," p. 46.

25. On Flint, see Meyerowitz, "Women in the UAW"; Patricia Yeghissian, "Emergence of the Red Berets," *Michigan Occasional Papers in Women's Studies*, no. X (1980); and the documentary film, *With Babies and Banners* (Women's Labor History Film Project, 1978). According to Philip Foner, this verse of the song, written by Woody Guthrie, as added by Millard Lampell of the Almanac Singers. See Foner, *Women and the American Labor Movement: From World War I to the Present* (Glencoe: Free Press, 1980), p. 334.

26. Meyerowitz, "Women in the UAW," p. 113.

27. *Proceedings* of 1938 UE Convention (New York City: UE, 1938), pp. 165-66; see also mimeo Report of District #3 to the 1937 UE Convention, p. 4.

28. Nyden, "Women Electrical Workers," p. 58.

29. "Fifteen Years with 201: August 1933-August 1948," pamphlet in Records of UE District 2, UE Archives, File Folder 166.

30. "Mansfield, Ohio, October 1, 1941," notes on meeting with UE officials, in Records of the U.S. Women's Bureau, National Archives, Record Group 86, Box 1416, Folder: "Region V, Magee, Lowrie, Settle and Manning—Early 1941 thru 6/1943." Information about a similar case at the Schenectady GE plant may be found in Records of UE District 3, UE Archives, File Folder 214.

31. George Myers to UE/GE Conference Delegates, August 28, 1940, in Records of UE District 9, UE Archives, File Folder 594.

32. James B. Carey to Herbert R. Bates, January 20, 1938, in Records of UE District 9, UE Archives, File Folder 219. See also the letter from Alice Roth, "Should Married Women Work?" in *UE News* 1, no. 20 (May 29, 1939): 4.

33. *Proceedings* of 1939 UE Convention, p. 140.

34. Local #2 Edition of the newspaper *United Automobile Worker*. (Copy in Joe Brown Collection, WSU Archives, Box 34, Folder: "Women—Employment.")

35. Ware, *Beyond Suffrage*, p. 116.

36. Scharf, in *To Work and To Wed*, stresses the way in which feminism was underplayed by social feminists. See especially Chapter 6.

37. For more discussion of the war period, see Milkman, "Organizing the Sexual Division of Labor."

A New Deal for Women: Government Programs, 1933-1940*

Winifred D. Wandersee

Until very recently, it would have been difficult for any historian to have given an account of American women and how they related to the New Deal, and in fact, few would have considered the topic worthy of attention. In spite of the fact that women of the 1930s had acquired the vote, that the "new woman" of the 1920s had made her colorful imprint on American values, and that women reformers participated in public and private welfare agencies across the country, the New Deal era was, nonetheless, the only major period of reform since the American Revolution that did not include a strong feminist component.[1] Futhermore, traditional historians of the New Deal have been prone to ignore the presence of women in Washington, aside from a polite recognition of Frances Perkins and, very occasionally, Molly Dewson or Mary Anderson.[2] Even the recent historians of women have tended to slight the New Deal era and emphasize the more dramatic advances of World War II.[3]

Yet in the last few years, several important studies have appeared that attest to women's active participation in the events of the 1930s, and to the fact that although their experience was not necessarily "feminist" per se, it was nonetheless distinct from that of men and worthy of its own historical account.[4]

What can we learn from these recent studies—about the New Deal, about women's historical experience during the 1930s, and about a historical profession that has dissected in minute detail every aspect of the New Deal but has waited for nearly

* The author would like to acknowledge financial assistance from Hartwick College in the form of a Board of Trustees Summer Research Grant.

fifty years to evaluate the role of women in this watershed event? The current generation of historians that seeks the answers to these questions is primarily female and basically feminist. That is, the writers have tried to interpret history as if it were something experienced by women, in a manner distinct from that of men.[5] The approaches have varied, emphasizing work, reform, feminism, and family. But the record that is emerging from this wide range of issues indicates clearly that the significance of women's interaction with the New Deal has been greatly understated in the past.

Basically, women's experience during the 1930s can be divided into three broad categories: work and family life under the pressures of economic crisis; the debate over feminism and careerism; and the New Deal itself, its impact upon women, and the role that women played in creating and carrying out the reforms of the New Deal. It is this last category of concerns that is the focus of this paper. Although the decade of the thirties was a time of economic stagnation, stress, and deprivation for women as well as for men, on the whole, the New Deal opened more doors than it closed. Furthermore, as a broad program of public policy reform, the New Deal was, in fact, the culmination of more than three decades of social feminism. It was the social reformers' "finest hour," as Secretary of Labor Frances Perkins quite clearly stated in June of 1940, when she read in a newspaper that the Republican Party convention had adopted all the social security programs in its platform. "God's holy name be praised! No matter who gets elected we've won."[6]

What had been won, from Perkins's point of view, was a long struggle for industrial and social insurance programs that stretched back to the early years of the Progressive era. This struggle was carried on largely, though not exclusively, by the social feminists.[7] But if social feminism achieved a victory in the form of the New Deal, the emphasis of that victory was certainly upon the social rather than the feminism. And herein lies the irony of this success—an irony which has been noted by other historians, in particular William O'Neill and Jill Conway. [8] The reform program of the New Deal, to the extent that it focused upon the problems of women, served to reinforce traditional notions of what women could and should do. Perhaps it was inevitable that the reformers would adhere to the societal pressures that were characteristic of the era, but the consequence, nonetheless, was a concrete and theoretical limitation upon the advancement of women and the cause of feminism. Thus, the New Deal was a catalog of contradictions that paradoxically represented great advances for women in some areas, while severely limiting their long-range opportunities by reinforcing age-old stereotypes.

A crucial issue for women during the 1930s was the tension between work and family—a tension which has characterized women's domestic and economic experience since the origins of the industrial era.[9] Kessler-Harris notes in her recent study *Out to Work* that the Depression delivered to women a curious double message. On the one hand, it imposed economic pressures on the family that pushed women into wage work. On the other hand, it fostered a public stance that encouraged family unity and urged women, in the interest of jobs for men, to avoid paid work for themselves.[10]

The reforms of the New Deal reflected a similar ambiguity. The programs for women were an honest and sometimes creative attempt to meet the needs of women workers, but they were based upon limited views of women's roles and their long-range place in the labor market. Finally, women leaders themselves, as reformers and feminists, contributed to that ambiguity.

The impact of New Deal legislation upon women workers has been addressed in three recent studies: Lois Scharf's *To Work and to Wed*; Wandersee's *Women's Work and Family Values*; and Kessler-Harris's *Out to Work*. All three historians note the ambiguities inherent in policies that were designed to protect women, but that ultimately had the effect of restricting them.

The classic example is the National Industrial Recovery Act (NIRA), which established codes covering about one-half of all employed women—mainly those in manufacturing, trade, clerical work, communications, and certain large service groups. Many women not covered by the codes were working in occupations in which the worst conditions prevailed, such as domestic service, laundries, dressmaking, and public service. At the other end of the occupational spectrum were the 1.5 million women in professional services who were also neglected by the NIRA codes.[11]

More to the point, although the NIRA codes did cover many women in industry, they also reflected the general view that women needed less money than men. By September 1, 1934, there were 233 NIRA codes, and 135 of them fixed minimum wage rates for women below those of men. The differences ranged from 6.3 percent lower in three cases, to as much as 30 percent lower in several cases. However, in most cases the difference was from 10 percent to 20 percent.[12]

The establishment of NIRA codes had a much more complicated effect than the rather simplistic fact of wage discrimination. Kessler-Harris points out that the codes succeeded in raising minimum wage levels dramatically. They also reduced the average number of hours worked for all workers, but particularly for women and other low-skilled, poorly paid, hourly employees. For instance, in the textile industry, where hours had been particularly long, they declined by 25 to 28 percent. Of course, this was a mixed blessing. Shorter hours usually resulted in lower weekly wages. Also, the better-paid workers often had their wages reduced to benefit the lower-paid workers.[13]

The labor clause of the NIRA, Section 7a, and its successor, the Wagner Act, both had a somewhat ambiguous impact upon women workers. The Wagner Act, often considered the most far-reaching piece of labor legislation ever signed by a President, revitalized the labor movement and encouraged the formation of the CIO in 1935. Scharf points out that the organizing drive through both the AFL and the CIO had a definite impact upon woman workers. The estimated number of women affiliated with unions increased fourfold during the 1930s. Major women-hiring industries that were affected included textiles, paper and paper products, cigar and confectionary manufacturing, restaurants, and laundries. The major thrust of the CIO was, of course, toward heavy industry. The automobile and the rubber industries were the most significant of those organized by the CIO as far as women workers were concerned. About 20 percent of the rubber workers were women. They had suffered severe wage reductions and extended hours earlier in the decades, but the recognition of the United Rubber Workers increased the wage rate twofold and made prevalent the eight-hour-day. On the other hand, the contract also designated "men's jobs and women's jobs," with women's wages averaging 20 percent less than men's.[14]

So, although women workers in major CIO-organized industries gained improved work standards and job security along with their male colleagues, discriminatory features were a part of most contracts. Wage differentials, sex-defined job categories, and separate seniority lists were accepted practices, and further-more, some unions opposed the hiring of married women. Also, women continued to play a very minor role in union leadership.[15]

The special position of women, both on the job and in the organized labor movement, was a reflection of the public debate which characterized societal attitudes toward women and work in the 1930s and which was carried on at another level through governmental programs. Therefore, the New Deal programs for unemployed women were never as far-reaching as those for men. Tentative and short-range in their goals and objectives, they reflected an honest concern with the special problems of women, but an unwillingness to see the problems as more than temporary.

The Federal Emergency Relief Administration, the National Youth Administration, and the Works Progress Administration (WPA) all had programs geared to the special needs of women. The programs tended to emphasize job skills that would prepare the women as domestic servants or housewives, but they did little to prepare them to compete on the job market. An article in the September 1938 *Women Worker* reported that more than one-half of the 372,000 women employed on WPA projects were working on projects such as canning and sewing. They made garments and supplies to be distributed to relief clients and to hospitals and other public institutions. They preserved, canned, and dried surplus food for needy families and for school lunch projects.

Many of the women involved in work relief under WPA were in a special program set up in July 1937 called the Household Service Demonstration Project. The program provided training for women who were seeking domestic employment, but it also provided for the employment of women who acted as teachers and demonstrators in the courses. Some seventeen hundred women were involved in giving a two-month training course in methods of cooking and serving food, care of the house, care of children, washing, ironing, and marketing. A survey of the project, done in December 1939, showed that in the more than two years of operation, twenty-two thousand women had received training and eighteen thousand trainees had been placed. Those who were not placed had either dropped out of the training course, found employment, married, or left the community. For those who stuck with the full course, placement was almost 100 percent.[16]

The WPA also employed another thirty thousand women on housekeeping aid projects. Women who were good homemakers but had no other skills were sent into the homes of needy families to help out in times of illness or other distress. In addition, during the 1937-38 school season, eight thousand women were employed on school lunch projects.[17]

Of course, women were employed in the various professional projects as well as those emphasizing menial domestic work. In fact, their occupational distribution was much more favorable than their male counterparts. Women on WPA projects were more likely to be placed in a white-collar occupation than were men. Almost 40 percent of all clerical workers and of all professional and technical workers were women. And surprisingly, women had as large a proportion in the category of project supervisors and foremen as men. These three categories together occupied nearly a third of all WPA women workers.[18]

The statistics indicate that women workers, as a whole, were underrepresented on WPA projects, although this was the work relief agency most sympathetic to the needs of working women. Only 17.5 percent of all WPA workers were female, at a time when women made up about 24 percent of the total labor force and their unemployment rates were comparable to men's.[19]

The major programs directed at youth—the Civilian Conservation Corps and the National Youth Administration (NYA)—focused most of their efforts, training, and funding on the needs of young men. Although women were included, at least in the NYA, they were never the primary object of concern. For example, the resident educational camps, established first under the Federal Emergency Relief Administration and later transferred to the NYA, reflected a class and sex role bias that steered young women into limited channels of achievement and ignored their potential for higher achievements. Also, the educational camps were in existence for only about three years, and reached less than ten thousand young women.[20]

Thus, the New Deal addressed the problems of women, but it tended to further relegate them to their traditional roles, thereby reinforcing their already low economic status. The employment of women on relief projects was seen as a temporary necessity, geared toward their basic economic survival.[21] The New Deal reformers saw a woman's long-range security as linked to her position in the family and supported by the primary family wage earner.

Nowhere was this commitment to family security more evident than in the most important piece of New Deal legislation, the Social Security Act of 1935. Under the terms of this legislation, adults who did not work for wages were not eligible for Social Security. Therefore, women who chose marriage over employment gave up government protection as well as their careers. The implication was obvious. The security of women was dependent upon men. Also, Social Security excluded many occupations that employed women, such as domestic service, farm labor, and educational, charitable, and hospital personnel. The exclusion of domestic workers left one-third of all married working women outside of a social welfare program. On the other hand, there was an Aid to Dependent Children (ADC) component to Social Security. In fact, some local WPA officials tried to take advantage of ADC by switching women from work relief to ADC as quickly as possible. The women themselves tended to prefer work to cash relief, and in a few cases they actually protested with sit-down strikes at welfare offices.[22]

Interestingly enough, the Social Security Act, as much as any part of the New Deal, was the creation of the social feminists, and as such it reflected their attitudes toward the poor, the welfare state, and the role of women. However, most of the studies that deal with Social Security give little consideration to the feminist-reformer aspect of the issue. Clearly this key piece of legislation not only laid the foundations for the social welfare state, but it institutionalized female economic dependency and reinforced attitudes about women's traditional role that were to affect women's economic lives for decades to come.[23]

It is perhaps unrealistic to suppose that government policies, programs, and projects of the 1930s would work toward the elimination of the sex role biases that were so thoroughly ingrained in the American social and occupational structure. Yet given the fact that women played such a large role in initiating, formulating, and implementing the New Deal, it is somewhat surprising that there was not a more aggressive stance taken on the potential of women—and a more creative effort to move beyond conventional stereotypes of women's role. The generation of women who were behind the New Deal were the first group of women to play an active and influential role in policymaking. Yet although they developed a network of support among themselves, and were directly concerned with women's issues, they seldom defined themselves as feminists. Their attitude was that of the social feminists of the Progressive era, and, of course, many, if not most, began their careers during that era. They were primarily concerned with the need to protect women and children caught in a harsh, competitive world. The hardships of the Depression understandably increased rather than decreased that tendency.

Historian Susan Ware has pointed out in her study *Beyond Suffrage: Women in the New Deal* that the experimental, reformist atmosphere of the New Deal encouraged and facilitated progress for women, particularly those who pursued careers in public life. The women who came to Washington during the New Deal era were able to rise to positions of power and prominence in many of the new government agencies. They came from similar backgrounds, with similar career patterns, and many of them knew each other from social welfare and reform activities going back to the Progressive era. The interaction of these women, on both the personal and professional level, formed a "network" which became an important force in enlarging women's influence in the New Deal.[24]

As Ware points out, women in the New Deal network took an active interest in furthering the progress of their sex. They recruited women for prominent government positions, demanded increased political patronage, and fostered an awareness of women as a special interest group. Although promoting the advancement of women always remained a central concern of the network, the women identified themselves as social reformers rather than feminists. They pursued social welfare goals benefiting both men and women. Ware argues that they also advanced the cause of women by taking on new and unprecedented roles in the public sphere. Yet they neither set an example for future generations—at least not one that was imitated—nor broke down the sexual stereotypes of their day that governed economic activity, vocational training, and public policy.[25]

Even recognizing the humane concern that the New Dealers had for women, children, and youth, the question must be asked: why did they not play a more aggressive role in breaking down sexual barriers and advancing the cause of feminism from their position of public influence? The answer lies partly in the general conditions which underlay the climate of opinion in the 1930s. The Depression was in itself a problem of such immediacy and magnitude that feminism as an issue and an ideology was remote from the concerns of most social reformers. Thus even limited benefits for women were seen as victories. The New Deal broke new ground in establishing employment, training, and welfare programs for women, and the reformers themselves were willing to accept that half-loaf. In part this was typical of the time and the temperament of the New Deal, but it was also partly related to the personal characteristics of the women in the New Deal network. As her biographer notes, Frances Perkins's career was built on the premise that in daily work there was no essential difference between men and women. She was widely quoted for her remark that being a woman in government was a handicap "only in climbing trees."[26]

This rather cavalier dismissal of the many slights that Perkins endured on a regular basis was quite typical of this generation of reformers. Ware points out that the women in the network naively believed that since they had done so well in government, conditions would continue to improve for women who wanted to pursue careers in government and politics. Eleanor Roosevelt stated in the *Democratic Digest* in 1938 that "the best way to advance the equal rights of women is for every woman to do her job in the best possible way so that gradually the prejudice against women will disppear."[27]

This kind of public feminism was perhaps adequate for those women who had strong individual talents and particular social and professional advantages. But such an approach was not going to produce basic changes for women in American society, no matter how impressive an example was being set. Because the women in the New Deal network were exceptional, they failed to question women's second-class status in American society. They never delved deeply into the causes of discrimination against women; they never challenged the stereotypes of "women's nature." And finally, because their won political impact was so dependent upon individual contributions, it was difficult to institutionalize even the limited gains that were won in the 1930s.[28]

The lack of feminist consciousness within the New Deal network can also be attributed to the split in the postsuffrage women's movement between the social reformers and the equal rights feminists. Susan Becker addresses this issue in her book *The Origins of the Equal Rights Amendment*, in which she argues that the National Women's Party (NWP) was the only "true" feminist organization in the United States during the interwar period. Party members kept feminism alive during these years, alerted women to the legal and economic discrimination that they faced, and probably prevented many of these discriminations from becoming worse. In formulating the Equal Rights Amendment, NWP feminists pointed the way to a future potential equality before the law.[29]

But the NWP's legalistic approach to feminism, with its unbending commitment to the Equal Rights Amendment, lost it many supporters among the social feminists and tended, perhaps, to give feminism a bad name among those who saw the need for protective legislation for women when the security of family life had failed them. Furthermore, the relationship between women's work and family values was the primary issue for most working women of the Depression years. To gain a wide base of support, the feminist ideology would have had to adapt to the basic fact that the great majority of American women were committed to a traditional pattern of family life that had little to do with equal rights or "careerism."[30]

To a certain extent, the lack of a strong feminist consciousness among New Deal reformers can be attributed to a simple expediency—a desire to cooperate and consolidate the gains that had been made among this first generation of women in government. These gains had often been made for those less fortunate than themselves. Certainly expediency was characteristic of some of the members of the so-called Negro cabinet, in particular Mary McLeod Bethune, head of the Negro's division of the National Youth Administration. B. Joyce Ross, in a recent article on Bethune, points out that Bethune adopted a pragmatic approach to desegregation and equal treatment of blacks. In her efforts to advance Negro interests in the New Deal agencies, Bethune necessarily had to accept limited progress in overall racial equality; in the presence of white audiences, she often spoke the language of the "accommodationist."[31]

In fact, in some ways, the experiences of blacks and of women in the New Deal are parallel and provide a good opportunity to compare the advances, the benefits, and the overall impact of expanded governmental activity upon two groups traditionally outside of the mainstream of American politics. In both cases, there were definite, though limited, gains. In both cases, old stereotypes were reinforced and certain structural inequities became an accepted part of the trappings of the New Deal welfare state—inequities that were to remain as unresolved issues to haunt future generations.

One historian has said, "Not even with the benefit of historical perspective is it a simple exercise to untangle the web of beneficial and victimizing effects of New Deal legislation."[32] Certainly this is true, but it is nonetheless the task of the historian to move beyond the traditional interpretations of the New Deal which note its "pragmatism," its lack of ideological rigidity, and its peculiar inability to challenge existing mores and values, to consider an equally interesting question: why was one-half of the population pragmatically dismissed from mainstream America, and why has it taken American historians so long to address this issue?

1. Three major reform eras—the antebellum years, the Progressive era, and the 1960s—all had a strong feminist movement, whereas the 1930s are generally viewed as a retreat from feminism. This traditional interpretation is, however, being challenged to some extent by the recent literature.

2. The best overall biography of Perkins, which focuses on her New Deal years, is George Martin's *Madame Secretary* (Boston: Houghton Mifflin, 1976). Two books on social welfare by Clarke A. Chambers underline the role of women as social reformers and their influence on New Deal legislation. See *Seedtime of Reform: American Social Service and Social Action, 1918-1933* (Minneapolis: University of Minnesota Press, 1963); and *Paul U. Kellogg and the Survey: Voices for Social Welfare and Social Justice* (Minneapolis: University of Minnesota Press, 1971). Arthur M. Schlesinger, Jr., in *The Politics of Upheaval, 1935-1936* (Boston: Houghton Mifflin, 1966), pp. 338-40, notes the role of women in the New Deal through the influence of Molly Dewson. He also has a number of references to Frances Perkins. See also, James T. Patterson, "Mary Dewson and the American Minimum Wage Movement," *Labor History* 5 (Spring 1964).

3. See especially, William H. Chafe, *The American Woman: Her Changing Social, Economic, and Political Roles, 1920-1970* (New York: Oxford University Press, 1972), pp. 39-47, which describes the 1930s as a period of reform, but a time of withdrawal from the feminist ideal. His analysis is not necessarily incorrect, but it is limited and inconclusive.

4. Four books on women and the 1930s have appeared in the last few years: Susan D. Becker, *The Origins of the Equal Rights Amendment: American Feminism between the Wars* (Westport: Greenwood Press, 1981); Lois Scharf, *To Work and to Wed: Female Employment, Feminism, and the Great Depres-*

sion (Westport: Greenwood Press, 1980); Winifred D. Wandersee, *Women's Work and Family Values, 1920-1940* (Cambridge: Harvard University Press, 1981); and Susan Ware, *Beyond Suffrage: Women in the New Deal*(Cambridge: Harvard University Press, 1981). In addition, there have been several articles: Ruth Milkman, "Women's Work and the Economic Crisis: Some Lessons from the Great Depression," *Review of Radical Political Economics* 8 (Spring 1976); Winifred D. Wandersee Bolin, "The Economics of Middle Income Family Life: Working Women during the Great Depression," *Journal of American History* 65 (June 1978): 60-74; and Wandersee, "American Women and the Twentieth-Century Work Force: The Depression Experience," in *Women, Identity and Vocation in American History*, ed. Mary Kelley (Boston: G. K. Hall, 1979). See also, Alice Kessler-Harris, *Out to Work: A History of Wage-Earning Women in the United States* (New York: Oxford University Press, 1982), ch. 9. See also, Susan Ware, *Holding Their Own: American Women in the 1930s* (Boston: G. K. Hall, 1982). A recent interest in Eleanor Roosevelt has also stimulated interest in the 1930s. See especially Lois Scharf, "ER and Feminism," and Martha Swain, "ER and Ellen Woodward: A Partnership for Women's Work Relief and Security," in *Without Precedent: The Life and Career of Eleanor Roosevelt*, ed. Joan Woff Wilson and Marjorie Lightman (Bloomington: Indiana University Press, 1984).

5. See Gerda Lerner, *The Majority Finds Its Past: Placing Women in History* (New York: Oxford University Press, 1979), p. 162, for a discussion of the feminist perspective of history.

6. Quoted in Martin, *Madame Secretary*, p. 431. Martin points out that Perkins included in that "we" not only the New Dealers, but also Al Smith, Florence Kelley, and every other man and woman who had fought for the social programs finally established through the New Deal.

7. For a more detailed analysis of the reform activities of social feminists before the New Deal, see Chambers, *Seedtime of Reform*; and J. Stanley Lemons, *The Woman Citizen: Social Feminism in the 1920s* (Urbana: University of Illinois Press, 1973).

8. Although William O'Neill gives very little attention to the New Deal era, his basic argument is that the social feminists stressed the unique qualities of women and the need for women to work out their special destiny which, by logical extension, was sexual in character. See William L. O'Neill, *Everyone Was Brave: A History of Feminism in America* (Chicago: Quadrangle Books, 1969), p. 315. See also, Jill Conway, "Women Reformers and American Culture, 1870-1930," in *Our American Sisters: Women in American Life and Thought*, ed. Jean E. Friedman and William G. Shade (Boston: Allyn and Bacon, 1976), pp. 301-12.

9. For a full development of this theme, see Carl Degler, *At Odds: Women and the Family in America from the Revolution to the Present* (New York: Oxford University Press, 1980).

10. Kessler-Harris, *Out to Work*, p. 251.

11. Wandersee, *Women's Work and Family Values*, pp. 95-96.

12. See Scharf, *To Work and to Wed*, pp. 110-14, for a broader discussion of this issue.

13. Kessler-Harris, *Out to Work*, pp. 263-65.

14. Scharf, *To Work and to Wed*, p. 131; and Kessler-Harris, *Out to Work*, pp. 268-69.

15. Scharf, *To Work and to Wed*, pp. 131-32.

16. "Women and the W.P.A.," *Woman Worker* 18 (September 1938): 8. See also, Ellen S. Woodward, "W.P.A.'s Program of Training for Housework," *Journal of Home Economics* 31 (February 1939): 86-88; and Florence Kerr, "Training for Household Employment: The W.P.A. Program," *Journal of Home Economics* 32 (September 1940): 439.

17. "Women and the W.P.A.," p. 8.

18. "Occupations of W.P.A. Workers," *Monthly Labor Review* 49 (August 1939): 355-56.

19. Ibid.

20. For a more complete discussion of the resident educational camps for women and other NYA programs, see Wandersee, "A New Deal for Youth: Government Relief Policies and Perceptions of Sex Roles in the 1930s," paper delivered at the Duquesne University History Forum, Pittsburgh, Pennsylvania, October 21-23, 1982.

21. An example of an educational program geared especially to women was the category of activities that came under the heading "Education for Family Living," under the WPA. See Doak A. Campbell et al., *Educational Activities of the Works Progress Administration*, Advisory Committee on Education Staff Study No. 14 (Washington, D.C.: U.S. Government Printing Office, 1939), ch. 10, pp. 103-19.

22. For a discussion of the impact of the Social Security Act upon women, see Scharf, *To Work and to Wed*, pp. 128-30. Ware, in *Beyond Suffrage*, gives a less critical account, pp. 97-101. See also, Martin, *Madame Secretary*, pp. 343-48.

23. A good recent discussion of Social Security is in James T. Patterson, *America's Struggle against Poverty, 1900-1980* (Cambridge: Harvard University Press, 1981), pp. 67-77.

24. Ware, *Beyond Suffrage*, pp. 6-7.

25. Ibid., p. 7.

26. Martin, *Madame Secretary*, p. 338; pp. 210-11.

27. Quoted in Ware, *Beyond Suffrage*, p. 129.

28. Ibid., pp. 129-30.

29. Becker, *The Origins of the Equal Rights Amendment*, p. 279.

30. Wandersee, "Epilogue," *Women's Work and Family Values*, pp. 118-22.

31. B. Joyce Ross, "Mary McLeod Bethune and the National Youth Administration: A Case Study of Power Relationships in the Black Cabinet of Franklin D. Roosevelt," *Journal of Negro History* 60 (January 1975): 1-28.

32. Scharf, *To Work and to Wed*, p. 111.

VIII

NEW DEAL
FARM POLICY

THE NEW DEAL
FARM PROGRAMS: THE MYTH
AND THE REALITY*

Wayne D. Rasmussen
Gladys L. Baker

What were the New Deal farm programs? Whatever they were, they must have been of substance, because, with virtually no exceptions, they were in effect fifty years later, modified this way and that but still in effect. At the very least, they have had the passive, if not the active, support of a majority of the American people for half a century.

Since the 1930s, assessment of these programs has ranged from high praise to strong denunciation. In recent years a number of scholars have challenged the value of the programs, not because they did not accomplish what they set out to do, but because the underlying goals were wrong. The New Deal offered an opportunity to overturn the traditional structure of American farming and reestablish a new and better order on the ruins of the old. Or, looking at the problem from a slightly different angle, some critics say that the New Deal programs encouraged the flight of people from the farm, reductions in the number of farms, and increased farm mechanization, thus continuing the erosion of the traditional small family farm.

There has been a major change in the structure of American agriculture since the Great Depression. The number of farms has declined from 6.3 million in 1930 to 2.4 million in 1980. The average size of farms has increased from 157 acres to 431 acres in the same period. The farm population fell from 30 million to 6 million, while the percentage of the labor force made up of

* The research for this paper was financed in part by a cooperative project with the History Department, Iowa State University.

farmers declined from 21 to 2.8. Most of this change has taken place since 1945. Many analysts ascribe it to the impact of World War II, though the question has been raised as to whether or not the New Deal farm programs made it possible.[1]

We hope to address this question in the present paper. We shall outline the major New Deal farm programs, with some discussion as to what was hoped for in each particular program and what scholars and others have felt its impacts to have been, looking at both the past and the present. We shall then attempt to relate the impact of these programs taken together on the world of a half-century later.

In 1933, President Franklin D. Roosevelt and his Secretary of Agriculture, Henry A. Wallace, faced a time of unprecedented crisis in American agriculture. In his inaugural address, Roosevelt had said, "This Nation asks for action, and action now." There had been sporadic outbreaks of violence on American farms and, on January 25, 1933, the president of the American Farm Bureau Federation, traditionally the most conservative of the farm organizations, had said, "Unless something is done for the American farmer we will have revolution in the countryside within less than twelve months."[2] On March 8, the board of directors of the Federation sent the President a telegram urging that he recommend immediate action to Congress on the restoration of price parity, monetary reform, guarantee of new deposits of all banks, and relief for distressed mortgage indebtedness.[3] This appeal was obviously directed at maintaining the traditional structure of agriculture, not at bringing about a major restructuring.

Wallace's response to these pressures was to urge Roosevelt to ask Congress to take up farm problems at the special session of Congress called for March 9 to act on the banking emergency. The President agreed and asked Wallace to call a farm leaders' conference to reach agreement on legislation.[4] The fifty leaders proposed to the President that legislation conferring broad emergency powers be recommended to the Congress.[5] The President then asked Wallace to have legislation drafted. He turned the job over to Mordecai Ezekiel, a longtime Department economist, and to Frederic P. Lee, a Washington lawyer employed by the American Farm Bureau Federation, with advice from Rexford G. Tugwell, the new Assistant Secretary of Agriculture.[6]

Roosevelt sent the draft to Congress on March 16, saying: "I tell you frankly that it is a new and untrod path, but . . . an unprecedented condition calls for the trial of new means to rescue agriculture."[7] As he said later, "It was the most drastic and far-reaching piece of farm legislation ever proposed in time of peace."[8] Congress made a number of changes in the bill that had been proposed, partly because Marvin Jones of Texas, Chairman of the House Committee on Agriculture, insisted on emphasizing the voluntary and self-determining concepts of the legislation.[9] Congress passed the legislation, and it was signed on May 12, 1933, as the Agricultural Adjustment Act.

Meanwhile, Secretary Wallace had been planning shifts in both the programs and the organization of the Department to put the legislation into effect immediately upon its signature by the President. He asked Nils A. Olsen, career agricultural economist and Chief of the Bureau of Agricultural Economics, to assist in establishing committees of Department personnel to compile statistics needed to administer major commodity programs under the new law.[10] Wallace also decided upon the major leaders of the new agency. For the most part, political pressures dictated these choices. This led to the most studied of all conflicts in Wallace's Department of Agriculture, a conflict that saw a group of conservatives defeat a number of liberals or radicals in their struggles to control the new agency and its far-reaching programs.

The first head of the Agricultural Adjustment Administration (AAA) was George N. Peek, who had been calling for government intervention since 1920. Peek believed that the surplus problem should be solved through encouraging exports, by subsidies if necessary. However, Wallace, Tugwell, M. L. Wilson, and others were committed to controlling production through restricting acreage planted. Within a year, Peek was succeeded by Chester Davis as administrator.[11]

Soon after Peek was appointed as administrator, Wallace persuaded him to accept Jerome Frank as General Counsel of the Agricultural Adjustment Administration. Frank was a brilliant lawyer, with a deep concern for consumers and for social issues and was often at odds first with Peek and then with Davis. Frank felt that since the law vested authority in the Secretary, he was responsible to Wallace as well as to the administrator. He worked, at least to some extent, with a group of so-called liberals in the Secretary's office.[12]

A major explosion came early in 1935 over the fate of the cotton sharecropper. In the 1934-35 contract between cotton producers and the Department for the reduction of acreage, it was stated that, insofar as possible, the landlord would maintain the normal number of tenants and other employees, and that the landlord should permit all tenants of good conduct to continue in the occupancy of houses rent free for the years 1934 and 1935. Spokesmen for tenants and sharecroppers, particularly the newly organized Southern Tenant Farmers' Union, contended that the landlord had to keep the same tenants. Frank and several others in the Agricultural Adjustment Administration agreed. Cully Cobb, Chief of the Cotton Production Section of the Agricultural Adjustment Administration, said that the landlord was to not necessarily keep the same tenants, but the normal number of tenants. For a few months the Department appeared to be a hotbed of intrigue and counterintrigue over the issue. Finally, Wallace agreed that Davis should fire Frank, and others in the AAA identified with Frank. For a time at least, Wallace had been forced to narrow the scope of the Department's interests as the conservatives had urged.[13]

The decision to fire Frank was regarded at the time and has been since as an indication that the Department was dedicated to preserving American agriculture as it was rather than to bringing about major structural changes. While Wallace did not reverse Davis's decision, he asked Mordecai Ezekiel to look into tenancy matters. After investigating the distribution of benefits from the cotton program, Ezekiel reported that the increase in landlords' income was substantially greater than that for all tenants. Farms with sharecroppers had an increase of 97 percent in income for landlords and 27 for tenants.[14]

In 1965, historian David E. Conrad concluded a history of sharecroppers in the New Deal by stating:

> Combining the facts about the decline of cotton tenancy with a knowledge of the workings of the AAA's cotton program leads naturally to the conclusion that AAA failed to benefit great numbers of Southern tenants and even harmed many of them. In a way, AAA accomplished an unintended reform in helping to drive tenants from the land, because those evicted were forced to seek new occupations and most of them eventually found a better life. However, it was usually years before they could make the adjustment, and in the meantime they suffered terribly. A great, humanitarian nation as rich as the United States can find

better ways to achieve such reforms.[15]

Recently, Pete Daniel, another historian, has written: "When the New Deal acreage reduction forced them off the land, sharecroppers did not ask for reform. They wanted to continue sharecropping; they wanted to stay on the land."[16]

The Agricultural Adjustment Act was declared unconstitutional by the Supreme Court on January 6, 1936. The president of the American Farm Bureau Federation said, "There will be neither surrender nor compromise, as we move forward. . . . The principle of farm adjustment, in terms of supply and demand, is not dead." In a letter to Secretary Wallace, a group of Iowa farmers wrote: "The vehicle by which the accomplishments were made possible has been discarded, but the spirit which drove that vehicle is still here, more determined than at any time the AAA was in operation. . . . We would remind you that not only the future of our industry but the future of our country is in the balance."[17]

In considering a replacement for the Agricultural Adjustment Act, Mordecai Ezekiel wrote to the Secretary: "There can be no question that the farm owners, constituting less than half of those engaged in agriculture, have been the dominant element in the preparation and administration of AAA programs heretofore. In certain commodities, notably cotton, this has resulted in their receiving the lion's share of the benefits resulting from the programs."[18]

The Agricultural Adjustment Act was replaced almost immediately by the Soil Conservation and Domestic Allotment Act, a law which lacked real production controls. President Roosevelt linked soil conservation with, as he wrote, "the reestablishment and maintenance of farm income at fair levels so that the great gains made by agriculture in the past 3 years can be preserved and national recovery can continue."[19] After the new act had been in effect about a year, Wallace wrote, "It will be necessary after supplies under the loan program have reached a certain point to keep the granary from running over by some practical program of production adjustment."[20]

The themes of maintaining farm income and adjusting production to demand were emphasized in the Agricultural Adjustment Act of 1938, which embodied the Soil Conservation and Domestic Allotment Act and added provisions for production control through compuslory marketing quotas under certain

conditions. The Federal Crop Insurance Corporation was established by the Agricultural Adjustment Act of 1938 and has
continued until the present.

The basic idea of federal crop insurance is to insure farmers
against loss from such unavoidable causes as weather, insects,
and disease. It does not ensure profit for the farmer or cover such
avoidable causes as neglect and poor farming practices. The
program has been modified first one way and then another. It
has never achieved the importance hoped for by its early supporters.

Crop insurance was often considered an alternative to disaster
payment or loans. Low-cost loans to victims of disaster began in
1918 and reached high points in the later 1920s and the 1930s,
particularly in the drought-stricken Great Plains. Grants were
also made. Eventually the Farmers Home Administration was
assigned responsibility for administering the loans.[21]

The 1938 Agricultural Adjustment Act, modified and remodi-
fied, is still in effect, and although details and terminology have
changed, the goals are still the same. We can conclude from this
that preserving and strengthening the traditional structure of
agriculture rather than replacing it with something else was a
basic goal of both Roosevelt and Wallace. At the same time, it is
clear that in fifty years agriculture has changed in ways unforeseen in the 1930s. Sharecropping in the old sense has ended—a
goal at one time eagerly sought by reformers. The number of
somewhat self-sufficient small farms has been declining very
rapidly, although in the early 1980s that decline slowed.

Roosevelt and Wallace both had plans to ease the transition
from sharecropping. The first step in this direction was the
establishment of the Resettlement Administration on April 30,
1935, as an independent agency headed by Rexford G. Tugwell.
Its immediate objective was the short-term relief of impoverished
farm people, but its long-term purpose was to rebuild the land
and the lives of the people who lived on it. Roosevelt gave the
program strong support, calling it "extraordinarily effective."
However, critics called it extravagant and impractical, particularly opposing the key programs of assisting families in the
worst situations to find new and more economic farms or to
locate elsewhere in other occupations with a prospect of work
and income.[22]

A subsistence homestead program, first established under the
National Industrial Recovery Act, became part of the Resettle-

ment Administration. Its head, M. L. Wilson, saw the program as a means of shifting poverty-stricken rural families from sub-marginal land to part-time farming communities where they could grow their own food and perhaps find jobs in new industries. Suburban resettlement projects, called greenbelt communities, were also planned, and three were completed. Some community or cooperative type of resettlement projects were organized. In some instances, the settlers worked the community farmland as a unit, leading to charges of Socialism or Communism.[23]

The Resettlement Administration also established a number of farm labor camps, first in California, to provide minimum sanitary facilities for one of the most disadvantaged groups in America, the migratory farm laborers. The program was continued by the Farm Security Administration. By December 1941, that agency operated seventy-four camps, which would serve more than thirteen thousand families at any one time. During World War II, the camps were operated by the Office of Labor, a wartime agency of the Department, to house interstate and foreign seasonal farm workers. The federal camps generally met the standards established for foreign workers, but the housing provided by individual growers was sometimes the subject of complaint. After World War II, the camps were sold or given to local governments, growers associations, and other groups.[24]

Meanwhile, the Resettlement Administration was transferred to the Department of Agriculture. In 1936, Roosevelt asked Congress for legislation that would encourage farm ownership, calling that the foundation for an enduring agricultural civilization.[25] At the suggestion of Tugwell, Roosevelt appointed the Special Committee on Farm Tenancy with Wallace as chairman. After visiting the Southern states to study the conditions of sharecroppers and tenants, Wallace saw that the problem was far from solved. As he said, this poverty represented a generation or more of limited opportunity and social handicap, and revealed the existence of longtime undermining forces in American agriculture.[26]

The committee recommended that the Resettlement Administration become the Farm Security Administration. The new Administration would be responsible for a tenant purchase program, with the government buying land to be sold under long-term contracts at low interest rates to disadvantaged farm families; for a rehabilitation loan program providing technical guidance; for continuance of camps for migratory farm workers; and for continuation of a program to retire submarginal land.[27] Legal authorization was provided by the Bankhead-Jones Farm Tenant Act of July 22, 1937, to carry out a substantial part of the recommended program (50 Stat. 522).

The Resettlement Administration, which had become a part of the Department on January 1, 1937, became the Farm Security Administration on September 1, 1937. The new tenant purchase program proved to be the most popular of those assigned to the new agency. It could, however, reach only a small percentage of the farm tenants, sharecroppers, and laborers who wanted to qualify for farm ownership loans. During the first year, loans were made to fewer than two thousand of thirty-eight thousand applicants. Within its limits, the program was successful.

While the tenant purchase program continued to be accepted by Congress, others fell more and more into disfavor. By 1943, the agency was under heavy attack. Wallace, who was now Vice-President, and Roosevelt were concentrating on World War II, while Secretary of Agriculture Claude R. Wickard and War Food Administrator Chester C. Davis had never been particularly strong supporters of the Farm Security Administration. The conservative farm organizations, notably the American Farm Bureau Federation, led the attack, backed by a number of Southern congressmen. The agency made a strong plea for making small farms a central part of the effort to secure increased food production. However, its plea was rejected, it lost direction of the farm labor camps, and it had its appropriations sharply cut.[28]

The longtime adminstrator of the Farm Security Administration, C. B. Baldwin, was forced to resign. Two years later his successor, Frank Hancock, reported to Congress that 60 of the 152 resettlement projects had been liquidated and that the remainder would soon be gone. Fourteen of 15 cooperative farming associations had been discontinued, and no loans were being made to cooperative associations. Most of the government-owned land controlled by the Farm Security Administration had been sold, and all long-term leases had been cancelled. Strict limits had been placed on the amount of money that could be loaned to individuals in the rural rehabilitation program. A year earlier, when a congressman asked Hancock why he had taken the job, Hancock replied: "I still have some humanity left in my soul."[29]

The Farm Security Administration was succeeded by the Farmers

Home Administration by an act approved by President Harry Truman on August 14, 1946. The law authorized the Secretary of Agriculture to make production and subsistence loans to farmers who could not secure credit elsewhere. These loans were in lieu of the emergency and rural rehabilitation loans made previously. The liquidation and disposal of rural-rehabilitation and resettlement projects and farm labor camps were to be completed. The law continued the tenant purchase program and authorized a program of insured farm mortgages (60 Stat. 1062). In the early 1980s the Farmers Home Administration was still carrying out these programs, with emphasis on low-cost loans to farmers who could not secure credit elsewhere, and was responsible for rural development.

The transformation of the Resettlement Administration to the Farm Security Administration and then to the Farmers Home Administration is a clear indication that as the farm crisis eased, the American people, as represented by the Congress, were unwilling to continue agricultural reform programs aimed at overturning or redirecting the traditional structure of the nation's agriculture. However, rural poverty is still to be eliminated even though literally millions of farmers and farm workers have left the country for the city, and many of the families who started out with rural rehabilitation and tenant purchase loans have firmly established themselves in farming. The author of a recent study critical of the programs as totally inadequate concedes that the Farm Security Administration did stabilize the best risks left on the land. Another historian concludes that Wallace saw rural reform in terms of promoting self-sustaining family-owned farms rather than in experimenting with collectivist types of organization.[30]

Both the agricultural adjustment and the rural resettlement programs were related to the problem of soil erosion. The situation was particularly alarming in the 1930s because a series of droughts centered in the Great Plains but reaching far to the East in 1936 had driven tens of thousands of families out of the Plains and had stripped irreplaceable topsoil from millions of acres. Wallace was concerned and kept President Roosevelt informed.[31]

Soil erosion was not a new problem. It had plagued parts of the nation from colonial times, but as long as there was cheap unsettled land to the west farmers gained economically by moving rather than by maintaining soil fertility and controlling erosion. Many reformers called for change. In 1928, Hugh Hammond Bennett, a Department of Agriculture soil scientist, pointed out in a circular called *Soil Erosion, A National Menace* that the problem was one facing the entire nation, not just the individual farmer. The next year, Congress appropriated funds to study the causes of soil erosion and methods for its control.

The new research program got underway at about the time of the New Deal and the first of several years of severe drought. Some of the earliest of the New Deal legislation and agencies— including the National Industrial Recovery Act, under which the Civilian Conservation Corps was established, and the Public Works Administration—established conservation programs using relief labor. The Public Works Administration funds financed the Soil Erosion Service, established in the Department of the Interior in 1933 under the direction of Bennett. After some political maneuvering the agency was transferred to the Department of Agriculture in 1935. On April 2, 1935, Bennett was testifying before the Senate Public Lands Committee on the need for a permanent program when the sky suddenly became dark with dust from the drought-stricken west. Nothing could have been more convincing. On April 27, 1935, Congress passed a law that became known as the Soil Conservation Act. This act declared soil erosion to be a national menace, established the soil conservation program on a permanent basis, and changed the name of the agency to the Soil Conservation Service. Secretary Wallace shifted the program from research and demonstration to working directly with farmers.[32]

President Roosevelt was interested in virtually all aspects of soil conservation. On April 23, 1935, he wrote to Alfred M. Landon regarding conditions in Kansas: "I fully realize the deep seriousness of the wind erosion problem and you can be sure that between now and next year we will use every effort to attack this unprecedented situation."[33]

Progress in persuading farmers to adopt soil conservation practices was slow. In 1939, some 200 million acres of cropland in use were subject to severe or moderate erosion, but conservation plans had been developed for only 39 million acres.[34] By 1980, only about 46 million acres of the 1 billion acres in farms were protected from soil erosion by soil conservation practices, although it must be noted that some farm land does not need such protection.

Another type of soil conservation program, operated by the Agricultural Adjustment Administration and its successor agencies, has existed side by side with the Soil Conservation Service's program. The Agricultural Conservation Program undertook cost-sharing conservation practices in direct cooperation with the farmers. These were often of a short-term rather than a long-term nature. Unfortunately, in spite of the continuing efforts made under these programs for fifty years, soil erosion is still a major threat to the soil of the nation.

Perhaps the most widely accepted of the New Deal farm programs was rural electrification. The campaign to electrify the farms came about because of the demonstrated unwillingness of the private utilities to furnish these services to most farmers. The question as to whether or not the federal government could undertake an effective program was answered when the Tennessee Valley Authority reached an agreement with a group of farmers and businessmen to supply electricity to a local cooperative that would be organized to work with rural people.

Shortly thereafter, Roosevelt created the Rural Electrification Administration (REA) by executive order. It was financed by money from a public works appropriation. At first an attempt was made to construct power lines with labor from relief rolls. However, this effort failed because of the skilled nature of the work. The basic responsibility was turned over to the cooperatives.[35]

The success of and competition from the rural electric cooperatives pushed some of the private power companies into more effort in the countryside. This sometimes took the form of a "spite" line, serving the more lucrative rural customers in the hope of heading off REA. In 1933, about one farm in ten had electric service. By 1941, 35 percent had service. After World War II, the program moved ahead again and by 1979, 99 percent were covered.[36]

The rural electrification program was one of the significant contributions of the New Deal to farmers and the nation. It made possible a fuller and more rewarding life on the farm.[37] However, it never succeeded in stemming the flow of people from the farms to cities, even though President Roosevelt wrote that an objective of the progam was to make farms and farming more attractive to present and future generations.[38]

The essential ingredient in the success of rural electrification was making loans at very low interest rates to local cooperatives. In fact, revising the entire structure of federally sponsored farm credit programs was one of the first of the New Deal actions to aid farmers.

A system of Land Banks had been established by Congress in 1916. This was followed in 1923 by the Federal Intermediate Credit Banks. While the credit banks had helped many farmers during the 1920s, they were not able to stem the forces of the Great Depression. During the early 1930s, farm foreclosures were becoming so widespread that the whole traditional system of land owning seemed threatened. On March 27, 1933, President Roosevelt established the Farm Credit Administration by executive order. All federal agencies dealing primarily with agricultural credit were consolidated into the new agency, both to maintain a sound program of cooperative agricultural credit and to achieve economy in administering the programs—a rather unusual justification by President Roosevelt. A week after issuing the executive order, Roosevelt asked Congress for legislation to provide for the refinancing of farm mortgages. By this time foreclosures were at a rate of about thirty-nine for each one thousand farms as compared with a rate of seventeen for each one thousand for the years 1926 to 1930. Congress complied by passing the Emergency Farm Mortgage Act of 1933, approved on May 12, 1933. This act was Title II of Public Law 10. Title I was the Agricultural Adjustment Act.[39]

When Roosevelt signed the bill, he urged creditors to delay foreclosures until applications for refinancing could be acted upon. The Reconstruction Finance Corporation was directed to make $200 million immediately available for refinancing. In general, creditors responded to the appeal, in part because some banks and insurance companies already had more farm land on hand than they wished to operate. From May 1, 1933, to September 3, 1937, federal land bank loans were made on about 540,000 farms—a loan on one farm out of every thirteen in the United States.[40]

Roosevelt never declared a moratorium on farm foreclosures. However, foreclosures during the year ending March 15, 1936, were only twenty per thousand as compared with thirty-nine per thousand in the spring of 1933. This record may have been due in some small part to the Frazier-Lemke Farm Mortgage Act, signed by the President on June 28, 1934. This law stopped foreclosures, but was shortly declared unconstitutional. A new Frazier-Lemke Act was approved on August 28, 1935. It delayed but did not stop foreclosures.[41]

According to Roosevelt, the farm debt refinancing program of the Farm Credit Administration provided assistance to the whole recovery program by, first, enabling farmers to rearrange their debts so that they could meet their obligations, and, second, by paying off existing creditors so that a vast amount of money was released into circulation as increased purchasing power.[42]

Increasing the purchasing power of Americans was a key to reducing surpluses, but until this happened, other steps were necessary. In the 1930s the nation faced a paradox of hungry people and surplus food. To some, it seemed that the problem was underconsumption rather than surplus. The White House called it "one of the most flagrant maladjustments of American economic well-being."[43]

When the Department of Agriculture began to purchase surplus hogs for slaughter in 1933, public questions were raised about the possible destruction of food when people were hungry. Wallace quickly made arrangements to ship the hogs to slaughter houses, where the usable meat was canned or smoked. It was then turned over to the Relief Administration for distribution. President Roosevelt announced an expansion of the food distribution program on September 21, 1933. On October 4, 1933, the Federal Surplus Relief Corporation, later the Federal Surplus Commodities Corporation, was organized to handle the work. From its organization through December 23, 1935, the Corporation distributed about 281,000 carloads of commodities.[44]

On August 24, 1935, President Roosevelt approved a series of amendments to the Agricultural Adjustment Act. These included, as Section 32, a provision appropriating an amount equal to 30 percent of the customs receipts to encourage the domestic consumption and export of agricultural commodities. For almost fifty years, this has remained a financial base for programs to purchase and distribute surplus commodities. In recent years, however, purchases with these funds have generally been limited to perishable commodities.

Surplus commodities were distributed to school lunch programs, some of which were operated as work relief projects by the Works Progress Administration. Then in 1939, the Federal

Surplus Commodities Corporation undertook a marked expansion of the school lunch program, making it a major outlet for surplus foods. A school milk program was started in 1940, using Section 32 funds.

Helpful as they were, these programs did not solve the farm income and city underconsumption problems. Early in 1938, Frederick V. Waugh, an agricultural economist in the Department, wrote a memorandum to Secretary Wallace proposing a graduated price program to increase the consumption of surplus foods. The idea appealed to Wallace on both humanitarian and practical grounds. He began to discuss it, calling it a two-price system whereby low-income families would be able to buy more of the food they needed through the regular channels of trade by paying a lower than regular price.[45]

After careful planning by Wallace and the Department, working with the organized food trade and congressional leaders, the food stamp program was announced. Under the plan, families receiving public assistance would be able to obtain food stamps that would provide them food for substantially less than the usual price. The plan began on an experimental basis on May 16, 1939, and soon came to be very useful. World War II brought it to an end.[46]

By the 1950s, many farm products were again in surplus, and many Americans were existing below the poverty level, unable to buy needed food. The Department of Agriculture began donating surplus foods to states and counties that were willing to distribute them.

During the 1960s, the question of ending hunger in America came to the fore, with many studies showing needs that were not being met. There was even a hunger march on Washington, centered on the Department. After considerable controversy, the direct distribution program was substantially enlarged and a new food stamp program was begun.[47]

On January 11, 1971, new food stamp legislation was approved. The direct distribution of food to individuals was discontinued except for such special programs as the cheese distribution of 1982. Food stamps became the principal vehicle for attempting to assure every American an adequate diet. Thus, a program dating from the early New Deal of providing food to needy people while reducing agricultural surpluses has become a cornerstone of America's programs for assisting the poor, the dis-

advantaged, and the unemployed. Not long after the food distribution programs began, Secretary Wallace wrote, "Not many
people realized how radical it was—this idea of having the
Government buy from those who had too much, in order to give
to those who had too little."[48]

The New Deal programs, then, ranged from those increasing
farm income to those distributing food to the poor and unemployed. The major programs becoming effective between 1933
and 1940 were price support and production adjustment, crop
insurance, disaster relief, resettling farmers from poor land and
aiding tenants to acquire farms, soil conservation, rural electrification, farm credit, and food distribution. All of these programs,
with one exception, are still in effect. The exception is the
program for resettling farmers from poor land and aiding tenants
to acquire farms. However, today's program to provide credit at
reasonable rates and terms for those in rural America who are
unable to get credit from other sources is a direct descendant of
the earlier program.

This complex of New Deal programs appears to have met the
immediate goals of President Roosevelt and Secretary Wallace.
While campaigning in 1932, Roosevelt said that the root of the
economic problems of the nation lay in the lack of equality for
agriculture. While the New Deal programs did not bring farmers
to full equality, they moved a long way in that direction.[49]

Wallace felt by 1936 that the economic programs had been
essential. The most significant contribution, though, was a
change in outlook among farmers, with the old defeatist attitudes
rapidly disappearing.[50]

In 1961, Wallace gave a notable address at the Department of
Agriculture in Washington, in his first return to public life
since 1948. He reviewed the New Deal farm programs, giving an
assessment of several of them. As he said early in his talk, the
situation was so desperate in 1933 that more than one approach
was required to meet his goal of restoring the farm economy.
The Agricultural Adjustment and Soil Conservation programs
were valuable, but, as Wallace put it, "Saving of physical resources
is not an end in itself and cannot be accomplished without
saving the people on the land." Through the rural rehabilitation
and tenant purchase programs, marked progress was made in
conserving human as well as natural resources. The Rural Electrification Administration was another agency of major impor-

tance in raising the standard of living of farm people. Only half of the farm problem, though, was to be found on the farm. The other half consisted of the plight of city consumers. Wallace saw the food stamp plan and the school lunch program as two of the most promising devices used to enable the disadvantaged to buy adequate food at market prices. Wallace concluded his assessment by expressing his philosophical approach to agriculture: "Scientific understanding is our joy. Economic and political understanding is our duty. Our objective is the understanding of life in all its varied levels."[51]

In considering the stated views of President Roosevelt during the New Deal and of Secretary Henry A. Wallace during the same period and later, one can conclude that both were primarily interested in restoring the farm economy. They did not plan to change the basic structure of American agriculture, even though they supported efforts to improve the lot of the most depressed, including sharecroppers and other tenants, migrant laborers, and drought victims. When some of these efforts ran into strong opposition, particularly in the Congress, neither Roosevelt nor Wallace risked their overall programs by giving all-out support to the more controversial reform measures.

The New Deal was successful in maintaining the basic structure of American agriculture. Critics say that the nation missed a unique opportunity to truly reform American agriculture and to ensure the continued existence of a large number of small or medium-sized, family-owned-and-operated farms. Instead, the economic restoration of the existing system provided the base for the rapid changes that took place after World War II, marked by a sharp decline in the number of farms and in the farm population. Others say that these trends had been in evidence since World War I, with changes slowed by the Depression and then accelerated by World War II. The programs were effective in ensuring that the countryside did not move into armed revolt and that farm ownership did not suddenly become concentrated in banks, insurance companies, and other creditors. The programs were diverse and were aimed at easing a number of problems. They were carried out by a Department which, under the leadership of Henry A. Wallace, was one of the best administered agencies in the federal government during the New Deal period.[52] That these programs, controversial as some of them were, met a national need is seen in the fact that they have survived, fundamentally unchanged, for fifty years.

1. Wayne D. Rasmussen, "The Mechanization of Agriculture," *Scientific American* 247, no. 3 (September 1982): 77-89.

2. U.S. Congress, Senate Committee on Agriculture and Forestry, *Hearings . . . Agricultural Adjustment Relief Plan*, 73d Cong., 1st sess., 1933.

3. American Farm Bureau Federation, *Official News Letter*, Washington, D.C., March 9, 1933.

4. Henry A. Wallace, *New Frontiers* (New York: Reynall and Hitchcock, 1934), pp. 162-64.

5. American Farm Bureau Federation, *Official News Letter*, Washington, D.C., March 21, 1933.

6. Theodore Saloutos, *The American Farmer and the New Deal* (Ames: Iowa State University Press, 1982), pp. 44-46.

7. Franklin Delano Roosevelt to the Congress of the United States, Mar. 16, 1933, National Archives, Record Group 16.

8. Franklin Delano Roosevelt, *Public Papers and Addresses*, vol. 2 (New York: Random House, 1938), p. 79.

9. Irvin M. May, Jr., *Marvin Jones: The Public Life of an Agrarian Advocate* (College Station: Texas A&M University Press, 1980), pp. 101-4.

10. Henry A. Wallace to Marvin Jones, Mar. 20, 1933, and H. A. Wallace to Nils Olsen, Mar. 6, 1933, National Archives, Record Group 16; and Richard Lowitt, ed., *Journal of a Tamed Bureaucrat* (Ames: Iowa State University Press, 1980), pp. 151-57.

11. Gilbert C. Fite, *George N. Peek and the Fight for Farm Parity* (Norman: University of Oklahoma Press), ch. 15.

12. Gladys L. Baker, "And to Act for the Secretary: Paul H. Appleby and the Department of Agriculture, 1933-1940," *Agricultural History* 45 (October 1971): 246-51.

13. Roy V. Scott and J.G. Shoalmire, *The Public Career of Cully A. Cobb: A Study in Agricultural Leadership* (Jackson: University and College Press of Mississippi, 1973), ch. 8.

14. Mordecai Ezekiel to the Secretary, Mar. 5, 1935, National Archives, Record Group 145.

15. David E. Conrad, *The Forgotten Farmers: The Story of Sharecroppers in the New Deal* (Urbana: University of Illinois Press, 1965), p. 209.

16. Pete Daniel, "The Transformation of the Rural South 1930 to the Present," *Agricultural History* 55 (July 1981): 234.

17. Quoted in Gladys L. Baker et al., *Century of Service: The First 100 Years of the United States Department of Agriculture* (Washington, D.C.: Centennial Committee, U.S. Department of Agriculture, 1963), p. 165.

18. Mordecai Ezekiel to Henry A. Wallace, Feb. 5, 1936, National Archives, Record Group 16.

19. Roosevelt, *Public Papers and Addresses*, vol. 5, p. 95.

20. Henry A. Wallace, "Definition of the Ever Normal Granary," *Agricul-

tural Situation 14, no. 2 (February 1937): 9.

21. Baker, *Century of Service*, pp. 140-41, 178-81, 298-99, 333, 369, 397.

22. Rexford G. Tugwell, "The Resettlement Idea," *Agricultural History* 33 (October 1959): 159-67; and Roosevelt, *Public Papers and Addresses*, vol. 4, pp. 143-55.

23. Saloutos, *American Farmer and the New Deal*, pp. 150-63.

24. Wayne D. Rasmussen, *The History of the Emergency Farm Labor Supply Program, 1943-47*, Agriculture Monograph No. 13 (Washington, D.C.: U.S. Department of Agriculture, September 1951), pp. 10-11, 176-185.

25. Franklin D. Roosevelt to John H. Bankhead, Sept. 17, 1936, National Archives, Record Group 16.

26. Baker, *Century of Service*, pp. 204-5, 211-12; U.S. Department of Agriculture, Press Release Nos. 1060-37, Jan. 23, 1937.

27. U.S. Special Committee on Farm Tenancy, *Farm Tenancy, Report of the President's Committee* (Washington, D.C.: U.S. Government Printing Office, 1937), pp. 11-12.

28. Sidney Baldwin, *Poverty and Politics*, pp. 383-400; Saloutos, *American Farmer and the New Deal*, pp. 164-78.

29. U.S. Congress, House Committee on Appropriations, *Hearings . . . Agricultural Appropriation, 1946*, 79th Cong., 1st sess., 1945, pp. 508-22; *Hearings . . . Agricultural Appropriation, 1945*, 78th Cong., 2d sess., 1944, p. 1001.

30. Daniel, "Transformation of the Rural South," p. 237; and Edward L. Schapsmeier and Frederick H. Schapsmeier, *Henry A. Wallace of Iowa: The Agrarian Years, 1910-1940* (Ames: Iowa State University Press, 1968), p. 206.

31. H. A. Wallace to the President, May 10, 1934, National Archives, Records Group 16.

32. Wayne D. Rasmussen, "History of Soil Conservation, Institutions and Incentives," in *Soil Conservation Policies, Institutions, and Incentives*, ed. H. G. Halcrow, E. O. Heady, and M. L. Cotner (Ankeny, Iowa: Soil Conservation Society of America, 1981), pp. 5-8; Baker, *Century of Service*, pp. 190-200.

33. Franklin D. Roosevelt to Alfred M. Landon, Apr. 23, 1935, Franklin D. Roosevelt Library, OF732 (Soil Erosion).

34. Saloutos, *American Farmer and the New Deal*, p. 258.

35. H. S. Person, "The Rural Electrification Administration in Perspective," *Agricultural History* 24 (April 1950): 70-89.

36. D. Clayton Brown, *Electricity for Rural America* (Westport, Conn.: Greenwood Press, 1980).

37. Saloutos, *American Farmer and the New Deal*, pp. 220-21.

38. Roosevelt, *Public Papers and Addresses*, vol. 4, pp. 172-75.

39. W. Gifford Hoag, *The Farm Credit System* (Danville, Ill.: Interstate Printers and Publishers, 1976), pp. 1-2.

40. Roosevelt, *Public Papers and Addresses*, vol. 2, pp. 84-90, 100-102, 180-83.

41. Ernest Feder, "Farm Debt Adjustments during the Depression—The Other Side of the Coin," *Agricultural History* 35 (April 1961): 78-81.

42. Roosevelt, *Public Papers and Addresses*, vol. 3, pp. 331-33.

43. Roosevelt, *Public Papers and Addresses*, vol. 2, pp. 361, 370-71.

44. Baker, *Century of Service*, pp. 181-83.

45. Frederick V. Waugh to the Secretary, Jan. 21, 1938, Files, Agricultural History Branch, Economic Research Service, USDA.

46. Baker, *Century of Service*, pp. 183-84.

47. Wayne D. Rasmussen and Gladys L. Baker, *The Department of Agriculture* (New York: Praeger Publishers, 1972) pp. 135-59; Don F. Hadwiger, "The Freeman Administration and the Poor," *Agricultural History* 45 (January 1971): 21-32.

48. Wallace, *New Frontiers*, pp. 183-84.

49. Roosevelt, *Public Papers and Addresses*, vol. 1, p. 697.

50. H.A. Wallace to R. M. Evans, May 26, 1936, National Archives, Records Group 16.

51. Henry A. Wallace, "The Department As I Have Known It," in *Growth Through Agricultural Progress*, ed. Wayne D. Rasmussen (Washington, D.C.: USDA Graduate School, 1961), pp. 25-31.

52. John M. Gaus, *Public Administration and the United States Department of Agriculture* (Chicago: Public Administration Service, 1940), pp. 91-93, 277-88, 378-86; Baker, "And to Act for the Secretary," pp. 235-58; and Theda Skocpol and Kenneth Finegold, "State Capacity and Economic Intervention in the Early New Deal," *Political Science Quarterly* 97 (Summer 1982): 255-78.

Henry A. Wallace as Agricultural Secretary and Agrarian Reformer

Edward L. Schapsmeier
Frederick H. Schapsmeier

In March of 1933 a former Republican from Iowa by the name of Henry Agard Wallace was to make his appearance on the stage of history as Secretary of Agriculture in the newly formed cabinet of President Franklin D. Roosevelt. While virtually unknown to the national media, the Wallace name was a household word among the rural population of the Midwest. They knew him as a crusading editor of the journal *Wallaces' Farmer* who championed federal relief for agriculture, gave expert advice on farming, espoused his own brand of agrarianism, and sermonized about the need for universal social justice.

Through his role in the formulation and implementation of the Agricultural Adjustment Act of 1933, the Soil Conservation and Domestic Allotment Act of 1936, and the Agricultural Adjustment Act of 1938, Wallace helped create an enormous economic infrastructure whose nucleus still exists. There is no doubt that Wallace contributed mightily to the shift away from free market farming to one managed in part by the federal government. In achieving this goal Wallace helped forge a welfare state for farmers. From the perspective of the present, it is indeed his primary legacy to this nation's history.

The permanency of this legacy, since it was conceived when different economic problems were in existence, depends in large measure upon the fate of the welfare state itself. Can it survive the dangers of deficit spending and high inflation? Will it be replaced by a New Federalism and decentralization or, on the other hand, evolve into full-scale socialism with increased government centralization? Only time will tell.

The role Henry A. Wallace played in the New Deal was threefold. First, he contributed to the pool of ideas that constituted the basis for much of the New Deal farm legislation and then helped to convince Franklin D. Roosevelt it was the best legislative basis for alleviating the economic hardships faced by farmers during the desperate days of the Great Depression. Second, he was an important factor in influencing the social, economic, and political orientation of the farmer in order to ensure rural acceptance of federal involvement in agricultural matters. Finally, he helped to gain passage of legislation intended to benefit farmers and successfully implemented massive agricultural programs never before attempted in the United States. Another significant achievement, although parallel to and aside from Wallace's political activity and administrative endeavors, was his personal contribution to the cause of scientific farming. Wallace's prowess as a geneticist and econometrician was significant in terms of giving impetus to a green revolution that may yet feed the world's growing population.

By the time Henry A. Wallace departed permanently from the political scene in 1950, he was perceived by most of the electorate, ironically, as a renegade New Deal radical more in tune with urban causes than those of agriculture. Yet his agrarianism was deep-seated and fundamental to his socioeconomic mode of thinking. The origin of Wallace's political ideology stemmed from his rural background, the teachings of his grandfather (the venerable "Uncle Henry"), and his long association with agriculturalists and rural reform movements. Uncle Henry, an appellation he used as owner and editor of his farm journal, *Wallaces' Farmer*, referred to the first Henry Wallace. He was the venerable patriarch of the family. He was a former clergyman, onetime farmer, and an astute student of scientific farming. The elder Wallace viewed the rural population as society's moral leaven and was sure the yeoman farmers were God's chosen people a la Jefferson's agrarian credo. He instilled in young Henry the need to serve as a champion of the rural sector in order to secure needed reforms on its behalf. In sociotheological terms the old man taught his grandson that the time had come to modify the older, individualistic Protestant work ethic with spiritual tenets drawn from the new and more relevant Social Gospel. This had to be achieved so that the divisive competition among farmers might be replaced with attitudes that promoted mutual cooperation. In this manner, the eldest Wallace believed, rural America would become the model for a society that could evolve into a Christian commonwealth where social justice was a universal reality.[1]

Upon the foundation of this agrarian oriented, religio-economic paradigm, Henry A. Wallace added certain Progressive concepts he acquired on his own. From his reading of the works of economist Thorstein Veblen, Wallace became cognizant of the fact that prices in the supposedly laissez-faire market actually could be manipulated by what Veblen called "sabotage" (i.e., deliberate curtailment of production). He also became aware that while the business community deliberately reduced output only to increase profits, social scientists (technocrats, engineers, economists, and social planners) could, according to Veblen, manage the economy for the good of the general welfare. Wallace also accepted Veblen's dictum that free trade would promote international peace by fostering mutually interdependent economies on a world scale.[2]

Henry A. Wallace set about to apply the tenets of Veblen's institutional economics to agriculture. In Wallace's first book, *Agricultural Prices* (1920), he sought a means to eliminate the existence of price-depressing commodity surpluses. He recommended that the federal government establish a Price Publicity Committee, composed of farm economists, for the purpose of determining profitable levels of production for major agricultural commodities and, in turn, advising farmers when it was necessary to reduce total output. Farmers were urged to cooperate with one another instead of competing. This shift away from individualism to collective action would, ostensibly, benefit all of them economically. Wallace also advised moving away from high tariffs to a policy of reciprocal trade. This would, in his estimation, help dispose of farm surpluses abroad while simultaneously fostering world peace.[3]

During the 1920s Wallace was involved in the McNary-Haugen movement. Congressional members of the Farm Bloc, who were the key element in the movement, sought enactment of the McNary-Haugen Bill. It would authorize the creation of the Federal Farm Board, which was supposed to promote the overseas sale of agricultural commodities and thus lessen the negative impact of farm surpluses on the domestic market. Under the leadership of Henry Cantwell Wallace, who was H. A.'s father and then Secretary of Agriculture, Congress was induced to pass the McNary-Haugen Bill twice only to have it vetoed both times by President Calvin Coolidge.[4]

By the early thirties Henry A. Wallace was looking for another alternative farm program when he learned of the Voluntary Domestic Allotment Plan (VDAP) of Professor M. L. Wilson of Montana State University. The primary emphasis of this scheme was to have the Department of Agriculture, through a newly created government agency, determine and assign to participating farmers legally binding acreage allotments for all basic agricultural commodities. The major objective was to reduce overall production and thereby prevent the accretion of surpluses. This policy of induced scarcity, ostensibly, would reduce the total output in order to keep commodity prices high. Via editorials in *Wallaces' Farmer*, and by speaking out at numerous agricultural conferences, Wallace widely publicized the alleged merits of the VDAP in farm circles all over the country. Through his contacts with Rexford G. Tugwell (then an economist at Columbia University and a member of the Brain Trust) and Henry Morgenthau, Jr. (a farm editor at the time and FDR's Hyde Park neighbor), Wallace helped persuade the 1932 Democratic presidential nominee to accept the VDAP as a proposal upon which to campaign for rural votes. In his key farm speech, delivered at Topeka, Kansas, on September 14, Franklin D. Roosevelt committed himself to the VDAP as a means of alleviating the economic plight of the nation's farmers.[5] It subsequently became the heart of the Agricultural Adjustment Act of 1933.

When the time came for FDR to name a Secretary of Agriculture, the agricultural establishment (consisting of economists, rural editors, and heads of farm organizations) tended to favor the appointment of Henry A. Wallace to this post. Dr. John D. Black, Professor of Agricultural Economics at Harvard University, eloquently summarized the viewpoint of this group. In a letter to President-elect Roosevelt, he wrote:

> In considering the usefulness of various persons for the job of Secretary of Agriculture, you may be interested to know that those of the circle of agricultural economists, in which I am included, consider Mr. Henry A. Wallace well qualified. Personally, I have had much contact with Mr. Wallace's work ever since 1921, and I have followed his thinking closely.

I have thought almost from the beginning that surely Mr. Wallace would be Secretary of Agriculture someday. A person with his ability, his great familiarity with the intimate problems of agriculture, his heritage and his connections could expect no other fate. It seems to me to be the opportune time for Mr. Wallace to render his predestined great service to American agriculture.[6]

Utilizing a Farm Bloc coalition in Congress, whose members were from the Midwest and South (the so-called marriage of corn and cotton plus Western wheat growers), Wallace spent long days testifying and lobbying for enactment of the Agricultural Adjustment Act of 1933. Although he had no previous experience shepherding legislation through Congress, Wallace worked adroitly with Representative Marvin Jones (D-Tex.) and Senator Ellison D. ("Cotton Ed") Smith (D-S.C.). Both of these legislators were rustic agrarians and pragmatic politicians who maneuvered skillfully to get a comprehensive farm bill that would satisfy all segments of the agricultural community. As idealistic as Wallace's rhetoric might be on the stump, he was realistic and practical when it came to legislative compromise. The final version of the measure included some amendments Wallace did not desire, but Title I of the law set up the Agricultural Adjustment Administration (AAA). It would be the function of the AAA to carry out the provisions of the domestic allotment plan.[7]

Under the Triple-A program, farmers who joined (and practically all of them did) were given acreage allotments for basic crops. If farmers complied, they became eligible for government price support payments. The latter were based on a parity ratio of 52 percent. The milk and cheese production of dairy farmers was controlled by marketing agreements. An excise tax was levied on food processors (who passed it on to consumers) to pay for the federal subsidies given to farmers. The Supreme Court invalidated this tax in the famous Butler case, much to Wallace's chagrin; thus, after 1936 the funding came from the general treasury or was financed by deficit spending. County Committees, composed of farmers who were elected by their neighbors, had the task of ensuring compliance. Considering the magnitude of the overall program it was an outstanding administrative feat by Wallace to oversee its implementation. Due to his expertise in agriculture, the AAA worked while the

New Deal companion National Recovery Administration soon showed signs of disintegrating. [8]

An important federal agency Wallace induced FDR to create by executive order was the Commodity Credit Corporation (CCC). The CCC was still another governmental device for preventing agricultural commodities from glutting the markets. This invariably happened after the fall harvest season, when the collective output of the nation's farmers created a deluge of such farm products as corn, wheat, and cotton. Wallace got the idea for the CCC from the Joseph Plan of the Old Testament. He later dubbed it the Ever Normal Granary. To carry out the main goal, namely, that of preventing a sharp autumn drop in farm income, the government would utilize planned storage to keep agricultural commodities off the market until such time as it would be economically advantageous to farmers to dispose of it. Farmers were given nonrecourse loans for their stored crops. Storage was made available in CCC elevators or, at times, farmers were paid to keep it on their own farms (as in the case of placing corn in cribs).

Farmers had the enviable choices of letting the CCC keep their commodity if the market price fell below the loan figure or of selling the crop, paying back the loan, and pocketing the profit if prices were above the loan value. This mechanism was made the focal point of the Agricultural Adjustment Act of 1938. It put Wallace in good stead with FDR when the nation went to war in 1941 with huge food reserves on hand. In fact, the concept of stockpiling was emulated in other areas.

During World War II the Triple-A machinery was reversed from its policy of reducing production to one of increasing it. [9] Price supports were raised from 52 percent of parity to a high, rigid 90 percent (and even 100 percent on some commodities) to induce greater output. This policy was continued until 1948, when the Republican-controlled Eightieth Congress set price supports at a flexible rate of from 75 to 90 percent of parity.

Having won the rural vote in 1948 by accusing the GOP of sticking a pitchfork in the backs of farmers, President Harry S. Truman got the Democrat-controlled Congress to raise price supports back up to 90 percent of parity. The number of commodities to be covered was also enlarged, including the addition of perishables. A two-year program for potatoes alone, for example, cost the taxpayers one-half-billion dollars before it was discontinued.[10] By the time Dwight D. Eisenhower occupied the White House in 1953, the CCC held over a billion dollars' worth of stored commodities with another three billion dollars' worth under loan. These reserves were costly to store, some stocks were deteriorating, and the net effect was to depress prices. Ike's Agriculture Secretary, Ezra Taft Benson, had to fight hard just to get the price support figure reduced to 82½ percent of parity.

Through the Agricultural Trade and Expansion Act of 1954 (PL480—later dubbed Food for Peace), huge surplus stocks were sold abroad or given away as foreign aid to underdeveloped countries. Despite Benson's herculean efforts, the avalanche of food kept pouring into CCC storage facilities. Despite smaller acreage allotments, production kept increasing due to widespread use of hybrid seed, chemical fertilizers, herbicides, and pesticides. Even though he was an advocate of free market agriculture, Benson had to resort to the Soil Bank. Enacted in 1956, it sought to prevent surpluses by taking some fertile and much marginal land completely out of production.[11] Subsequent presidential administrations have also been plagued with the inevitable accretion of agricultural surpluses. Even the Reagan Administration, despite its low-price-support policy, found itself in a position of having to give away cheese and butter to make way for new supplies. The one sector of the economy that suffers economically from its successes, ironically, is the farm community. Thus it was during the thirties and so it remains today.

From our contemporary vantage point, Henry A. Wallace's many books and writings appear dated due to the distinct emotional tone generated by the Great Depression. In them he defined New Deal liberalism in highly idealistic terms. In their totality they did, no doubt, exert a positive influence on the voters of that time. In *New Frontiers*, written in 1934, Wallace defended the New Deal as the necessary means to attain economic planning so that social and economic reforms might be achieved. The "Old Frontier," as he defined it, was the past period of rugged individualism and laissez-faire capitalism. The "New Frontier," in contrast, was a forthcoming era of an evolving welfare state (later called "progressive capitalism") where true "economic democracy" (i.e., social justice) would become a reality. He described the New Deal in rhetorical terms that were unabashedly idealistic, Social Gospel oriented, and which contained elements of agrarianism. Wallace was not above quoting Isaiah of the Old Testament, Uncle Henry, or FDR as if all were coequals in their advocacy of social justice. Using a religious idiom, Henry A. Wallace claimed the New Deal would usher into existence the "Kingdom of God" on earth where the "general welfare" would be fostered by the federal government so as to guarantee economic security for every American.[12]

In his unique and forceful style Wallace reiterated his vision of a new society in numerous other works. These included *Statesmanship and Religion* (1934), *America Must Choose* (1934), *Whose Constitution, An Inquiry into the General Welfare* (1936), *Technology, Corporations, and the General Welfare* (1937), and *Paths to Plenty* (1938).

FDR personally chose Henry Wallace to be his vice-presidential running mate in 1940. This was done against the wishes of many Democratic leaders who believed the Iowan was far too visionary and idealistic to be in a position where he might well become Roosevelt's successor. However, Wallace's status as a highly visible New Deal philosopher and his record as an able administrator were beyond question.[13] FDR sought to make use of Wallace's talent by appointing him, first, head of the Supply Priorities and Allocation Board, and then Chairman of the Board of Economic Warfare (BEW). Thus, Wallace was the first Vice-President to have an executive function in addition to his constitutional prerogatives. Wallace would surely have been renominated for the Vice-Presidency in 1944 had he not antagonized Roosevelt in 1943 by getting himself involved in a bitter public dispute with Commerce Secretary Jesse Jones over problems that existed between the BEW and the Reconstruction Finance Corporation.[14]

As the Vice-President, Wallace began to envision an extension of the New Deal on a global basis. His views were contained in the following books written during World War II: *Price of Free World Victory* (1942), *The Century of the Common Man* (1943), *Christian Bases of World Order* (1943), *Our Job in the Pacific* (1944), and *Soviet Asia Mission* (1945). The United States, asserted Wallace, was to be the leader of the "Free World" to promote international peace within the context of the United Nations. Furthermore it was to seek attainment of Roosevelt's Four Freedoms on a worldwide basis. Reciprocal trade, postwar cooperation with the Soviet Union, and promotion of the general welfare for all people on an international scale were to replace high tariffs, spheres of influence, and armed alliances. Wallace believed that by making practical application of science (including atomic energy) and motivating people by the spiritual principles enunciated in the Sermon on the Mount, world peace and universal abundance were in the offing. The new world order conceived by Wallace was even more grandiose than the one envisioned by Franklin D. Roosevelt.[15]

After Franklin D. Roosevelt passed from the scene in 1945, the leftwing element of the Democratic Party regarded Wallace as the chief spokesman for New Deal liberalism and an altruistic internationalism based upon amicable relations with the Soviet Union. As Commerce Secretary in the cabinet of Harry S. Truman, Wallace continually championed the expansion of New Deal policies. In his book *Sixty Million Jobs* (1945), he argued for passage of the Full Employment Bill (it became the Employment Act of 1946) to ensure federal intervention into the economy when needed to make sure there were jobs available for all. Concerned over what he believed to be U.S. blame for heightening Cold War tensions, Wallace opposed Truman's "get tough" policy with regard to the Soviet Union. After being fired from the cabinet and taking a position as editor of *The New Republic*, Wallace challenged Truman's containment policy but seldom criticized the expansionism of Russia. In his *Toward World Peace* (1948) he advocated patient cooperation with Joseph Stalin, sharing atomic secrets with the Soviets, unilateral disarmament, and wholehearted support for the United Nations.

Running as presidential candidate of the Progressive Party in 1948, Wallace alienated most Democrats and, as well, was seen by a large segment of the voting public as an apologist for Soviet imperialism. It was only after the onset of the Korean War in 1950, in which he supported U.N.-U.S. participation, that Wallace admitted he had misjudged the intentions of the Communist leaders.[16]

Parallel to Wallace's lifelong endeavors to engender the reform spirit in America was his work as a scientist. In 1925 Wallace founded the Pioneer Hi-Bred Corn Company to sell commercially the hybrid seed corn he personally had developed. In that same year he coauthored *Correlation and Machine Calculation* to foster the use of statistical correlation studies to develop new techniques for improving agronomy and farm management. Later in life, when he resumed his work in genetics, he also coauthored the study *Corn and Its Early Fathers* (1956). Before he died Wallace developed other hybrids for underdeveloped countries, thus helping to forestall the famine that haunts many peoples of this earth. Even while dying of amyotrophic lateral sclerosis (Lou Gehrig disease) in 1965, Henry Wallace allowed medical researchers to conduct experiments on his pain-racked body so that he might make one last contribution to science and humanity.[17]

In retrospect it is obvious that Henry A. Wallace made a considerable impact upon agriculture. The farm programs he helped forge into existence still remain, although in amended and modified form. The federal government still gives farmers deficiency payments (price supports) to make up the difference between target prices and those of the marketplace if they agree to crop set-asides (acreage allotments). But forces unforeseen by Wallace have made it much more difficult for this system to assist farmers, especially those with small farms.[18]

In the 1930s the circumstances surrounding rural life were far different than now. Farmers constituted 25 percent of the nation's population, the scale of farming was smaller, retail food prices were relatively low, taxes were low, cheap land existed, interest rates ranged from 1 to 2 percent and the country suffered from deflation. In the 1980s farmers constituted only about 3 percent of the nation's population, large-scale agribusiness came into being, retail food prices were high (due among other things to widespread unionization of labor), taxes were high, land prices went sky high, interest rates rose dramatically, and the country suffered from inflation. Although Henry Wallace and others in the New Deal era faced farm problems of the Great Depression with great verve and imagination, their formulas are inadequate for present conditions. Salvaging small farms today is tantamount to subsidizing Mom and Dad stores to prevent them from succumbing to the competition of supermarkets. The huge outlay of capital needed for farming at present makes the small-scale unit obsolete.[19] It also seems repugnant in this day and age to pay farmers for not producing, when food is needed for the world's exploding population. Likewise, intensive cultivation using fertilizers, pesticides, and herbicides encouraged by acreage allotments has led to serious ecological problems such as water pollution and soil depletion. Also, a national debt in excess of one trillion dollars requires a drastic reduction of deficit spending.

In contemporary rural America, small towns are disappearing at a fast rate. Farming is big business and no longer reflects the old agrarian way of life. The very rural rhetoric uttered by Henry Wallace seems archaic now. Yet in the judgment of the authors, Wallace, who was born and reared in the heartland of America, influenced agriculture as few persons before or after him. In 1968 we wrote, "In the span of his lifetime, the agrarian years represent the finest hour of Wallace's presence on the stage of history. In the final evaluation the place of Henry A. Wallace as the nation's greatest Secretary of Agriculture seems secure."[20] With the possible exception of the dubious wisdom of introducing commodity cartels with the International Wheat Agreement of 1933 (to be emulated by OPEC), nothing has happened subsequently to alter this assessment.

1. Summarized from our *Henry A. Wallace of Iowa: The Agrarian Years, 1910-1940* (Ames: Iowa State University Press, 1968), chapter 15, "The First Henry Wallace: Preacher, Publisher, and Patriarch." For more information on the first Henry Wallace's life and philosophy, see his memoirs, *Uncle Henry's Own Story of His Life, Personal Reminiscences* (Des Moines: Wallaces' Publishing Company, 1919). See also Edward L Schapsmeier and Frederick H. Schapsmeier, "The Wallaces and Their Farm Paper: A Story of Agrarian Leadership," *Journalism Quarterly*, 44 (Summer 1967): 289-96.

2. Specific books by Thorstein Veblen that influenced Wallace's thinking were: *An Inquiry into the Nature of Peace and the Terms of Its Perpetuation* (New York and London: Macmillan Company, 1917); *The Theory of Business Enterprise* (New York: Charles Scribner's Sons, 1932); and *The Theory of the Leisure Class: An Economic Study of Institutions* (New York: Modern Library, 1931).

3. Summarized from *Henry A. Wallace of Iowa*, chapter 3, "Agricultural Economics: Prelude to Politics."

4. Summarized from *Henry A. Wallace of Iowa*, chapter 7, "McNary-Haugenism: The Battle Cry of the Farmers' Fight for Federal Relief." See also Edward L. Schapsmeier and Frederick H. Schapsmeier, "Disharmony in the Harding Cabinet: The Hoover-Wallace Conflict," *Ohio History* (Summer 1966): 126-36; and Donald L. Winters, *Henry Cantwell Wallace as Secretary of Agriculture, 1921-1925* (Urbana: University of Illinois Press, 1970).

5. Summarized from *Henry A. Wallace of Iowa*, chapter 10, "Roosevelt and Rural Leaders: The Democrats Adopt the Domestic Allotment Plan." See also Bernard Sternsher, *Rexford Tugwell and the New Deal* (New Brunswick: Rutgers University Press, 1964), 144-64; and Raymond Moley, *The First New Deal* (New York: Harcourt, Brace and World, 1966), 70-79.

6. Quoted in *Henry A. Wallace of Iowa*, 160.

7. Summarized from *Henry A. Wallace of Iowa*, chapter 11, "The New Deal for the Farmer: The First AAA and the Emergency Phase of Agricultural Recovery." See also Edward L. Schapsmeier and Frederick H. Schapsmeier, "Farm Policy from FDR to Eisenhower: Southern Democrats and the Politics of Agriculture," *Agricultural History* 53 (January 1979): 352-71; and Irwin M. May, Jr., *Marvin Jones: The Public Life of an Agrarian Advocate* (College Station: Texas A&M Press, 1980), 98-125.

8. Edward L. Schapsmeier and Frederick H. Schapsmeier, "Henry A. Wallace: Agrarian Idealist or Agricultural Realist?" *Agricultural History* 51 (April 1967): 133-36.

9. Summarized from *Henry A. Wallace of Iowa*, chapter 15, "Agricultural Statesmanship: The Ever-Normal Granary and the 1938 Agricultural Adjustment Act." See also Derke Bodde, "Henry A. Wallace and the Ever-Normal Granary," *Far Eastern Quarterly* (August 1946): 411-26.

10. Allen J. Matusow, *Farm Policies and Politics in the Truman Years* (Cambridge, Mass.: Harvard University Press, 1976), 130.

11. Summarized from our *Ezra Taft Benson and the Politics of Agriculture: The Eisenhower Years, 1953-1964* (Danville, Ill.: Interstate Publishers, 1975), chapter 5, "Formulation of a New Farm Program." See also Ezra Taft Benson's memoir, *Cross Fire: The Eight Years with Eisenhower* (Garden City, N.Y.: Doubleday and Company, 1962); and Peter A. Toma, *The Politics of Food for Peace: Executive-Legislative Interaction* (Tucson: University of Arizona Press, 1967).

For a comparison of Benson and Wallace see our "Religion and Reform: A Case Study of Henry A. Wallace and Ezra Taft Benson," *Journal of Church and State* 21 (Autumn 1979): 525-35.

12. Summarized from *Henry A. Wallace of Iowa*, chapter 9, "Utopia and Utility: The Synthesis of Agrarian Idealism with Agricultural Realism."

13. Edward L. Schapsmeier and Frederick H. Schapsmeier, "Henry A. Wallace: New Deal Philosopher," *Historian* 22 (February 1970): 177-90.

14. Summarized from our *Prophet in Politics: Henry A. Wallace and the War Years, 1940-1965* (Ames: Iowa State University Press, 1970), chapter 2, "Wartime Administrator: The Board of Economic Warfare." See also our article, "A Prophet in Politics: The Public Career of Henry A. Wallace," *Annals of Iowa* 39 (Summer 1967): 1-21.

15. Summarized from *Prophet in Politics*, chapter 3, "Idealism, Ideology, and Ideas for the Postwar World"; and chapter 6, "Philosopher without Portfolio: Planning for Worldwide Reforms."

16. Summarized from *Prophet in Politics*, chapter 9, "The Commerce Department: Plans for Postwar Prosperity"; chapter 10, "Cold War Critic: The Cabinet Crisis of 1946"; chapter 11, "*The New Republic* and the Fight for Peace"; and chapter 12, "The Progressive Party and the Presidential Campaign of 1948."

17. Summarized from *Henry A. Wallace of Iowa*, chapter 2, "The Young Henry Agard at College: The Making of a Scientist," and *Prophet in Politics*, chapter 15, "Profile of a Scientist: The Final Contribution."

18. Willard W. Cochrane delineates ten fundamental forces which affected agriculture from the time of colonial subsistence farming to contemporary commercial-mechanized farming. They are: (1) fertile land, (2) scientific farming, (3) economic infrastructure, (4) social infrastructure, (5) government intervention, (6) international trade, (7) status of the economy, (8) beliefs and value systems, (9) energy, and (10) environmentalism. See Cochrane's *The Development of American Agriculture: A Historical Analysis* (Minneapolis: University of Minnesota Press, 1979), chapter 15, "The Forces in Review," pp. 303-19. See also our *Abundant Harvests: The Story of American Agriculture* (St. Louis: Forum Press, 1973). For an analysis of agricultural legislation which followed the New Deal, see our *Encyclopedia of American Agricultural History* (Westport, Conn.: Greenwood Press, 1975), 12-16.

19. The trend toward "cannibalism" or tendency for farms to get ever larger in order to be profitable is discussed in Cochrane's *Development of American Agriculture*, pp. 387-419.

20. Quoted from *Henry A. Wallace of Iowa*, 285.

Comment by Richard Lowitt

In setting up this conference its planners apparently believed that Henry Wallace could be separated from a discussion of New Deal farm policy. Though the four authors of these two fine papers made an effort to separate the two topics, clearly they have failed, much to our benefit. Together they provide an excellent overall review of farm policy and programs during Henry Wallace's tenure as Secretary of Agriculture. The Schapsmeiers' concise examination of Wallace's career is based largely on summary statements from their biographical studies of Henry Wallace and Ezra Taft Benson. Their paper, though laudatory in its conclusion, seemingly indicts Wallace for helping create an "ever-normal granary" based on parity payments from the public treasury that posed grave problems for Secretary Benson in the 1950s. Benson was hostile to the idea of a welfare state for agriculture, a concept the Schapsmeiers credit Wallace with inaugurating. In viewing Henry Wallace's efforts from the perspective of the present with an angle of vision close to that of Ezra Taft Benson, they have doubts as to the efficacy of New Deal programs in the postwar years.

Wayne Rasmussen and Gladys Baker, in their carefully crafted and concise paper, take note of the situation New Dealers faced and then review the various programs administered by the U.S. Department of Agriculture (USDA) to revive, more so than to reform, American agriculture and to improve the lot of the farmer and his family. They conclude that, while there has been a major change in the structure of the farm economy, the programs instituted during the New Deal are still in place, "fundamentally unchanged" a half century later. They also remark that although the New Deal's primary concern was to restore the farm economy, Henry Wallace and his associates in the Department of Agriculture "supported efforts to improve the lot of the most depressed, including sharecroppers and other tenants, migrant laborers, and drought victims." But they refuse, except by implication, to pass judgment on the long-range validity of the New Deal programs. Instead they note, what I think is more important, that "the programs were effective in ensuring that the countryside did not move into armed revolt and that farm ownership did not suddenly become concentrated in banks, insurance companies, and other creditors."

What I propose in my remarks is to comment on Henry Wallace and his tenure as Secretary of Agriculture. In this way, perhaps, I can bring these two papers into sharper focus and further elaborate on Wallace's contribution as Secretary of Agriculture.

In 1933, when Wallace became Secretary, it was abundantly clear that free enterprise and competition had not resolved the farm problem and, if anything, had exacerbated it. Wallace understood this and understood as well that careful planning to provide necessary stabilizers within capitalism would be a necessary component of any farm program. He also recognized that the department would have to be reorganized to include action agencies, heretofore never prominent in its affairs.

The Federal Farm Board, like the Agricultural Adjustment Administration (AAA) that followed it, was concerned with immediate and pressing problems and was staffed in many instances with key personnel from bureaus within the department, which played a more passive role in the shadow of the action agency. This situation, involving in effect a second Department of Agriculture, created problems for Arthur M. Hyde, Hoover's Secretary of Agriculture, who loyally supported the Federal Farm Board although it helped shatter morale and created difficulties within the department. The problems became more pronounced with the advent of the New Deal because the Agricultural Adjustment Administration was housed within the department with the specific mandate "to relieve the existing national economic emergency" by the then drastic step of supporting prices by having farmers adjust production to demand.

Both papers develop and amplify this theme. What I can note is that Henry Wallace helped project into reality what his father and others were suggesting in the 1920s: production must be limited if price levels are to be raised, and government must play a role in the process. The approach championed by Herbert Hoover—that prices were the result of conditions affecting supply and demand and that the best way to secure fair prices was through individually adjusted production and expanding markets—was now markedly modified if not reversed. This shift in viewpoint caused most of the individuals engaged in agricultural research and educational and service work to modify their views to keep abreast of New Deal farm programs. Those who could not adjust their thinking became dissatisfied, critical, and hostile.

Within the department, employees had little time to make this adjustment. Wallace had to hurriedly organize and staff agencies to meet situations demanding immediate and drastic action. The department, in part owing to these tensions, was reorganized several times. Finally, Wallace created the Office of Land Use Coordination and the Mount Weather agreement in 1938 and achieved what he considered a satisfactory arrangement with the Bureau of Agricultural Economics as the chief planning agency.

Planning, however, was involved in the operation of all action agencies of the department: the AAA, the Farm Security Administration, and the Soil Conservation Service, among others. And it was planning, particularly as its results affected people in the rural regions, that posed a grave concern for Wallace. How to involve people at the grassroots and how to bring county officials, educators at land grant institutions, and others into the process were matters of importance to Henry Wallace, who long before the term came into common parlance was interested in "participatory democracy" and who always capitalized the phrase "the Common Man."

How well Wallace succeeded was suggested by Charles A. Beard in 1939 at a time when he was becoming increasingly critical of other aspects of the New Deal. Beard, writing from his experience as a dairy farmer in Connecticut, testified to the broad democratic approach of the department:

> I have had numerous and intimate contacts with officials and employees in the Department both in Washington and in rural regions. I have carried local issues up to Washington for consideration and action. I have seen agents of the Department in fields and barns and farmers' meetings. I have watched them make studies of soils, of erosion, of conservation problems. With my neighbors in Connecticut I have sat down in conferences with representatives of the Department to debate, thresh out and settle complicated and vexatious issues of marketing, production and land uses. And I can bear witness to the fact that the representatives of the Department with whom I have come in contact in offices, farmers' meetings, on the land and in forests have the

> capacity to make clear the work they are engaged in, to give the
> reasons for it, and are fair minded and exacting in requiring
> compliance with law and rule.

Beard concluded his remarks with the following tribute: "I can
truly say that nowhere in its work have I seen a spirit of bureaucratic regimentation made manifest in word or deed. Social
order itself requires laws and rules, but in a democratic society
these commands are expressions of popular opinion matured
into decisions and accepted in the light of such reason as we can
command. The Department of Agriculture operates in this
spirit."

Moreover, I can observe in response to a point stressed in the
Schapsmeiers' paper about the long-range effects of the cost of
the various programs coming from the public treasury that this
was *not* the original intent of Henry Wallace and others in the
USDA. It was the Supreme Court in 1936 with the flimsiest of
legal reasoning in the Butler decision that forced Wallace to
seek government financing of his ever-normal granary approach.
The Court rejected a self-financing plan for crop adjustment.

Another observation I can offer is that Wallace had a more
difficult task than other New Deal administrators in achieving
meaningful results. Success depended upon production controls,
getting farmers to cooperate, market conditions, coping with
forces of nature, and so on. Few material results could be
exhibited: for example, no massive public works projects were
constructed and millions of people were not put to work. Many
New Deal farm programs, unlike those of other departments
and agencies, were predicated on limited horizons: curbing
production, limiting land use, suggesting in some instances
that there were too many farms, and the like. Most results, like
the shelterbelt program, would take several years to manifest
themselves. For a people of plenty, this approach ran against
the American grain. Moreover, what many considered USDA
failures quickly gained national attention: the 1935 purge in
the department, and particularly the plight of sharecroppers in
the South. And what some people considered Wallace's eccen-
tricities—his so-called mysticism alone with some of his remarks—were used in a whispering campaign that subjected
him to scorn and ridicule. Since he was a man of many parts and
did not fit into any category, except possibly that of genius,
some of his contemporaries in politics and agricultural affairs

found him hard to understand.

What the critics ignore is that Wallace was aware of the plight of sharecroppers. For example, Calvin Hoover, a leading economist on leave from Duke, was completing a study of the situation. Wallace, however, was faced with a crisis situation which could have cost him the services of Chester Davis, the AAA administrator who was just then getting the program into full gear. While he was criticized at the time for ignoring the plight of the rural poor, particularly blacks, his commitment to civil rights can not be seriously questioned. Wallace had to choose in February 1935 between the revival of commercial agriculture and needed reforms. He chose to get rid of some of the reformers in order to keep the larger program going. The New Deal could function without the socially conscious lawyers recruited by Jerome Frank, but it risked paralysis without the support of conservatives in and out of the Agricultural Adjustment Administration. Wallace, in sum, was faced with a difficult choice; whatever he did damned him in the view of one or the other parties to this controversy and their supporters.

Ignored too by those who regarded Wallace as something of a crackpot was the high regard in which he was held by the scientists and economists within the department and the academic community. As Secretary he managed to find time to deliver papers at professional meetings, publish in scholarly journals, write timely books and articles, and efficiently administer what by 1940 was one of the largest agencies of government in the world. Along with David Lilienthal, he became a leading philosopher of the New Deal and had a significant voice in domestic policymaking. Also worth reiterating is the point made by Baker and Rasmussen that Wallace understood that only half the farm problem was to be found on the farm, that farmers had a responsibility to city consumers, and that their livelihood depended upon the purchasing power of consumers. They note that during his tenure two significant programs, the food stamp and the school lunch plans, were utilized to provide better nutrition for families unable to purchase adequate food at market prices.

In short, as both papers have indicated, Wallace was an effective and practical administrator in good part because as Secretary he was able to provide "sufficient harmony of function to tie everything together in a sense of purposeful service." Like his father before him, he achieved notable breakthroughs in mobilizing intellectual power for social purposes. He turned the USDA completely around, making it an instrument of direct assistance to farmers in planning production and in supporting agricultural prices. In doing so he had to make hardheaded compromises with politicians. Nevertheless, Wallace's approach to farm and food policy was innovative and forward-looking. In the 1930s the whole farm population was poor, and there was not the wide dispersion in farm sizes, levels of income, and wealth that occurred in later decades. In coping with the farm crisis of the 1930s, Wallace was a man for his times. He was also ahead of his time, and he was painfully aware of it when he observed, toward the end of his career, that "it may be more difficult to live virtuously and wisely with abundance than with scarcity."

IX

ROOSEVELT AND HIS ADVISERS

Brandeis, FDR, and the Ethics of Judicial Advising

Bruce Allen Murphy

Fifty years ago, the man whom many now proclaim to have been our greatest President, Franklin Delano Roosevelt, faced the dual problems of organizing his Administration for the challenges ahead as well as searching for the solutions that would bring this nation out of the worst depression in our history. As with all new administrations in such a period of transition, there was the usual jockeying back and forth among all of the new President's advisers to see which ones would gain the most power in charting the course over the next few years. These advisers—some in formal positions of governmental power and others outside of government—came from the expected sectors of American society: prior administrations, state governments, universities, Congress, industry, interest groups, and the like. Yet, in tallying up the list of prominent advisers to FDR, one must place another prominent American on the list. During this formative period in our history, this other man, who many might not expect to be so involved because of the nature of his formal position, quietly and patiently labored behind the scenes and out of the public eye, until many of those policies that were most dear to him were finally adopted in some fashion.

United States Supreme Court Justice Louis D. Brandeis—a man who by this time in his career was well on his way to being put on everybody's list of our greatest justices—had been waiting many years for this Administration. In addition to his formal judicial accomplishments, Brandeis had developed over the years an extensive list of political programs that he very much wanted to have adopted. However, most of that agenda had been lost in the preceding decade of Republican administrations. Part of that failure can be attributed to the adverse political

243

winds that faced Brandeis, but another reason for the failure stemmed from the constraints placed on him by the norms of his position. He simply could not afford to get into the political trenches in order to fight his battles because of the consequences for himself and his Court if such efforts were discovered by the public. However, in 1933, Brandeis, then in his middle seventies, was willing to extend himself and become one of the most extrajudicially active justices in history in the hopes of seeing his blueprint for American society adopted.

Because of the nature of Brandeis's position, it is not enough merely to consider his efforts to affect the course of the New Deal. One must not only reflect on the style of that behavior, but attempt to set both style and substance into the norms governing all members of the Supreme Court when they choose to become political advisers. This paper will set out some of the considerable efforts of Brandeis during the New Deal with the intention of suggesting both the strategies of such a presidential adviser and the importance of these actions in light of the principal normative standards confronting all members of the Supreme Court.

Brandeis well knew that in considering involvement in informal political efforts to shape public policy as a member of the Supreme Court he faced two general rules. First, the public expected members of the judiciary to be as pure as Caesar's wife when it came to politics. That is, members of the Court were expected to do more than merely stay out of politics; they were not even to consider such involvement in the first place. The reasons for this expectation cannot be found in the Constitution directly, but more in the myths that the general public holds regarding the ruling institutions in Washington.[1] Members of the Court are expected to adhere to the concept of the separation of powers, which proscribes members of one branch of government from exercising the powers of the other branches. Specifically, this is intended, with respect to members of the Court, to keep them from privately advising about policies that might later come before their body for constitutional review or statutory interpretation. In addition, members of the Court are expected to be totally nonpartisan, unconcerned with politics, so that they can sit at the pinnacle of the nation's judicial system and resolve controversies using only their interpretation of the Constitution rather than any partisan political instincts.

While it is of course theoretically possible for a justice to engage in politics and still independently decide cases on similar issues at a later time, history has shown that the public reacts negatively to the discovery of such extrajudicial conduct because it suspects that the independent judicial function is being compromised.[2]

Just as surely as Louis Brandeis knew about this rule regarding public expectations of totally nonpolitical justices, he was equally aware of the other rule on this subject: one can generally ignore the first rule. The notion of a Supreme Court secluded from politics was then, and is now, a myth. Two-thirds of the members of the Supreme Court have engaged in some type of extrajudicial political behavior. To be sure, the extent of this activity has varied among different individuals and has taken a number of different forms. But if Louis Brandeis was inclined toward extrajudicial involvement, there was more than adequate precedent to support his decision.

When one considers the range and extent of extrajudicial conduct by earlier members of the Supreme Court, it is difficult to understand how the public had continued to believe in a nonpolitical judiciary by the time Brandeis came to the Court. During the previous century, a number of the justices had developed close advisory relationships with sitting Presidents: Roger Brooke Taney with Andrew Jackson, John Catron with James K. Polk (via letters which contained the admonition to "Throw this in the Fire"), David Davis with Abraham Lincoln, and William Moody with Theodore Roosevelt. Justice Thomas Todd had helped the war hawks in Congress plan strategy for the War of 1812. Joseph Story became virtually a legislator on the bench—writing and lobbying for reforms of the organization of the judiciary and the United States criminal code. Five members of the Court served on the 1877 Electoral Commission resolving the disputed Hayes-Tilden presidential election. Moreover, several justices—James Moore Wayne, Salmon P. Chase, and Stephen Field among them—actively ran for the White House. One member of the Court, John McLean, even placed his hat in the presidential ring during every election from 1832 to 1860. It was also common for justices to write articles, deliver speeches, and propose both executive and judicial appointments.[2]

From the time Brandeis came on the Court in 1916 until the Roosevelt election in 1932, the main change in the standard of propriety for such behavior concerned the nature of informal advisory relationships between justices and Presidents. The norms began to relax during World War I because of Brandeis's own activities with Woodrow Wilson. Close friends for many years, Brandeis continued to openly advise the President even after his judicial appointment. Toward the end of the war, the justice became a participant in the writing of the Balfour Declaration, which established a British mandate for Palestine. In fact, he even helped Wilson in 1922 to formulate a Progressive platform designed to aid the Democratic Party in its return to power.[3]

Over the next decade, two other justices continued and expanded this practice of close advisory relationships. Chief Justice William Howard Taft took these activities to new heights by his involvement with Presidents Harding and Coolidge. Not only did he significantly affect many of the judicial appointments during that period, but he helped to write and lobby for a series of acts which entirely reorganized the federal courts. In addition, he advised the President on dealing with striking coal and railroad workers as well as oil leasing rights in the Red River.[4]

Justice Harlan F. Stone continued this practice by working closely with Herbert Hoover. As a member of the President's "Medicine Ball Cabinet," the two men daily discussed matters of mutual interest. In this informal advisory capacity Stone reviewed Hoover's speeches, gave advice on public policy, and even drafted a section of the President's inaugural address which discussed the need for a commission on law enforcement. Occasionally he even used journalist Irving Brant to promote his policies in the lower levels of the executive branch.[5]

Though he was well aware of the many precedents that would support a close advisory relationship with the newly elected Franklin D. Roosevelt, Justice Brandeis decided for a number of reasons to offer his counsel from a greater distance on most occasions. By remaining apart from the political world Brandeis believed that he would be insulated from public discovery and any potential scandal, should his enemies attempt to characterize his behavior as judicially indiscreet. Moreover, Brandeis wanted to keep his distance from an Administration that was likely to adopt policies which would later require his independent judicial review on the Supreme Court. The last thing that he wanted was a call from within the Administration for him to recuse himself from such cases. Finally, concerned by the growing anti-Semitism in the nation, Brandeis did not wish to add to what was perceived to be the increasing sentiment in some quarters that FDR was too heavily influenced by the Jewish community.

As wary as Brandeis was of developing an overly close relationship with the Roosevelt Administration and with the President personally, he was equally moved by the powerful impulse to press for the adoption of the economic recovery program that he had formulated. This plan was grouped into four general areas. First, Brandeis believed that only by massive spending on public works projects, such as "wholesale afforestation" and "control of waters," could economic recovery be achieved. In addition to the general economic benefits of such expenditures, the justice argued that the programs would "put two million men to work directly by the United States and the States within six months and another million or so indirectly."[6] The next set of proposals was designed to pay the costs of these programs. Brandeis argued that the income tax system had to be made much more progressive. Thus, he said, the "super rich," of which he was one, should be taxed out of existence by means of a prohibitive inheritance tax, and the money should be funneled to programs for the poor. He also called for the closing of various tax loopholes, such as certain gift and estate levies, and for the abolition of "outrageously large" contingency fees collected by tax attorneys who were filing claims against the government.

Brandeis's third set of plans concerned a number of financial reforms which would either help to prevent or mitigate the effects of future economic downturns. Here he called for reforms in banking practices and Wall Street operations, the control of holding companies used by large industries to evade government taxes and regulations, and the adoption of a comprehensive unemployment compensation program for the relief of American workers. In order to help secure the adoption of all the above, Brandeis's final concern was that the New Deal be adequately staffed with lawyers not only of great ability, but also possessing the proper progressive outlook.

Since such an ambitious governmental program would require close supervision on its way to adoption, and Brandeis was not willing to place himself in the political trenches because of the nature of his position, the justice needed to develop a unique style for pressing his ideas on the Roosevelt team. So, as he had in earlier years, Brandeis chose to work through various allies. The justice's primary ally was Harvard Professor of Law Felix Frankfurter. Over the years Frankfurter had proven himself to be incredibly able in translating the ideas he received from Brandeis's letters into either government programs or published articles.[7] Since the requests that Brandeis made of Frankfurter to direct the outside "political" world frequently carried with them certain expenses, for years the multimillionaire justice had been providing the often underfunded professor with money for just such purposes. To Brandeis, Felix Frankfurter not only represented "the most useful lawyer in the United States," but also his "half brother-half son."[8] On the one hand, the justice sent a torrent of letters with "suggestions" for political action, while on the other Frankfurter became the only person outside of the members of the Court to be made privy to many of the secrets of Brandeis's judicial life.

This political partnership had great benefits for both men. For Brandeis, it represented a method for satisfying his reformist urges while still displaying the nonpolitical temperament that the general public expected of its justices. In addition to helping him maintain a physical distance from politics, this relationship also enabled Brandeis to get all of the necessary information on a given topic from a very reliable source before proposing his programs. For Frankfurter, the relationship opened up new vistas for political involvement as well as ensuring that he would never suffer from a lack of funds for such endeavors.

While Frankfurter was a central ally in Justice Brandeis's political affairs, he was by no means the only one. During the New Deal period alone, the justice also consulted or worked through such people as editor Norman Hapgood; former journalist and then member of the Agricultural Adjustment Administration's Consumers' Counsel, Gardner Jackson; former Secretary of the Navy, Josephus Daniels; lawyer Huston Thompson; banker J. Lionberger Davis; and presidential speechwriter Samuel I. Rosenman. All of these other figures, though, were used by the justice only on occasion, and only Frankfurter seemed to have the full picture of the range and extent of extrajudicial activities being undertaken.

Not surprisingly, Brandeis's initial moves during the New

Deal, sometimes on his own but largely through Felix Frankfurter, were concerned mainly with widening his circle of influence in the Administration. By helping to staff some of the departments and agencies in the rapidly expanding "Alphabet Soup" government, the justice would increase both his information sources and the contact points through which he could press his programs. Many of Brandeis's suggestions for appointments, which were successfully lobbied for by Frankfurter, became part of the legion of Harvard Law School graduates in the Administration that were later known as "Felix's Happy Hot Dogs." While their main successes came in the Departments of Labor, the Interior, and Agriculture, the full range of their collective appointments spanned the Administration. Among their new young allies were Department of Labor solicitor Charles E. Wyzanski, Department of the Interior solicitor Nathan Margold, and TVA Board member David Lilienthal. Besides serving as the "eyes and ears" in the Administration for Brandeis and Frankfurter, they also became the means by which other appointments at the lower levels of their departments and agencies were successfully pushed.[9]

Once again, Brandeis felt the need to develop a somewhat distant means for counseling the rapidly expanding legion of his followers in the New Deal. While on occasion some of them had personal appointments with the justice, one of the main techniques used to advise them (besides directing his comments through Felix Frankfurter in his letters) was to have them invited to one or several of his weekly teas. These social affairs, held in Brandeis's apartment, might include fifteen or twenty people drawn from all the sectors of the Washington community— presidential assistants, members of federal commissions, several members of the executive departments and agencies, members of the Brookings Institution, corporate heads and labor union figures, and even members of the diplomatic community. While the guests chatted, each of them was brought over to Brandeis for a short discussion in the corner of the room. Inevitably, the conversation turned to the problems facing that guest in his daily chores. Through a series of cross-examination-style questions, Brandeis would "squeeze [them] like an orange" until he "drained [them] dry of every little bit of information that [they] knew."[10] Then, through a series of Socratic questions that Brandeis used to "stretch the mind" of his guest, the justice would make that individual fully aware of the direction of his desired solution. In this fashion, Brandeis was able to make his own policy views apparent without having to discuss in detail the specifics of any particular policy.[11]

In considering the means by which Justice Brandeis indirectly advised Felix Frankfurter and the other younger New Dealers in the course of their political efforts, it is important to keep the views of these allies in perspective. Brandeis was the distant prophet, nicknamed Isaiah by the New Dealers, who seemed devoutly uncompromising in describing and pressing for his vision for America. For him, passage of the "right" solution was as important as the passage of any solution at all. Perhaps his almost mystical qualities had been best captured by one visitor, Assistant Secretary of State James Grafton Rogers, several years earlier: "Brandeis is something between Lincoln and Christ in the strange poetical impression he leaves. Life to him is a great moral web, a complex of good and evil forces, an organ composition. Gentleness, sweetness, yearning, listening, hoping are the sensations you get from him. . . . He is not a socialist. He is a moralist. He is scarcely of this world at all."[12]

However, Frankfurter and the other allies cannot be assumed to have been puppets on the end of the justice's string. They did not simply carry out all of his instructions on command—though Brandeis was always available for consultation when necessary. Rather, these other men were simply of a similar mind and philosophical bent with Brandeis, and given some general hints and encouragement, it was not surprising to find them frequently acting in a manner that was consistent with his private wishes. If there was one area in which they differed frequently with the justice, it was that Frankfurter and the others were constantly aware of the political implications of the various proposals. They had to be concerned with both the difficulty of passing these programs and the implications for the future of the Roosevelt regime upon so doing. Consequently, it was not unusual to find these men frequently adjusting the specifics of Brandeis's ideas to make them more palatable to politicians searching for "expediency" and "compromise" rather than "rightness" in their programs.

Even with all of their early efforts, Brandeis and Frankfurter soon realized that if they were to have any major impact on the Administration they would have to secure an ally who had daily access to the President. With Brandeis necessarily removed from the action on the Court and Frankfurter in Cambridge, they soon realized that their policies, no matter how correct and well formulated, would be lost in the shuffle of all the policies coming from those who were operating from within the White House.

This search for an intermediary to the President became even more important to the justice when he realized that FDR's central advisers were advocates of the collectivist policies which were anathema to him. While Brandeis and Frankfurter favored policies that were designed to restore competition among industries and businesses, reestablish trust in the banking and investment communities, and increase the importance of state governments, the Roosevelt "Brain Trust" of Rexford Tugwell, Raymond Moley, and Adolf Berle—who were actually involved in the daily planning of the New Deal—had just the opposite view. These "collectivists" believed that the answer to economic recovery lay in central planning by large-scale national programs.

Over the years an image grew in the literature about the New Deal that these two groups fought an internecine battle for the attention of the President. Frankfurter himself disputed this portrait, once writing historian Arthur Schlesinger, "I must reject your assumption that there was a real clash of views between Moley-Tugwell and FF-Brandeis."[13] However, there is much evidence to show a distinct lack of harmony between certain members of the two advisory groups. Rexford Tugwell saw Brandeis's views as "outmoded," Frankfurter as being his "satellite," and in his unpublished diary even blames the two men for his eventual downfall ("They had implacable hostility to me. They were determined to check me everywhere, to discredit and eject me from government [and] they succeeded").[14] There seems to be some evidence that Tugwell's assessment was right— at least so far as it concerned one of the Frankfurter proteges, Thomas Corcoran. When the subject of Rexford Tugwell was raised during a conversation with Raymond Moley, Corcoran's views were made quite explicit:

> I've never seen anything like him for arrogance. He picked up the draft of a speech the Skipper [FDR] was to make, laid it in front of me, pointed to the word "competition" and said: "That ought to come out." When I paid no attention he turned to the President and said: "You know you don't believe in it." The

President ignored him. Can you imagine the nerve of that bastard?
Well, we've got the knife in the sheaf and we'll take care of him.
Not that he doesn't serve a useful function. He is a sort of catfish
to keep the herrings from getting sluggish when the fishermen
have taken them back in tanks to port. But the Skipper shouldn't
get the idea that he is an edible fish.[15]

But it seems that at least with respect to one of the members of
the Brain Trust, there was more of a connection between the
two groups of advisers than has been previously thought. Despite
his philosophical differences with Frankfurter and Brandeis,
Assistant Secretary of State Raymond Moley was prepared to
work with them on occasion. Moley not only helped to arrange
a meeting between Brandeis and FDR, but after an exchange of
several letters, he also personally met with the justice in order
to be lectured regarding the "right" plan for economic recovery.
Though he later wrote that he found Brandeis's proposal of
financing a vast public works program by closing loopholes in
the tax code and "by waiting for the super rich to die" to be
"frivolous to the point of absurdity," he had given the two men
what they were looking for—a point of access on a continual
basis to the inner White House circle.[16]

After this meeting, Frankfurter viewed the Assistant Secretary
of State as a main conduit to FDR. Whenever an Administration
crisis arose, or there was a need for Frankfurter or Brandeis to
express their views on policy to FDR, Moley would find on his
desk either a letter or a telegram pleading with him to "call
collect." During the first months of the Administration, then,
Frankfurter was able to propose through Moley many of the
ideas for legislation and staff appointments that he and the
justice viewed as desirable. Moley was successful at keeping a
considerable distance from the two men whenever necessary,
but he also frequently provided them with exactly what they
needed.

Even after Moley left the government, Brandeis was able to
enjoy another indirect point of access to the inner White House.
Two of Frankfurter's prize students—Thomas Corcoran and
Benjamin V. Cohen—working from their respective positions
in the Reconstruction Finance Corporation and the Public
Works Administration, soon formed a legendary partnership
for drafting New Deal legislation. In the course of these duties,
it turns out that they not only served as Brandeis's and Frankfurter's "eyes and ears" in Washington, but they also did much

of the legwork in drafting some of the justice's desired proposals into law.

Once again, in working with these two young New Dealers, the justice developed a means of both advising them while also keeping his distance from the Administration.[17] Corcoran and Cohen would initiate the process by visiting Brandeis at his apartment and discussing the activities as well as the problems of the Administration. Their purpose was not to receive policy ideas, but only to inform him of the situation in the executive branch. For his part, Brandeis would frame his questions so that he gathered the desired information, while making no effort to instruct his visitors regarding the possible alternative solutions to the problems facing the Roosevelt Administration. Then, after these conferences, the justice would send his specific policy ideas to Frankfurter in a detailed letter that on occasion even suggested areas of needed study by his "boys" at Harvard Law School. The professor would then gather the necessary material and send it to FDR, along with Brandeis's legislative ideas (sometimes even saying that the justice had "passed" on the proposal). The President then completed the circle by suggesting some of these ideas to Corcoran and Cohen for drafting. The two young New Dealers would research the issue, draft the legislation (often in conjunction with their many allies in the Administration), and do whatever was necessary to see that passage was secured.

Using this ingenious style of advising the Roosevelt Administration from behind the scenes, Louis Brandeis was able to help shape the course of the New Deal while remaining relatively free of the fear of public discovery. On the one occasion that his involvement in politics did become an issue during this period, the justice was able to escape from the public criticism following the disclosure with a minimum of difficulty.[18] But like all presidential advisers, Brandeis had his successes and his failures in pushing for his proposals. A brief examination of the major elements of the justice's efforts on behalf of one program— unemployment insurance—will perhaps illustrate not only the style and extent of his political behavior, but it will also highlight some of the normative considerations raised by such actions by a member of the Supreme Court.

Since the early 1900s Brandeis had had a passionate hatred for "irregular employment," which he termed the "greatest industrial waste." In fact, starting in 1911, he advocated a "plant reserves" program to deal with the problem. In this program, each employer contributed to a fund benefiting un-employed workers in their own firm; the employer would then receive back either all or a certain portion of the money remain-ing at the end of the year depending on the firm's record of employment. By thus tapping the self-interest of the employers, Brandeis hoped that they would be encouraged to minimize the causes of unemployment by regularizing their work schedules. Before Roosevelt's election, Brandeis had worked with his daugh-ter and son-in-law, Elizabeth and Paul Raushenbush, who helped to secure passage of a similar program in Wisconsin. When no other state adopted the plan, Brandeis was forced to seek the enactment of a national program.[19]

In the discussions at the national level, Brandeis's plant reserves system was opposed by those who advocated that all of the insurance funds for an industry be pooled at the state level in order to equalize the monetary risks for each corporation. This program, the so-called Ohio plan, was a pure insurance system by which the employers, the employees, and the govern-ment all contributed to the fund which was to help laid-off workers.[20]

In searching for the means by which the plant reserves system could be adopted by the federal government, Brandeis suggested to the Raushenbushes that the federal tax power be used as a lever to encourage states to adopt such employment plans. The idea was that the federal government could apply a uniform payroll tax for unemployment insurance against which the employers might credit any similar taxes they might have paid into a state unemployment program. Thus, each state would be encouraged to adopt an unemployment plan in order that they might be able to use the incoming funds.[21]

The justice became so excited over the prospects for his tax offset-plant reserves unemployment program that he dropped his usual guard against direct involvement in politics to lobby for the plan. During the fall of 1933 he met personally with a number of New Dealers—Raymond Moley, NRA head General Hugh Johnson, NRA counsel Donald Richberg, and United States Commissioner of Labor Statistics Isador Lubin, among others—to explain the aspects and merits of his program. More-over, he made some attempts at encouraging a "national figure," such as Senator Robert Wagner or Labor Secretary Frances Perkins, to make a public statement on the need for national action in this area.[22]

Once he had secured some modicum of support for the program in the upper echelons of the Administration, Brandeis made an indirect effort to influence those who would actually be drafting the measure. At the suggestion of the justice, Massachusetts businessman A. Lincoln Filene, an old Progressive ally, organized a meeting of the supporters of the unemployment insurance program at his daughter's house in Georgetown in January 1934.[23] Among those present were Elizabeth Raushenbush, Charles E. Wyzanski, Jr., Thomas G. Corcoran, Frances Perkins, and Senator Robert Wagner. Filene, careful never to mention the justice's name but making quite clear who was being discussed, presented the Brandeis program for unemployment insurance. In the course of this discussion, Filene made clear that he thought this plan would survive a test by the Supreme Court, and both Perkins and Wagner, who were equally concerned with such an eventuality, seemed to be convinced that this was true.

Perkins assigned the drafting of the bill to the assistant solicitor of her department, Thomas H. Eliot, and Brandeis's son-in-law, Paul Raushenbush. The proposal, which eventually became the Wagner-Lewis Act, called for a uniform payroll tax on employers of 5 percent with the tax offset provision that was designed to encourage states to adopt their own unemployment insurance plan. Justice Brandeis was so pleased with the plan, which was introduced in Congress on Februrary 5, 1934, that he referred to it in a letter to Felix Frankfurter as "my federal excise tax . . . to offset irregularity of employment."[24] But the justice could not have been happy with what happened after the initial bill had been drafted. Because President Roosevelt was unwilling to commit himself definitely to the passage of this program (writing to Rexford Tugwell that the plan would "require a good deal of overhauling"), the bill was allowed to die in committee.[25]

In early June, Brandeis dispensed with his usual unwillingness to meet personally with President Roosevelt and spoke for forty-five minutes with FDR on the need for an unemployment insurance program. By this time, though, the President was interested in developing a more comprehensive social security program. Though the justice left his meeting at the White House believing that he had been successful in influencing the President, he discovered over a week later, by way of Thomas Corcoran, that FDR was actually leaning toward an entirely federally administered plan. However, the young New Dealer had also indicated that FDR might still have some room for compromise.[26]

For the justice the events seemed to be getting away from him in mid-1934 when FDR established the Committee on Economic Security, which was charged with developing a program that was "national in scope." This group soon seemed to be leaning toward a centralized, national administration of the unemployment program. In order to secure uniformity of standards and benefits, they were arguing for a subsidy system by which the federal government would collect all of the payroll taxes and return portions of the funds to those states with compensation laws that met federal standards, and this money would in turn be used to support unemployed workers. Brandeis opposed this idea, thinking that it would thwart state innovation and experimentation.

So, on the justice's instructions, Felix Frankfurter met with Raymond Moley, who was now out of government but still retained close contacts to the President. Frankfurter reported in a letter to Brandeis that he had tried to "indoctrinate [Moley] with [the] difficulties and doubts" about the insurance programs, as well as to impress on him "the importance of going slow and avoiding premature commitments" when the Administration was considering which plan to support. Though Frankfurter reported back that he had a significant impact on Moley, both he and the justice understood the need for much further action in the fight.[27]

For reasons that are unclear, Frankfurter at this point seems to have weakened in his devotion to the Brandeis proposal. Perhaps he thought that the plan was not really in the President's best political interests, or perhaps he had never been truly wedded to the idea in the first place. In any event, Frankfurter's usual passion in proposing a Brandeis plan was missing. It was not out of character for Frankfurter to advise caution in the announcement of which program was to be adopted, as he had already done with Moley, but it was out of character for him not to press forcefully for the justice's unique plan with either

Moley or FDR. In fact, Frankfurter became scrupulously neutral whenever discussing the various unemployment insurance plans with either the President or any of his men.

While the justice does not seem to have discovered that his chief ally was not wholeheartedly committed to the cause, there is no question that he did not have the same totally devoted friend in this battle that he had enjoyed in others. Apparently torn between Brandeis's ideological rigor and Roosevelt's political needs, Frankfurter seems to have decided to let the President make his own judgment. In one letter to Raymond Moley, who was then writing a campaign speech for FDR, Frankfurter even seemed to have been diverging considerably from Brandeis's "true faith":

> I think FDR should point out emphatically that we need a national program, but a national program does not mean exclusively *national* Congressional legislation. It means nationwide action and national leadership but such leadership may be executed in part by State legislation or by regional legislation in conjunction with Congressional action. [Italics in original][28]

This tolerance for something other than individual state administration of the program—by leaving it perhaps to regional compacts—seems to be indicative of the professor's willingness to couch his advice in terms that were acceptable to the Roosevelt Administration.

By this time, August 1934, Brandeis seems to have become very concerned about the prospects for the adoption of his program. Advised by his son-in-law that Edwin Witte, a Wisconsin economics professor who was the executive director of the Committee on Economic Security, seemed not so willing to fight for the inclusion of the plant reserves system in his state as part of the federal unemployment program, the justice met personally with him in mid-August to discuss the issue.[29] Then, knowing that Felix Frankfurter would be meeting with the President following the professor's year-long journey to Oxford, Brandeis sent his longtime ally some instructions as to the message he wanted conveyed: "When you see FDR . . . it will be advisable to reinforce what I said to him on employers bearing the whole cost—which seemed to impress him favorably."[30]

Unfortunately from the justice's perspective, when Frankfurter did confer with FDR over a two-day period in late August, he maintained a strict neutrality when the topic turned to unemployment insurance programs. Rather than fully exploring the elements of Brandeis's "true faith," Frankfurter reported that he had decided to let "Witte's Committee impress FDR with the facts as to the national show."[31] Of course, the problem with this from the justice's perspective was that there was no guarantee that the committee, then in active deliberations, would reach the conclusion that the plant reserves-tax offset proposal was the desirable solution.

There can be little doubt that Brandeis's position on the Court was affecting his ability to function as a presidential adviser. Unable to make the political arguments on his own, he was forced to rely on the efforts of men such as Felix Frankfurter to make his views known to different politicians and then lobby effectively for their adoption. When these allies failed to make the requisite moves, Brandeis's programs were placed into jeopardy. However, the justice's sense of ethics prevented him in nearly all cases from making the sort of direct appeal that not only might be more successful politically, but might also risk placing the Court in jeopardy.

Fortunately for Brandeis, the President soon began leaning toward the state-oriented approach to administering the unemployment insurance program. This became clear in November 1934 when FDR delivered an address in favor of the federal-state approach. By late December, Rexford Tugwell, who realized that his efforts on behalf of a purely federal system were ineffective, complained in his personal diary that the influence of Brandeis and Frankfurter on FDR had just been too strong.[32]

The bill that was included in the 1935 legislative program was a compromise unemployment insurance plan. Like the Wagner-Lewis proposal, a payroll tax was placed on employers only, but it was limited to 3 rather than 5 percent, and states that adopted the Brandeisian plant reserves plan were required to pool one-third of the contributions from each industry. Even these changes were too much for the uncompromising Isaiah. He pleaded with Frankfurter to have "Tom and Ben . . . finish away this compromise . . . [and to] strive for the simon-pure article."[33] But the efforts of some of the supporters of the original Wisconsin program of plant reserves—Philip and Robert La Follette, and Paul Raushenbush—were unsuccessful in removing some of what Brandeis termed the "objectionable features" of the proposal. In the end, the disappointed justice wrote to

Frankfurter that he believed "political considerations [to be] the main cause of the unfortunate abandonment [by FDR] of the Wagner-Lewis bill."[34] Unknown to the justice, it was perhaps these same political considerations that had led his main ally, the Harvard professor, to consider seriously the same compromises in the latter stages of the drafting process.

Despite his disappointment, Louis Brandeis got much of what he wanted in the way of an unemployment compensation program when FDR signed it into law on August 14, 1935. Unique among the many lobbyists inside and outside the Administration, though, Brandeis had one additional weapon— fear. It is quite apparent that some members of the Administration were affected in listening to the justice by the knowledge that he had the final constitutional nay-saying power over their programs should they ever be tested in the Supreme Court. While there is little doubt that Brandeis saw himself as a private citizen in pressing for the unemployment compensation law, the fact is that others could and did perceive him as a powerful member of the Supreme Court. And in the world of political lobbying, it is the perception of the targeted individual that is crucial. Thus, it becomes important to reflect on the normative considerations raised by Louis Brandeis's efforts to affect the course of the New Deal.

The special nature of Brandeis's official position as it affected his role as a presidential adviser, together with the controversy stirred by the publication of my book on this topic in 1982, indicates a need to reflect on the ethics of such behavior. Must we deny ourselves the political advice of brilliant men simply because they are clothed in a judicial gown? Saying that Brandeis engaged in such behavior with little damage to the Supreme Court is inadequate, for the next individual might not be so careful or so concerned with the public's opinion. There are clearly two dimensions to the problem. First, given the norms which existed during the time that he served on the Court, were the actions of Brandeis ethical? Second, what lessons can be drawn from this behavior for establishing an objective normative standard to guide present and future Supreme Court justices? The initial question is one of propriety, while the latter focuses on the concept of advisability.

The search for a normative standard by which to judge Brandeis's and Frankfurter's conduct should begin with an examination of three areas: the intention of the nation's founders, the history of the actions by earlier justices, and the dictates of the canons of judicial ethics. Unfortunately, the lessons from the founding period are not terribly useful for determining the propriety of political involvement by the Supreme Court. The problems posed by the relative lack of discussion on this issue at the Constitutional Convention are compounded by the vast disagreement among those who were concerned with it. While some, such as James Madison, sought to institutionalize political involvement by the justices, others were violently opposed to any such arrangement. Then the early Congresses delegated several specific extrajudicial duties to the Court, only to have the justices themselves, in the *Hayburn* case,[35] reject the notion of obligatory political duties. Each justice, then, was left to make his own determination regarding the ethics of individual conduct.

Turning to the behavior of justices who served on the Court before Brandeis, we discover some limited guidance on the matter. A vast majority of them freely engaged in all sorts of extrajudicial political conduct. Yet, only a much smaller number of these men—John Jay, Salmon P. Chase, Stephen Field, and Samuel Miller—were involved in activities as extensive as that of Brandeis. Through the actions of his predecessors, a set of informal norms had been developed which led Brandeis to believe that his involvement in political actions was permissible. Really all that can be gleaned from this history of the Court is one "golden rule": "Engage in political work if you wish, but keep it secret." Brandeis's unique indirect style of lobbying succeeded in doing just that.

The canons of judicial ethics, adopted by the American Bar Association on July 9, 1924, offered no apparent reason for Brandeis to modify his standards. Perhaps the most telling argument against the notion that these norms were ever intended to restrict extrajudicial behavior is the fact that they were drafted and advocated by a premier "judicial politician"—Chief Justice William Howard Taft. Moreover, the vagueness of these standards makes it unclear whether, or how, they could be used to limit such political conduct. Quite obviously, these norms had little effect on the political inclinations of the rest of the Court; so Brandeis and Frankfurter felt unconstrained by these proscriptions as well.

A close examination of the canons indicates that Brandeis was careful never to violate the *letter* of the ethical standards. As an attorney and then as a justice, he was well trained for this exercise of acting just within the bounds of judicial propriety. The use of words was his stock and trade. Consequently, the careful construction of Brandeis's questions to his lieutenants enabled him to roam freely in politics while still remaining within the bounds of the standard of ethics. If asked to defend his actions now, it would be relatively easy for Brandeis, given the vagueness of the few relevant canons.

The only canons which might be construed to deal with Brandeis's extrajudicial conduct during the New Deal would create little difficulty for him were he asked to justify his behavior. A jurist is instructed to remain "free from impropriety and the appearance of impropriety." Generally, this standard was satisfied simply because most of his actions were hidden from public view. Then a judge is warned not to "be swayed by partisan demands, public clamor or considerations of personal popularity." Here Brandeis appeared to be fully satisfied that he could keep his judicial and political roles completely separate. On those occasions when the two sets of interests overlapped, actions were taken to restore that distinction. Further, the canons advise that a judge should "not accept inconsistent duties; nor incur obligations, pecuniary or otherwise."[36] Brandeis is free from criticism on this score, for he never acted for selfish gain or lessened his attention to official duties in order to accomplish political tasks. The final canon which has any relevance to this question is the one dealing with "a summary of judicial obligations":

> In every particular [a judge's] conduct should be above reproach. He should be conscientious, studious, thorough, courteous, patient, punctual, just, impartial, fearless of public clamor, regardless of public praise, and indifferent to private political or partisan influences . . . he should not allow other affairs or his private interests to interfere with the prompt and proper performance of his judicial duties.[37]

People may well have criticized Brandeis at certain times for his involvement in political activities, but never during his tenure on the Court was there any question regarding his motivation in making judicial decisions. Never was he seen as biased or partisan in his judgments, for even if he remained secluded from politics he still would have had the same private views and made the same decisions.

While the vagueness of the canons makes it possible to defend Brandeis on the basis of the *letter* of the norms, some may wonder whether he violated their *spirit* in isolated instances. Over the years two practices have developed to shield the Court from possible controversy in the exercise of their duties. First, the "ethical" judge will recuse himself whenever an issue on which he has had prior involvement is being litigated before the Court. Second, the "ethical" judge will refuse to hear the case of litigants with whom he has had a prior or ongoing relationship. Brandeis did fail to observe these accepted practices. Repeatedly, he allowed his judicial and political roles to overlap by hearing cases which raised issues on which he had privately given advice. After warning some Administration officials against the direction of the National Recovery Administration (NRA) and the Agricultural Adjustment Administration (AAA) during the New Deal, owing to the centralized direction of their approach, Brandeis reviewed those measures in two separate cases—*Schechter Poultry Corp.* v. *United States*[38] and *United States* v. *Butler*.[39] Despite having indirectly helped to formulate the unemployment provisions of the Social Security Act, Brandeis later voted to uphold the constitutionality of that law in *Steward Machine Co.* v. *Davis*.[40] The failure to recuse himself in these cases is especially puzzling given pre-New Deal recusals in other cases raising conflict-of-interest questions. Because of his connection to the Sacco-Vanzetti defense team, and his prejudicial efforts for minimum wage legislation, Brandeis refused to sit during challenges on both of these matters—*Sacco and Vanzetti* v. *Massachusetts*[41] and *Adkins* v. *Children's Hospital*.[42] Moreover, it is difficult to understand how the same man whose personal sense of ethics compelled him to reimburse his law firm for the time involved in doing pro bono publico legal work could so blatantly ignore existing judicial norms. Quite clearly, Brandeis perceived no ethical problem here whatsoever.

There are three possible explanations for this atypical behavior. The first, and most cynical view, is that the justice deliberately ignored these ethics in the belief that the public would never discover the violations. Accordingly, in the *Sacco-Vanzetti* and minimum wage cases, he decided to step down because his

involvement with these issues was well known. The next explanation is that Brandeis believed that during times of national
crisis such as war or the Depression, all normative standards
were temporarily abolished. But, if this were the case, why did
none of his colleagues engage in politics to a similar extent?
Thus the final, and perhaps best, explanation is that, rightly or
wrongly, Brandeis viewed his political advising and judicial
decisionmaking as being entirely separate. The *Butler* case
seemingly demonstrates this ability to compartmentalize his
life, in that Brandeis upheld the very Agricultural Act which he
was privately trying to destroy. The difficulty with this behavior,
and the failure of any justice to recuse himself in such cases, is
that very often the personal standard of the individual involved
is not as important as how the public perceives this action. For
this reason, the spirit of the canons of ethics clearly dictated
that Brandeis should have stepped down in these cases.

The only useful concept for assessing Brandeis's behavior is
the nebulous "separation of powers." No matter what the theoretical understanding of this "separation" might be, it is really
public opinion which sets the bounds of acceptable interaction
among the various governmental branches. This can be applied
equally to formal and informal activities of public officials. We
have certainly seen this to be true with regard to public willingness to permit political behavior by members of the Supreme
Court. Over the years this standard of propriety has changed in
reaction to various controversies. In those eras when the public
approved of collaboration between justices and members of
other branches of government, that became the acceptable norm.
Since this is an ever-changing standard, the politically inclined
justice determines its limits through trial and error—gradually
learning how far he can go before the public will object. Consequently, Brandeis must be judged in the context of his perception of the public's standard of propriety during the time that
he served on the Court.

Throughout that period, public opinion placed very few
restrictions on such conduct. Virtually any wartime judicial
appointment and reform or literary endeavor was condoned.
However, public expectations regarding the existence of advisory
relationships between a justice and a political figure make this
aspect of his behavior somewhat more difficult to judge. To be
sure, during this period the public was aware of and accepted

several of these arrangements—for example, Justice Stone with Herbert Hoover. The only requirement seemed to be that the justice be discreet in his extrajudicial dealings. While Brandeis was circumspect in his behavior, none of his colleagues was as involved in as extensive political activities as he was during his tenure on the Court. Moreover, when one of these actions was discovered, public reaction was swift and extremely negative. Had the general public been made aware of the incredible array of extrajudicial actions by Brandeis—the personal advising, the influencing of key appointments, and even the counseling on public statutes—it is safe to say that the justice would have become the subject of great public debate and would perhaps have been driven from the bench entirely. By maintaining a high degree of discretion, Brandeis illustrated his regard for, if not strict adherence to, this final standard.

Technically, Louis Brandeis did not violate any specific standards of propriety in his endeavors simply because no real set of proscriptions existed at that time. However, that does not entirely free him from any criticism. Determining the ethics of these activities according to the norms of that period only compels one to question further the *wisdom* of his involvement. Brandeis was engaged in politics on a wide scale and yet, because most of it was kept secret, he is remembered only as a paragon of judicial virtue. Should we thus condone Brandeis's establishment of one of the most unique financial relationships in the history of the Supreme Court in order to engage in politics? Even in a time of crisis, was it wise for him to become so intimately involved with the Roosevelt Administration? When one considers the risks of discovery not just to the individual justice, but to the entire Court, some may well view such behavior as unwise. Not only did Brandeis continually gamble that the public would not discover the depth of his involvement, but by acting in this manner he set an example for later politically inclined justices—such as Felix Frankfurter—to follow. Thus, it is left to each of us to weigh the wisdom of involvement by a brilliant justice such as Brandeis or Frankfurter in the face of the knowledge that discovery of these actions could prove disastrous for the entire institution. For many, the risks may outweigh the possible benefits of the political efforts of these nine individuals.

1. The only provision of the Constitution remotely relating to this subject is Article I, Section 6, which bars members of one branch (the executive branch) from simultaneously serving in Congress.

2. For the details of these extrajudicial incidents, their effect on the normative standards, and the corresponding citations to primary and secondary sources, see Bruce Allen Murphy, "Toward the Monastery: A Survey of Justices in Politics from 1789 to 1916," in *The Brandeis-Frankfurter Connection* (New York: Oxford University Press, 1982), pp. 345-63.

3. Ibid., pp. 46-60, 74.

4. Henry F. Pringle, *The Life and Times of William Howard Taft* (New York: Farrar and Rinehart, 1939), pp. 1004-63.

5. Alpheus T. Mason, *Harlan Fiske Stone: Pillar of the Law* (New York: Viking Press, 1956), pp. 266, 270-71, 285, 474N, 707N.

6. Letter, LDB to FF, January 31, 1933, Felix Frankfurter Papers, Manuscripts Division, Library of Congress (hereinafter cited as FF/LC), Box 28. For other letters describing Brandeis's plans, see: Letters, LDB to FF, January 21, 1933, February 5 and February 9, 1933, and April 29, 1932, FF/LC, Box 28; memoranda written by Frankfurter, "Memo on Public Works Program" and "Memorandum Regarding Financing of the Public Works Program," undated FF/LC, Box 226; and Letter, LDB to Elizabeth Brandeis Raushenbush, November 19, 1933, in Melvin Urofsky and David Levy, eds., *Letters of Louis D. Brandeis*, vol. 5 (Albany: State University of New York Press, 1978), pp. 527-28.

7. For examples, see Murphy, *Brandeis/Frankfurter Connection*, chapter 3; and David Levy and Bruce Allen Murphy, "Preserving the Progressive Spirit in a Conservative Time; The Joint Reform Efforts of Brandeis and Frankfurter," *Michigan Law Review* 78 (1980): 1275-78.

8. The quotations are drawn from two letters: LBD to Harold Laski, November 29, 1927, Brandeis MSS, Louisville Law School, Box M18; and LBD to FF, September 24, 1925, FF/LC, Box 26. For the details of the financial relationship between Brandeis and Frankfurter, see Murphy, *Brandeis/ Frankfurter Connection*, pp. 40-44; and Levy and Murphy, "Preserving the Progressive Spirit," pp. 1261-63.

9. For more, see Murphy, *Brandeis/Frankfurter Connection*, pp. 158-59, 164-65, 138-41, 163, 103-5, and 130.

10. Interview with Joseph L. Rauh, Jr., July 9, 1979, Washington, D.C.

11. For more on the Brandeis teas, see the text and footnotes in Murphy, *Brandeis/Frankfurter Connection*, pp. 121-23.

12. Letter, James Grafton Rogers to Robert Stearns, undated, James Grafton Rogers papers, Hoover Institution, Folder 19025-10V.

13. Letter, FF to Arthur Schlesinger, Jr., June 18, 1963, FF/LC, Box 101. For an example of Professor Schlesinger's depiction of the differences between the two groups to which Frankfurter disagreed, see *The Age of Roosevelt: The Crisis of the Old Order* (Boston: Houghton Mifflin Co., 1957), pp. 419-20.

14. Rexford Tugwell, *Roosevelt's Revolution: The First Year—A Personal Perspective* (New York: Macmillan Co., 1977), pp. 284-86; and Tugwell, "Introduction" to his New Deal Diary, pp. 13-15, Tugwell MSS, Franklin Roosevelt Library, Box 13, as quoted in Murphy, *Brandeis/Frankfurter Connection*, p. 107.

15. Undated memorandum, Raymond Moley Papers, Hoover Institution on War, Revolution, and Peace, Stanford, California, Box 1.

16. Raymond Moley, *The First New Deal* (New York: Harcourt, Brace and World, 1966), p. 275.

17. This process was first described in an interview with Thomas Corcoran, September 29, 1977, Washington, D.C., and then confirmed by an analysis of the letters written by the major actors during these legislative campaigns.

18. The one occasion when this involvement did come to the public's attention, due to a remark by NRA head General Hugh Johnson, was an accidental mention which was beyond Brandeis's control. For details, see Murphy, *Brandeis/Frankfurter Connection*, pp. 144-50.

19. For an early description of Brandeis's plan, see "Memorandum of Mr. Brandeis on Irregular Employment," June 1911, FF/LC, Box 226.

20. For more on the entire unemployment compensation issue, see Daniel Nelson, *Unemployment Insurance: The American Experience, 1915-35* (Madison: University of Wisconsin Press, 1969), chapter 9.

21. Reminiscences of Paul and Elizabeth Raushenbush, Columbia Oral History Collection, pp. 140-41.

22. Ibid., p. 143; see also, letters LDB to FF, September 20, 1933, FF/LC, Box 28, and LDB to Donald Richberg, December 10, 1933, Richberg Papers, Library of Congress, Box 1; LDB to Elizabeth Raushenbush, September 30 and November 17, 1933, in Urofsky and Levy, eds., *Brandeis Letters*, vol. 5, pp. 523, 426-27; and memorandum, Mr. Stoddard to A. Lincoln Filene, December 27, 1933, Brandeis MSS, Louisville Law School, Box G-7.

23. Raushenbush Reminiscences, Columbia Oral History Collection (COHC), pp. 142-48, contains an account of these meetings.

24. Letter, LDB to FF, January 25, 1934, FF/LC, Box 115. See also Raushenbush Reminiscences, COHC, pp. 149-55.

25. Memorandum, FDR to Rexford Tugwell, February 28, 1934, Roosevelt Library, PSF 73.

26. Letters, Thomas Corcoran to FF, June 18, 1934, FF/LC, Box 149; and LDB to Elizabeth Raushenbush, June 8, 1934, in Urofsky and Levy, *Brandeis Letters*, vol. 5, pp. 539-40.

27. Letter, FF to LDB, July 24, 1934, Brandeis MSS, Box G9.

28. Letter, FF to Moley, July 25, 1934, Moley MSS, Hoover Institution on War, Revolution, and Peace, Box 17.

29. Letter, LDB to FF, August 8, 1934, FF/LC, Box 28.

30. Letter, LDB to FF, July 26, 1934, FF/LC, Box 28.

31. Letter, FF to LDB, August 31, 1934, Brandeis MSS, Louisville Law School, Box G-9.

32. Tugwell Diary, December 31, 1934, Tugwell MSS, Roosevelt Library, Box 16.

33. Letter, LDB to FF, December 31, 1934, FF/LC, Box 28.

34. Letter, LDB to FF, February 7, 1935, FF/LC, Box 28. See also letters, FF to LDB, January 18, 1935, Brandeis MSS, Louisville Law School, Box G9, and LDB to FF, January 23, 1935, FF/LC, Box 28.

35. 2 Dallas 409 (1792).

36. Canon Numbers 4, 14, 24, as reprinted in U.S. Congress, Senate Committee on the Judiciary, "Nonjudicial Activities of Supreme Court Justices and Other Federal Judges," *Hearings before the Subcommittee on Separation of Powers*, 91st Cong., 1st sess., 1969.

37. Canon Number 34, in ibid.

38. 295 U.S. 495 (1935).

39. 297 U.S. 1 (1936).

40. 301 U.S. 548 (1937).

41. 275 U.S. 574 (1927).

42. 261 U.S. 525 (1923).

BERNARD BARUCH AND THE VOCATION OF PRESIDENTIAL ADVISER

Jordan A. Schwarz

To the best of my knowledge, there is no job description for presidential adviser. It is a position that does not fit into a flowchart of institutional structure and responsibilities. It is not the sort of job that seeks an applicant, either through the classified ads or a university placement office. It has no particular course of study in academe and, while its occupants are ambitious people, I cannot imagine that they declared early in life a goal of becoming a presidential adviser. Nevertheless, the book on presidential advisers ought to have been written as a collaboration of two astute and knowledgeable minds—Franklin D. Roosevelt and Bernard M. Baruch—Roosevelt because he drew upon an eclectic pool of advisers and employed them in myriad ways during his long tenure in office, and Baruch because he performed adroitly at the game long before Roosevelt and long after, thereby allowing him to claim the title of presidential adviser to every President from Woodrow Wilson through Lyndon Johnson. However, before we examine what drew these two experts on presidential advising together, we ought to scrutinize the sources of advisers for President Roosevelt.

Roosevelt found his advisers in different fields that varied with the episodes of his life. To begin, there was Louis Howe, who, despite what I already said, seemed to have no other life's ambition than to make Franklin Roosevelt President.[1] Of course, the former governor of New York was bound to bring some advisers with him from Albany to Washington: Harry Hopkins and Frances Perkins are the outstanding examples of that transition.[2] However, prior to 1932, Roosevelt had few people who could combine the requisite functions of politics and policy;

Howe was a political animal while Hopkins and Perkins performed policy functions. Moreover, Roosevelt needed advisers who could transcend the state level while combining political with policy expertise.

For such versatility, two uncelebrated names stand out: Cordell Hull and Homer Cummings.[3] Both were party men whose ties went far beyond the boundaries of state or region and whose experience in national affairs antedated the beginnings of the Wilson Administration. In fact, that Roosevelt had earned their support prior to 1932 is a tribute to his shrewdness. Both men had been Chairman of the Democratic National Committee, Cummings from 1919 to 1920, Hull from 1921 to 1924. They had been loyal to Wilson in times of adversity, and they had been forces for healing party divisions during and following the trauma that accompanied the Democratic Convention of 1924 and its aftermath. Cummings was a skilled lawyer, as was Hull a skilled legislator in Congress, Hull's service there dating from 1909 when he helped pilot the income tax through the House of Representatives and remained one of the key men on the Ways and Means Committee until he went to the Senate in 1931. In an age when presidential primaries mattered less than they do now, Hull and Cummings were indispensable promoters of Roosevelt throughout the preconvention maneuverings of 1932. Hull would be rewarded with the position of Secretary of State, Cummings with Attorney General. Both served Roosevelt with loyalty, discretion, and finesse, protecting and advancing New Deal programs at home and abroad—Cummings until 1939, Hull until 1944. Both superbly combined the political and policy functions of the presidential adviser. However, whereas Roosevelt valued Cummings and Hull chiefly for their political astuteness, he primarily looked to others for their wisdom on policy matters.

His famous Brain Trust, composed of three Columbia University professors—Raymond Moley, Rexford Tugwell, and Adolf A. Berle—provided him with ideas as well as words with which to express them.[4] But it would be difficult to identify specific major policy strategies they contributed, although Berle wrote the famous San Francisco Commonwealth Club speech that gave the Roosevelt campaign its most progressive tone. To all intents and purposes, the Brain Trust ceased to exist following the inauguration. Moley became Assistant Secretary of State and Tugwell Assistant Secretary of Agriculture, but neither lasted long as Roosevelt's adviser. Moley made the mistake of attempting to upstage Cordell Hull and found himself cast out of the New Deal in a matter of months. Tugwell knew the value of loyalty and endured in a variety of minor roles, eventually making his mark as a perceptive chronicler of the New Deal.

Berle was a different story altogether. Unlike Moley and Tugwell, Berle combined a law practice with his academic interests and chose to return to New York rather than accept lower-level assignments. Again he distinguished himself as an adviser, this time to Fiorello La Guardia. He became Treasurer of the City of New York, where he devised the financial strategies that rescued New York City from the brink of bankruptcy and put it on a three-decade road to solvency. Roosevelt, mindful of the federal system, appreciated Berle's local tack and creativity in public finance. Berle made frequent brief excursions to Washington in temporary assignments for the Reconstruction Finance Corporation and visited the White House and Hyde Park often during the first term. Also, his letters, which began with the puckish salutation "Dear Caesar," received FDR's careful attention. Considered by most New Dealers as the most creative mind in public life, Berle left La Guardia in 1937 and the following year became Assistant Secretary of State, where he remained until the 1944 State Department shake-up that saw Hull retire and Berle go to Brazil as Ambassador. Of all the Brain Trusters, only Berle was a Roosevelt adviser to the end.[5]

One Brain Truster does not fit the mold. Hugh Johnson was not a Roosevelt man before the Chicago convention.[6] Neither a politician nor an academic, Johnson was a former general in the army whose personality was such that words like *colorful* and *pugnacious* are too mild to describe it. Although he had spent some time on the Mexican border, Johnson had been a desk general, trained as a lawyer and assigned to the War Industries Board in 1918, where he was taken under the wing of its chairman, Bernard M. Baruch. Employed by Baruch in the 1920s, Johnson scouted companies in various markets for possible transactions by the venerable speculator; in their words, Johnson was Baruch's "bird dog." In 1932, Johnson's analysis of the Depression was insightful and vivid; Baruch's influence with Democrats was extensive and powerful. Moreover, he was the Democratic Party's principal financial angel. Accordingly, when Baruch marched into Roosevelt headquarters with Johnson in tow immediately following Roosevelt's nomination and offered the general's uses as a member of the Brain Trust, Louis Howe accepted. In the months that followed, Johnson's role as an adviser grew from that of conservative speechwriter to that of industrial spokesman on policy questions. In the Hundred Days, Johnson's was a voice to be reckoned with. Then, to the consternation of Baruch, who considered Johnson "my number three man" and unfit to lead,[7] Johnson was designated by the President to lead the National Recovery Administration (NRA). In time Roosevelt would rue Johnson's elevation from adviser to policymaker, and eventually Johnson would go the way of Raymond Moley as a New Deal adversary. But Baruch would endure as an undesignated presidential adviser.[8]

Rexford Tugwell would later write, "Baruch's was a history few people were familiar with."[9] That was only partly true. To a provincial academic from Morningside Heights, Baruch's role in the Democratic Party and in Washington was terra incognita, but Franklin Roosevelt knew that history well and selectively appreciated it. Tugwell remembered the special pains Roosevelt took to inform him of Baruch's power: "He leaned over the desk to tell me that Baruch owned—he used the word— sixty congressmen. That, he said, was power around Washington. He said he didn't know himself why this effort was made and this control established. That could be speculated about. But those sixty congressmen had to be kept in line."[10]

Roosevelt knew that Baruch had been in 1918 a principal economic adviser to President Wilson, and in the War Cabinet he had sat at the President's left hand. In 1919 he went with Wilson to the Paris Peace Conference, thereby enabling Baruch to enlarge his knowledge of men and issues to an international sphere. He could reject Wilson's offer of Secretary of the Treasury with no diminution of prestige, and it was said that by 1932 the only position he coveted was that of Secretary of State. He had not been much of an adviser to Republican Presidents Harding and Coolidge, chiefly because he remained loyal to the Democratic Party and subscribed to Democratic war chests much like a reckless bull in a bear market. Nevertheless, Baruch's generous contributions were shrewdly selective, being mostly confined to Southern and Western Senate races where the outcome was resolved in the primaries. Thus, in 1933 Roosevelt knew that Senate Majority Leader Joe T. Robinson of Arkansas, Senate Foreign Relations Committee Chairman Key Pittman of Nevada, Senate Finance Committee Chairman Pat Harrison of Mississippi, and rising Democrats such as Senators James F. Byrnes of South Carolina and Alben Barkley of Kentucky were unmistakably on "Baruch's string."

A simple but insufficient explanation of Baruch's influence would be that he had "bought" what he "owned." But that does not give credit to his formidable intellect and personality. He cultivated powerful people and sought to persuade them to subscribe to his system of ideas—which could best be described as private enterprise corporatism facilitated by government supervision intended to achieve stabilization of a capitalist economic system whose worst enemy was its own competitive chaos. This system of ideas had flourished in Washington during the Great War and after, counting among its subscribers such Wilsonians as Herbert Hoover and Franklin Roosevelt. It was from those ideas and that wartime experience that they would draw their recovery programs in the 1930s. When Democratic majorities took control of Congress in 1931, Baruch became the most powerful Democrat in President Hoover's Washington. The bipartisan consensus that went into the writing of the Reconstruction Finance Corporation owed much to Baruch's sway over the Democrats in Congress.[11] For that matter, he influenced the writings of several prominent columnists of the day such as Mark Sullivan, Frank Kent, William Hard, and Arthur Krock.

In summary, to answer the question that much of Washington and Roosevelt could not answer—"why this effort was made and this control established"—it was to generate more influence with which he could guide the body politic to achieve an elusive economic stabilization. Prior to his reputation as an adviser to Presidents he had been an adviser to senators. His influence with the Senate increased his influence with the press and public because it demonstrated that politicians gave him their attention. And this in turn brought him access to the White House. In short, he was a kibitzer who became an institution by himself in Washington.

But what a kibitzer! Superficially one could argue that the early New Deal had been inspired by Baruch. The Hundred Days did not follow a coherent course on prices, but it was decidedly deflationary in cutting the budget at a time when the principal spokesman for deflation was Baruch. The speculator played a strong advisory hand in the Administration's decision not to cooperate with Europe at the London Economic Conference. George Peek lead the Agricultural Adjustment Administration (AAA) partly because he was a "Baruch man," just as Hugh Johnson *appeared* to be his puppet at the National Recovery Administration. Both Peek and Johnson had been with Baruch in the War Industries Board (WIB), had been partners with him in public and business ventures during the twenties, and remained loyal acolytes who hailed him as their "chief." But Baruch deserved neither the credit nor the blame for the New Deal recovery program. He was hardly the only deflationist in the Brain Trust; almost fourteen months after Roosevelt's inauguration, Tugwell would confide to his diary that he and Baruch "agree that there is considerable deflation which still has to be undertaken."[12] As for the London Economic Conference, the President himself was the man decidedly in charge and was very suspicious of European designs. As for Peek, he had been the chief publicist for the McNary-Haugen farm relief movement in the 1920s—a consensus choice to lead any agricultural recovery program, but philosophically in disagreement with the AAA program he implemented. Johnson's NRA was seen as the reincarnation of Baruch's WIB by Johnson, the press, and most historians since then; but Baruch denied authorship for the very reasons that undermined its success—it coerced industrial cooperation rather than employing incentives and sweet persuasion. In truth, Baruch was both a Roosevelt adviser and a New Deal critic.

Why was Baruch suddenly an outsider? He had been more powerful under Hoover and, as he told Joe Robinson early in 1934, "I have kept away from men like you and Pat Harrison because you are in a somewhat different position under a President who is the leader of the party."[13] Even with this inevitable diminution of influence, Baruch's memoranda concerning politics and policies received quick follow-ups at the White House, and the man himself was always welcome to visit FDR, a coin that Baruch was careful not to use too often. It was said that Baruch relished having his back "stroked the right way by an occasional audience with F.D.R." But why should the President bother to stroke him? As Roosevelt told Frances Perkins late in the 1930s when foreign policy issues began to intrude and the Administration encountered heavy resistance to its social and economic proposals from Southern conservatives, "Baruch can raise rumpeses [sic]. He can put things in our paths. He's got a lot of influence on the Congress still. We kind of need him to keep [congressmen] in line. . . . He helps out tremendously in keeping the more wild members of Congress, kind of down and reconciled. . . . Barney's a great help to us in keeping them in line, keeping them pacified, keeping them from doing reckless things."[14] At that late date, Baruch's influence on Capitol Hill still made him a Roosevelt adviser.

But the New Dealers who operated in the bureaucracy either did not see those uses of Baruch or did not understand them. Most of them were followers of Felix Frankfurter and Harry Hopkins, detractors of Baruch. They resented his conservatism, his ties with reactionary Southern congressmen and businessmen, his money which seemed to account for his power, and his lack of office that could have legitimized his authority and required accountability. Also, they suspected that, although he kept silent with them, he privately opposed New Deal programs.

In that they were correct—and they were not. He possessed nuances of disagreement. He defended their relief programs because they were both humane and eminently practical. Wilsonians celebrated terms such as *practical idealism* and *enlightened selfishness*. Most of the social programs, Baruch believed, were long overdue and did not deserve the opposition of conservatives or businessmen. Still, he did not like overtones of a welfare state that suggested the deathknell of individualism and voluntary cooperation. Whatever trepidations he had for the future of capitalism came to the fore with the passage of the 1936 tax bill and its capital gains and undistributed profits taxes. Baruch lobbied with Roosevelt and Morgenthau against their imposition and, failing that, finally dared to go public against the New Deal tax program in 1938. By that time there were many doubters of the taxes within the Administration, although few of them would have gone so far as to agree with Baruch that the taxes actually contributed to the Depression of 1937-38. Congress defeated the Administration's revenue bill, provoking FDR to allow the tax bill to become law without his signature—the first time this happened since Grover Cleveland in 1894. The outcome was hailed as a triumph for Baruch.

Baruch was not a New Dealer, but it would be wrong of a New
Dealer to consider him the enemy. Politics and policymaking
make strange bedfellows. New Dealers and Baruch seldom trav-
eled in the same circles. It was easier for liberals to deal with his
image as an ogre than with his humanity. The Brandeisians
depicted him as the personification of Democratic Bourbonism.
"We met at 10 in Baruch's study," Herbert Feis reported to his
friend, Felix Frankfurter; "Baruch was cordial and contrary to
all pictures I had built up of the man. He is of a rather smiling
and understanding nature."[15] Not only was he a genial and
warm personality, but he was perceptive and insightful too—
not at all the moneyed lightweight the lawyers and academics
of the New Deal imagined. "Baruch is an intelligent man,"
Rexford Tugwell finally admitted to himself more than a year
after he first met Baruch. "So now I find myself in substantial
agreement with him on what must be done."[16]

As the New Deal waned, Baruch's role as a White House
adviser took on greater significance. Baruch had not been a
New Deal adviser; however, he had been a Roosevelt adviser,
albeit a distant one, even through all his disagreements with
the President. And, as domestic quarrels began to take a backseat
to the Fascist threat, Baruch' stature as a political ally and
policymaker grew within the Administration.

Baruch's influence in Washington during World War II bur-
geoned because (1) he recognized that the principal issue of the
times was whether a capitalist society could simultaneously
achieve growth and stabilization in a revolutionary environment such as war, and (2) even as a septuagenarian he was
determined to employ all his resources in personal contacts
within the government and through public relations to attain
the objectives of economic expansion and social stability. In
other words, the New Deal failure, acknowledged by 1938, to
achieve those twin goals made Baruch's role as a Roosevelt
adviser during 1939-45 all the more imperative.

Relations between Baruch and the Roosevelt Administration
depended upon the issue. For instance, on the neutrality bills,
Assistant Secretary of State Adolf Berle and others frequently
called upon Baruch for lobbying or publicity assistance.[17] But,
when it came to mobilization of the economy and preparedness
for war, Roosevelt and the New Dealers would have no part of
his efforts to move the Administration toward the revival of

1918's War Industries Board. Roosevelt was as determined to avoid the Great War's organizational design as Baruch was determined to revive it. Baruch remained skeptical of the Administration's partial mobilization measures between 1939 and 1942, which deliberately excluded Baruch and any taint of his influence. Ironically, his public dissent from partial measures contributed to his popular esteem as the "Park Bench Statesman" and the "sage of Lafayette Square" who put national needs above politics. His popularity made him virtually indispensable when the Administration was compelled by events to seek the total mobilization Baruch wanted.

In the stabilization crisis of 1942, liberals and Roosevelt found it imperative to employ Baruch's prestige as well as his influence with the public, the Congress, and even within the bureaucracy Roosevelt headed. For nearly two years he had dueled with policymakers and economists over the selection and timing of price controls; in 1941 economist Alvin Hansen virtually conceded that the so-called Baruch Plan for price controls defined the issue that most economists and New Dealers had hitherto hoped to avoid.[18] Without him, Roosevelt's Economic Stabilization Program and the office of Price Administration's General Maximum Price Regulation of April 1942— which controlled prices for the duration of the war and enabled the United States to achieve its enormous output of war materials without incurring the runaway inflation attendant to any wartime economy—might not have been possible. Moreover, Baruch intruded himself into political debates such as the rubber crisis of June 1942. Without analyzing here the circumstances that brought Baruch to the White House on June 6, 1942, it is enough to note that Baruch's suggestion to Roosevet to appoint someone with judicial stature and political sagacity to study and to propose obvious remedies for the rubber shortage resulted in the Baruch Rubber Survey Report that stabilized the production and distribution of petroleum while setting a precedent for other critical materials in widespread use.

How was it possible for one individual without constituency or portfolio to wield such corporate influence in a pluralistic society? Of course, wartime exigency did much to make it possible, but few people understood the problems of war organization and the attendant issues and relationships engendered by the crisis as well as did Baruch. He could achieve in war what he and the New Deal had failed to attain, full production and stabilization. He accomplished it by establishing a special relationship with President Roosevelt, maintaining his prestige with the Cognress, creating new relationships within the old regular bureaucracy and the special wartime bureaucracy, and anticipating issues that Washington would have to engage.

The President defined his relationship with Baruch. He heeded Baruch's advice selectively, paying careful attention to messages that treated monetary matters, distrusting Baruch's advice on fiscal concerns. He treated Baruch as a handy conniver who, although unworthy of public trust, could be of personal service if dealt with carefully, or a public nuisance if unnecessarily alienated. They were friends out of convenience and associates out of necessity. The President valued Baruch as a ubiquitous self-appointed troubleshooter. The problems of the Presidency at war were complex, and Roosevelt was intent upon hoarding as much power and authority as he could. He needed extra eyes and ears about him to avoid various domestic pitfalls. More than before, the New Dealers were in awe of Baruch, both fearing and respecting him. [19] He was the "Old Man."

The war atmosphere of Washington was more conservative than it had been a few years before. Secretary of the Interior Harold Ickes, an old progressive who formerly considered Baruch an anathema and now considered him an ally, wanted Roosevelt "to recall Bernie Baruch and give him the authority that he so well carried out twenty years ago. I beleive that this would be particularly reassuring to the country at this time."[20] Roosevelt gave Baruch no permanent official position, just temporary ones, but the Old Man's power grew with the war anyway. Eleanor Roosevelt, for instance, admonished Harry Hopkins that liberals would need Baruch's assistance in the coming struggle over reconversion because "he does have more influence at the present time than any of us. We do have to work with Congress, you know, and he has more influence than you or I or the CIO, or most people who feel as we do."[21] Planning for the Bretton Woods conference, a Treasury Department official advised Secretary Morgenthau, "If Baruch were with us, he could be a lot of help. He is too big for anybody else around here." Morgenthau was urged to get Baruch's help and he did just that.[22]

Power in Washington depends upon both appearances and

tangibles; it is safe to say that Baruch possessed the illusion and the trappings of influence. This power was all the more remarkable because Baruch's cronies in the Senate had by 1941 passed from the scene. Robinson, Pittman, and Harrison were dead. Jimmie Byrnes, however, had moved into the Administration as the top mobilization man. Byrnes's prominence increased Baruch's prestige, but the Old Man possessed his own clout. The war bureaucracy was honeycombed with administrators who had been the beneficiaries of a Baruch favor or who feared Baruch because they knew of so many other people who owed Baruch a political debt, or businessmen and lawyers who had not been New Dealers and just appreciated Baruch as an informal liaison who spoke their language and could cut bureaucratic red tape for them. Always he operated pro bono publico as part scold, part cheerleader, part solicitor, part mediator, and part arbiter. He was both a bureaucratic politician and a publicist par excellence. Only his enemies considered him a nuisance. Thus, without intending it, Roosevelt had increased Baruch's importance and functions by endeavoring to personalize his wartime leadership in the White House with Harry Hopkins as designated chief adviser and weak leaders such as Donald Nelson heading the mobilization agencies.

In conclusion, Baruch survived the Roosevelt Presidency with his status as presidential adviser enhanced. Considering that he had been a New Deal outsider, Baruch's power tells us something about the way Roosevelt exercised presidential power as well as the ways in which circumstances changed during 1933-45. Never wholly antagonistic in their policies and always respectful of each other's guile, both men appreciated the limitations of presidential authority vis-a-vis the Congress and the bureaucracy and the changing temper of their times. The latter, however, made the twin goals of prosperity and stabilization better suited for Baruch's influence than for Roosevelt's. In that sense the war was the fulfillment of the New Deal, and Baruch's pragmatism made him the ideal Roosevelt adviser.

1. Alfred Rollins, Jr., *Roosevelt and Howe* (1962).

2. Robert E. Sherwood, *Roosevelt and Hopkins* (1948); Frances Perkins, *The Roosevelt I Knew* (1946).

3. Cordell Hull, *The Memoirs of Cordell Hull* (2 vols., 1948); "Homer

Stille Cummings," in *Dictionary of American Biography*, ed. John A. Garraty, Supp. 6 (1980), pp. 136-38.

4. Raymond Moley, *After Seven Years* (1939), *The First New Deal* (1966); Rexford Tugwell, *The Democratic Roosevelt* (1957), *The Brains Trust* (1968), *Roosevelt's Revolution* (1977); Beatrice Bishop Berle and Travis Beal Jacobs, eds., *Navigating the Rapids 1918-1971* (1973); Frank Freidel, *Franklin D. Roosevelt: Launching the New Deal* (1973); Elliot A. Rosen, *Hoover, Roosevelt, and the Brains Trust* (1977).

5. I confess that Berle is the subject of the book I am currently researching.

6. Hugh Johnson, *The Blue Eagle from Egg to Earth* (1935).

7. Frances Perkins, Columbia University Oral History Collection (hereafter cited as COHC), V: 94-104.

8. Jordan A. Schwarz, *The Speculator: Bernard M. Baruch in Washington, 1917-1965* (1981).

9. Tugwell, *The Brains Trust*, p. 274.

10. Ibid., p. xxviii.

11. Jordan A. Schwarz, *The Interregnum of Despair: Hoover, Congress and the Depression* (1970).

12. Diary, May 19, 1934, Tugwell Papers, Roosevelt Library.

13. Baruch to Joe T. Robinson, January 17, 1934, Baruch Papers, Selected Correspondence, Mudd Library, Princeton University.

14. Schwarz, *The Speculator*, p. 306; Perkins, COHC, V: 427.

15. Herbert Feis to Felix Frankfurter, February 23, 1933, Frankfurter Papers, Library of Congress.

16. Diary, May 19, 1934, Tugwell Papers.

17. Adolf A. Berle to Baruch, June 22, 1939, Berle Papers, Box 29, Roosevelt Library.

18. Alvin H. Hansen, "Some Additional Comments on the Inflation Symposium," *Review of Economic Statistics* 23 (February 1941): 93.

19. Schwarz, *The Speculator*, pp. 389-96.

20. Harold L. Ickes to President Roosevelt, December 11, 1941, President's Personal Files, Roosevelt Library.

21. Eleanor Roosevelt quoted in Joseph P. Lash, *Eleanor and Franklin* (1971), p. 904.

22. "Bretton Woods," Treasury Department conference, February 16, 1945, Morgenthau Diaries, 820: 29-30, Roosevelt Library.

COMMENT BY MICHAEL B. STOFF

Few presidents and their advisers have attracted as much attention as Franklin Roosevelt and his circle. Even before his inauguration in 1933, President-elect Roosevelt's famous "Brain Trust" had entered the public limelight. The circle, of course, was wider than that, and in early 1934 the Washington *Post* began a series of vignettes of the "New Dealers" just to keep track of them.

Some were old hands, such as Frances Perkins, Louis Howe, and Harry Hopkins, brought down to Washington from Albany. Others, like Hugh Johnson, Harold Ickes, and George Peek, had little prior affiliation with Roosevelt but soon found homes at the pinnacles of his jerry-built bureaucracy. Louis Brandeis and Bernard Baruch stood mainly outside the circle. Often as not they criticized New Deal policies but still managed to penetrate the inner domain. Sometimes they approached the President directly; mostly they moved along his flank, making contact through surrogates. The recent explosion of literature on the Roosevelt years has been dominated by biographies, a testament to the influence of so many people on the New Deal.

Such attention to individuals is appropriate. Those who channeled their energies into federal service during the 1930s were an uncommon lot acting in desperate times. To meet the urgent needs of a depressed economy and a discouraged people, Roosevelt assembled a stable of thoroughbreds and quarter horses: high-spirited and temperamental; strong and gritty. As Professor Schwarz has pointed out, the President drew talent from no one sector, no single ideology. There were a disproportionate number of college professors and social workers, lots of lawyers and economists. Most were well educated. Many were young, some astonishingly so. (Charles Wyzanski was twenty-six years old when he became solicitor of the Labor Department.) They all valued ideas, often disagreed over them, and fought vigorously to promote their own. It is unusual for laissez-faire liberal Democrats like Lewis Douglas and Cordell Hull to serve the same President as radical planners like Rex Tugwell and deficit spenders like Marriner Eccles. It is remarkable that *both* Louis Brandeis and Bernard Baruch could influence the same administration.

The anomaly becomes more comprehensible when one examines the leader of this uneasy cohort. Shallow and fathomless, accessible and remote, charming and acidic, a ruthless politician who could not bear to dismiss incompetent aides, Franklin Roosevelt surrounded himself with a staff whose contradictions and competitiveness matched his own. The diversity of his circle also betrayed the President's uncertainty. For all his confidence, Roosevelt never knew quite which way to go, only where he wanted to be. He described the place over and over. It was free from want and fear, with adequate food, housing, and clothing for all who lived there. Decency was respected and so were the dispossessed. He wasted no time drawing a map that led precisely to his destination; he just opened the throttle and sped in the general direction, switching tracks whenever he hit a dead end. If the New Deal therefore suffered from confusion, it nonetheless manifested the uncommon vitality of its engineer. To be sure, confusion impeded economic recovery, but vitality helped to induce pyschological recovery. This alone is noteworthy, even more so because the psychological revival preceded the economic one.

More than Roosevelt's ambivalence accounted for the variety of those who served as his guides. Diversity was also a function of the setting within which he worked. Too often the New Deal is depicted as the work of Franklin Roosevelt. The New Deal, for all of Roosevelt's considerable importance, had to contend with a number of shaping hands. Chief among them were congressmen and Supreme Court justices, with whom Baruch's and Brandeis's influence was strongest. Sometimes they pushed Roosevelt farther than he wanted to go, as in the instances of the Federal Deposit Insurance Corporation and the Wagner Act. Sometimes they refused to go far enough, as with the Supreme Court plan or executive reorganization.

Professors Schwarz and Murphy add rich detail to the picture by marking some sources of New Deal policies, together with the paths and limits of personal influence. More than that, their work is characteristic of current directions in New Deal scholarship. Early study of the New Deal proceeded from the top down, with Franklin Roosevelt as the focal point. More and more, study now percolates from the bottom up, with the happy results that the true complexity of the New Deal is emerging and being documented.

That men with public philosophies as disparate as those of Bernard Baruch and Louis Brandeis could exert some sway over the course of the New Deal suggests the range of impulses from which public policies flowed. Above all else, Baruch sought to stabilize the economy. His favored instruments were the private corporation and the trade association, whose success would be facilitated by cooperation, voluntarism, and the coordinating influence of government. Enlightened collaboration would replace killing competition; chaos would yield to order.

Brandeis disagreed. Competition, he maintained, generated and maintained prosperity. Consolidation, of the kind envisioned by Baruch and fostered during the First World War, led to monopoly practices and to concentration of financial and political power. Bigness, either in business or in government, was a curse, not a talisman. So as Baruch pressed for private collectivism and public cooperation, Brandeis urged decentralization, taxes on size, and economy in government. Baruch's star ascended during the early days of the New Deal, Brandeis's in the years after 1935.

However elemental their philosophical differences, Baruch and Brandeis shared strong commonalities of origin and experience, which indicate the social breadth and tolerance of the New Deal. Both men were southerners, the sons of immigrant parents. Both were deracinated ethnics who never escaped their heritage—and never truly wanted to. Both also cultivated the Protestant establishment; both gained entry to its *sanctum sanctorum*; and neither was completely welcome there. Both supported Woodrow Wilson and saw in his capacious vision of the New Freedom room enough to realize their separate dreams. Both were, in Professor Schwarz's excellent phrase, "Roosevelt advisers and New Deal critics." In their day, both were considered the most famous Jewish octogenarians in America.

More important, both Brandeis and Baruch were master wire-pullers, though their wires ran in different directions. Brandeis's ran toward executive departments and agencies, where so many of his sympathizers found employment; Baruch's ran toward the Senate, particularly toward southern Democrats, in whose hands so much of his money found employment. And both, despite the credit they have received for making it, were never fully pleased with public policy during the New Deal, even when it turned their way. The National Recovery Administration, as a case in point, was seen by some as a child of Baruch's philosophy, inspired by his War Industries Board and run by his lieutenant, Hugh Johnson. In fact, the old speculator was unhappy with both its administrator and his coercive ways as well as with the inflationary effects of his price floors. In similar fashion, Brandeis criticized the wording of the Public Utilities Holding Company Act and its weak methods of enforcement. Even at the height of his power, he failed to obtain the rigorous taxation he believed necessary to kill gargantuan enterprise.

In the end, these polar opposites were only two poles among many. Roosevelt, a broker and manipulator, performed a tricky balancing act within his administration. It left no single group of advisers ever in control. If Brandeisians such as Corcoran and Cohen drafted securities legislation, men closer to Baruch's thinking (such as Joe Kennedy) were appointed to administer the resulting programs. When the centralized planning agency for industrial recovery was invalidated in 1935, partial planning replaced it and private concentration continued apace.

Those results and the interplay that produced them occurred in the world of politics. And that real world, as Brandeis's apprentice Felix Frankfurter knew, mediated all outcomes and wreaked havoc with all theorists, no matter how compelling their advice. "I can not," Frankfurter once said, "compress my life into a formula." Neither could Franklin Roosevelt, the man he loved, nor the New Deal, the program he and countless others helped to fashion.

X

THE NEW DEAL
AND THE COURTS

The New Deal and Judicial Activism

Paul L. Murphy

Recently a journalist, looking at the Supreme Court over the last fifty years, wrote: "From Franklin Roosevelt in the 1930s, the Supreme Court got scorn. 'Nine old men,' he said, 'were thwarting the people by nullifying the reforms their Congress had voted.' From conservatives, in the 1950s, the Court got anger. 'Impeach Earl Warren,' they said, 'for requiring reforms no legislature had approved.' Liberals in the 1970s became conservatively protective. They said, 'What if a Nixon majority repeals those judicial reforms, which the voters have now accepted?' "[1] One could go further in reciting public perceptions of the Court. But for our purposes, what all this says is that the interaction between the New Deal and the Supreme Court, and the forces and controversies which that interaction produced, pinpointed both a form of judicial behavior and a controversy about that form of judicial behavior that have not diminished since that time. This paper will confine itself to the origins of that controversy in the late 1930s, but in the process it will argue that that late 1930s turning point was a vitally important moment in the history of public policy and public policymaking in this country.

The issue of the role of judicial activism is hardly new in the twentieth century. Thomas Jefferson, one of the great saints in the Democratic Party Valhalla, had, after many years of bruising and usually losing battles with John Marshall, deplored the Supreme Court as a regrettably undemocratic element in our democratic society and as a "subtle corps of sappers and miners constantly working to undermine the foundations of our confederated fabric." "It is an irresponsible body," Jefferson argued, "setting itself in opposition to the common sense of the nation, usurping legislation, practicing on the Constitution by inferences, analogies, and sophisms, . . . bidding defiance to the spirit of the whole nation, . . . making the Constitution a mere thing of wax which they may twist and shape into any form they please."[2]

What Jefferson was protesting was excessive judicial activism in the sense that the Court, rather than being a body narrowly defining constitutional rights and wrongs through the careful interpretation of doctrine, had become a policymaking agency. It was thus determining such vital political decisions as the legitimacy of the National Bank, the permissible limits of federal regulation of interstate commerce, and the extent to which the states could regulate before they excessively impaired the obligation of contracts and interfered destructively with private economic growth. A great many democratic leaders over the subsequent nineteenth and early twentieth century continued to deplore the extent to which the country was subjected to "government by judiciary,"[3] particularly during periods in which that judiciary rendered highly conservative rulings which in turn had a massive and frequently partisan impact upon public policy matters. This was true whether the ruling was in Dred Scott,[4] or in invalidating the Reconstruction amendments for blacks,[5] or in throwing out a federal income tax;[6] or whether it constituted the actions of the Taft Court of the 1920s in reversing child labor laws,[7] minimum wage laws for women,[8] or other forms of economic regulation which legislatures felt were legitimate exercises of their police power.[9]

In the 1920s, this controversy took particularly classic form as it reemerged with great vitality. Chief Justice William Howard Taft, who dominated the high tribunal during that decade, seldom missed an opportunity to state that the role of judges was a passive one. Judges, Taft argued, should not assume a responsibility for active policymaking. Nonetheless, he also contended that "the cornerstone of our civilization is the proper maintenance of the guarantees of the 14th and the 5th amendments."[10] And in that regard he directed his Court in the active curtailment of social legislation and economic regulation designed to interfere with the liberty of property without due process of law. Judicial activism, camouflaged by its denial, was thus to be the instrument for the recreation of these laissez-faire policies, especially in light of executive and legislative inactivism. But to Taft, such inactivism was desirable, since these branches were dangerously susceptible to the pressures of "democratic idiocy," which the insulated Court was not.[11]

This view led Taft to move to strengthen judicial power during the decade. The Judiciary Act of 1925, referred to at the time as the "Judges' bill,"[12] expanded greatly the Supreme Court's discretion in picking and choosing cases. It was lobbied through Congress largely by the carefully orchestrated efforts of Taft, and resulted in upgrading the importance of the cases the Supreme Court did agree to hear. It also stimulated a commensurate enhancement of the Court's own prestige and power.

Liberal critics, on the other hand, especially hostile to judicial supremacy since Progressive days, viewed these developments with considerable hostility. Even a mainline Republican like Charles Evans Hughes questioned the wisdom of the Court's exercising more discretionary authority.[13] But Hughes's position was mild compared with that of leaders such as Samuel Gompers, who rejected judicial policy rulings contending that "the Courts have abolished the Constitution as far as the rights and interests of the working people are concerned."[14] Or Robert LaFollette, whose 1924 presidential platform began with a categorical assertion that "the fundamental rights of Americans were endangered by the tyranny of the monopoly system. And the principal instrument for maintaining such a system on the backs of the people was the sanction by a judiciary usurping their power and their rights."[15]

The legal realist movement of the 1920s and 1930s added further such argumentation.[16] Its leaders questioned particularly the knowledge of constitutional command on the part of justices, and stressed that constitutional adjudication was largely a matter of judicial preference in policy matters. But in the process, the iconoclasm of such critics of traditional Constitution interpreting made their freewheeling countermovement of rejecting such constitutional game-playing considerably tenuous. The Constitution's grip on the American mind and soul led many traditionalists to bristle at Walton Hamilton's "realist" assumption that constitutionalism "is the name given to the trust which men repose in the power of words engrossed on parchment to keep a government in order."[17] Government by Constitution may have been superseded by government of men in the eyes of the realists, but for many Americans it was still actual and proper reality.

But already, by this time, a corner had been turned away from the excesses of Taftian rigidity, symbolized by the 1930 appointment of Charles Evans Hughes to the Chief Justiceship. Within a short time, the Court under his leadership began the process of enforcing seriously the Bill of Rights against the states in a series of decisions,[18] which were supported by a number of the more conservative members of the high bench. In fact, in one of the famous *Scottsboro* cases,[19] it was Justice Sutherland, one of the famed four horsemen, who demanded a higher standard from state courts in the area of the right to counsel. And in *DeJonge* v. *Oregon*,[20] all four of the conservatives voted with the majority to extend federal protection of the right of freedom of assembly against state interference, in a situation in which high-handed local police tactics, clearly a projection of conservative local hostility to radicals, had been the instrument for assailing and breaking up a peaceful meeting.

Thus, active judicial extension of provisions of the Bill of Rights against the states was well under way by the mid 1930s and in theory seemed to represent a reconciling of the double standard of the 1920s, in which the Court had thrown out, in case after case, state police power legislation when it adversely affected economic interests, but had sustained most laws curtailing the freedom of expression and freedom of action of radical union leaders and more militant social reformers. Thus, in a small way, Taft's expanding of Supreme Court discretion was turned on him by a more liberal court now willing to use that discretion in a new, more socially conscious way.

But the action in the early 1930s of which the public was most aware was not in the Court. That action was at the executive and legislative levels. And it was action based upon a new, and for some even a radical, reconceptualization of the Constitution and of proper constitutional government in a modern industrial state. "The glory of our Constitution," Franklin Roosevelt stated in his first inaugural address, is that it is "so simple and practical that it is possible always to meet extraordinary needs by changes in emphasis and arrangement without loss of essential form. That is why our constitutional system has proved itself the most superbly enduring political mechanism the modern world has produced."[21]

And the early New Deal reflected that general sense of flexibility. The two central pieces of legislation in the first New Deal's broad program for relief and recovery, the National Industrial Recovery Act (NIRA),[22] and the Agricultural Adjustment Act (AAA) of 1933,[23] had extremely tenuous constitutional bases. Their framers talked of a theory of emergency power which warranted such extraordinary federal action, and defended the NIRA's broad delegation of legislative policymaking to the President as essential. But one relied upon an extremely expansive interpretation of the commerce clause, and the other on the taxing power and the general welfare clause, to justify positive intervention in business and in agriculture.

For two laws which were somewhat revolutionary in moving toward positive government, superstatism, and massive centralization of power, the constitutional base was troublingly dubious. Their framers were thus virtually asking for trouble, particularly from a Supreme Court which had already tipped its hand as still being antistatist in the civil liberties area, and which could hardly have been expected to be wildly enthusiastic about such statism in the area of economic development and massive national planning. In fact, the Supreme Court did void both measures, expressing in general a strong concern for the distressing lack of strictures and provisions which might serve as an impediment to the abuse of federal power.

But the problem, for our purposes, was really more the kind of repudiational action which the Court took in nullifying these two constitutionally flawed pieces of legislation. In the *Schechter* case,[24] all nine Justices agreed that the provisions of the NIRA, particularly the codes of fair competition which authorized the President in his discretion to "effectuate the policy" of the Act, constituted an illegal and unconstitutional delegation of legislative power. More importantly, however, Chief Justice Hughes in his majority opinion turned to an extremely restrictive and ancient interpretation of the commerce clause, one which even the Taft Court of the 1920s had modified,[25] in order to challenge the federal government's positive use of its regulatory authority. Further, although the Court had seemed to condone certain use of the doctrine of emergency powers in an earlier decision, here it rejected that concept, while suggesting, somewhat creatively, that if action was to be taken along these lines, such action was limited by the Tenth Amendment to the states. Asked to comment on the ruling at a press conference, FDR singled out particularly the strictness of its commerce clause interpretation, complaining that "we have been relegated to the horse-and-buggy definition of interstate commerce."[26]

Roberts' ruling invalidating the AAA (*US* v. *Butler*)[27] was even more confining in its suggestions regarding the limitations of positive federal authority. Charging that the measure's processing tax was a coercive "scheme for purchasing through Federal Funds, submission to Federal Regulation of a subject reserved to the States," Roberts went on to construct an elaborate argument that the federal government possessed the power to tax and appropriate for the general welfare apart from the other enumerated powers of Congress. However, he argued, this was not a circumstance entailing a legitimate use of that process. Little wonder that Justice Harlan Fiske Stone, in a dissent written with the concurrence of Justices Brandeis and Cardozo, accused the majority of a "tortured construction of the Constitution," and sharply reminded them that "courts are not the only agency of government that must be assumed to have capacity to govern."[28] While admitting that governmental power of the purse can be abused, he stated that the majority's inference that such power, unless judicially limited, might be put to undesirable and constitutionally prohibited ends, "hardly rises to the dignity of an argument." "So may judicial power [be abused]," he commented curtly.[29]

However, the judicial activism dimension of these cases, and particularly of Butler, are our real concern here. Both decisions constituted a form of negative activism with seemingly little concern for any possible alternative. As David Minar once wrote, these and several other pre-1937 rulings concerning the national economic regulatory power "failed quite deliberately to come to terms with the proper scope of political authority as such."[30] All one learned from such rulings was the precise nature of the commerce and taxing power and the dead areas of the Constitution—the lacunae in which no power existed, either state or national, to deal with the problems of government. They revealed virtually nothing of the extent to which the electorate could use its supposedly democratic authority to control and shape society.

Further, the process by which this was done, as self-consciously and defensively described by Owen J. Roberts (the Court in constitutional litigation "has only one duty—to lay the Article of the Constitution which is invoked beside the statute which is challenged and to decide whether the latter squares with the former"),[31] seemed almost a form of latter-day scholasticism which basically suggested that an adaptable constitution, condoning a positive state, was not to be found by the careful, semimechanical process which conservatives argued was the judges' proper role. Thus these two opinions seemed to say, "Don't try this kind of thing again." Conspicuously absent were suggestions as to any prescription for future correct constitutional action. That fact, in turn, made clear to at least some of the more vocal critics that these judges were really imposing their own policies on the country, rather than those of the Constitution, as implemented through federal and state legislation. "What we face now," wrote Dean Lloyd K. Garrison of the University of Wisconsin Law School, "is not how government functions shall be shared, but whether in substance we shall govern at all."[32]

It thus had to be a legislative and executive constitutionalism to which the leaders of the second New Deal would turn if substitute legislation for that so sharply invalidated were to be placed on the statute books. Franklin Roosevelt said as much at the time, urging Congress to pass a new coal conservation act regardless of any doubts, "however reasonable," that it might have about the bill's constitutionality.[33] Critics complained that the President was urging Congress to disregard the Constitution. More astute observers realized he was challenging the unique claim which the Court seemed to be making of the finality of its interpretations of that document.

The "replacement" legislation which constituted the second New Deal, although more discreet and specific (and some have argued more Brandeisian) than the first, still contemplated positive federal intervention in a variety of economic matters.[34] It was thus equally distasteful to conservatives from the Liberty League to the high bench. The fact that it was more carefully framed, with conscientious attention to its constitutional basing, hardly masked its political thrust.

It was when the Supreme Court majority persisted in its earlier path and set out almost automatically to exorcise this latest heresy from the statute books that the partisanship of the body began to show much too strongly through its members' robes, and that an altered perception of the Court itself began to take a hold on segments of the better-informed public. Now confirmation seemed to exist for the allegations which the legal realists had been making for the previous decade: that judges made law; that political and social predilections were a central component of judicial decisionmaking; that the Constitution contained ambiguities, not absolute truths; and that the process of judging was one of temporarily choosing among competing principles, more than one of declaring the law for all time. People came to see, in other words, that the first principles of law were not perfect symmetry and certainly were not simply the reenunciation of traditional jurisprudence so rooted in past values as to be inappropriate for contending with contemporary issues.

Roosevelt, in launching his Supreme Court "packing" plan, however, mistakenly exaggerated the degree to which that perception was embraced by Americans. His hope of showing that it was the composition of this particular court, not the Constitution itself, that was the obstacle to New Deal success, clearly underestimated the degree of blind symbolic adherence there was to both the Court and the Constitution as stable symbols in unstable times.[35]

After the smoke had cleared and the dust had settled, and particularly after the Court had capitulated and sanctioned most of the second New Deal, no one was quite sure what the future role of that body was to be.[36] As to the Justices, they were understandably anxious to dispel the "rubber stamp" charges which their alleged cave-in brought from many quarters. But this speaks more to ambiguity than to clarity. Certainly, if one views the situation through lenses ground by any sensitivity to the significance of power relations, one can empathize with what was going through their minds and the minds of those concerned about the Court's future function at that time. The Court certainly had no desire to emerge from this confrontation powerless, helpless, and out of business. As one of the three coequal branches, its members clearly saw the need for its continued exercise of public authority. And the public itself could not help but react, either consciously or unconsciously, to certain realities of life at that time. On one hand, the President had a massive mandate to govern positively, to continue attempting to extract the United States from the Depression, and to impose needed regulation over many aspects of the economy in the public interest. But the same public was increasingly aware of the overseas models of the modern centralized state then threatening the world, whether they be German National Socialism, Italian Fascism, Russian Communism, or Japanese militarism. In some way American positive government had to respect the rights and guarantee the liberties of the American people as part of its overall function. Minority rights had, allegedly from the days of Thomas Jefferson, been the responsibility of the Supreme Court, and the Constitution embodied a view of liberty which entailed the protection of individual rights against all government encroachment, but particularly encroachment by legislative bodies. Therefore it is not surprising that certain Court members began early to explore the most constructive, and at the same time judicially defensible, avenues for accepting those responsibilities.

All of which brings us to Harlan Fiske Stone—without a doubt, in my opinion, the central figure in attempting to come to terms with the degree of judicial activism which the post-1937 Court should seek to exert.[37] Attorney General and subsequently Justice Robert H. Jackson, whose 1941 book *The Struggle for Judicial Supremacy* was a strong statement against the excessive negative aggressiveness of the pre-1936 Justices, viewed the post-1937 circumstances quite matter-of-factly. He pointed out:

> Ordinary legislation whose basis in economic wisdom is uncertain can be redressed by the processes of the ballot box or the pressures of opinion. But when the channels of opinion and of peaceful persuasion are corrupted or clogged, these political correctives can no longer be relied on, and the democratic system is threatened at its most vital point. In that event, the Court, by intervening, restores the processes of democratic government.[38]

Justice Stone had begun moving down that path two years earlier. Generally comfortable with the second New Deal's use of the commerce clause to underwrite its labor and agricultural policies and its programs of security regulation, as well as with its move for a national wage and hour law, Stone sustained the latter in an expansive ruling in *U.S.* v. *Darby* in 1941.[39] Specifically overruling the narrow commerce clause interpretation in the 1918 child labor case of *Hammer* v. *Dagenhart*,[40] he returned to the *McCulloch* v. *Maryland* principle that the enumerated powers of the national government could be implemented by Congress through whatever necessary and proper means Congress might determine. He also delivered the coup de grace to the use of the Tenth Amendment to block federal commerce-based legislation, and completed the process, begun by Hughes at the height of the court-packing furor, of taking the Supreme Court out of the business of evaluating the constitutionality of such measures once enacted. He thus utilized judicial activism to move the Court out of the role of a censor over congressional economic enactments.

But in the area of personal rights and the integrity of the democratic process, Stone was suspicious of majority control. His now famous *Carolene* footnote[41] (which one authority referred to as "the manifesto in a footnote")[42] charted a path of civil liberties activism which ultimately was to produce a new flurry of controversy over the Court's imposing its will, its standards, and its policies upon the body politic. For Stone articulated different standards for judicial review of legislation in accordance with the character of the interests involved.

The Court was to assume a new and more assertive role in eliminating prejudice against "discreet and insular minorities."[43] But such civil liberties activism was to be accompanied by economic self-restraint, wherein the Court was to assume the legitimacy of economic regulation at the same time it was questioning the legitimacy of laws restricting civil liberties and civil rights. This, critics charged from the start, would require the Court to pursue a new double standard which was as inde-fensible as that of the Taft Court in the 1920s, which had done just the opposite. The rejoinder was that economic interests had easy access to the elective branches for relief, whereas "dis-crete and insular minorities" needed and deserved judicial help in gaining meaningful access to the political process, including the freedom of expression and participation necessary to become part of that political process. Thus, Stone had charted early on what one current commentator, John Hart Ely, has called his "representation-reenforcing theory."[44] Quite early on.

But if this paper is to make any point strongly, it is that during the New Deal era this controversy remained generally in the incubatory stage in the years to 1945. *Carolene* by no means became accepted doctrine in that period. Instead, its "new direction" was subject to controversy on the high bench and off, and even its supporters differed as to the best means to achieve its somewhat unclear goals. Initially, Stone's rhetorical position seemed attractive. But even if one accepted the assumptions of the position, the manner of implementing the "manifesto" was not obvious.

Stone's own actions initially seemed uncomplicated and consistent. He reiterated, in his aroused dissent in the first of the flag salute cases in 1940,[45] and in his expansive majority opinion in *U.S.* v. *Classic* in 1941, [46] the new obligations of the Court to protect the civil and political rights of minorities from the abuse of both public and private power. But his brethren diverged in both cases. In *Gobitis*, eight of the Justices agreed with Frankfurter that the interests of the state were here more fundamental than the rights of the minority. The legislative judgment which clearly infringed those rights should be respected. But to the majority's allegation that it was not the Court's duty to question the wisdom of such legislation, Stone replied somewhat heatedly: "When confronted with legislation that stifles the freedom of helpless minorities, the Supreme Court should not hesitate to assume the role of protector, even if in doing so it supplants the legislative judgment with its own conception of what is appropriate."[47] But his was a lone voice crying in the wilderness. And the *Carolene* argument was rejected.

In *U.S.* v. *Classic* (1941), a case involving the conviction of a New Orleans politician guilty of the crudest kind of election frauds, Stone made clear that the Court was no longer prepared to tolerate official local misaction under the color of law. He thus not only struck a clear blow at this abuse of governmental power, but followed the program which Attorney General Frank Murphy had recently begun in the new Civil Liberties Unit of the Justice Department of seeking to ferret out and discipline such abuses of civil liberties. But three dissenters—Douglas, Black, and Murphy himself—were unconvinced.[48] They denied that a seventy-year-old congressional statute intended the constitutional power of Congress to authorize federal monitoring of congressional primaries. This Old Civil Rights Act of 1870, to which Stone had turned, was not sufficiently specific to allow such prosecution, they contended, despite Stone's feelings about its overriding constitutional purpose. Primaries, they pointed out, were not in existence when the Act was passed, and it took far too loose a reading of the Act to use it as the basis for prosecution. Thus these civil libertarians saw Stone's protection of one set of individual rights as an infringement on another set—the freedom of individuals from federal prosecution based on vague, questionable, and implied federal standards.

After Stone was elevated by FDR to the Chief Justiceship (in part because of his dissenting role in opposing the earlier judicial emasculation of the New Deal), the Jehovah's Witness situation, at least, turned in his favor. In the second flag salute case in 1943,[49] Justice Jackson, speaking for Stone and four others, and relying heavily upon Stone's *Gobitis* dissent, found that flag salute statutes violated the First and Fourteenth Amendments. He further argued that under the federal constitution, compulsion by statute of minority individuals, as there employed, was not a permissible means of achieving a national or even local social purpose. Further, he condoned civil liberties judicial activism, contending that the very purpose of a Bill of Rights was "to withdraw certain subjects from the vicissitudes of political controversy, to place them beyond the reach of majorities and officials; and to establish them as legal principles to be applied by the courts."[50]

What Stone won in *Barnette*, however, he gave away in the Japanese cases.[51] While he struggled hard to achieve some sort of delicate balance between national security, military necessity, and war-time civil liberties, his approach was too vulnerable to majority political emotions to serve as a consistent doctrine for the Court to follow. His flexible definitions of the discretionary powers of the military left minorities far too vulnerable and threatened. It was not enough to see to it that the discretionary power in the military had been reasonably exercised. The treatment of the Japanese involved per se untoward violations of civil liberties, and for Justices like Jackson and Murphy, the Court should not have entertained such violations.

But Stone's *Carolene* approach to civil liberties was only part of his view of the Court's role and function. *Carolene* inferred a certain kind and quality of activism. Other parts of Stone's philosophy militated to some degree against its careless use. This was particularly true as the Court confronted cases entailing legislation promoting or restricting the power of labor unions. Here, as the issue took the form, in the eyes of many, of a decidedly result-oriented jurisprudence, Stone tended to view what was taking place with a certain uneasy caution.

There was, and had long been, on the statute books a body of legislation which had been utilized in dealing with unions and union activities. The issue was largely whether it had been used fairly and equitably. That raised complex and difficult issues of statutory interpretation. For certain prounion justices—particularly Black, Douglas, and Murphy—the path seemed clear: such statutes should be interpreted by the courts in a decidely prounion manner. Stone, on the other hand, was prepared to move cautiously. And while he had no reluctance to review older situations in which the antitrust laws, particularly, had been twisted into devices for sharply curtailing unions, overcompensation was to him hardly the remedy. Rather, a search for moderation and restraint, based upon fidelity to statutory language and a gradualist approach to change, was to him the responsible judicial course. Political accommodation was important. There were, in his views, definite limits to the process of judicial lawmaking. The Court should avoid being imprisoned by a set of social attitudes, attitudes which had so guided the "four horsemen," even if now those social attitudes were liberal ones, aimed at more constructive and progressive social ends. The dimensions of this controversy again revealed the lack of consensus regarding the permissible limits of judicial activism which pervaded the period prior to 1945.

Stone had initially read the central purpose of the National Labor Relations Act as to effectuate the creation of even-handed machinery through which labor and management could negotiate their differences.[52] As the National Labor Relations Board (NLRB) evolved, however, its rulings exhibited an increasing sympathy with the views of labor unions. Stone also became concerned about the emergence of administrative construction of a statute, since he thought this could well be used to circumvent the statute's primary purposes. Thus as NLRB cases moved from inquiries as to whether unions possessed any power to questions about the scope of their power, Stone sought to restrict what he thought were indiscriminately prounion constructions of the Act on the part of the NLRB. Here, however, he got caught to some degree in his desire to correct previous abuses.

The case *Apex Hosiery* in 1941[53] is a revealing example. There Stone, for the majority, sharply curtailed the use of the Sherman and Clayton Anti-Trust Acts as restraints on labor unions. Previously it had been necessary to establish the liability of unions, to prove only that there existed an intent to restrain interstate commerce, coupled with a direct and substantial restraint. Now, Stone ruled, it had to be shown that the union's activities had the effect of suppressing a free and competitive market, either by monopolizing the supply or controlling the prices or discriminating between would-be purchasers. But in U.S. v. Hutcheson,[54] the Court, to Stone's distress and to the ire of Justice Roberts, strode on to a position which threw to the winds Stone's Apex reasoning, which had sought to keep unions subject to Court intervention when their practices resulted in actual market restraint. Felix Frankfurter for the Court engaged in some remarkable broken-field running through the Sherman, Clayton, and Norris-LaGuardia Acts and virtually took organized labor entirely out from under the antitrust structure. Reading the applicable statutes in what a commentator called a "spirit of mutilating broadness,"[55] he somehow discovered in Norris-LaGuardia a congressional intention to repudiate the construction put on the Clayton Act by earlier rulings. Roberts, in a dissent which Stone joined, denounced the majority's action as a "usurpation by the Courts of the function of the Congress, not only novel but fraught, as well, with the most serious danger to our Constitutional system of division of powers."[56] But the real loser was Stone, who had hoped for a more balanced ruling that would have kept the old line of precedents behind the door, just in case, and kept the Court's result-oriented labor proclivities more constitutionally camouflaged, if not controlled.

It thus seems clear that the post-1937 Justices were responding in many ways to their own history and experience. That experience made further negative judicial activism, or at least negative economic activism, an unacceptable route. Only two federal laws were ruled unconstitutional in the next decade, in Tot in 1943,[57] and in Lovett in 1946,[58] and in both cases the issue was narrow and turned on individual rights.

The extent to which the Carolene "manifesto" was to be followed was less clear. Barnette seemed to reinforce its thrust, but the Japanese cases hovered ominously in the background. Nonetheless, it did seem clear that in the area of constitutional interpretation, if Carolene was to be pursued, the type of activism which it entailed would be directional in guiding public policies toward the expansion of democratic opportunities.

As to statutory construction, only the future would tell. The criticisms of Hutcheson, and the even more vigorous criticisms of subsequent prounion rulings in *Allen Bradley*[59] and *Hunt* v. *Crumboch*,[60] left the Court ambivalent about its proper role. So did *U.S.* v. *Classic*, even though the issue there turned on a civil rights question. As with constitutional interpretation, in statutory construction the rules needed clarification as to the parameters and nature of the Justices' role. The older and more traditional view had been that courts could go no farther than the ordinary or plain meaning of words in a statute. Such a view also rejected readings that substituted what Judge Learned Hand once referred to as "what a judge thought the government ought to have said."[61]

Learned Hand had long sought to achieve a middle ground between the perspective of the mechanical jurisprudes and that of the legal realists by the use of the concept of statutory purpose. A judge began with statutory language, but refrained from interpreting it too liberally or ignoring it altogether. Instead, he examined it as a manifestation of the general purposes of the statute, the broad social policies that the legislature intended to implement. Where specific statutory coverage was lacking, a judge was to deduce the application of its general statutory purposes to the particular situation. This theory assumed that a court was capable of determining the primary purpose of a statute, but that assumption was itself controversial. While some judges found it comparatively easy, others did not. The latter assumed far greater discretion to apply legislation creatively so that its subsequent interpretations would best serve the general social purpose which the legislature intended, or surely must have meant to intend.

The fine line, then, was where judicial creativity ceased to become a process of seeking legislative intent and became one of judges substituting their own views of the proper role and function of statutes. More than this, the concept involved the process of applying a general intent to unanticipated specific situations. When judges were called upon to rule, how creative should they be? Again, however, there was no closure on this question in the New Deal years.

We are thus left with a situation which partly, at least, paraphrases a recent popular play title; "Nine Justices in Search of a Judicial Role," with a possible subtitle; "Ambitious Judicial Politicians Trapped in the Events of Their Own Recent History." Clearly, the struggle to define that role went on bitterly and without resolution through the remaining life of FDR. Indeed, the Stone Court, made up almost entirely of New Deal liberals, was one of the most acrimonious in the Court's history. But I would contend also that there is another historical circumstance here, which is not as obvious, but may be more central than the ones I have detailed.

Up until 1945, and in many ways well beyond it, a type of latent progressivism still dominated majority judicial thinking. New Deal justices still thought in terms of a beneficent government, staffed by nonpartisan experts out to fight social evils, with the goal of making a majoritarian system work better. Such affirmative government, however, had never had great concern for minorities. And progressivism certainly did not incorporate a concept of protecting rights. For many members of that generation, rights were still an outmoded nineteenth century idea, a rhetorical justification for the power asserted by entrenched special privilege. Undeserving racial or ethnic minorities had better not call upon the state for protection. California is a classic case in point, where progressive political reform had always gone hand and hand with oriental racism, a fact demonstrated in the 1940s by Earl Warren's willing compliance with the incarceration of the Nisei during World War II. The liberalism to which Black, Douglas, and later Warren himself came by the 1950s and 1960s, embraced, by sharp contrast, the idea of individual rights against the state—rights translated in time into a presumptive claim by all Americans to be treated equally. With this came the second goal of liberalism, the idea of affirmative action by government to protect disadvantaged persons—a minoritarian view foreign to mainline progressive assumptions.

But this was to be a debate of a later generation. Even Black at this time was not pushing preferred position and blanket nationalization. The greater dimensions of the argument came in the 1950s and 1960s, starting with *Brown* v. *Board*,[62] and aggravated and agitated by *Baker* v. *Carr*,[63] *Miranda*,[64] *Engle* v. *Vitale*,[65] and all the other cases we know so well. In 1945, the fact that this would become the agenda for a national debate over the Supreme Court was not foreseen. Or if it was, the dimensions and implications—ideological, political, and judicial—of that debate were not yet sharply drawn.

1. Anthony Morley, "A Judicial Standard of Rights," *Minneapolis Tribune,* July 17, 1977, 9A.

2. Quoted in Henry S. Commager, *Majority Rule and Minority Rights* (New York, 1943), p. 38.

3. A generation of such criticism was ably distilled in Louis B. Boudin, *Government by Judiciary* (New York, 1932), 2 vols. This powerful critique assaulted the abuses as well as the premises of judicial power. On Raoul Berger's modern *Government by Judiciary* (Cambridge, Mass., 1977), primarily a conservative attack on the post-1937 Court, see Stanley Kutler, "The Judiciary and Social Policy: Usurpation or Acquiescence?" *Reviews in American History* 6, no. 2 (June 1978): 263-71.

4. *Dred Scott* v. *Sandford,* 19 Howard 383 (1857).

5. The Slaughterhouse Cases, 16 Wallace 36 (1873); the Civil Rights Cases, 109 U.S. 3 (1883); *Hurtado* v. *California,* 110 U.S. 516 (1884); *Plessy* v. *Ferguson,* 163 U.S. 537 (1986).

6. *Pollock* v. *Farmers' Loan and Trust Co.,* 157 U.S. 429 (1895); *Pollock* v. *Farmers' Loan and Trust Co.,* 158 U.S. 601 (1895).

7. *Bailey* v. *Drexel Furniture,* 259 U.S. 20 (1922).

8. *Adkins* v. *Children's Hospital,* 261 U.S. 525 (1923).

9. For a summary of such rulings, see Paul L. Murphy, *The Constitution in Crisis Times* (New York, 1972), p. 63 ff.

10. William Howard Taft to Elihu Root, December 21, 1922, Taft Papers, Library of Congress.

11. Alpheus T. Mason, *William Howard Taft: Chief Justice* (New York, 1964), pp. 14, 264-65. Taft had, at one point, referred to the U.S. Senate as "a most Bolshevik body, . . . to be kept under constant surveillance by the Court" (Walter Murphy, *Elements of Judicial Strategy* (Chicago, 1964), p. 167).

12. 43 Stat. 936 (1925). On Taft's skill in obtaining the measure, see Felix Frankfurter and James M. Landis, *The Business of the Supreme Court* (New York, 1927), p. 280 ff.

13. Murphy, *Constitution in Crisis Times,* p. 46; Mason, *Taft,* p. 111.

14. Samuel Gompers, "The Courts vs. Natural Rights and Freedom," *American Federationist* 31 (November 1924): 865.

15. Kirk H. Porter and Donald B. Johnson, *National Party Platforms* (Urbana, Ill., 1956), p. 252.

16. On the legal realists, see Wilfred Rumble, *American Legal Realism: Skepticism, Reform, and the Judicial Process* (Ithaca, N.Y., 1968); and Edward A. Purcell, *The Crisis of Democratic Theory: Scientific Naturalism and the Problem of Values* (Lexington, Ky., 1973).

17. Walton H. Hamilton, "Constitutionalism," *Encyclopedia of the Social Sciences,* vol. 4 (New York, 1935), p. 255.

18. *Stromberg* v. *California,* 283 U.S. (1931); *Near* v. *Minnesota,* 283 U.S. 502 (1931); *Powell* v. *Alabama,* 287 U.S. 45 (1932); *Norris* v. *Alabama,* 294 U.S 587

(1935); *Herndon* v. *Georgia*, 295 U.S. 441 (1935); *Hamilton* v. *Board of Regents*, 293 U.S. 245 (1934). On the *Near* case see Paul L. Murphy, *"Near* v. *Minnesota* in the Context of Historical Developments," *Minnesota Law Review* 66, no. 1 (November 1981): 152 ff.

19. *Powell* v. *Alabama*, 287 U.S. 45 (1932).

20. 299 U.S. 353 (1937).

21. Samuel I. Rosenman, ed., *The Public Papers and Addresses of Franklin D. Roosevelt*, vol. 2 (New York, 1938), pp. 14-15.

22. 48 Stat. 31 (1933). On the framing of the measure, see Oliver P. Field, "The Constitutional Theory of the National Industrial Recovery Act," *Minnesota Law Review*, 18 (February 1934): 269-318.

23. 48 Stat. 195 (1933). See Murray R. Benedict, *Farm Policies of the United States* (New York, 1953), p. 276 ff.; and William E. Leuchtenburg, *Franklin D. Roosevelt and the New Deal* (New York, 1963), pp. 48-50.

24. *Schechter Poultry Co.* v. *U.S.*, 295 U.S. 495 (1935).

25. The Taft Court in *Stafford* v. *Wallace*, 258 U.S. 495 (1922), had greatly expanded the permissible use of the commerce clause to justify federal economic regulation. Hughes went back to *U.S.* v. *E.C. Knight*, 151 U.S. 1 (1895), a far more restrictive ruling.

26. Rosenman, *Public Papers*, vol. 4, pp. 206, 221.

27. 297 U.S. 1 (1936).

28. Ibid., p. 87.

29. Ibid.

30. David W. Minar, *Ideas and Politics: The American Experience* (Homewood, Il., 1964), pp. 309-10.

31. 297 U.S. 1, 62 (1936).

32. Lloyd K. Garrison, "The Constitution and the Future," *New Republic* 85, (January 29, 1936): 328-30.

33. See Alexander M. Bickel, *The Least Dangerous Branch* (New York, 1962), p. 263.

34. The central measures included the National Labor Relations Act, the Bituminous Coal Act, the Public Utility Holding Company Act, the Social Security Act, the Fair Labor Standards Act, and new agricultural legislation. On the latter see Paul L. Murphy, "The New Deal Agricultural Program and the Constitution," *Agricultural History* 29 (1955): 160-69.

35. Congressional Quarterly, *Guide to the U.S. Supreme Court* (Washington, 1979), p. 702. On the impact of the Court/Constitution symbolism, see Sanford Levinson, "The Constitution in American Civil Religion," *The Supreme Court Review, 1980* (Chicago, 1980), pp. 123-215. On the background of the Roosevelt strategy, see William E. Leuchtenburg, "The Origins of Franklin D. Roosevelt's 'Court Packing' Plan," *The Supreme Court Review, 1966* (Chicago, 1967), p. 376 ff.

36. E. S. Corwin, who had been actively involved in the court-packing episode, wrote: "The Court, having abandoned guardianship of property, would still have plenty to do if it intervened 'on behalf of the helpless and oppressed'; it would then be 'free, as it has not in many years, to support the humane values of free thought, free utterance, and fair play.' Surrender of its role as protector of economic privilege would allow the Court 'to give voice to the conscience of the country.'" Quoted in Alpheus T. Mason, "The Warren Court and the Bill of Rights," *Yale Review* 56, no. 2 (Winter 1967): 201.

37. On Stone, see Alpheus T. Mason, *Harlan Fiske Stone: Pillar of the Law* (New York, 1956), especially pp. 405-18; 511 ff.

38. Robert H. Jackson, *The Struggle for Judicial Supremacy* (New York, 1941), p. 285.

39. 312 U.S. 100 (1941).

40. 247 U.S. 251 (1918).

41. *U.S.* v. *Carolene Products,* 304 U.S. 144, 152-53 (1938).

42. Leo Pfeffer, *This Honorable Court* (Boston, 1965), p. 342.

43. *U.S.* v. *Carolene Products* 304 U.S. 153 (1938).

44. John Hart Ely, *Democracy and Distrust: A Theory of Judicial Review* (Cambridge, Mass., 1980).

45. *Minersville School District* v. *Gobitis,* 310 U.S. 586, 601 (1940). See also Mason, *Stone,* pp. 528-31.

46. 313 U.S. 299 (1941).

47. 310 U.S. 586, 607, (1940).

48. 313 U.S. 299, 329 (1941).

49. *West Virginia State Board of Education* v. *Barnette,* 319 U.S. 628 (1943).

50. Ibid., 638.

51. *Hirabayashi* v. *U.S.,* 320 U.S. 81 (1943); *Korematsu* v. *U.S.,* 323 U.S. 214 (1944); ex parte *Endo,* 323 U.S. 283 (1944). On Stone's role, see Sidney Fine, "Mr. Justice Murphy and the Hirabayashi Case," *Pacific Historical Review* 33 (May 1964): 199 ff.

52. Mason, *Stone,* p. 494 ff.

53. *Apex Hosiery Co.* v. *Leader,* 310 U.S. 469 (1940).

54. 312 U.S. 209 (1941).

55. Mason, *Stone,* p. 500.

56. *U.S.* v. *Hutcheson,* 312 U.S. 209, 246 (1941). On Frankfurter's "activism," Roberts fulminated: "I venture to say that no court has ever undertaken so radically to legislate where Congress has refused to do so" (p. 245). Walton H. Hamilton and George D. Braden, "The Special Competence of the Supreme Court," *Yale Law Journal* 50 (June 1941): 1363, observed that when he felt the end proper, Frankfurter could "discover the true intent of Congress; write a marginal note into the Norris-LaGuardia Act; use this to resolve the ambiguities

of the Clayton Act; and eventually bring the moving gloss to rest within the Sherman Act itself." See also Charles O. Gregory, "The New Sherman-Clayton-Norris-LaGuardia Act," *University of Chicago Law Review* 8 (Winter 1941): 503-16. For a more recent assessment of the Justice, see H. N. Hirsch, *The Enigma of Felix Frankfurter* (New York, 1981).

57. *Tot* v. *U.S.*, 319 U.S. 463 (1943).

58. *U.S.* v. *Lovett*, 328 U.S. 303 (1946).

59. *Allen Bradley Co.* v. *Local Union, I.B.E.W.*, 325 U.S. 797 (1945).

60. *Hunt* v. *Crumboch*, 325 U.S. 821 (1945).

61. Learned Hand, *The Spirit of Liberty* (New York, 1952), p. 109.

62. *Brown* v. *Board of Education of Topeka*, 347 U.S. 483 (1954).

63. *Baker* v. *Carr*, 369 U.S. 186 (1962).

64. *Miranda* v. *Arizona*, 377 U.S. 201 (1966).

65. *Engle* v. *Vitale*, 370 U.S. 421 (1962).

REFLECTIONS ON FDR's APPOINTEES TO THE SUPREME COURT

Henry J. Abraham

In a number of ways, my assignment to reflect upon Franklin Delano Roosevelt's appointees to the Supreme Court of the United States is a happily broad-gauged and open-ended one. For one, the pleasant noun "reflections" encourages a product that may blend fact, analysis, and evaluation, thus eschewing more disciplined or narrow specificity. For another, by confining the parameters to FDR's own appointees, I can indulge in the luxury of sidestepping such seminal questions as, for example, who among those other eight Justices that served during the twelve-year Roosevelt era from January 1933 through April 1945 is properly classifiable as jurisprudentially, decisionally, and/or predispositionally "pro-" or "anti-" New Deal. Thus I forego the temptation to comment upon the role contributions of the following members of the Court, who served during portions of the twelve-year period, but who had been appointed by FDR predecessors: Chief Justice *Hughes* (Hoover-appointed in 1930, retired in 1941) and the following seven Associate Justices: *Van Devanter* (Taft, 1910, retired in 1937); *McReynolds* (Wilson, 1914, retired in 1941); *Brandeis* (Wilson, 1916, retired in 1939); *Sutherland* (Harding, 1922, retired in 1941); *Butler* (Harding, 1922, died in 1939); *Roberts* (Hoover, 1930, resigned in 1945); and *Cardozo* (Hoover, 1932, died in 1938). Because the 1925-Hoover-appointed *Stone* was elevated to the Chief Justiceship by FDR in 1941, I include him in what I have always counted as the President's *nine* Supreme Court appointments. (Incidentally, contrary to common parlance, that is not record: it belongs to President George Washington, whose Senate-confirmed appointments totaled thirteen, although only ten

307

actually served.)[1]

In reflecting on the nine FDR appointments, I have considered three general rubrics: (1) their qualifications for the high post; (2) FDR's reasons or motivations for their selections; and (3) their performance on the Court, both in terms of presidential expectations and in the evaluative eyes of students of the judicial process and the Court.

Certainly far more than any other nominations to the federal bench, those to the highest tribunal in the land are not only theoretically, but far more often actually, made with a considerable degree of *scienter* by the Chief Executive. This may well not be true with regard to the initial "fingering" of the candidate, but once the percolating nominating process of a Supreme Court aspirant has reached its penultimate stage, the President *knows* whom he is about to submit to the Senate's confirmation tasks. Even President Harding knew something about his nominees—although a good case could be made for the contention that his selections were in effect made, cleared, or at least not vetoed, by his Chief Justice, William Howard Taft. As President, the latter was intimately acquainted with the profiles of the six he sent to the Court—three of whom, incidentally, were avowed Democrats. President Washington insisted on a veritable Wasserman test *cum smorgasbord* of six essential criteria for his record-setting number of Supreme Court appointments.

After having made what he would later categorize as "my two biggest mistakes—and they are both on the Supreme Court,"[2] President Eisenhower insisted on being fully au courant of the characteristics and qualifications of the other three appointments fate permitted him. While President Nixon fortunately did not get what he wanted by way of his ill-fated nominations for the second vacancy on the Court, it was assuredly not for lack of trying. And although the Nixon tapes record Keystone-cops-like references to "Renchquist" and "Renchburg,"[3] the President was fully alive to the cosmos of nominees Rehnquist and Powell.

President Truman knew very well why he chose his four arguably less-than jurisprudentially-distinguished appointees, Burton, Vinson, Clark, and Minton: he knew them well personally and professionally; they were his friends; they were political allies; they were tried-and-true Democrats or, in Senator Burton's case, a compatible and reasonable Republican. With the exception of aspects of Justice Clark's on-bench performance, he would not be disappointed in his expectations. President Kennedy, aided and encouraged by his Attorney General brother, personally selected his two appointees, White and Goldberg. This was not the case in President Ford's sole designee, John Paul Stevens, but Ford's faith in the judgment of his able Attorney General, Edward Levi, was abiding. President Reagan had neither met nor heard of Sandra Day O'Connor—nor, for that matter had anyone else close to him—but she was highly recommended by two sitting Justices whom he could trust eminently, namely Chief Justice Burger and Justice Rehnquist, and she richly fitted the prescriptive needs of the contemporary political scene.

In sum, in more or less understandable, indeed all but necessary, contrast to lower federal bench selections, a President makes a reasonable effort to know *whom* he is about to send to the Supreme Court; *why* he is doing so; and what he *expects* of his choice's performance on the institution of government (as to which the sage Alexis de Tocqueville had commented a century-and-a-half ago that "no other nation ever constituted so powerful a judiciary as the Americans"[4]—[without which] he added, "the Constitution would be a dead letter").[5] De Tocqueville was fully alive to Hamilton's famed *Federalist #78* half-accuracy, namely, that because the Court's only power is the power to persuade, the purse and sword being in other hands, the Court constitutes government's "least dangerous branch." Yet he correctly perceived the Court's powerful claims not only to authenticity but to its very real clout—as history has amply demonstrated.

Any set of criteria for the selection of future members of the Supreme Court is quite naturally informed, and discountable, by eye-of-the-beholder conceptualizations, by subjectivity. Yet it is not impossible to advance certain standards that, at least in theory, ought to govern eligibility, regardless of the degree to which a President's motivation may permit them to play a governing role in his decision to make a particular appointment. Thus, Professor Sheldon Goldman, a close observer of the judicial selection process—particularly at the trial and intermediate appellate levels—identified, in a recent *Annals* article, "eight qualities, characteristics, or traits that most would agree are associated with the ideal type of a judge."[6] The eight are, in his language: (1) neutrality as to the parties in litigation; (2) fair-mindedness; (3) being well versed in the law; (4) ability to think and write logically and lucidly; (5) personal integrity; (6) good physical and mental health; (7) judicial temperament; and (8) ability to handle judicial power sensibly.[7] It is hard to argue with the octet. To apply it to specific instances of selection, however, makes for considerably more complexity and introduces controversy in at least some of the stated components. The same observation, I confess, may well apply to the somewhat shorter roster of six components of merit I had suggested as *de minimis* qualification guidelines in the Seventh Annual Address to the Supreme Court Historical Society in 1982:[8]

> One, demonstrated judicial temperament. Two, professional expertise and competence. Three, absolute personal as well as professional integrity. Four, an able, agile, lucid mind. Five, appropriate professional educational background or training. Six, the ability to communicate clearly, both orally and in writing, especially the latter.[9]

Others have voiced similar requirements and qualifications.

And that the above may be broadly attainable in whole or in part is demonstrated by the composite of the 101 men and the one woman who have to date sat on the Supreme Court. The Holmesian tongue-in-cheek aphorism requires that a jurist be a "combination of Justinian, Jesus Christ and John Marshall";[10] if this combination may not always have been attainable, it is apposite to note that with one possible exception even that trio may not have been perfect! Even though political party affiliation has almost always played a role, there are just as many qualified Democrats as there are qualified Republicans, and just as many qualified Republicans as there are qualified Democrats. Nor is there any gainsaying a nominator's resolve to select a nominee with whom he is ideologically and jurisprudentially comfortable. You would, and I would, act similarly— always, it is to be devoutly hoped, assuming the presence of threshold merit. How FDR viewed his attendant responsibilities will be essayed presently.

At first, however, I ought to attempt to identify what history demonstrates as the ascertainable decisional reasons or motivations for the presidential selections of members of the Supreme Court. A quartet of steadily occurring criteria appears to emerge quite clearly, pace specific assertions or analyses to the contrary. In no particular order of avowal or numerology, that quartet embraces: first, objective merit; second, personal friendship; third, balancing "representation" or "representativeness" on the Court; and fourth, "real" political and ideological compatibility.[11] Obviously, more than one of these factors—and indeed sundry others—were present in most nominations to the Court, and in some cases all four were. Yet it is entirely possible to point to one as the overriding one. Thus, a classic and well-known illustration of presidential selection based purely on the first category, objective merit qua merit, is that of Democrat Benjamin Nathan Cardozo by Republican Herbert Hoover to succeed Justice Holmes early in 1932. That public opinion and senatorial insistence practically had to put the President on a rack to prompt him to choose Cardozo is beside the point. He did—and he would ultimately be credited for it as "the finest act of his career as President."[12]

Examples abound in the second category, that is, personal and political friendship as the overriding causation for presidential choice. Among the several illustrations that come to mind quickly—yet were nonetheless unquestionably characterized by merit—is President Andrew Jackson's selection (or, more accurately, selections) of Roger Brooke Taney for Associate Justice (unsuccessful) and Chief Justice (successful). Taney had been Jackson's longtime close friend, loyal adviser, and confidant. All of President Truman's aforementioned appointments fall into this category, as do those by Taft of Horace H. Lurton and by Lyndon B. Johnson of Abe Fortas.

The third category, the "representation" or "representativeness" of a putative selectee has become increasingly prevalent. Thus such "representative" or "equitable" factors as race, gender, religion, and geography never fail to be advanced as a major consideration, sometimes as the controlling one. Among a host of illustrations are the recent selections of Thurgood Marshall (race) and Sandra Day O'Connor (gender) by Presidents Lyndon Johnson and Reagan, respectively; President Lincoln's fruitful search for "an outstanding trans-Mississippi lawyer" (whom he found in Samuel F. Miller); President Cleveland's insistence upon "geographic appropriateness" in the person of his new Chief Justice, Melvin Fuller of Illinois; and President McKinley's choice of Joseph McKenna (religion).

The fourth criterion, political and ideological compatibility, may well be *the* controlling factor. It has been that demonstrably in a large majority of instances, and understandably so. The legion of examples include, for one, President Harding's Chief Justice Taft-inspired selection of ex-U.S. Senator and Congressman George Sutherland from Utah (one of the very few of foreign birth—England—to reach the Court). An experienced lawyer as well as legislator, Sutherland's alliance with Harding began when the two served together in the U.S. Senate, the association culminating in the role of "brain truster" to the President. He could have had any position in the latter's Administration, but he preferred to accept spot troubleshooting assignments at home and abroad—in the frank anticipation of a Court vacancy.

I now turn to FDR's nine appointees: Chief Justice Stone and Associate Justices Black, Reed, Frankfurter, Douglas, Byrnes, Jackson, Murphy, and Rutledge.

Putting the proverbial cart before the horse, how did Court students and Court watchers rate or rank the nine men once the FDR period had entered history? While the massive commentaries on the era during which the nine served do not, of course, fully agree on their individual achievements, the collective judgment on the group as a whole places them not only considerably above average in the constellation of the members of the Court, but far above average. While the 1970 Blaustein-Mersky study contains some inherent deficiencies, and utilizes dubious adjectival criteria—for example, "great," "near great," "average," "below average," and "failure"—without providing meaningful guidelines, it does provide an interesting compendium.[13] Sixty-five law school deans and professors of law, of history, and of political science (of whom I was privileged to be one, as were Wallace Mendelson, Charles Alan Wright, and several other University of Texas professors) were asked to evaluate all ninety-six Justices who had served on the Supreme Court from its establishment until just prior to the appointment of Chief Justice Burger in 1969 (thus including all of the Roosevelt appointees, of whom Black and Douglas were then still sitting members). Only one Justice received all sixty-five votes under the rubric of "great": John Marshall; next came Brandeis with sixty-two followed in third place by Holmes with sixty-one; Black was fourth with forty-two, with Frankfurter just behind him. The sixty-five evaluators designated a total of twelve as "great" (I rested my own case at nine). In addition to those just mentioned, Story, Taney, Harlan I, Hughes, Stone, Cardozo, and Warren were accorded the top evaluation—with FDR's appointees thus garnering three of the twelve "great" slots (a remarkable 25 percent of the total).

It may be of interest to note that in a celebrated 1957 address at the University of Pennsylvania, "The Supreme Court in the Mirror of Justices,"[14] Felix Frankfurter listed "his" choice of "greats." Excluding all those appointed *after* 1932, and thus the FDR group, the Frankfurter compendium numbered fifteen, including all those similarly ranked in the Blaustein-Mersky study (except the post-1932 FDR appointees Black, Frankfurter himself, Stone, and Eisenhower's appointee Warren). Four years later, Court-watcher John P. Frank issued his list of rank-perceptions in his *Marble Palace*,[15] which was a longer and perhaps less exclusive one, also refraining from rating any post-1932 appointees. Frank's top choices included, as had Frankfurter's, all the pre-1932 "greats" designated by the Blaustein-Mersky poll, thus pointing to a rather general index of agreement.

With Black, Frankfurter, and Stone designated as "great", how did the other six fare at the hands of the sixty-five lawyers and academicians? Three—Douglas, Jackson, and Rutledge—were ranked as "near great," Reed and Murphy as "average," and Byrnes as a "failure" (the last being patently an unfair designation since Byrnes served for but one term of Court, 1941-42). FDR would have rejoiced in the face of these evaluations—and he would have largely agreed. But I do not intend to rest on the above-described "poll" approach to analyze the qualifications and performances of the nine FDR appointees; let me attempt to examine them and their selection individually.

All but convinced that death and retirement had taken a holiday, that the fates were conspiring against him, and that he was about to be beaten in battle on his "Court-packing" plan (although the "switch-in-time-that-saved-nine" had been more or less accomplished in late March and early April 1937),[16] FDR at last received news that he would have his first appointment to the Supreme Court, just a bit short of four-and-one-half years of drought. On May 18, a jubilant President was advised by the seventy-eight-year-old Justice Willis Van Devanter that he would retire from the high bench, on which he had served for twenty-seven years, on June 1, 1937! FDR was ready. He had contemplated fully his criteria for appointments. There were

three major ones: (1) absolute loyalty to the principles of the
New Deal, particularly to governmental regulatory authority;
(2) firm adherence to a libertarian and egalitarian philosophy
of government under law; and (3) (once it had become clear that
war clouds would cover the New World as well as the Old) full
support of his war aims—which necessitated a generous interpretation of the extent of executive power. Of lesser importance
were age and geography; nevertheless, he considered such factors with great care. With occasional exceptions, all of FDR's
appointees lived up to his expectations during his lifetime: few
Presidents had been rewarded with judicial performances so
pleasing.

When Justice Van Devanter announced his retirement, the
leading candidate for the vacancy was Joseph T. Robinson of
Arkansas, the Democratic Majority Leader of the Senate. A
faithful New Dealer who had supported every New Deal measure
that FDR had sent to Congress, the popular, hard-working
Robinson had also been an early and key backer of the President's
Court-reorganization bill. Everything pointed to his designation. FDR had evidently promised him a Supreme Court seat,
although not necessarily the first available one. But according
to the then still high-riding Postmaster General and Democratic
National Committee Chairman James A. "Jim" Farley, Roosevelt had said that Robinson could count on being nominated.[17]
And in an unusual move the Senate as a body endorsed the
candidacy of its Democratic Leader. Yet FDR would bide his
time. He liked and was grateful to "Arkansas Joe"; still, there
was just enough basic conservatism in Robinson's past to cast
doubt on his reliability.

Then fate intervened: on July 14, while leading the floor
fight for the Court-packing bill, Senator Robinson suffered a
fatal heart attack. Roosevelt at once instructed Attorney General
Homer S. Cummings to canvass the field of other "suitables,"
keeping in mind that the nominee had to be absolutely loyal to
the New Deal program, and report back. By early August the
search had narrowed to four loyal New Deal Democrats: U.S.
Solicitor General Stanley F. Reed of Kentucky, Senator Sherman
Minton of Indiana, Senator Hugo L. Black of Alabama, and
Assistant Attorney General Robert H. Jackson of New York.
All four would become Supreme Court Justices eventually; it
was Black's turn now (although there have been assertions—

denied by Justice Douglas for one—that FDR offered Minton first refusal). "Jesus Christ!" exclaimed White House Press Secretary Stephen Early when FDR disclosed his choice to him on August 11.[18]

Steve Early's reaction was understandable. At first glance there was precious little in the impoverished rural background of the then fifty-one-year-old Senator—the eighth (and last) child of a small-town rural merchant—to qualify him for the Supreme Court. True, he had had considerable experience as a lawyer among country sharecroppers, as a county solicitor, and as a police court judge and prosecutor in Birmingham; he had read widely; and he had a lucid, profound mind. His educational background made that amply clear: he never finished high school, moving straight into the Birmingham School of Medicine, where he finished two years of curricula in one. He then took three years of law school at the University of Alabama (Tuscaloosa), where he was so bored that he completed an entire liberal arts curriculum concurrently, graduating with highest honors in 1907![19] But was he *really* the best FDR could do?

The President, of course, knew precisely what he was doing: Black, now in his second term in the Senate, had not only demonstrated enthusiastic and outspoken support of the New Deal, but he had staunchly supported the Court-packing bill. Those two factors were decisive. However, FDR also happily noted that Black had a long and effective record of siding with "little people" and "underdogs" and that he was from a part of the country that he, FDR, wanted to see represented on the Court. The nomination's announcement was met with approbation by most of Senator Black's colleagues and most New Deal spokesmen throughout the land. Yet it also evoked loud protests from both public and private sources. The intellectual and soft-spoken liberal was portrayed as being utterly unqualified by training, temperament, and constitutional dedication; as being blindly partisan; as being a radical rather than a liberal; as being, in fact, a phony liberal when it was revealed that he had been a member of the Ku Klux Klan (KKK) in the 1920s. The press—no more a friend of the Senator's than of his President—roasted Black for "combined lack of training on the one hand and extreme partisanship on the other,"[20] with the *Chicago Tribune* declaring that the President had picked "the worst he could find."[21] But the Senate, although treated to the somewhat unaccustomed spectacle of a public debate on the merits of a sitting member, quickly confirmed its colleague (backed thirteen to four in the Judiciary Committee) by a vote of sixty-three to sixteen on August 17.[22] (Sixteen senators abstained from voting or absented themselves.)

When the verdict was in, Justice-designate and Mrs. Black sailed for a European vacation. In their absence, Ray Sprigle, a reporter on the *Pittsburgh Post-Gazette*, published a six-day series of articles repeating the known facts of Black's erstwhile KKK membership. While acknowledging written proof of Black's resignation from the Klan in 1925, Sprigle alleged that, in fact, Black—notwithstanding on-the-floor denials by such powerful non-Democratic colleagues as W. E. Borah (R.-Idaho), for example—not only was still a member of the hooded organization but that he had been secretly elected to life membership in 1926. Black was besieged abroad by reporters, but he characteristically disdained any comment until he stepped before radio microphones on October 1 to make the statement which was heard by the largest radio audience ever, save for those who listened to Edward VIII's abdication:[23]

> My words and acts are a matter of public record. I believe that my record as a Senator refutes every implication of racial or religious intolerance. It shows that I was of that group of liberal Senators who have consistently fought for civil, economic, and religious rights of all Americans, without regard to race or creed. . . . I did join the Klan. I later resigned. I never rejoined. I have never considered and I do not now consider the unsolicited card given to me shortly after my nomination to the Senate as a membership of any kind in the Ku Klux Klan. I never used it. I did not even keep it. Before becoming a Senator I dropped the Klan. I have had nothing whatever to do with it since that time. I abandoned it.[24]

The public was generally sympathetic and persuaded of his sincerity. Again characteristically, Mr. Justice Black—whose personality Gerald T. Dunne has described as "steel wrapped in silk"[25]—said no more on the subject, refusing to discuss or reopen the matter during the remainder of his long life. "When this statement is ended," he had said, "my discussion of the question is closed." Three days after the broadcast he donned the robes—"he need not buy but only dye his robes" was a favorite contemporary cocktail quip[26]—of Associate Justice of the Supreme Court to begin a tenure of more than thirty-four years. It was one marked by a distinction and an influence rare in the annals of the Court. How right the *Montgomery Advertiser* had been when it observed: "What a joke it would be on Hugo's impassioned detractors if he should now turn out to be a very great justice of the Supreme Court. Brandeis did it when every Substantial Citizen of the Republic felt that Wilson should have been impeached for appointing him."[27]

Few jurists have had the impact on law and society as did Justice Hugo Lafayette Black. A constitutional literalist to whom every word in the document represented a command, he nonetheless used the language of the Constitution to propound a jurisprudence that has had a lasting effect on the development of American constitutional law. His contributions were towering. They stand as jurisprudential and intellectual landmarks in the evolving history of the land he loved so well.[28] In Paul Freund's view, Black was "without a doubt the most influential of the many strong figures" who sat on the Court during the thirty-four years of his tenure.[29] In that of Philip Kurland, only one other member, John Marshall, "left such a deep imprint on our basic document."[30]

He fully met FDR's expectations, of course—but that was in the short run; the New Deal as such had run its course by the end of the 1930s. In the long run, Black's achievements encompassed securing the central meaning of the Constitution and the Bill of Rights. At the pinnacle of his legacy stands the now-all-but-complete nationalization of the Bill of Rights, its application to all of the states through the due process clause of the Fourteenth Amendment. In what was probably his most influential opinion in dissent, the *Adamson* case of 1947[31]—he considered it the best he ever wrote—Hugo Black called for that nationalization, dramatically expanding and elaborating the Cardozo position in the 1937 *Palko* case.[32] He lost by only one vote. But by constantly reiterating the theme of constitutional intent as he perceived it in the Fourteenth Amendment—"I cannot consider the Bill of Rights to be an outworn eighteenth-century 'straight jacket,'" he had thundered in *Adamson*—he coaxed the Court step by step to his side. By the late 1960s the Warren Court had, in effect, written into constitutional law its concurrence.[33]

It is generally agreed that the nationalization of the Bill of

Rights was Black's most visible achievement; yet it is but one of
many. Among those achievements were his leadership in propounding an "absolutist" theory of the First Amendment's
freedom of expression guarantees, a theory that contributed
heavily to the Warren Court's liberal definition of obscenity
and to its striking down of much of the "subversive activities"
legislation of the McCarthy era; his assertive majority opinions
defining the line of separation between church and state; his
tenacious, literal interpretation of the protective *specific* provisions of the Constitution in the administration of justice, including those against coerced confessions, compulsory self-
incrimination, double jeopardy—he did have considerable reservations about the Fourth Amendment—and those defining the
conditions of trial by jury and the availability of counsel; and
his victory over Justice Frankfurter in the arena of "political
questions" that legalized the egalitarian representation ("one
man, one vote") concept now broadly taken for granted.

Probably the most moving of the 969 opinions Black authored
was written for a unanimous Court in the celebrated case of
Gideon v. *Wainwright* (1963),[34] which overruled a decision of
more than two decades earlier from which he had vigorously
dissented.[35] *Gideon* enshrined the principle that any criminal
defendant in a state as well as a federal proceeding who is too
poor to pay for a lawyer has a constitutional right to be assigned
one gratis by the government. For Black the opinion represented
the affirmation of another moving plea written twenty-three
years earlier in the famed case of *Chambers* v. *Florida*. Still
viewed as one of his finest opinions, it held for a unanimous
Court that the confessions obtained by Florida authorities to
condemn four black defendants to death were patently coerced
and therefore a clear violation of due process of law. In the most
celebrated passage, at the close of his opinion, Black wrote:

> Under our constitutional system courts stand against any winds
> that blow as havens of refuge for those who might otherwise
> suffer because they are helpless, weak, outnumbered, or because
> they are non-conforming victims of prejudice and public excite-
> ment. Due process of law, preserved for all by our Constitution,
> commands that no such practice as that disclosed by [the *Chambers*
> case record] shall send any accused to his death. No higher duty,
> no more solemn responsibility, rests upon this Court, than that
> of translating into living law and maintaining this constitutional
> shield deliberately planned and inscribed for the benefit of every

human being to our Constitution—of whatever race, creed, or persuasion.[36]

One week after ill health compelled his retirement in September 1971 at eighty-five, Justice Black died. "The law," as one of those who knew him best wrote, "has lost a kindly giant."[37] Friends who called at a funeral home in Washington before his burial in Arlington National Cemetery received a poignant parting gift—a copy of the Constitution. On a desk bearing a book for visitors' signatures was a pile of small paperbound copies of the document Black had so often referred to as "my legal bible"—a copy of which he always carried in his pocket. He would have approved.

FDR's second appointment opportunity came within six months of Black's when Justice George Sutherland, second of the Four Horsemen to retire, stepped down in January 1938. FDR's choice was no surprise: Stanley F. Reed, the Solicitor General, had been high on the list when FDR nominated Black. He was approved without objection on January 25. Reed had studied law at—although never graduating from—Columbia and Virginia, later practicing law in his native Kentucky. In the late 1920s he had entered government service in response to President Hoover's successive invitations to serve as general counsel to the Federal Loan Board and the Reconstruction Finance Corporation. He then moved to the Attorney General's office as a special assistant, serving there until FDR, conscious of Reed's faithful New Deal adherence, named him Solicitor General in 1935. It was a crucial period for the New Deal and its legislation, and the President needed an individual in the post who could be trusted to back the Administration fully. Given the composition of the Court, Reed won few cases before the Court until the 1937 switch occurred, but he always ardently supported New Deal principles.

In terms of his fundamental commitment to FDR's governmental philosophy, Reed was a logical choice. But he also was an attractive candidate because of his age (fifty-three); his state (the border states were then not "represented" on the Court); his impressive legal reputation; his solid character and personal popularity; and his noncontroversial image.

Reed, who authored more than three hundred opinions during almost two decades of service, was the least glamorous and least mercurial of the Roosevelt Justices. He faithfully backed the

President's program, but observers generally label him as being far more of a conservative than a liberal on the bench—probably because he moved more slowly and cautiously than his colleagues on the frontiers of constitutional change, and because he was reluctant to side with his more liberal associates in their rulings favoring individuals vis-a-vis government. This was especially true in national security and criminal justice cases, in which Reed usually fit into the "law and order" mold. Yet he solidly backed the Court's developing position on racial segregation; thus, in 1946, he wrote the opinion in *Morgan* v. *Virginia* invalidating racial segregation in interstate buses[38] and, in 1944, the opinion in *Smith* v. *Allwright*[39] striking down for an eight-to-one court the "White Primary" of the Texas Democratic Party as an unconstitutional violation of the Fifteenth Amendment. Ironically, Chief Justice Stone had initially assigned the case to Justice Frankfurter but, given the emotional nature of the controversy, had yielded to Mr. Justice Jackson's plea that it be given to someone else—someone more amenable to the South than a foreign-born Jew and a Harvard-educated, none-too-loyal Democrat.[40]

Felix Frankfurter was the next man to be selected for the Court. This, Roosevelt's third opportunity to appoint a Supreme Court Justice, came with the untimely death of the jurist and man Frankfurter revered, Benjamin N. Cardozo (whose seat had been formerly occupied by Frankfurter's hero, Oliver Wendell Holmes, Jr.). For almost a quarter of a century Frankfurter would serve with brilliance, dedication, and persuasiveness, almost—but not quite—equaling the performance of Hugo L. Black in lasting impact and influence. Black and Frankfurter were often in fundamental Court-role and jurisprudential disagreement, but usually with mutual respect and appreciation. These two, who towered over a Court replete with probably more talent than any other in the tribunal's recent history, left a legacy for American constitutional law and jurisprudence that was not only profound but seminal.

FDR, who had known Frankfurter since his days as Assistant Secretary of the Navy, had fully intended to send him to the Court, and told him so. Yet on Cardozo's death the President informed his friend and adviser that he could not do so now; that he hoped to appoint him when and if Brandeis resigned; that he felt a genuine need to choose someone from west of the

Mississippi to counterbalance a bench now entirely made up of Easterners. He then asked Frankfurter to prepare dossiers on prospective candidates from the desired area.[41] Roosevelt made no secret of his stated intentions which, in turn, set into motion a veritable ground swell of support for Frankfurter, reminiscent of the events surrounding Hoover's nomination of Cardozo. Unlike Cardozo, however, Frankfurter actively promoted his own candidacy, with FDR "braintrusters" Benjamin V. Cohen and Thomas Corcoran serving as his almost daily advocates with the President. Fifty-six years old, Frankfurter was a brilliant scholar and teacher (he had taught for twenty-five years at the Harvard Law School); a superb lawyer; a powerful advocate for the underdog; an effective, shrewd administrator; a connoisseur of personnel; and a highly effective public servant with considerable experience in federal and state government. He had become a close presidential adviser and confidant in the evolving New Deal; he had aided in the drafting of legislation; and he had recommended many able young appointees to the Roosevelt Administration—often derisively referred to as "Felix's Happy Hotdogs" because of their alleged political coloration and fealty to "F.F."

The pressure on FDR to designate Professor Frankfurter became intense: his closest personal and political advisers, such as his Solicitor General, Robert H. Jackson; his Secretary of the Interior, Harold L. Ickes; his Man Friday, Harry Hopkins; his friend and political ally, Senator George Norris; and, perhaps most persuasively, Justice Stone, all implored the President to place excellence over geography. Jackson scored points by urging FDR to choose F.F., if for no other reason than naming "someone who can interpret [the Constitution] with scholarship and with sufficient assurance to face Chief Justice Hughes in conference and hold his own in discussion."[42] The President yielded, announcing to his entourage that "there isn't anybody in the West . . . who is of sufficient stature."[43] Frankfurter himself recorded that at 7:00 p.m. on January 4, 1939, while he was in his B.V.D., late to receive a dinner guest, the phone rang in his study, "and there was the ebullient, exuberant, resilient, warmth-enveloping voice of the President of the United States, 'Hello. How are you?'" Then, after asking about Frankfurter's wife, Marion,[44] FDR told him not once, but several times: "You know, I told you I don't want to appoint you to the Supreme

Court of the United States. . . . I mean it. . . . I mean this. I mean this. I don't want to appoint you. . . . I told you I can't name you." Underwear-clad, and eager to go down to dinner, Frankfurter agreed again and again with his caller, becoming more and more exasperated. He was hardly prepared for the President's next words: "But wherever I turn, wherever I turn and to whomever I talk that matters to me, I am made to realize that you are the only person fit to succeed Holmes and Cardozo." Adding: "Unless you give me an insurmountable objection I'm going to send your name in for the Court tomorrow at twelve o'clock." The overwhelmed Frankfurter replied softly, "All I can say is that I wish my mother were alive."[45] Senate confirmation, by unanimous voice vote, came twelve days later, after some protracted opposition by Senator Pat McCarran (D.-Nev.), who tried to link the nominee with Communism.

Senator McCarran need not have worried. Frankfurter may have been a native of Vienna, but he loved his adopted country and its institutions as few men did. This longtime champion of the poor, the oppressed, the underdog, and the persecuted had but one aim: to make America an even better place to live for an ever greater number of people. A passionate believer in the democratic process with an abiding regard for the British concept of legislative supremacy, he would dedicate his twenty-three years on the Court to the proposition that the people should govern, but that it was up to their representatives in the legislature, not the judiciary, to make laws. Thus Frankfurter became increasingly known as an articulate and persuasive advocate of judicial abnegation in favor of legislative action. "When in doubt, don't," became the Frankfurter maxim. So dedicated was he to the principle of judicial restraint—pace the recent documentations of his extracurricular activities as a surrogate of Brandeis[46]—that Fred Rodell referred to him as "the Supreme Court's Emily Post."[47] Walton Hamilton characterized him as "weaving crochet patches of legalism on the fingers of the case."[48] Frankfurter's jurisprudential philosophy, of course, enabled him to back the New Deal's program to the fullest—enacted as it was by the people's duly chosen representatives. FDR was pleased, indeed.

In social and economic legislation Frankfurter could be found with the other Justices appointed by Roosevelt. But when it came to the interpretation of the Bill of Rights, he and Black and the other "libertarian activists" (especially Douglas, Murphy, and Rutledge) would often part company—for Frankfurter brought the same sense of judicial restraint to legislation concerning human rights as he did to legislation concerning economic issues. He could be a powerful spokesman on behalf of due process of law: as the author for a unanimous Court in *Rochin v. California* (1952),[49] he delivered a magnificent lecture to Los Angeles County police authorities on the requirements of procedural due process. He accorded the Fourth Amendment's safeguards against unreasonable searches and seizures a place second to none in the Bill of Rights. Yet this champion of human freedom who had fought so hard to save Sacco and Vanzetti stood like Canute against his personal convictions when it came to his role as a jurist. Thus, notwithstanding his abhorrence of capital punishment, he could not bring himself to provide the necessary fifth vote to save Willie Francis, a teenage Louisiana black, from a second trip to the electric chair (the malfunctioning instrument had failed to do its grim job the first time).[50] Frankfurter felt bound by what he viewed as the commands of the Federalist division of powers—in spite of his outcry to Justice Burton, whose dissenting opinion he had seen: "I have to hold on to myself not to reach your result."[51] Yet he had used all of his considerable influence—unsuccessfully—in trying to commute Willie's sentence.

Frankfurter's scrupulous adherence to his duty as a judge despite his personal commitments is perhaps even better illustrated by his most famous dissenting opinion in a civil liberties case. It came in 1943 when a six-to-three Court, overruling an earlier Frankfurter opinion,[52] declared unconstitutional a West Virginia statute that compelled school children to salute the flag as a daily exercise.[53] Frankfurter, of course, would not have voted for such a law had he been a legislator, since it compelled saluting even by those, like the Jehovah's Witnesses, who regarded the act as paying homage to a graven image. But as a jurist he could not bring himself to join the majority opinion that the compulsory salute was an unconstitutional invasion of the free exercise of religion and freedom of expression guaranteed by Amendments One and Fourteen:

> One who belongs to the most vilified and persecuted minority in
> history is not likely to be insensible to the freedoms guaranteed
> by our Constitution. Were my purely personal attitude relevant I

should wholeheartedly associate myself with the general libertarian view in the Court's opinion, representing as they do the
thought and action of a lifetime. But as judges we are neither
Jew nor Gentile, neither Catholic nor agnostic. We owe equal
attachment to the Constitution and are equally bound by our
judicial obligations whether we derive our citizenship from the
earliest or the latest immigrants to these shores. As a member of
this Court I am not justified in writing my private notions of
policy into the Constitution, no matter how deeply I may cherish
them or how mischievous I may deem their disregard.[54]

Frankfurter's conception of the judicial function is also tellingly illustrated by his continuing battle, successful until the
momentous 1962 *Baker* v. *Carr*[55] reapportionment-redistricting
decision, against the Court's dealing with "political questions."
In an impassioned sixty-eight-page dissenting opinion, joined
by his disciple-ally John Marshall Harlan, he warned the Court
that it was about to enter a "mathematical quagmire," that it
must stay out of such "a political thicket." He further admonished
the majority of six: "There is not under our Constitution a
judicial remedy for every political mischief. In a democratic
society like ours, relief must come through an aroused popular
conscience that sears the conscience of the people's representatives."[56] But, asked his opponents tellingly, what happens when
there are no electoral channels open to "sear" that conscience?

Felix Frankfurter died on February 22, 1965, ill health having
dictated his retirement at the age of eighty, three years earlier. A
great jurist in defeat as well as in victory, he left a major
imprint on the American scene. In a memorial editorial the
New York Times summed up eloquently: "As a philosopher
and scholar of the law, a judicial craftsman, a master of prose
style and a formative influence on a generation of American
lawyers and public officials, Felix Frankfurter was a major
shaper of the history of his age."[57] And dozens of newspapers
ended their obituaries with the above-quoted sentences from
his *Baker* v. *Carr* dissenting opinion.

Four weeks after President Roosevelt had nominated Frankfurter, Justice Louis D. Brandeis retired after twenty-three years.
FDR thus had his fourth vacancy in little more than three-and-
a-half years. How matters had changed since those first frustrating
years of similar duration! The President still wanted a Westerner,
and his youthful Chairman of the Securities and Exchange
Commission, William O. Douglas, born in Ottertail County,

Minnesota, and raised in Yakima, Washington, was a likely candidate. But Douglas—an FDR favorite and an "insider" on whom the President had often called for advice and speech-writing duties—had spent half of his forty-one years in New York (Columbia Law School), in New Haven, Connecticut (Yale Law School Faculty), and in Washington, D.C. (government service); Roosevelt viewed him as two-thirds Easterner. He had promised a "true Westerner" and, besides, the Court was in his corner, though perhaps not by a comfortable margin. Thus he took no immediate action.

Yet pressure began to build from his close advisers as well as Brandeis, who strongly urged FDR to nominate Douglas. The latter, after all, was personally as well as philosophically close to Brandeis on social, economic, political, and constitutional policy. Douglas, moreover, was an ardent and articulate New Dealer; he believed that the law had to be alive to the demands of the times; he had an outstanding legal mind; and he was a proved expert in the intricacies of public finance and corporation problems. Further persuasion came with a press conference dramatically called by Senator William Borah of Idaho, now ranking member of the Senate Judiciary Committee. In that conference he "claimed" Douglas as "one of the West's finest and brightest sons."[58] FDR, now convinced, telephoned Douglas on a golf course to inform him of his decision. FDR teased Douglas "for five minutes—I thought he was offering me the Federal Communications Chairmanship—but then he offered me the job."[59] Douglas's name went to the Senate on March 20. He was confirmed promptly by a vote of sixty-two to four—at a mere forty-one years of age the youngest appointee since Justice Joseph Story in 1811. Ironically, the four "no" votes (cast by Republican Senators) categorized Douglas as a "reactionary tool of Wall Street"![60]

Justice William O. Douglas remained as a member of the Court for more than thirty-six-and-a-half years. Still incredibly vigorous both physically and intellectually until his late seventies, and despite a pacemaker in his chest and a fourth wife almost fifty years his junior, he was felled by severe circulatory illness and, most reluctantly, was prevailed upon to retire in 1975. He died in 1980. Although all of FDR's appointees came through for him and the New Deal, no one did more so, with more consistency and with more concern for the results of decisions, than Douglas.

And, ultimately, Douglas compiled a civil liberties record on the bench second to none: in close to 96 percent of all cases involving line drawing between the rights of the individual and those of society, he sided with the former. The Douglas human-rights-activist posture thus would not be checked by the verbiage of the Constitution: if that document and its Bill of Rights did not provide the kind of protection for the individual Douglas deemed necessary to bring about justice under law, well, he would find it—as he did in his famed and controversial precedent-setting, "privacy"-constitutionalizing opinion in the *Connecticut Birth Control Case* of 1965, in *"penumbras*, formed by emanation from those guarantees of the Bill of Rights that help give them life and substance."[61] It was *the* opinion that became midwife to the momentous *Abortion Cases* of 1973.[62]

Often embattled off as well as on the Court, this colorful and brilliant scholar eloquently articulated his posture again and again—in cases at law as well as from the lecture podium, in books as well as journals, including *Playboy* magazine. As he put it on one occasion, "the American Government is premised on the theory that if the mind of man is to be free, his ideas, his beliefs, his ideology, his philosophy must be placed beyond the reach of government."[63] While unquestionably doctrinaire and result oriented, Douglas deserves the "near great" rating of the Court historians just as did his jurisprudential opposites Field and Sutherland. His term on the court constitutes the longest to date; his record 1,232 majority, concurring, and dissenting opinions appear in nearly one-quarter of the more than 450 volumes of the *United States Reports*; and, with the total of 586, he of course had become the Court's leading dissenter.

No hesitation whatever attended FDR's filling of his fifth vacancy. On November 16, 1939, Pierce Butler, one of the two remaining Four Horsemen, died after seventeen years on the Court. On the same morning, the President informed Frank Murphy, his forty-six-year-old Attorney General, that he was his choice to succeed the New Deal's nemesis. Murphy at first demurred, feeling "utterly inadequate,"[64] but he ultimately accepted and was officially nominated on January 4, 1940. The Senate confirmed him a few days later. The tall, gaunt Murphy was in many ways a "natural" for the position. Like Butler he was a Midwesterner and a good Irish Catholic of middle-class origin. Widely known as a crusading New Deal liberal, he had served in the 1920s as a U.S. Assistant Attorney and as a Detroit judge—a post he held until, successfully courting the support of the numerous Irish and black citizens, he was elected Mayor of Detroit in 1929. During the Depression, which affected the Motor City severely, Murphy became a strong and articulate advocate of federal aid. After Roosevelt's election in 1932, for which he worked tirelessly, Murphy was chosen President of the Conference of Mayors and later was appointed Governor of the Philippines by FDR. In 1936 Murphy gave up that post not only to aid in the presidential campaign but to run (successfully) for the governorship of Michigan, and thus to aid the national ticket in securing that key industrial state.

Two years later Murphy lost his bid for reelection, and Roosevelt appointed him his Attorney General. The repeated suggestions that Murphy was later "kicked upstairs" to the Court from the Justice Department may hold some truth, but FDR might very well have appointed Murphy anyway, if perhaps not quite so soon. Murphy, not an interested or conscientious administrator, paid little heed to the modus operandi of his department; he placed heavy emphasis on antitrust litigation, neglecting such crucial areas as internal revenue; and, like many Attorneys General before and after him, he did not get along well with the powerful head of the FBI, J. Edgar Hoover. In view of Murphy's other qualifications, FDR quite conceivably decided to expedite his promotion and to give the Attorney Generalship to the man who was supposed to get it in the first place, Solicitor General Robert H. Jackson. "Bob, I suppose you know that you're to come into this office," Murphy told Jackson, "that I am here only temporarily."[65]

Frank Murphy was cut down by a fatal heart attack little more than nine years later. During that time he established himself as not only 100 percent loyal to the New Deal but as the Court's most advanced civil libertarian, outscoring all others in his generous support of individual rights and claims. He alone among the libertarian block of Black, Douglas, and Rutledge dissented (together with Justices Roberts and Jackson) from the 1944 landmark decision of *Korematsu* v. *United States*, written by Black,[66] which upheld the wartime evacuation from the West Coast of more than one hundred thousand Japanese Americans, of whom three-quarters were American-born citizens.

In his emotion-charged opinion,[67] Murphy assailed the evacuation program as one that "goes over the 'very brink of constitutional power' and falls into the ugly abyss of racism." Pronouncing it a flagrant violation of due process of law, he angrily and sarcastically characterized the military order, now sanctioned by the Court, as "based upon an erroneous assumption of racial guilt" and justified upon "questionable racial and sociological grounds not ordinarily within the realm of expert military judgment." And once again it was Murphy who, with Rutledge, wanted to strike down as unconstitutional the military trial and conviction of Japanese General Yamashita, Commanding General of the Japanese army group that had wrought such havoc in the Philippines. Black and Douglas were with the majority opinion by Chief Justice Stone in that 1946 decision,[68] but Murphy argued in defeat that the Court's failure to extend the guarantees of the Fifth and Sixth Amendments to General Yamashita was crassly unconstitutional and would hinder the "reconciliation necessary to a peaceful world."[69]

Murphy would all but inevitably side with the underdog— were he an enemy alien, a rank offender at the bar of criminal justice, or a member of a beleaguered religious sect. In *Adamson v. California* (1947),[70] with Rutledge concurring, he articulated the doctrine that if the specific provisions of the Bill of Rights did not provide sufficient safeguard against abusive governmental action, "constitutional condemnation in terms of a lack of due process despite the absence of a specific provision in the Bill of Rights" would be warranted. To Black, who also dissented in that landmark case (but for different reasons), the Murphy-Rutledge posture was an obvious invocation of natural law, which he regarded as an "incongruous excrescence on our Constitution."[71] Very likely because his concerns and productivity on the Court were essentially one-dimensional, no matter how noble and hortatory, Murphy was accorded, with considerable justice, only an "average" rating by the Court watchers. Yet he was a major influence in the spectrum that concerned him most—man's freedom and dignity.

The last of the Four Horsemen, and probably the most tenacious and reactionary member, announced his retirement early in 1941. James McReynolds had been on the Court for twenty-seven years, was nearing eighty, and simply decided that there was no point in staying on. FDR heartily agreed! Most Court observers believed that the President would now turn to his Attorney General, but Bob Jackson had been in office scarcely a year, and Roosevelt felt he could not spare him. Moreover, many of his most influential party leaders, including Senators Alben W. Barkley of Kentucky, Pat Harrison of Mississippi, and Carter Glass of Virginia, were pushing hard for FDR's political and personal ally, Senator James F. Byrnes of South Carolina, who had often and prominently been mentioned as a possible candidate and who held a barrelful of I.O.U.'s for loyal Democratic party service. The President himself had mentioned the Court to Byrnes on sundry occasions but, because of Byrnes's role as an influential, articulate, and shrewd Administration stalwart in the Senate, he hesitated to move him—especially since he no longer had to worry about the Court's posture on his programs. Byrnes was unquestionably more conservative than any of the other members of the Court FDR had appointed, but the President was not genuinely concerned on that score— the Court was now safely "pro-New Deal" and "pro-libertarian."

What finally determined Byrnes's selection was his failure to receive the vice-presidential nomination in the Democratic Convention of 1940. Byrnes, who himself had harbored presidential ambitions, but had staunchly supported FDR for a third term, was grievously disappointed. The President was eager to please his loyal lieutenant, and he responded to Senator Glass's entreaties: "Of course, I will appoint him. . . . He is just as much my friend as yours—I wanted him to be my running mate in 1940. . . . My only regret in appointing him is that I need him so much in the Senate."[72] And appoint him he did—but only after delaying for close to five months because of crucial pending legislation in the Senate. On June 12, 1941, Byrnes's colleagues proudly confirmed him unanimously and without reference to the Judiciary Committee. Wesley McCune, a chronicler of the Roosevelt Court, reported that FDR remarked during Byrnes's swearing-in ceremony:

> He wished he were Solomon and could halve Jimmy Byrnes, keeping one half in the Senate and the other half on the Court. At that moment, he was losing the smoothest, most effective worker he had ever had in the Senate, at the same time acquiring an unknown quantity for his Court.[73]

The sixty-two-year-old Byrnes—who would live on for another three decades, most of it in a variety of federal and state governmental posts—had a remarkable record of governmental experience. After brief executive and judicial service in his native South Carolina, he served seven terms in the U.S. House of Representatives and two in the Senate. He had first met FDR when the latter was Governor-elect of New York; the two men had formed a lasting political and personal alliance. Byrnes gave important support to Roosevelt in the 1932 presidential election, and he went on to become one of his most trusted advisers. An invaluable leader in the Senate, he even backed the Court-packing bill. And the President could count on him fully in such vital legislation as selective service and lend-lease.

Jimmy Byrnes lasted for little more than a year on the Court; a man of action, a doer and planner, he was not comfortable as a jurist. Thus in the fall of 1942, when Roosevelt asked him to step down to assume the post of Assistant President for Economic Affairs, he readily assented—he was simply delighted to be able to return to the active political arena. With the possible exception of his authorship of a case propounding the right of free interstate travel,[74] he left no mark on the Court, whose observers have rated him a failure—a grossly unfair judgment in view of the brevity of his membership.

On June 2, 1941, ten days before the Byrnes confirmation, the great Charles Evans Hughes, in his eightieth year, advised FDR of his intention to retire on July 1. He had served admirably for eleven difficult years. His declining health dictated an earlier withdrawal, yet he wanted to see a replacement for the McReynolds vacancy before creating a new one. Roosevelt, with five of his appointees on the high bench and the sixth one certain to be approved by the Senate, felt no pressure to nominate a successor quickly, especially since the Court was about to adjourn until October. But Hughes and his colleagues strongly implored FDR not to delay, and the President acquiesced. For some time he had been pondering a successor to Hughes, and it was widely assumed that his choice lay between two eminent lawyers: Associate Justice Harlan F. Stone and Attorney General Robert H. Jackson.

FDR's heart was clearly with Jackson, a New Deal loyalist of long standing who had fought with him all the way. Moreover, he had more than once mentioned the Chief Justiceship to Jackson, who had made clear to his President that he wanted the position very much. Still, FDR hesitated—being acutely aware that a professional ground swell of support was about to arise for Stone. He called Hughes to the White House to discuss his successor; the retiring Chief immediately volunteered that "Stone's record gave him first claim on the honor."[75] Hughes also approved Jackson's candidacy but stuck to his preference, based on Stone's judicial performance. Roosevelt later conferred with Justice Frankfurter and asked point-blank which of the two men he would prefer as Chief Justice. Wishing FDR had not asked that question, Frankfurter replied:

> On personal grounds I'd prefer Bob. While I've known Stone longer and our relations are excellent and happy, I feel closer friendship with Bob. But from the national interest I am bound to say that there is no reason for preferring Bob to Stone—quite the contrary. Stone is senior and qualified professionally to be C.J. But for me the decisive consideration, considering the fact that Stone is qualified, is that Bob is of your personal and political family, as it were, while Stone is a Republican. . . . when war does come, the country should feel you are a national, the Nation's President, and not a partisan President. Few things would contribute as much to confidence in you as a national and not a partisan President than for you to name a Republican, who has the profession's confidence, as Chief Justice.[76]

The President did not commit himself, but Frankfurter was fairly confident that the choice would be Stone, and he so informed his fellow Associate Justice. A few days later FDR discussed the matter with Jackson, explained the persuasiveness of Frankfurter's logic, and again assured his Attorney General that he would send him to the Court. Jackson concurred fully with Frankfurter and received the President's permission to advise Stone himself. Not many years later, after he had become a member of the Court, Jackson would write that the need for judicial leadership and the "desirability for a symbol of stability as well as progress" were evidently the reasons for the Coolidge-appointed Stone's elevation "in the interest of [the fostering of the] judiciary as an institution."[77]

A nationwide chorus of praise and acclaim greeted Stone's nomination on June 12, 1941. The press was ecstatic, the judiciary delighted, the intellectual community reassured, Congress happy. When the nomination officially reached the floor of the Senate on June 27, he was confirmed viva voce without a single objection.

Harlan Fiske Stone was almost sixty-nine when he succeeded

Hughes in the center chair. He would live for less than five years, but—although those years proved far less satisfactory, less happy than his sixteen as Associate Justice—they did not deter the experts from ranking him as one of the great jurists to grace the bench. Yet he was clearly more comfortable in being a member of the team than in leading it. Not a first-rate administrator like Taft, not a skillful and disciplinary Court-master like Hughes, not a ruthless craftsman like Marshall, not so persuasive as Taney, and not so innovative as Warren, his reluctance to crack down and his aversion to do battle with warring factions contributed to a marked divisiveness on the Court during his Chief Justiceship, led by the prolonged and nasty feud between Black and Jackson. Moreover, he really disdained the routine of administrative detail that he now found incumbent upon him. Yet there were precious few who understood and followed the commands and restraints of the Constitution, who supported the essence of limited government, who enhanced the concept of popular government under law, and who furthered respect for the Bill of Rights as fully as Stone did.

Since he could not be groom, Robert H. Jackson would be best man, and it was to no one's surprise that the forty-nine-year-old Attorney General was selected to fill the vacancy created by the Stone promotion. His appointment took a while longer to be approved than had been anticipated, chiefly because of the opposition of Senator Millard E. Tydings (D.-Md.), who had been unhappy with Jackson ever since he had refused to prosecute columnist Drew Pearson for publishing an alleged libel against Tydings. But the Judiciary Committee unanimously approved Jackson after but a few minutes' deliberation, and the Senate confirmed him on July 11 with only Tydings dissenting.

Jackson was eminently qualified to serve on the Court. Although his formal legal training had been meager indeed (he passed the New York bar exams without having been graduated from law school), he achieved a reputation as a brilliant private and public lawyer in upstate New York, where he had built a lucrative practice and become active in Democratic policies. He achieved early national exposure as a close ally of Roosevelt when the latter was Governor of New York, and as an effective campaigner for him at the Democratic National Convention as well as during the election of 1932. Initially Jackson refused to follow his friend and idol to Washington, but ultimately he yielded, accepting Roosevelt's appointment as General Counsel of the Bureau of Internal Revenue. A vigorous defender of and spokesman for the New Deal programs (including the Court-packing scheme), Jackson began a rapid climb through sundry posts, notably in the Department of Justice. Beginning as an Assistant Attorney General in the Antitrust Division, he succeeded to the Solicitor Generalship (where he did so well in his role as the "Government's Lawyer" that Justice Brandeis was moved to comment that "Jackson should be Solicitor General for life")[78] and then to the Attorney Generalship. In each of his posts he combined hard work and expertise with persuasiveness, charm, and a superb, indeed elegant, command of English.

The Court historians have recognized Jackson's achievements as "near great." But his tenure was not an entirely happy one. He had really wanted to be Chief Justice; tragically, his path was blocked in considerable measure by a doctrinal and personal feud with Hugo Black. Largely because of Jackson's strong feelings, some of their controversy was carried on in public— harming Jackson far more than Black and exacerbating Chief Justice Stone's problems in maintaining a harmonious Court. Jackson's acceptance of President Truman's request in 1945 for him to become the United States Chief Prosecutor at the Nuremberg Nazi War Crimes Trials, and his subsequent absence from the Court for an entire term, compounded his difficulties with his colleagues—not to mention the business of the Court, which had to operate with eight Justices and the attendant all-too-present danger of four-to-four tie votes.

Jackson was brilliant at Nuremberg, yet he returned from the trials a different man: the once libertarian judicial activist,[79] who had so often sided with Black, Douglas, Murphy, and Rutledge, had become profoundly cautious, a markedly narrow interpreter of the Bill of Rights. He now more often than not sided with the Frankfurter wing of the Court, which took a generally restrictive stand in matters affecting national security and state criminal justice procedures. [80] This intriguing meta-morphosis may well have resulted from his Nuremberg experiences, his firsthand perception of the melancholy events resulting in the destruction of the Weimar Republic and the rise of Nazism. It was his conclusive judgment that one of the major contributory factors was the failure of the Weimar Government to crack down on radical dissenters and groups.

Yet he remained an apostle of judicial restraint in the economic-proprietarian sphere, supporting governmental authority to regulate and thus remaining true to his basic New Deal commitments. And even if there were no other justification for holding Jackson in high esteem as a jurist, his magnificent prose—second in beauty and clarity perhaps only to that of Cardozo—has earned him a high regard. It would be hard to forget the haunting beauty of his phrases, such as those in his memorable opinion striking down the West Virginia flag salute in 1942: "Those who begin coercive elimination of dissent," he warned his countrymen, "soon find themselves exterminating dissenters. Compulsory unification of opinion achieves only the unanimity of the graveyard." And elaborating:

> If there is any fixed star in our constitutional constellation, it is that no official, high or petty, can prescribe what shall be orthodox in politics, nationalism, religion, or other matters of opinion or force citizens to confess by word or act their faith therein. . . .
> The very purpose of a Bill of Rights was to withdraw certain subjects from the vicissitudes of political controversy, to place them beyond the reach of majorities and officials and to establish them as legal principles to be applied by the Courts. One's right to life, liberty, and property, to free speech, a free press, freedom of worship and assembly, and other fundamental rights may not be submitted to vote; they depend on the outcome of no elections. [81]

On October 9, 1954, death came to Robert Jackson. He had still participated that May in the Court's unanimously decided, momentous *Public School Desegregation Cases*, [82] unpersuaded by the Court's reasoning but supportive of the results. [83] In some ways he died a bitter and disappointed man—never having attained the coveted Court leadership—but he left a legacy as "America's Advocate." [84]

Roosevelt had now appointed eight Justices in less than four years. Barring unforeseeable illnesses or resignations, that certainly would be the end of the line. Yet in October 1942 came Justice Byrnes's resignation from the Court and the ninth vacancy! This time there was no obvious successor, no obvious political debt to be paid. Such major New Deal supporters as Messrs. Black, Reed, Frankfurter, Douglas, Murphy, Jackson, and Byrnes had been sent to the Court; others, such as Francis Biddle, the able Attorney General, were not interested. At last FDR might indulge his desire to nominate someone from west of the Mississippi. There was no rush as far as he was concerned, and he asked Biddle to look around carefully for a likely candidate. The ultimate nominee—pressed on the Administration by Biddle as well as by such allies as Senator Norris, Justices Murphy and Douglas (Stone and F.F. still wanted Learned Hand), and particularly by the distinguished *Des Moines Register* and *Chicago Sun* journalist Irving Brant—was a rather "marginal" Westerner, but with more claims to that region than Douglas: Judge Wiley Rutledge of the United States Court of Appeals for the District of Columbia. Rutledge was the only Roosevelt appointee with federal judicial experience (four years), and one of only three with any judicial background—the other two being Black and Murphy. FDR was not personally acquainted with Rutledge, but after chatting with him at the White House ("Wiley, you have geography," FDR said to him with his infectious grin) [85] and being assured by Biddle that the candidate was a bona fide libertarian, an early and solid New Dealer who had ardently championed the Court-packing plan, and a judge whose opinions demonstrated a solid commitment to the presidential philosophy, he nominated him in February 1943. Confirmation came readily without a formal roll call.

Born in Kentucky, brought up there and in North Carolina and Tennessee, schooled in Tennessee and Wisconsin, Rutledge had taught and worked in the public school systems of Colorado, Indiana, and New Mexico before becoming Professor of Law at the University of Colorado, Professor of Law and Dean at Washington University in St. Louis, and Dean at the University of Iowa's School of Law. In 1939 he was appointed to the federal bench. Rutledge, who genuinely loved people of all walks of life, promptly demonstrated his libertarian colors. Indeed, his Supreme Court score in behalf of individual claims against alleged violations by government was higher than any of his colleagues (followed closely by Murphy's). Thus it was Rutledge who joined Murphy's generous extensions of civil liberty safeguards beyond the Constitution's verbiage when he concurred in the latter's famed dissenting opinion in *Adamson* v. *California* in 1947:

> I agree that the specific guarantees of the Bill of Rights should be carried over intact into the first section of the Fourteenth Amendment. But I am not prepared to say that the latter is entirely and necessarily limited by the Bill of Rights. Occasions may arise where a proceeding falls so far short of conforming to

fundamental standards of procedure as to warrant constitutional condemnation in terms of lack of due process despite the absence of specific provisions in the Bill of Rights. [86]

During his scant six-and-a-half years on the bench, Rutledge's scholarship, his mastery of law, his articulate explication of difficult issues, and his prodigious workmanship combined to establish him as a jurist who well earned the second-highest rating that the Court's students bestowed upon him. The years of Rutledge's tenure saw the Court at its libertarian apogee; after his death it would not return to a similar posture until the heyday of the Warren Court.

Rutledge left a proud record, highlighted by some celebrated dissenting opinions, such as those for *In re Yamashita*, and *Everson* v. *Board of Education of Ewing Township*. The former decision upheld seven to two Japanese General Tomoyuki Yamashita's summary military commission conviction for violating the rules of war. The latter sanctioned five to four state-subsidized transportation of parochial as well as public school students. Rutledge regarded these opinions as his best. Thus he admonished the Stone-led majority in *Yamashita* that it "is not in our tradition for anyone to be charged with crime which is defined after his conduct, alleged to be criminal, has taken place; or in language not sufficient to inform him of the nature of the offense or to enable him to make defense. Mass guilt we do not impute to individuals." [87] And, in *Everson*, before appending Madison's "Memorial and Remonstrance Against Religious Assessment," Rutledge warned the Black-led majority: "Like St. Paul's freedom, religious liberty with a great price must be bought. And for those who exercise it most fully, by insisting upon religious education for their children mixed with secular, by the terms of our Constitution the price is greater than for others." [88] When he succumbed to a cerebral hemorrhage at the early age of fifty-five while vacationing in Maine in September 1949, an era came to an end. Wiley Rutledge had been the last Roosevelt appointee: the three (Burton, Vinson, and Clark) whom President Truman would send to the Court in the years between FDR's death in April 1945 and that of Rutledge four-and-a-half years later were of a far different philosophical and jurisprudential stripe, indeed; so would prove to be Rutledge's replacement, the likable but ineffectual and misplaced Sherman Minton.

During the relatively brief deliberations on the staffing of the judicial branch down on Fifth and Chestnut Streets in Philadelphia in 1787, Mr. Madison voiced the expectation cum hope that the Supreme Court would constitute "a bench happily filled." Notwithstanding a number of both lay and professional detractors—many of whom are but questionably qualified to pass judgment—it has been just that: a bench happily filled. We may confidently apply that verdict to the FDR Justices collectively and, with but minor reservations, individually. I have little, if any, quarrel with the herein-described collective judgment of Court watchers, Court students, and that still sparse but slowly increasing coterie of judicial biographers who are in general concordance that, omitting Byrnes, six of the eight FDR appointees (all of whom still served at the time of FDR's death) rightfully belong in the highest or second-highest category, and in the instances of Reed and Murphy in the third or "average." Forged by the towering intellectualism of a Black and a Frankfurter; the burning zeal of a Douglas; the applied conscience of a Stone; and the beautifully communicated teachings of a Jackson, it was a Court of veritable giants. FDR had every right to be pleased with his choices: their qualifications were abundant, their professional performance superior. His expectations were not disappointed. It was worth having had to wait for that first opening for what had seemed an endless four-and-a-half years. His constitutional *weltanschau-ung* had been well served and so, on balance, had the nation's.

1. See Appendix in Charles Warren, *The Supreme Court in United States History* (Boston: Little, Brown, and Co., 1923), vol. 3.

2. See my *Justices and Presidents: A Political History of Appointments to the Supreme Court* (New York: Oxford University Press, 1974 and Penguin Press, 1975), p. 246.

3. *The Riverside California Press*, July 19, 1974, p. 11.

4. *Democracy in America*, trans. George Lawrence, ed. J. P. Mayer (Garden City, N.Y.: Doubleday and Co., 1969), p. 149.

5. Ibid., p. 150.

6. "Judicial Selection and the Qualities That Make a 'Good' Judge," *Annals*, (AAPSS) 462 (July 1982): 112.

7. Ibid., pp. 113-14.

8. Restored Supreme Court Chamber, U.S. Capitol, April 30, 1982. Some-

what shortened and adapted, the address was published in *Judicature* 66, no. 7 (February 1983).

9. MSS, Supreme Court Chamber, pp. 11-12.

10. As quoted by Judge Irving R. Kaufman, "Chartering a Judicial Pedigree," *New York Times*, January 24, 1981, p. 23.

11. See my *The Judicial Process: An Introductory Analysis of the Courts of the United States, England, and France*, 4th. ed. (New York: Oxford University Press, 1980), pp. 65-80.

12. *New York Times*, March 2, 1932, quoting Senator Clarence Dill (R.-Wash.).

13. Albert P. Blaustein and Roy M. Mersky, "Rating Supreme Court Justices," *American Bar Association Journal* 58 (November 1972): 1183-89. See also the same authors' book-length study, *The First One Hundred Justices: Statistical Studies on the Supreme Court of the United States* (Hamden, Conn.: Shoe String Press, 1978).

14. *University of Pennsylvania Law Review* 105 (1957): 781.

15. *Marble Palace: The Supreme Court in American Life* (New York: Alfred A. Knopf, 1961), pp. 43-44.

16. See the two seminal 5:4 decisions in *West Coast Hotel Co.* v. *Parrish*, 300 U.S. 379 (1937), and *N.L.R.B.* v. *Jones & Laughlin Steel Corp.*, 301 U.S. 1 (1937).

17. *Jim Farley's Story* (New York: McGraw-Hill, 1948), p. 86.

18. As quoted in Virginia Van der Veer Hamilton, *Hugo Black: The Alabama Years* (Baton Rouge: Louisiana State University Press, 1972), p. 275.

19. Hugo Black, Jr., *My Father: A Remembrance* (New York: Random House), pp. 16-17.

20. As the *Washington Post*, for one, put it editorially on August 13, 1937.

21. *Judicature* 60, no. 7 (February 1977): 350.

22. Sixty Democrats and three Republicans—Robert LaFollette of Wisconsin, Arthur Capper of Kansas, and Lynn J. Frazier of North Dakota—voted "aye"; ten Republicans and six Democrats voted "naye."

23. John P. Frank, *Mr. Justice Black: The Man and His Opinions* (New York: Alfred A. Knopf, 1949), p. 105.

24. *New York Times*, October 2, 1937, p. 1.

25. *Hugo Black and the Judicial Revolution* (New York: Simon and Schuster, 1977), p. 43.

26. *New York Times*, October 2, 1937, p. 52.

27. As quoted in Frank, *Mr. Justice Black*, p. 102.

28. See his poignant valedictory publication, *A Constitutional Faith* (New York: Alfred A. Knopf, 1968).

29. "Mr. Justice Black and the Judicial Function," *UCLA Law Review* 14 (1967): 473.

30. "Hugo Lafayette Black: In Memoriam," *Journal of Public Law* 20 (1971): 362.

31. *Adamson* v. *California*, 332 U.S. 46 (1947).

32. *Palko* v. *Connecticut*, 302 U.S. 419 (1937).

33. See my *Freedom and the Court: Civil Rights and Liberties in the United States*, 4th ed. (New York: Oxford University Press, 1982), especially chapter 2.

34. 372 U.S. 335.

35. *Betts* v. *Brady*, 316 U.S. 455 (1942).

36. *Chambers* v. *Florida*, 309 U.S. 227 (1940), at 241.

37. John P. Frank, "Hugo L. Black: He Has Joined the Giants," *American Bar Association Journal* 58 (January 1972): 25.

38. 328 U.S. 373.

39. 321 U.S. 649.

40. See the fascinating account in Alpheus Thomas Mason, *Harlan Fiske Stone: Pillar of the Law* (New York: Viking Press, 1956), pp. 614-15. See also my *Judicial Process* pp. 221-22.

41. See Liva Baker, *Felix Frankfurter* (New York: Coward-McCann, 1969), pp. 201-6.

42. As quoted in Eugene C. Gerhart, *America's Advocate: Robert H. Jackson* (Indianapolis: Bobbs-Merrill Co., 1958), p. 165.

43. As quoted in Harold L. Ickes, *The Secret Diaries of Harold L. Ickes* (New York: Simon and Schuster, 1954), vol. 2, p. 539.

44. In 1919, New York State Court of Appeals Judge Cardozo had married Felix Frankfurter and Marion A. Denman.

45. *Felix Frankfurter Reminisces*, recorded in talks with Harlan B. Phillips (Garden City, N.Y.: Doubleday and Co., 1962), pp. 328-29, 334-35.

46. Bruce A. Murphy, *The Brandeis/Frankfurter Connection: The Secret Political Activity of Two Supreme Court Justices* (New York: Oxford University Press, 1982).

47. Fred Rodell, *Nine Men* (New York: Random House, 1955), p. 271.

48. Ibid.

49. 342 U.S. 165.

50. Louisiana ex rel. *Francis* v. *Resweber*, 329 U.S. 459 (1947).

51. As quoted in Marvin Braiterman, "Frankfurter and the Paradox of Restraint," *Midstream* (November 1970): 21.

52. *Minersville School District* v. *Gobitis*, 310 U.S. 586 (1940).

53. *West Virginia State Board of Education* v. *Barnette*, 319 U.S. 624 (1943).

54. Ibid., at 646.

55. 369 U.S. 186.

56. Ibid., at 270.

57. February 24, 1965, p. 40.

58. John P. Frank, "William O. Douglas," in Leon Friedman and Fred L. Israel, eds., *The Justices of the United States Supreme Court, 1789-1969* (New York: Chelsea House, 1969), vol. 4, p. 2453.

59. William O. Douglas, "An Intimate Memoir of the Brethren," excerpted from his *The Court Years, 1939-75*, in *New York Times Magazine*, September 21, 1980, p. 38ff. (See also his Obituary, *New York Times*, January 20, 1980, p. 28, col. 4.)

60. Frank, "William O. Douglas," p. 2454.

61. *Griswold* v. *Connecticut*, 381 U.S. 479 (1965), at 481.

62. *Roe* v. *Wade*, 410 U.S. 113 (1973), and *Doe* v. *Bolten*, 410 U.S. 179 (1973).

63. As quoted in *New York Times Magazine*, May 26, 1969, p. 26.

64. J. Woodford Howard, *Mr. Justice Murphy* (Princeton: Princeton University Press, 1968), pp. 215-16.

65. Gerhart, *America's Advocate*, p. 167.

66. 323 U.S. 214.

67. Ibid., p. 233ff.

68. *In re Yamashita*, 327 U.S. 1.

69. Ibid., at 29.

70. 332 U.S. 46. Murphy's dissent begins p. 124.

71. Ibid., at 75.

72. James F. Byrnes, *All in One Lifetime* (New York: Harper and Bros., 1958), p. 130.

73. *The Nine Young Men* (New York: Harper and Bros., 1947), p. 243.

74. *Edwards* v. *California*, 314 U.S. 160 (1941). For some interesting behind-the-scenes events surrounding the case's assignment to Byrnes, see my *Judicial Process*, pp. 227-28.

75. Merlo J. Pusey, *Charles Evans Hughes* (New York: Macmillan Co., 1951), vol. 2, pp. 787-88.

76. Ibid., p. 573.

77. As quoted in Mason, *Harlan Fiske Stone*, p. 191, fn. 30.

78. As quoted in Gerhart, *America's Advocate*, p. 191.

79. E.g., see his opinions in *West Virginia State Board of Education* v. *Barnette*, 319 U.S. 624 (1943); *Korematsu* v. *United States*, 323 U.S. 214 (1944); and *Thomas* v. *Collins*, 323 U.S. 516 (1945).

80. E.g., see his opinions in *Kunz* v. *New York*, 340 U.S. 290 (1951); *Dennis* v. *United States*, 341 U.S. 494 (1951); and *Adler* v. *Board of Education*, 342 U.S. 485 (1952).

81. *West Virginia State Board of Education* v. *Barnette* (1943), at 638, 642.

82. *Brown* v. *Board of Education of Topeka*, 347 U.S. 483 (1954) and *Bolling* v. *Sharpe*, 347 U.S. 497 (1954).

83. See Richard Kluger, *Simple Justice* (New York: Alfred A. Knopf, 1976) for a detailed account of Jackson's role in the *Brown* case (especially on pp. 678-99).

84. Gerhart, *America's Advocate.*

85. David Fellman to author, August 13, 1974.

86. 332 U.S. 46 (1947), at 124.

87. 327 U.S. 1 (1946), at 43.

88. 330 U.S. 1 (1947), at 59.